002400329

D1573199

The
Power of
Metaphor

The
Power of
Metaphor

Examining Its Influence on Social Life

Edited by Mark J. Landau,
Michael D. Robinson, and Brian P. Meier

American Psychological Association • Washington, DC

Published by
American Psychological Association
750 First Street, NE
Washington, DC 20002
www.apa.org

To order
APA Order Department
P.O. Box 92984
Washington, DC 20090-2984
Tel: (800) 374-2721; Direct: (202) 336-5510
Fax: (202) 336-5502; TDD/TTY: (202) 336-6123
Online: www.apa.org/pubs/books
E-mail: order@apa.org

In the U.K., Europe, Africa, and the Middle East, copies may be ordered from
American Psychological Association
3 Henrietta Street
Covent Garden, London
WC2E 8LU England

Typeset in Goudy by Circle Graphics, Inc., Columbia, MD

Printer: Maple Vail Press, York, PA
Cover Designer: Mercury Publishing Services, Inc., Rockville, MD
Cover Art: Jon Barwick, *Fustercluck*, 2011, Mixed Media on Canvas, 60″ × 60″

The opinions and statements published are the responsibility of the authors, and such opinions and statements do not necessarily represent the policies of the American Psychological Association.

Library of Congress Cataloging-in-Publication Data

The power of metaphor : examining its influence on social life / edited by Mark J. Landau, Michael D. Robinson, and Brian P. Meier.
     pages cm
  Includes bibliographical references and index.
   ISBN 978-1-4338-1579-9 — ISBN 1-4338-1579-6 1. Social perception. 2. Cognitive grammar. 3. Metaphor—Social aspects. 4. Metaphor—Psychological aspects. I. Landau, Mark J. (Mark Jordan)
   HM1041.P69 2014
   303.3'7—dc23
                                      2013024820

British Library Cataloguing-in-Publication Data

A CIP record is available from the British Library.

Printed in the United States of America
First Edition

http://dx.doi.org/10.1037/14278-000

CONTENTS

CONTRIBUTORS

Luciano Arcuri, PhD, Professor Emeritus, Department of Developmental and Socialization Psychology, University of Padova, Padova, Italy

Daniel Casasanto, PhD, Assistant Professor, Department of Psychology, University of Chicago, Chicago, IL

Gerald L. Clore, PhD, Professor, Department of Psychology, University of Virginia, Charlottesville

L. Elizabeth Crawford, PhD, Associate Professor, Department of Psychology, University of Richmond, Richmond, VA

Adam K. Fetterman, MS, Graduate Student, Department of Psychology, North Dakota State University, Fargo

Rebecca Fincher-Kiefer, PhD, Associate Professor, Department of Psychology, Gettysburg College, Gettysburg, PA

Raymond W. Gibbs Jr., PhD, Professor, Department of Psychology, University of California at Santa Cruz

Julian House, MA, Graduate Student, Rotman School of Management, University of Toronto, Toronto, Canada

Mark J. Landau, PhD, Associate Professor, Department of Psychology, University of Kansas, Lawrence

Spike W. S. Lee, PhD, Assistant Professor, Rotman School of Management, University of Toronto, Toronto, Canada

Anne Maass, PhD, Professor, Department of Developmental and Socialization Psychology, University of Padova, Padova, Italy

Brian P. Meier, PhD, Associate Professor, Department of Psychology, Gettysburg College, Gettysburg, PA

Victor Ottati, PhD, Professor, Department of Psychology, Loyola University Chicago, Chicago, IL

Erika Price, MA, Graduate Student, Department of Psychology, Loyola University Chicago, Chicago, IL

Randall Renstrom, PhD, Assistant Professor, Department of Psychology, Central College, Pella, IA

Michael D. Robinson, PhD, Professor, Department of Psychology, North Dakota State University, Fargo

Simone Schnall, PhD, Senior Lecturer, Department of Psychology, University of Cambridge, Cambridge, England

Abigail A. Scholer, PhD, Assistant Professor, Department of Psychology, University of Waterloo, Waterloo, Canada

Norbert Schwarz, PhD, Professor, Department of Psychology, University of Michigan, Ann Arbor

Gary D. Sherman, PhD, Postdoctoral Fellow, Harvard Decision Science Laboratory, Harvard University, Cambridge, MA

Caterina Suitner, PhD, Assistant Professor, Department of Developmental and Socialization Psychology, University of Padova, Padova, Italy

Chen-Bo Zhong, PhD, Assistant Professor, Rotman School of Management, University of Toronto, Toronto, Canada

I

METAPHOR AS
A COGNITIVE TOOL
FOR UNDERSTANDING
ABSTRACT SOCIAL
CONCEPTS

1

INTRODUCTION

MARK J. LANDAU, MICHAEL D. ROBINSON, AND BRIAN P. MEIER

Browse a bookstore's philosophy section and you will find hefty tomes devoted to the analysis of single concepts such as *friendship, authenticity, guilt, power, morality, freedom*, and *evil*. Scholars wrestle with the precise meaning of these concepts because they are inherently abstract. Unlike concepts that refer to categories of things that we experience with our senses, these concepts lack a concrete referent existing in the world outside ourselves—you cannot see *evil*, for instance.

It is therefore remarkable that, generally speaking, people seem to have little difficulty making sense of these and other abstract concepts. They form impressions of coworkers' friendliness and authenticity, suffer the pangs of guilt, buy luxury goods to advertise their power, judge the moral implications of political policy, and support wars to spread freedom and stem the tide of evil. The question then becomes: What cognitive processes do people normally use to grasp the abstract concepts that lie at the center of their social life?

http://dx.doi.org/10.1037/14278-001
The Power of Metaphor: Examining Its Influence on Social Life, M. J. Landau, M. D. Robinson, and
B. P. Meier (Editors)

This book explores the possibility that people understand and experience abstract social concepts using metaphor. From this perspective, metaphor is not—as conventional wisdom would have it—simply a matter of words; rather, it is a cognitive tool that people routinely use to understand abstract concepts (e.g., *morality*) in terms of superficially dissimilar concepts that are relatively easier to comprehend (e.g., *cleanliness*).

Although observations on metaphor's cognitive significance date back to Aristotle (circa 335 B.C.E./2006), the development of a formal theoretical framework, labeled *conceptual metaphor theory* (CMT), has recently stimulated systematic empirical study on metaphor's role in social psychological phenomena. This book summarizes current knowledge and integrates recent developments for readers interested in the topic of metaphor and the cognitive underpinnings of social life more broadly. We hope this book stimulates and guides future research on the causes and consequences of metaphoric thinking for how people perceive, act, and make judgments and decisions in their social environment.

This introductory chapter provides an overview of CMT. We then review recent developments in social psychology that have been useful for empirically studying metaphors' influence on thought, feeling, and action. We close with an overview of how the rest of the book is organized.

CONCEPTUAL METAPHOR THEORY

Metaphor is commonly known as a figure of speech through which we describe one thing in terms of another. When Romeo says, "Juliet is the sun," he cannot *really* mean that she is a giant spherical mass of hot plasma. Most of us are taught in grade school that metaphor is a decorative frill—a colorful but essentially useless embellishment to "normal" or even "proper" language—and that it is the special province of poets and other literary elites. But this is incorrect. English speakers utter about one metaphor for every 10 to 25 words, or about six metaphors a minute (Geary, 2011). Consider the following ordinary expressions:

- I can *see* your point (*understanding is seeing*)
- I'll *keep* that *in* mind (*the mind is a container*)
- Christmas is *fast approaching* (*events are moving objects*)
- That is a *heavy* thought (*thoughts are objects with weight*)
- I feel *down* (*feelings are vertical locations*)
- The national economy *veered off course* (*economy as a vehicle*)
- I *devoured* the book, but I'm still *digesting* its claims (*ideas are food*)
- Her arguments are *strong* (*arguments are muscle force*)

- I'm moving *forward* with the book (*progress is forward motion*)
- What a *sweet* person! (*agreeableness is sweet taste*)

Although these expressions strike most people as perfectly natural, they do not make sense in strict literal terms. For example, thoughts lack weight, feelings do not have an actual vertical location, and arguments cannot have muscle strength. Given such points, and the fact that linguistic metaphors are nevertheless pervasive (Geary, 2011), the big question is whether metaphoric language possesses deeper significance for understanding the representational processes that underlie thought.

According to many theories of language and, perhaps, common sense as well, the answer to this question is "no." Metaphoric expressions may be simply idioms (figures of speech) that do not convey any meaningful insight into how we think. If a person says, for instance, that she is "moving up in the company," we instantly understand that she is referring to her career without, it seems, accessing any information about her vertical position. Another possibility is that people speak metaphorically because they think doing so is somehow more powerful in communication. From this related perspective, we use expressions such as "a *cold* reception" to convey subjective experiences in a manner that might be more easily comprehended by others, but, critically, our private thinking about those experiences is essentially literal.

Yet there is a distinguished philosophical tradition that conceives of metaphor as fundamental to human thought (Gibbs, 1994, 2008). On this view, people speak metaphorically because they think metaphorically. This notion was advanced by Friedrich Nietzsche (1873/1974) and 20th century philosophers such as Julian Jaynes (1976) and Susanne Langer (1979), and it finds its clearest formulation in George Lakoff and Mark Johnson's 1980 book *Metaphors We Live By*. In what has come to be known as conceptual metaphor theory, Lakoff and Johnson made a compelling theoretical case for the view that metaphor pervades human thought processes (for an introductory overview, see Kövecses, 2010).

A conceptual metaphor consists of two dissimilar concepts, one of which is understood in terms of the other. The two concepts involved in metaphor have special names. The concept that one tries to understand is the *target*, whereas the concept used for this purpose is the *source*. Targets are generally abstract, complex, and difficult to comprehend, whereas sources represent relatively more concrete, perceptual, and embodied experiences (e.g., tasting something, seeing something, feeling something's texture)— experiences that are easier to comprehend and typically available from the earliest moments of life (Mandler, 2004). For example, although it is difficult to understand *intimacy*, it is easier to experience *warmth* as a bodily temperature. A metaphor involving these two concepts is conventionally denoted as *intimacy is warmth* and is expressed in idioms such as a *warm greeting* or an *icy stare* (devoid of intimacy).

What does it mean to understand a target in terms of a source? According to CMT, metaphor creates a *conceptual mapping,* defined as a systematic set of associations between elements of a target (i.e., features, properties, and relations) and analogous elements of the source (see Figure 1.1 for a graphical depiction). In the previous example, intimacy and warmth share elements because both are experienced as pleasant and in fact co-occur in our interactions with caregivers and romantic partners (Williams, Huang, & Bargh, 2009). In this way, a conceptual metaphor allows people to draw on their knowledge of the source as a framework for thinking about the target.

To illustrate, consider the conceptual mapping created by the metaphor *love is a journey,* depicted in Figure 1.2. The mapping puts elements of the two concepts into systematic correspondence, thereby allowing people to use their knowledge of journeys to inform how they think, feel, and act during a close relationship marked by love. For example, they can represent love-related experiences as having a *starting point* (initial attraction) and an intended *destination* (typically matrimony and increased intimacy over time). The relationship can *stall* or *move* in the wrong *direction,* such as when a partner feels they are *headed* for a breakup.

The metaphor also entails practical inferences. People generally understand that a person on a journey usually has to pass over difficult terrain to reach a destination. By understanding a close relationship as a journey, people can expect to encounter conflicts as their relationships progress. Of course, conceptual mappings are partial, meaning that not all elements of the

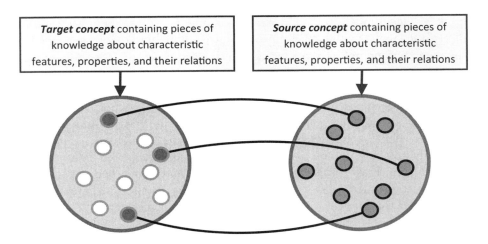

Figure 1.1. Graphical depiction of a conceptual mapping.

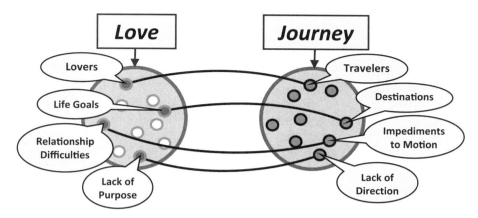

Figure 1.2. Graphical depiction of a portion of the conceptual mapping created by the metaphor *love is a journey.*

source are used to structure the target. When beginning a new relationship, for example, people do not usually worry about packing a suitcase.

A corollary of CMT is that the same target can be mapped onto different sources. Because mappings are partial, mapping a target onto one source will highlight (make salient) and downplay (inhibit) some elements, whereas mapping that same target onto an alternate source will pick out a different set of elements (see Figure 1.3 for a graphical depiction). For example, thinking of love as a *journey* will highlight the fact that relationships should head somewhere, whereas thinking of love as *a plant that needs to be nurtured* will deemphasize movement but perhaps better capture the idea that relationships can *wither* to the extent that we do not *water* them (e.g., by periodic expressions of kindness).

In this way, alternate conceptual mappings can produce systematic changes in perceptions, inferences, and attitudes toward the target. For example, conceptualizing *arguments* in terms of *war* ("I cannot *penetrate* her *defenses*") should promote a hostile orientation in which one party is the victor and the other is the vanquished. By contrast, conceptualizing *arguments* in terms of *locations* that are far apart ("Are we on different *planets?*") should downplay hostility and even promote efforts toward finding a 'common ground,' or compromise, between arguing parties.

What empirical evidence exists in support of CMT? Pioneering research in the area of cognitive linguistics analyzed speech acts and inferred the conceptual metaphors that gave rise to them (for a comprehensive review of this work, see Gibbs, 1994). This research has succeeded in an important respect: Metaphoric linguistic expressions are not isolated speech acts but rather are strikingly coherent in supporting a common conceptual metaphor.

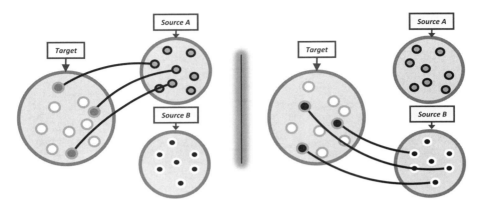

Figure 1.3. Alternate conceptual mappings.

For example, by positing a conceptual metaphor *ideas are food*, one can explain why so many linguistic expressions follow from this mapping (you *devour* a book, try to *digest* its *raw* facts, let the ideas *simmer* for a while, *regurgitate* those ideas when asked, although some ideas may be *half-baked*). Novel expressions consistent with such conceptual metaphors (e.g., that point could use some *seasoning*) are readily understood, further attesting to the active operation of a deep, conceptual mapping.

Even so, it must be recognized that this line of evidence is impressionistic and unconvincing to some researchers. There are many idioms (e.g., *kick the bucket*) that are often used but do not appear to be meaningful in conceptual terms in the modern day (Gibbs, 1994). Also, expressions that might have been conceptually motivated at some point in time (e.g., "feeling *down*") are now so conventional that one might doubt whether conceptual metaphors motivate their expression (McGlone, 2007). Gibbs (Chapter 2, this volume) sums up this controversy: "People may use metaphoric language as a matter of convention without necessarily having some underlying cognitive mapping occur between disparate source and target concepts" (p. 22). Such concerns have recently been surmounted in an impressive body of evidence for conceptual metaphor in social psychology, the focus of the present volume.

METAPHOR RESEARCH IN SOCIAL PSYCHOLOGY

By taking advantage of methodological advances in the study of social cognition, social psychologists have provided extensive, sometimes surprising, evidence for the role of conceptual metaphors in people's thought, feeling, and action. Researchers have primarily adopted one of two broad research strategies, the *metaphoric transfer strategy* and the *alternate source strategy* (Landau, Meier, & Keefer, 2010). The reasoning behind the metaphoric transfer strategy is that if people in fact think of an abstract target (e.g., *intimacy*) in terms of a relatively more concrete source (e.g., *physical warmth*), then manipulating how people understand or experience the source (e.g., inducing physical warmth) should "transfer" across the conceptual mapping, changing how they process analogous elements of the target (e.g., heightening felt intimacy). If, alternatively, metaphor does not shape thought, there would be no reason to expect such effects, because people's representations of the target would not be systematically structured around knowledge of the source.

The alternate source strategy is derived from the idea that the same target can be understood in terms of different sources (e.g., *love is a journey, a plant that needs to be nurtured,* and dozens of other concrete concepts; Kövecses, 2010). This strategy focuses on whether the activation of different conceptual metaphors for the same target differentially influences target processing in line with the respective source concepts (Landau et al., 2010).

Let's first consider research using the metaphoric transfer strategy in more detail. Researchers adopting this strategy have developed a number of experimental paradigms. Some have used reaction time and perception tasks borrowed from cognitive psychology. For example, Meier, Robinson, and Clore (2004) based their predictions on metaphors linking positive affect to brightness (e.g., a *bright* future) and negative affect to darkness (e.g., a *dark* thought). They randomly assigned positive (e.g., hero) and negative (e.g., liar) affect words to lighter or darker font colors and asked participants to evaluate them as quickly as possible. Despite the irrelevance of the font color manipulation, positive affect words were evaluated more quickly when assigned to the brighter color, and negative affect words were evaluated more quickly when assigned to the darker color. Meier and Robinson (2004) extended such results to manipulations of verticality. Positive affect words were evaluated more quickly when placed high on the computer screen (consistent with positive affect being *up*), and negative affect words were evaluated more quickly when placed low on the computer screen (consistent with negative affect being *down*). Other studies using related paradigms have shown that socially dominant stimuli are categorized faster when presented higher (Schubert, 2005), moral stimuli are classified faster when in a white font color (Sherman & Clore, 2009), and positive stimuli seem brighter (Meier, Robinson, Crawford, & Ahlvers, 2007) and shift attention upward (Meier & Robinson, 2004).

Other variations on the metaphoric transfer strategy use between-subject manipulations to examine whether priming a source concept produces metaphor-consistent changes in target processing. Williams and Bargh (2008a) used this approach to examine the metaphoric link between physical and interpersonal warmth. They based their hypotheses on studies showing that people commonly refer to interactions with others by using the concepts *warm* and *cold* (Asch, 1946; Fiske, Cuddy, & Glick, 2007), such as when one receives a *warm* welcome or a *cold* rejection. To determine whether this metaphor influences social perceptions, they had the experimenter, who apparently needed a free hand, ask participants to hold her coffee cup. Depending on condition, the cup was either warm or cold. Afterward, all participants were asked to read a brief description of another person and rate that person's friendliness and trustworthiness—that is, their interpersonal "warmth." As predicted, participants who simply held a warm (vs. cold) beverage subsequently perceived a target individual as friendlier and more trustworthy, suggesting that conceptual metaphors can influence social perceptions even in contexts in which metaphoric language is absent. Williams and Bargh (2008b) subsequently showed that priming closeness (vs. distance) leads people to feel more attached to their hometowns and families.

Theoretically predicted metaphoric transfer effects have now been found in dozens of published studies. Although this work began in a few labs, the study of metaphor and social cognition is now an enterprise shared among independent researchers across the globe, many of whom are contributors to this book. Subtle manipulations of source-relevant cognition and experience have been shown to influence how people perceive, remember, and make judgments and decisions related to a wide range of abstract social concepts that, on the surface, represent different kinds of things. In fact, studies show that source experiences influence, by means of metaphoric associations, outcomes that are commonly attributed to fixed personality traits (e.g., agreeableness) or intellectual capacity (e.g., creativity). Here are just a few of the fascinating results that have been found:

- Weight manipulations influence perceived importance.
- Smooth textures promote social coordination.
- Hard textures result in greater strictness in social judgment.
- Hot backgrounds bias perceptions of facial anger.
- Dirty rooms result in less tolerance of moral indiscretions.
- Fishy smells result in doubts about trustworthiness.
- Thoughts of body contamination activate anti-immigrant sentiments.

The success of this strategy is surprising in part because priming research in social psychology has mostly focused on the activation of knowledge structures that have a relatively obvious bearing on the target phenomenon (e.g., priming hostile thoughts produces hostile behaviors). That manipulating a perception-related concept would systematically influence processing with respect to a more abstract social concept represents a major departure from this traditional focus, one in favor of a fundamental role for metaphor in social cognition (Bargh, 2006; Williams et al., 2009).

A smaller body of research has used the alternate source strategy. A common method for activating a particular metaphor in people's minds is to expose them to a *metaphoric framing*—a communication (e.g., a newspaper headline) that compares an abstract target to a superficially unrelated, more concrete source. Researchers have tested whether situational exposure to a metaphoric framing guides people to use their knowledge of the source to think about analogous elements of the target, even those that are not explicitly described in the communication.

In one illustrative study, Morris, Sheldon, Ames, and Young (2007) asked participants to read stock market commentaries that framed a price trend in terms of either the deliberate action of a living agent (e.g., "This afternoon the NASDAQ started *climbing* upward") or as the activity of an inanimate object (e.g., "This afternoon the NASDAQ was *swept* upward"). Next, participants predicted what would happen to the price trend the next day. Morris et al. reasoned that because people generally know that living things move with intention toward destinations, participants exposed to an agent-metaphoric framing would infer that the price trend would continue along its current trajectory the following day, whereas those exposed to an object-metaphoric framing would not make this inference. This is exactly what they found. Related studies show that even incidental exposure to metaphoric framings produces metaphor-consistent changes in how people form attitudes, regulate their goal pursuit, and even cope with traumatic life events (Landau et al., 2010).

OVERVIEW OF THIS VOLUME

Evidence for conceptual metaphor and its importance to understanding social cognition and interpersonal behavior is rapidly expanding (Landau et al., 2010), and many of the relevant papers have been published in the best journals in the field (e.g., *Science*). Nevertheless, there are no edited volumes bringing such lines of research together, and therefore the present edited volume is both timely and necessary. Leaders in the field wrote the chapters, and their topics are diverse, encompassing individual differences, embodiment, morality, social judgments, decision making, cultural differences, and politics and persuasion, among others. Each author or set of authors was given a topic but allowed leeway in its coverage. What resulted from these efforts was a coherent but diverse consideration of the significance of CMT across many subdisciplines of psychology. Each chapter presents future research directions and discusses the practical implications of metaphor research for addressing social problems. The take-home point emerging from the chapters is the idea that people think, feel, and behave metaphorically to a much greater extent than has been appreciated in previous edited volumes in social (e.g., Kruglanski & Higgins, 2007) and personality (e.g., John, Robins, & Pervin, 2008) psychology.

The edited volume consists of 13 chapters divided into three parts. The chapters in Part I provide a broad introduction to CMT and its application within social and personality psychology. Following the present introductory chapter, Gibbs discusses how experimental research overcomes many of the empirical limitations confronting linguistic analyses of conceptual metaphor, and he offers novel suggestions for integrating these heretofore isolated literatures in future research.

The chapters in Part II examine how and why metaphors matter for a wide range of phenomena. Meier, Scholer, and Fincher-Kiefer review evidence that metaphors influence perceptions of other people and the self in realms as diverse as social status, religiosity, anger, mate value, and personality characteristics such as agreeableness. Crawford reviews studies showing that when people reconstruct memories of social stimuli, they often rely on metaphors linking the meaning of those stimuli to perceptual experiences and bodily activities. Lee and Schwarz highlight metaphors' role in judgment and decision making. The evidence reviewed crosses economic, consumer, and social domains.

In a challenge to traditional objectivist conceptions of morality, Zhong and House point to mounting evidence that people's judgments of right and wrong are influenced by metaphoric associations with superficially irrelevant aspects of their environments, particularly physical dirt and cleanliness. Robinson and Fetterman focus on emerging work on metaphor and individual differences in personality functioning. They present and discuss multiple lines of research showing that a number of dispositional characteristics of the individual (e.g., agreeableness) seem to operate in a metaphor-consistent manner.

Maass, Suitner, and Arcuri discuss how groups of people use metaphors to think about and relate to members of other groups. Drawing on research findings and real-world examples, the authors show how metaphors guide categorization, create and maintain stereotypes, and reinforce dehumanizing representations of outgroups. Building on theory and research on persuasion, Ottati, Renstrom, and Price outline a comprehensive model specifying how exposure to metaphors in mass political communication influences observers' attitudes toward social and political issues.

The study of metaphor in social psychology is still in its earliest stages, and we are just beginning to understand how metaphoric thinking structures, constrains, and guides thought, feeling, and action. Thus, there are many research topics that remain to be addressed. The chapters in Part III explore these issues.

Sherman and Clore propose that people draw on verticality, brightness, and size when conceptualizing value but call for new lines of research that can better support a metaphoric interpretation of such relationships. Schnall argues that experimental metaphor research would benefit from investigating which particular metaphors have the most extensive impact on social thought and behavior, and she suggests what such "basic" metaphors might be. Casasanto analyzes the origins of some basic conceptual metaphors in patterns of linguistic, cultural, and bodily experience. In the final chapter, Landau, Robinson, and Meier outline other directions for future research on metaphor's significance in social life.

INTENDED AUDIENCE

This book will benefit four types of readers. The primary audience is social and personality psychologists who have a broad interest in social cognition. CMT is novel in this context. Its inputs are often perceptual and nonverbal and cannot be completely captured by canonical social cognition views of mental representation and priming (Fiske & Taylor, 1991; Higgins, 1996). For example, in contrast to *schema*-based perspectives of social cognition (Fiske & Taylor, 1991), the results reported in this book will reveal that people's mental representations of social concepts are often structured by metaphoric analogy with knowledge that is not part of that concept per se, at least as traditionally conceived. In addition, CMT emphasizes processes that are typically embodied in nature and is therefore consistent with recent calls for a greater focus on the body's role in social cognition (Niedenthal, Barsalou, Winkielman, Krauth-Gruber, & Ric, 2005).

This book will also benefit professional researchers and students whose interests are in a particular topic, whether defined in process- or content-related terms. It includes chapters on language, person perception, emotion, memory, and decision making, topics of undergraduate courses and seminars that have not typically focused on metaphoric influences. Yet conceptual metaphors seem to pervade these operations of the human mind, and the relevant chapters will provide new ways of thinking about these topics. In terms of content areas, this book includes chapters on morality, personality, intergroup relations, political psychology, and culture, and again makes the case that CMT advances understanding of these phenomena. Taken as a whole, the chapters articulate the scope of CMT in terms of topics that have not typically been understood from this theoretical perspective but most decidedly benefit from doing so.

Third, researchers in multiple fields outside of psychology (e.g., anthropology, communication, philosophy) now recognize the value of experimental findings in understanding how human beings think and behave (Gibbs, 2008). Accordingly, metaphor research in social psychology may be valuable in arbitrating theoretical disputes in these fields that might be otherwise difficult to arbitrate. For example, many of the empirical results reviewed in this volume suggest a systematic relation between perception and thought, a relationship that has been heavily debated in the anthropology literature (Whorf, 1956/1998). With reference to language and communication, these results challenge prominent theories (Chomsky, 1995; Fodor, 1983) contending that there is a specialized language "module" that is dissociated from other modules related to perception and action. Reviewed results are also relevant to an important issue in philosophy—namely, how it is that individuals "ground" abstract thoughts in a way that can be more easily apprehended by both the self and others (Johnson, 1987).

Finally, this book might be of interest to curious laypersons as well. Several psychologists have written popular books whose central conclusions overlap somewhat with ours—namely, that decision making (Damasio, 1994), language (Pinker, 2007), and emotion (Goleman, 1995) are embodied in ways that challenge traditional views of human cognition. We focus on a specific form of embodiment posited by CMT (Lakoff & Johnson, 1999) and review relevant experimental results (Landau et al., 2010), and it is therefore hoped that this book will be of interest to thoughtful nonscientists who wish to apprise themselves of this important set of developments in understanding some central questions about human nature.

REFERENCES

Aristotle. (2006). *Poetics and rhetoric* (S. H. Butcher & W. R. Roberts, Trans.). New York, NY: Barnes & Noble Classics. (Original work published circa 335 B.C.E.)

Asch, S. E. (1946). Forming impressions of personality. *The Journal of Abnormal and Social Psychology, 41,* 258–290. doi:10.1037/h0055756

Bargh, J. A. (2006). What have we been priming all these years? On the development, mechanisms, and ecology of nonconscious social behavior. *European Journal of Social Psychology, 36,* 147–168. doi:10.1002/ejsp.336

Chomsky, N. (1995). *The minimalist program.* Cambridge, MA: MIT Press.

Damasio, A. (1994). *Descartes' error: Emotion, reason, and the human brain.* New York, NY: Grosset/Putnam.

Fiske, S. T., Cuddy, A. J. C., & Glick, P. (2007). Universal dimensions of social perception: Warmth and competence. *Trends in Cognitive Sciences, 11,* 77–83. doi:10.1016/j.tics.2006.11.005

Fiske, S. T., & Taylor, S. E. (1991). *Social cognition*. New York, NY: Random House.

Fodor, J. A. (1983). *Modularity of mind*. Cambridge, MA: MIT Press.

Geary, J. (2011). *I is an other*. New York, NY: HarperCollins.

Gibbs, R. W. (1994). *The poetics of mind: Figurative thought, language, and understanding*. Cambridge, England: Cambridge University Press.

Gibbs, R. W. (Ed.). (2008). *The Cambridge handbook of metaphor and thought*. New York, NY: Cambridge University Press. doi:10.1017/CBO9780511816802

Goleman, D. (1995). *Emotional intelligence*. New York, NY: Bantam Books.

Higgins, E. T. (1996). Knowledge activation: Accessibility, applicability, and salience. In E. T. Higgins & A. W. Kruglanski (Eds.), *Social psychology: Handbook of basic principles* (pp. 133–168). New York, NY: Guilford Press.

Jaynes, J. (1976). *The origins of consciousness in the breakdown of the bicameral mind*. Boston, MA: Houghton Mifflin.

John, O. P., Robins, R. W., & Pervin, L. A. (2008). *Handbook of personality: Theory and research* (3rd ed.). New York, NY: Guilford Press.

Johnson, M. (1987). *The body in the mind: The bodily basis of reason and imagination*. Chicago, IL: University of Chicago Press.

Kövecses, Z. (2010). *Metaphor: A practical introduction*. New York, NY: Oxford University Press.

Kruglanski, A. W., & Higgins, E. T. (2007). *Social psychology: Handbook of basic principles* (2nd ed.). New York, NY: Guilford Press.

Lakoff, G., & Johnson, M. (1980). *Metaphors we live by*. Chicago, IL: University of Chicago Press.

Lakoff, G., & Johnson, M. (1999). *Philosophy in the flesh*. New York, NY: Basic Books.

Landau, M. J., Meier, B. P., & Keefer, L. A. (2010). A metaphor-enriched social cognition. *Psychological Bulletin, 136*, 1045–1067. doi:10.1037/a0020970

Langer, S. (1979). *Philosophy in a new key: A study in the symbolism of reason, rite, and art*. Cambridge, MA: Harvard University Press.

Mandler, J. (2004). *The foundations of mind: Origins of conceptual thoughts*. New York, NY: Oxford University Press. doi:10.1111/j.1467-7687.2004.00369.x

McGlone, M. (2007). What is the explanatory value of a conceptual metaphor? *Language & Communication, 27*, 109–126. doi:10.1016/j.langcom.2006.02.016

Meier, B. P., & Robinson, M. D. (2004). Why the sunny side is up. *Psychological Science, 15*, 243–247. doi:10.1111/j.0956-7976.2004.00659.x

Meier, B. P., Robinson, M. D., & Clore, G. L. (2004). Why good guys wear white: Automatic inferences about stimulus valence based on brightness. *Psychological Science, 15*, 82–87. doi:10.1111/j.0963-7214.2004.01502002.x

Meier, B. P., Robinson, M. D., Crawford, L. E., & Ahlvers, W. J. (2007). When "light" and "dark" thoughts become light and dark responses: Affect biases brightness judgments. *Emotion, 7*, 366–376. doi:10.1037/1528-3542.7.2.366

Morris, M. W., Sheldon, O. J., Ames, D. R., & Young, M. J. (2007). Metaphors and the market: Consequences and preconditions of agent and object metaphors in stock market commentary. *Organizational Behavior and Human Decision Processes, 102*, 174–192. doi:10.1016/j.obhdp.2006.03.001

Niedenthal, P. M., Barsalou, L. W., Winkielman, P., Krauth-Gruber, S., & Ric, F. (2005). Embodiment in attitudes, social perception, and emotion. *Personality and Social Psychology Review, 9*, 184–211. doi:10.1207/s15327957pspr0903_1

Nietzsche, F. (1974). On truth and falsity in their ultramoral sense. In O. Levy (Trans. & Ed.), *The complete works of Frederick Nietzsche* (Vol. 2, pp. 173–192). New York, NY: Gordon Press. (Original work published 1873)

Pinker, S. (2007). *The stuff of thought: Language as a window into human nature*. New York, NY: Penguin.

Schubert, T. W. (2005). Your highness: Vertical positions as perceptual symbols of power. *Journal of Personality and Social Psychology, 89*, 1–21. doi:10.1037/0022-3514.89.1.1

Sherman, G. D., & Clore, G. L. (2009). The color of sin: White and black are perceptual symbols of moral purity and pollution. *Psychological Science, 20*, 1019–1025. doi:10.1111/j.1467-9280.2009.02403.x

Whorf, B. L. (1998). *Language, thought, and reality: Selected writings of Benjamin Lee Whorf*. Cambridge, MA: MIT Press. (Original work published 1956)

Williams, L. E., & Bargh, J. A. (2008a). Experiencing physical warmth influences interpersonal warmth. *Science, 322*, 606–607. doi:10.1126/science.1162548

Williams, L. E., & Bargh, J. A. (2008b). Keeping one's distance: The influence of spatial distance cues on affect and evaluation. *Psychological Science, 19*, 302–308. doi:10.1111/j.1467-9280.2008.02084.x

Williams, L. E., Huang, J. Y., & Bargh, J. A. (2009). The scaffolded mind: Higher mental processes are grounded in early experience of the physical world. *European Journal of Social Psychology, 39*, 1257–1267. doi:10.1002/ejsp.665

2

CONCEPTUAL METAPHOR IN THOUGHT AND SOCIAL ACTION

RAYMOND W. GIBBS JR.

Metaphoric language has the potential to alter how we think and feel about various topics. Consider one excerpt from a speech by President Barack Obama given early on during his first term of office in 2009, in which he described the nation's economic challenges:

> In this *winter of our hardship* . . . *let us brave* once more the *icy currents*, and endure what *storms* may come; let it be said by our children's children that when *we were tested* we refused to let this *journey end* that we *did not turn back* nor did we *falter*; and with *eyes fixed on the horizon* and God's grace upon us, *we carried forth* that great gift of freedom and *delivered it* safely to future generations. (as cited in Scacco, 2009, para. 25, italics added by Scacco)

We can debate the merits of Obama's vision, but his words convey different images (e.g., "journey," "did not turn back," "we carried forth"), the

http://dx.doi.org/10.1037/14278-002
The Power of Metaphor: Examining Its Influence on Social Life, M. J. Landau, M. D. Robinson, and B. P. Meier (Editors)

majority of which center on the basic metaphoric theme of *life is a journey* and the more specific idea that our experiences of economic hardship (the target concept) is a journey (the source concept). Some have argued that Obama, similar to many other U.S. presidents, used the *journey* metaphor precisely because it echoes "the historical frontier motif common in American history of settlers who traveled westward" (Scacco, 2009).

One major question in contemporary metaphor studies focuses on whether the presence of metaphoric language, such as the different tropes seen in Obama's speech, necessarily reflects enduring patterns of metaphoric thought. Does Obama really, unconsciously, think of economic hardship as a kind of journey? Or might his metaphoric phrases be created for their rhetorical power to communicate specific beliefs and attitudes to the American public? The answer to this question leads to very different understandings of metaphor's role in thought and language. If we assume that people first come to think about some, usually abstract, subject in metaphoric terms, then the presence of metaphoric discourse would be motivated by different kinds of metaphoric thought. However, if people use linguistic metaphor only on certain occasions to accomplish particular social goals, then metaphor would ultimately be seen as less a cognitive phenomenon and more a matter of communication.

This chapter offers an analysis of this debate on the origins and functions of metaphor in both thought and language. There is plenty of empirical evidence from linguistics, psychology, and related disciplines to support the "metaphor is part of thought" (or *conceptual metaphor*) thesis (Gibbs, 2011b). However, the move from viewing metaphor as a linguistic entity to a fundamental aspect of thought has led to some scholars downplaying metaphor's role in social action. My argument is that a broader examination of the ways people think metaphorically demonstrates how metaphor is a pervasive social action that allows us to better coordinate with both ourselves and others. This expanded vision of conceptual metaphor points to a dismantling of traditional divides between thought, language, and communication and highlights the emergence of metaphor as a context-sensitive tool for meeting all sorts of adaptive challenges in daily life.

LINGUISTIC ANALYSES OF CONCEPTUAL METAPHOR

The proposal that metaphor is as much a part of ordinary thought as it is of language has been voiced by rhetoricians, philosophers, and others for hundreds of years, but it became very prominent in the past 30 years with the rise of *conceptual metaphor theory* (CMT) starting with the publication of Lakoff and Johnson's (1980) *Metaphors We Live By* (for additional overview of

CMT, see Chapter 1, this volume). Lakoff and Johnson provided systematic linguistic evidence to support the claim that there are indeed metaphors of thought or *conceptual metaphors*. Although some linguistic metaphors clearly present novel conceptualizations of different objects and ideas, many conventional linguistic statements reflect the existence of enduring conceptual metaphors. For example, consider the following set of expressions about aspects of people's lives:

- "His life took an unexpected turn after he met her."
- "John is struggling to get someplace in his career."
- "Sally is off to a slow start working on her thesis."
- "Their relationship was moving along in a good direction."
- "Jack was spinning his wheels trying to solve the math problem."

Each statement reflects a particular way of thinking about life and more generally demonstrates the metaphoric concept of a life as a kind of journey. The *life is a journey* conceptual metaphor has as its primary function the cognitive role of understanding one concept (life) in terms of another (taking journeys). Conceptual metaphors arise when we try to understand difficult, complex, abstract, or less delineated concepts, such as the idea of life, in terms of familiar ideas, such as the physical taking of journeys. This mapping of journey onto life gives rise to a range of entailments, as shown in Table 2.1.

Each linguistic expression about life as a kind of journey typically reflects one or more of these different entailments arising, once more, from the conceptual metaphor of *life is a journey*. Obama's earlier statements are clearly motivated by this same metaphoric concept.

Since 1980, several hundred cognitive linguistic projects have demonstrated how systematic patterns of conventional expressions reveal the presence of underlying conceptual metaphors. These studies have explored a large range of target concepts and domains (e.g., the mind, concepts of the self,

TABLE 2.1.
The Mapping of Journey Onto Life

Journey	Life
Traveler	Person leading a life
Journey or motion toward a destination	Leading a life (with purpose)
Destinations	Life goals
Obstacles in the way of motion	Difficulties in life
Distance covered	Progress made
Path or way of the journey	The manner or way of living
Choices about the path	Choices in life

Note. From *Language, Mind and Culture* (p.116) by Z. Kövecses, 2006, New York, NY: Oxford University Press. Copyright 2006 by Oxford University Press. Adapted with permission.

emotions, science, morality and ethics, economics, legal concepts, politics, mathematics, illness and death, education, psychoanalysis), within a vast number of languages (e.g., Spanish, Dutch, Chinese, Hungarian, Persian, Arabic, French, Japanese, Cora, Swedish), including sign languages and ancient languages (e.g., Latin, Ancient Greek), and have investigated the role of conceptual metaphors in thinking and speaking/writing within many academic disciplines (e.g., education, philosophy, mathematics, theater arts, physics, chemistry, architecture, political science, economics, geography, nursing, religion, law, business and marketing, and film). Additional cognitive linguistic studies have revealed the fundamental importance of conceptual metaphors in other areas of linguistic structure and behavior, including historical language change, polysemy, the creation and interpretation of novel metaphors, child language acquisition, and even metaphors in Egyptian hieroglyphics (Gibbs, 2011b).

The main upshot of this varied research is that recurring patterns of conceptual metaphors have influence in people's thinking, speaking, and understanding. Certain conceptual metaphors, known as *primary metaphors* have a greater universal appeal because they reflect pervasive correlations in embodied experience typically shared by all people, such as *understanding is seeing* ("I can't see what you are saying in that article"), *intimacy is closeness* (e.g., "We have a close relationship"), *important is big* (e.g., "Tomorrow is a big day"), *more is up* (e.g., "Prices are high"), and *causes are physical forces* (e.g., "They push the bill through Congress"; Grady, 1997; see also Chapter 11, this volume). In this way, basic metaphoric schemes of thought are grounded in embodied experience, one reason why CMT is often linked to new developments in the embodied cognition movement in cognitive science (Gibbs, 2006a).

CRITICISMS OF CONCEPTUAL METAPHOR THEORY

The claim that one can find metaphor in both language and thought is highly controversial, despite the large literature in cognitive linguistics on CMT. Many scholars across several academic disciplines are openly skeptical about cognitive linguistic arguments in favor of conceptual metaphor (Haser, 2005; McGlone, 2007; Murphy, 1996; Pinker, 2007). The most general question voiced by these critics is whether the presence of metaphor in language necessarily indicates anything about the way people ordinarily think. Most everyone acknowledges that the production and adoption of novel metaphors may indicate that someone is drawing novel connections between dissimilar knowledge domains, as when the poet Robert Burns created a novel mapping in his famous line "My love is a red, red, rose." But the argument that systematic patterns of conventional expressions, novel metaphors, and polysemy indicate vitally alive metaphoric concepts is far less convincing. Consider a few of the general criticisms leveled against CMT by scholars from varying disciplines, especially in regard to the linguistic evidence presumably supporting this theory.

Isolated Constructed Examples

Many metaphor scholars complain that far too many of the linguistic analyses presented in favor of CMT are based on isolated examples often constructed by the research analyst (e.g., the analysis of *life is a journey* discussed earlier). But are these constructed examples representative of how people use metaphor in real discourse? Some linguists looking at metaphor in naturalistic texts find both dense clusters of expressions motivated by a single conceptual metaphor and many instances in which people flip back and forth between several metaphoric source concepts when talking about some abstract target concept. It is somewhat unclear how CMT would address this kind of variability in metaphoric talk. More generally, doubts about the ecological validity of linguistic analyses lead many to question the scientific basis of CMT, especially as a psychological account of human concepts.

Limitations of the Individual Analyst

Metaphor scholars, especially in fields such as psychology, suggest that linguistic analyses of conceptual metaphors, such as *arguments are wars*, are based on an individual linguist's own intuitions that may be theoretically motivated. More objective evidence is required, using naive research participants, to confirm the existence of particular conceptual metaphors. Critics also complain that it is impossible for people, even trained linguists, to introspect about fast-acting cognitive unconscious processes, such as if and when conceptual metaphors are used in ordinary thinking and metaphoric language use. Difficulty in introspecting about these rapid unconscious mental processes demands, once again, that more objective evidence be collected from individuals who do not hold theory-biased beliefs. There is also a great need for experimental evidence that tests previous empirical hypotheses about what people are likely to do when thinking and speaking metaphorically, rather than trying to explain their linguistic behavior after the fact given the existence of certain patterns of speech.

Lack of Explicit Criteria for Metaphor Identification

Some psychologists and linguists argue that many conventional expressions that cognitive linguists view as metaphoric are not metaphoric at all and are treated by ordinary speakers and listeners as literal speech (McGlone, 2007; Pinker, 2007). They suggest that simple expressions such as "He attacked every weak point in my argument" are entirely literal and not motivated by a conceptual metaphor such as *arguments are wars*. Most ordinary speakers, as well as traditional metaphor scholars in literary studies, do not believe that "Your criticisms were right on target," for example, is poetic or metaphoric. People may use metaphoric language as a matter of convention without necessarily having some underlying cognitive mapping occur between disparate source and target concepts. For instance, the simple phrase "John blew his stack" may be produced or understood to mean "John got very angry" without an individual having to access or compute some mapping between *anger* and *heated fluid in the bodily container*, as suggested by traditional cognitive linguistic analyses (Steen, 2006).

In fact, cognitive linguistic analyses on conceptual metaphor rarely provide explicit criteria about either (a) how to identify what is metaphoric in language or (b) how to infer what conceptual metaphors motivate different groupings of metaphoric discourse. Metaphor scholars need to find reliable and replicable criteria for both identifying metaphors in real discourse and then provide explicit steps for determining what patterns of language necessarily imply the existence of a particular conceptual metaphor.

CMT Is Unfalsifiable and Needs Nonlinguistic Evidence

Some psychologists maintain that CMT is unfalsifiable if the only data in its favor are the systematic groupings of metaphors linked by a common theme (Vervaeke & Kennedy, 1996). Consider the conceptual metaphor *argument is war*, which presumably motivates conventional expressions such as "He attacked my argument" and "He defended his position." Cognitive linguistic research suggests that any expressions about arguments that do not fit the war theme are really evidence for different conceptual metaphor themes, such as arguments are *weighing*, *testing*, or *comparing*. This line of reasoning implies that no linguistic statement can be brought forward as evidence against the *argument is war* metaphor, which makes the basic tenet of CMT impossible to falsify.

In a similar way, critics argue that CMT relies on circular logic. For example, a traditional analysis may start with an examination of different conventional expressions that in turn suggest the existence of an underlying conceptual metaphor. However, the final step in making the existence proof for any conceptual metaphor is to go back to the language to find other linguistic expressions that fit the same conceptual metaphor schema. This strategy appears to be circular according to many critics of CMT (Ritchie, 2003). Having nonlinguistic evidence would help eliminate this problem of circularity that may be inherent in most traditional cognitive linguistic analyses in favor of conceptual metaphor (Murphy, 1996).

CMT Is Vague in Its Claims About Metaphor Processing

What exact role do conceptual metaphors play in verbal metaphor understanding? Consider the novel metaphoric expression "My marriage is a rocky roller-coaster ride from hell." CMT generally asserts that people understand this linguistic expression by accessing from memory the underlying conceptual metaphor *love relationships are journeys*. Yet does one first access the conceptual metaphor from memory and only then apply it to infer metaphoric meaning of expression? If so, does the conceptual metaphor that is accessed come with a complete set of meaning entailments spelled out, or do these have to be computed each time given the specific linguistic utterance and context?

Or might conceptual metaphors only arise as after-the-fact products of linguistic understanding? For example, people could interpret "John blew his stack" to mean "John got very angry" and only then, in certain situations, tacitly recognize that this expression is motivated by the underlying conceptual metaphor *anger is heated fluid in the bodily container?* CMT scholars have not considered these different possibilities in their articulation of the theory.

Furthermore, cognitive linguistic analyses typically assume that only complete conceptual metaphors structure our understanding of certain metaphoric language. One plausible alternative is that many conceptual metaphors offer partial, probabilistic constraints on the interpretation process (Gibbs & Santa Cruz, 2012). Many psycholinguistic theories of language processing now adopt a "constraint-satisfaction" view in which many sources of information combine in, once more, partial, probabilistic ways to produce satisfactory, in the moment, interpretations of what speakers mean by what they say. CMT has not yet embraced this newer vision of discourse processing, which may provide a more complete and context-sensitive approach to linguistic interpretation.

CMT Ignores Other Factors

One of the most persistent criticisms of CMT is that the theory fails to consider a wide range of other alternative possibilities in its accounts of metaphoric thought and language. Even scholars working within cognitive linguistics often note that conceptual metaphors alone are not sufficiently powerful to enable many of the systematic patterns of metaphoric language use. For example, many scholars maintain that ideological and cultural forces shape people's adoption of particular metaphoric themes in specific discourses

(Goatly, 2007). Other scholars detail how CMT ignores specific linguistic (i.e., lexical and grammatical) factors that lead to people using particular linguistic forms when speaking and writing metaphorically (e.g., Svanlund, 2007), none of which can be explained simply in terms of conceptual metaphor activation.

CMT Is Reductionist

Finally, various metaphor scholars, mostly those working in linguistic poetics and the philosophy of aesthetics, complain that CMT is far too reductionist in its account of verbal metaphor (Haser, 2005). After all, CMT reduces the consideration of novel poetic language to static conceptual metaphors that are grounded in recurring embodied experiences and even neural processes.

Many metaphor scholars seek to understand the consciously produced aesthetic, poetic qualities of metaphors, which they believe have little to do with the possible embodied and conceptual foundations of metaphor (Steen, 2006). Along this line, much traditional research on metaphor focuses on how people interpret the novel, emergent meanings of classic "A is B" metaphors, such as "My love is a red, red rose" and see this activity as being related to artistic intentions and deliberate metaphor use on the part of speakers and writers (Gibbs, 2011a). CMT rarely considers any of these other possible constraints on why people produce metaphors in the ways they do or how we interpret verbal metaphors as having specific, poetic meanings.

PUTTING CMT ON FIRMER EMPIRICAL GROUND

The critical attention given to CMT reflects both the prominence of the theory in interdisciplinary metaphor studies and some of the limitations the theory has as a comprehensive account of metaphoric language and thought. Regardless of one's opinion of the criticisms of CMT, the various discussions of the theory have led to several new developments in cognitive linguistics, cognitive psychology, and elsewhere that now place CMT on firmer empirical ground. Some of this research also points toward viewing conceptual metaphor as social action.

Methods for Metaphoric Language Identification

First, several attempts have been made to offer reliable, replicable procedures for identifying metaphorically used words in discourse (e.g., Pragglejaz Group, 2007; Steen et al., 2010). These empirical methods have provided researchers with important tools for assessing the idea that metaphor is ubiquitous in language, an idea forwarded early on in the history of CMT. Not surprisingly, metaphorically used words appear to be make up only about 10% to 20% of all words in discourse, with different genres having varying rates of metaphor use (e.g., metaphors are not as frequent in fiction as in other genres; Steen et al., 2010).

Methods for Determining Conceptual Metaphors

Second, advances in corpus linguistic methodologies and databases have provided quantitative insights into the identification and counting of conceptual metaphors in discourse (Deignan, 2006; Stefanowitsch & Gries, 2006). At the same time, different computational schemes have been proposed for inferring the existence of conceptual metaphors in different discourse domains (e.g., economics; Martin, 1990; Mason, 2004). Much of this newer research, it is fair to say, offers confirming evidence for the idea that certain conceptual metaphors are pervasive in different discourse domains, as originally proposed by CMT. Still, the corpus linguistic research also highlights some of the linguistic factors (e.g., lexical and grammatical information) in metaphor use that critics argue CMT too often ignores.

Metaphor in Nonlinguistic Experience

Third, a growing body of research from many academic disciplines suggests the presence of conceptual metaphors in many nonlinguistic domains, including psychophysical judgments about time and space, gestural systems, mathematics, music, dance, pictorial advertising and comics, architecture, material culture, and other aspects of multimodal metaphor (for reviews, see Forceville & Urios-Aparisi, 2009; Gibbs, 2011b). These different lines of empirical research lend greater credence to the major claims of CMT that metaphor is fundamentally part of everyday cognition, not just a linguistic, rhetorical device as presumed by traditional theories of metaphor. Nonetheless, we still do not have a reliable, agreed on method for examining some stretch of metaphoric language (or gesture, music, or art) and then deducing that specific conceptual metaphors necessarily motivate systematic patterns of behavior.

Experimental Research on Conceptual Metaphor in Thinking and Verbal Metaphor Use

Perhaps the main development in placing CMT on firmer empirical ground is seen in the extensive experimental research on conceptual metaphors in psycholinguistics and social psychology. This work addresses some of the complaints about the purely linguistic evidence on CMT, especially the needs for studies that do not rely on individual analysts and that provide nonlinguistic data. Testing CMT as a psychological theory of metaphoric thought and communication requires, at the very least, that one determine (a) whether different metaphoric meanings are motivated by conceptual metaphors that are part of people's long-term memory and (b) whether conceptual metaphors are automatically recruited during immediate experiences, including people's producing and understanding of metaphoric language and gesture.

Numerous experimental studies provide a positive answer to the first of these questions (Gibbs, 1994, 2006a, 2011b; Gibbs & Colston, 2012). These include projects showing that conceptual metaphors shape people's tacit understandings of why conventional and novel metaphoric expressions have the meanings they do for idioms (e.g., "John blew his stack" being motivated by *anger is heated fluid in the bodily container*) and proverbs (e.g., "Don't put all your eggs in one basket"); people's context sensitive judgments about the meanings of idioms; people's judgments about the permissible mappings underlying primary metaphors, such as *desire is hunger* (e.g., "John hungered for fame"); people's answers to questions about temporal events, people's answers to questions about metaphorically motivated fictive motion (e.g., "The road runs along the coast"); and people's semantic and episodic memories for conceptual metaphors, such as *life is a journey*. These various studies, using a range of research methodologies, suggest that people's tacit understandings of why many metaphoric words and phrases have the meanings they do are motivated by enduring conceptual metaphors.

Other studies examined the role of conceptual metaphor in problem solving. For example, university students read a report about the crime rate in a fictitious city, named Addison (Thibodeau & Boroditsky, 2011). Some of the students saw the report in which the crime was early on described as "a beast preying" on Addison, and the other students saw the crime report with a metaphor of "a virus infecting" Addison. Both stories contained identical information, presented after the metaphor, about crime statistics. After reading their respective stories, the students had to propose a solution to the Addison crime problem. Once again, the specific metaphor people read influenced their proposed crime solutions. The participants reading the "beast preying" metaphor suggested harsher enforcement be applied to catching and jailing criminals. In contrast, participants who read the "virus infecting" metaphor proposed solutions that focused on finding the root causes of the crime and creating social programs to protect the community. The power that metaphor had on people's problem-solving solutions was covert as students did not mention the metaphors when asked to state what influenced them the most in coming up with their crime solution (i.e., most people mentioned the crime statistics). In general, reading of metaphoric statements activated conceptual metaphoric knowledge that constrained people's subsequent problem-solving abilities.

However, demonstrating that conceptual metaphors motivate the meanings of verbal metaphors does not imply that people always access conceptual metaphors each time they produce or interpret relevant metaphoric language. Different types of experiments, using online methodologies, indicate a positive answer to this possibility (see Gibbs, 2011b, for reviews of this work). Thus, people find it relatively easy to read verbal metaphors in which meanings are motivated by conceptual metaphors identical to those structuring the previous text or discourse. Priming tasks revealed that conceptual metaphors (e.g., *anger is heated fluid in a container*) are accessed during people's immediate processing of idioms motivated by those conceptual metaphors (e.g., "John blew his stack"). Other studies show that it takes people longer to process consecutive verbal metaphors in discourse when these are motivated by different underlying conceptual metaphors (Gentner, Imai, & Boroditsky, 2002).

Experimental Research on Embodied Metaphor in Verbal Metaphor Use

Many psycholinguistic studies also demonstrate how immediate bodily experience influences metaphor interpretations. For example, in one series of studies on metaphoric talk about time, students waiting in line at a café were given the statement "Next Wednesday's meeting has been moved forward two days" and then asked "What day is the meeting that has been rescheduled?" (Boroditsky & Ramscar, 2002). Students who were farther along in the line (i.e., who had thus very recently experienced more forward spatial motion) were more likely to say that the meeting had been moved to Friday, rather than to Monday. Similarly, people riding a train were presented the same ambiguous statement and question about the rescheduled meeting. Passengers who were at the end of their journey reported that the meeting was moved to Friday significantly more than did people in the middle of their journey. Although both groups of passengers were experiencing the same physical experience of sitting in a moving train, they thought differently about their journey and consequently responded differently to the rescheduled meeting question. These results suggest how ongoing sensorimotor experience has an influence on people's comprehension of certain metaphoric statements.

One new idea in psycholinguistics is that embodied simulations related to conceptual metaphors play a role in people's immediate processing of verbal metaphors (Gibbs, 2006b). Embodied simulation broadly refers to the reenactment of previous sensorimotor states during immediate processing of linguistic and nonlinguistic stimuli and when imagining different possible actions. People may create partial embodied simulations of speakers' metaphoric messages that involve moment-by-moment "what must it be like" processes that make use of ongoing tactile-kinesthetic experiences (Gibbs, 2006b). Understanding abstract, metaphoric events, such as *grasping the concept*, for example, is constrained by aspects of people's embodied experience as if they are immersed in the discourse situation, even when these events can only be metaphorically and not physically realized (i.e., it is not physically possible to grasp an abstract entity such as a "concept").

Several studies provide support for this view of embodied simulation. For instance, people's mental imagery for metaphoric phrases, such as "tear apart the argument," exhibit significant embodied qualities of the actions referred to by these phrases (e.g., people conceive of the "argument" as a physical object that when torn apart no longer persists; Gibbs, Gould, & Andric, 2005–2006). Furthermore, people's speeded comprehension of metaphoric phrases, such as "grasp the concept," is facilitated when they first make, or imagine making, a relevant bodily action, such as a grasping motion (N. L. Wilson & Gibbs, 2007). Finally, a novel study revealed that people walked farther toward a target when thinking about a metaphoric statement "Your relationship was moving along in a good direction" when the context ultimately suggested a positive relationship than when the scenario alluded to a negative, unsuccessful relationship (Gibbs, 2012). This same difference, however, was not obtained when people read the nonmetaphoric statement "Your relationship was very important" in the same two scenarios. People appear to partly understand the metaphoric statement from building an embodied simulation relevant to *love relationships are journeys*, such that their bodies simulate taking a longer journey with the successful relationship than with the unsuccessful one.

These different empirical studies on embodied simulation and metaphor understanding offer a view of CMT that differs from how the theory is typically interpreted within linguistics and psychology. People do not just access passively encoded conceptual metaphors from long-term memory during online metaphor understanding. Understanding a conventional metaphoric expression such as Obama's statement "We did not turn back" may not just arise from the simple activation of a conceptual metaphor such as *life is a journey*, which has been stored within some conceptual network. However, people may spontaneously create a particular construal of metaphors that are "soft-assembled" via simulation processes operating during thinking, speaking, and understanding. This possibility fits in nicely with the proposal, outlined subsequently, that conceptual metaphors primarily arise in specific moments of social thought and discourse.

Experimental Research on Conceptual Metaphor in Social Experience

Finally, one of the most exciting lines of empirical research related to conceptual metaphors comes from a wide variety of studies showing how metaphoric thought shapes social perceptions and cognition, as many of the chapters in this volume explore. For example, there is the widespread set of metaphors suggesting that *good is up* and *bad is down*. Studies show that people evaluate positive words faster if these are presented in a higher vertical position on a computer screen and recognize negative words faster if they appear in the lower part of the screen (Meier & Robinson, 2004). People judge a group's social power to be greater when these judgments are made at the top of a computer screen than when presented in the lower part of the screen (Schubert, 2005). These findings are consistent with the idea that people conceive of good and bad as being spatially located along some vertical dimension, a concept that arises from good experiences being upward (e.g., being alive and healthy) and bad ones being downward (e.g., sickness and death).

Physically engaging in certain actions often leads people to adopt metaphoric concepts that influence their social judgments. Having people hold warm, as opposed to cold, cups of coffee for a few seconds led them to judge another person's interpersonal traits as being warmer (Williams & Bargh, 2008), a finding that is completely consistent with the primary metaphor *affection is warmth*. Within a different experiential domain, having people make judgments about people's behavior in a dirty work area caused them to rate the behavior as more immoral than when the same judgments were made in a clean work area (Schnall, Benton, & Harvey, 2008). Asking people to recall an immoral deed, as opposed to an ethical one, made them more likely to choose an antiseptic wipe as a free gift after the experiment (Zhong & Liljenquist, 2006). Both these findings are consistent with the conceptual metaphors *good is clean* and *bad is dirty*. These few examples illustrate how conceptual metaphors can structure individuals' nonlinguistic experiences, including those related to making social judgments about other people and events. This social psychological research adds significant empirical evidence in favor of the claim that conceptual metaphors emerge in everyday experiences that are not tied to language or people's linguistic performances. More generally, there is a large, diverse body of research within psycholinguistics and social psychology that overcomes some of the earlier noted difficulties with linguistic analyses of conceptual metaphors. These experimental studies place CMT on a firmer empirical foundation by demonstrating how conceptual metaphors are part of how people think, reason, and understand one another in a variety of experimental tasks.

We must be careful, however, not to assume that embodied conceptual metaphors are omnipresent in language use and social experience. Some of the positive evidence on CMT may be dependent on the specific experimental task, and there are also clear individual differences in the extent to which people recruit conceptual metaphors in thinking, speaking, and understanding. One important challenge for the future is to articulate theories that can capture some of the empirical regularities and variations associated with conceptual metaphor behaviors both seen in the experimental literature and evident from linguistic analyses of metaphor in discourse (e.g., Cameron, 2011; Gibbs & Colston, 2012).

CONCEPTUAL METAPHORS FOR THOUGHT OR COMMUNICATION

The history of empirical research on CMT in linguistics and psychology has primarily shown how metaphoric mappings are conventional parts of the human conceptual system. Psychological studies have gone on to demonstrate that conceptual metaphors are routinely used in many aspects of thinking, speaking, and understanding. CMT scholars view this diverse research as contradicting the traditional idea that metaphor is a purely linguistic device used for social, communicative purposes.

The Social Nature of Metaphoric Thought

Nonetheless, the emphasis in CMT on metaphor as essential for thought vastly underplays the social nature of ordinary thinking. My claim, in fact, is that it may be impossible to disentangle private metaphoric thought from metaphoric social action. Even if metaphoric concepts are essential for certain aspects of abstract thought, they typically emerge in specific contexts in which people attempt to better coordinate their own actions and their interactions with other persons. In this way, conceptual metaphors are both cognitive, in the sense of shaping thinking, and social, in the sense of facilitating people's social behaviors. There are several possibilities to consider in making this argument.

First, many of the psycholinguistic studies on conceptual metaphor in language use have implicit social demands, either through the stimuli participants read or from the mere fact of being in an experiment in which instructions must be followed. Cognitive psychologists typically view their findings as evidence of private mental representations and processes. Yet many of the experimental effects discussed in the previous section can be readily interpreted as having social origins as in cases where participants make judgments about the contextual sensitive nature of metaphoric meaning or solve social-oriented problems.

Furthermore, people may think in multiple metaphoric ways depending on the social context. Imagine, for example, that I am thinking about my marriage (or past marriages, really). Several metaphoric themes can help me do this, including the cross-domain mappings of *marriage is a journey* and *marriage is a manufactured building,* among many others. Both conceptual metaphors offer concrete, even embodied, understandings for the abstract concept of marriage. I may recruit either of these metaphoric concepts in different contexts depending on my particular needs, such as when I sit and consider whether I am satisfied with the present state of my marriage. Thus, one metaphor, *marriage is a journey,* highlights the changing nature of marriage over time, with the people facing different obstacles and making various choices on how to proceed as the marriage continues, or not. The *journey* metaphor also emphasizes how different circumstances shape the path that any marriage takes. In contrast, the *marriage is a manufactured building* metaphor emphasizes the stable nature of marriage and how the participants need to build a solid foundation for their marriage as a more static entity. Adopting either of these conceptual metaphors entails rather different consequences for me as I evaluate the present status of my marriage and its possible future. In this way, conceptual metaphors serve intrapersonal needs in enabling me to coordinate my various plans and goals that may be active at any moment in life. This makes my metaphoric thinking, even when alone, communicative in the sense of how different conceptual metaphors help me implicitly understand and communicate with myself and decide my future actions.

My thinking of different marriage metaphors is also inherently social given the implied presence of others as I adopt different conceptual metaphors. I do not simply think of a specific marriage metaphor, for example, and then decide whether and how to communicate this view to others. Instead, my immediate metaphoric thinking about marriage is always relational given the constraints my adoption of that metaphor places on my marriage actions. As is the case with private emotional experiences (Fridlund, 1994), people's thinking without speaking episodes are implicitly social both for purposes of communicating with oneself and possibly interacting with others at a later time. Our tacit imagination of specific and generalized others shapes our so-called private cognition. This argument is consistent with various other empirical findings from cognitive psychology showing the context-sensitivity of how people report their understandings of various conceptual categories (Barsalou, 2008), where both the explicit task and people's implicit assumptions about what experimenters are looking for directly influence people's in-the-moment categorization behaviors. How people think and report the contents of their thoughts is always constrained by social factors, including assumptions about other people's implied expectations. Viewing metaphor as part of thought should not, therefore, imply that metaphors have little connection with our omnipresent need to better communicate with ourselves and with others in the social world.

Do Verbal Metaphors Give Rise to Conceptual Metaphors?

A related issue to consider in the *metaphor for thought* versus *metaphor for communication* debate is the degree to which conceptual metaphors develop within social context. Some scholars suggest that conceptual metaphors may "ultimately derive from the repeated use of linguistic metaphor, and thus arise from communicative rather than purely cognitive reasons" (D. Wilson, 2011, p. 192). One proposal along this line claims that metaphoric concepts should be understood as "features designed for the situational rhetoric of talk, rather than for displaying a person's abstract understanding of the world" (Edwards, 1991, p. 515). People possess enduring knowledge of cross-domain mappings, or conceptual metaphors, but these mental mappings are constructed "in the adoption of rhetorical practices" (Edwards, 1991, p. 525). Conceptual metaphors may become conceptually salient because people encounter certain verbal metaphors repeatedly in communicative situations, which leads them to conceive of some abstract targets in metaphoric ways.

For example, recall the empirical research from social psychology showing that people associate unethical or immoral behavior with dirt. Not surprisingly, people use many linguistic statements that refer to this association, such as seen in the following list (Stefanowitsch, 2011, p. 301):

- the stain of guilt, sin, illegitimacy
- impure thoughts, soul, character
- a dirty mind, look, word, secret
- an unclean thought, spirit, mind
- to contaminate a relationship
- to taint someone's reputation
- to pollute someone's mind, thoughts

The question is, "do we think of disagreeable things as *dirty* because there are linguistic metaphors that make this connection, or are the linguistic metaphors simply an expression of a preexisting mental connection," (Stefanowitsch, 2011, p. 302) such as the conceptual metaphors *good is clean* and *bad is dirty*? My suggestion is that we need not answer this question one way or the other. There is no reason to assume that the underlying motivation for verbal metaphor has to be either (a) embodied-cognitive or (b) social-communicative. Embodied and linguistic experience may both continually contribute to the emergence of different verbal metaphors. Thinking of the correspondences between dirt and immoral actions and then talking about this relationship mutually enhances the possibility of the other. Looking at correspondences, and possible differences, between people's use and exposure to various metaphoric language and their felt embodied experiences of metaphor (e.g., *good is clean*, *affection is warmth*) is one place to begin examining how verbal metaphor may shape metaphoric social action.

In general, people's bodily actions and their social experiences producing and interpreting verbal metaphors likely act as multiple, interacting constraints on the creation and continued reliance on entrenched conceptual metaphors. Cognitive linguistic studies and the empirical findings from psychology can easily be interpreted as support for the bidirectional relationship between metaphoric communication and cognition, not just as metaphoric concepts serving as the sole causal basis for linguistic metaphor.

Conceptual Metaphors as Emergent
From Metaphoric Speaking in Context

Dissolving the strict divide between *metaphor for thought* and *metaphor for communication* points to a new vision of CMT in which conceptual metaphors emerge not as prepackaged ideas from our private minds but from specific acts of thinking, speaking, and understanding that are always social. One proposal along this line, called the *discourse dynamic approach*, emphasizes the functions that metaphor has in "thinking and talking" rather than seeing verbal metaphors as mere linguistic manifestations of underlying conceptual metaphors (Cameron, 2011; Gibbs & Cameron, 2008).

Consider, for example, the following excerpt from a remarkable set of conversations between a woman, Jo Berry, whose father, Sir Anthony Berry, was killed by a bomb in 1984, and Patrick Magee, who planted the bomb on behalf of the Irish Republican Army (IRA) during their conflict with the British government (Cameron, 2011). Jo Berry had asked to meet Pat Magee after he was released from prison to understand more about why the bombing happened. This excerpt is taken from the second recorded conversation between Jo and Pat, about 20 minutes into their talk. The words and phrases underlined are the source terms of the metaphors (i.e., those used metaphorically in this context). Up to this point, both Jo and Pat had talked about how the two of them came to be together in a reconciliation meeting, using similar *journey* metaphors to those seen below.

> 644 Pat   . . . (1.0) 1984,
> 645   when your father was killed,
> 646   or when I killed your father,
> 647   .. when the republican <u>movement</u> killed your father.
> 648   . . . (3.0) er,
> 649   my <u>journey</u>,
> 650   . . . (1.0) preceded that you were <u>catapulted</u> <u>into</u> this <u>struggle.</u>

651		.. I think,
652		er,
653		. . . (1.0) my <u>journey</u> preceded that.
654		. . . (1.0) but,
655		. . . (1.0) our <u>journey</u> began that moment.
656		. . . and here we are.
657		.. today.
658		sixteen years later.
659		seventeen years later.
660		. . . (1.0) it's quite a remarkable <u>journey.</u>
661		I think.
662		er,
663	Jo	. . . (2.0) you —
664	Pat	[er]
665	Jo	[you] said that,
666		. . . (2.0) the <u>price</u> that er —
667		. . . you <u>paid,</u>
668		for <u>taking up</u> violence,
669		was <u>part</u> —
670		. . . <u>partly</u> <u>losing</u> some of your humanity.
671	Pat	.. hmh
672	Jo	. . . and that now you're .. <u>refinding</u> that.
673		. . . (1.0) <u>through</u> .. other meetings with —
674		. . . (1.0) ehm,
675		other victims,
676		and loyalists,

Metaphor performance is typically manifested through successive metaphor sources that shift and develop as people negotiate meaning, extend their ideas, or exploit potential opened up by the use of a source term. For instance, the journey source was used previously in the talk to refer to Jo's effort to understand her father's murder and, in the preceding excerpt, is successively reused and adapted to refer to two additional targets:

| Pat's early history of politicization | "my journey" | 649, 653 |
| the process of meeting and reconciliation | "our journey" | 655, 660 |

These microlevel shifts and changes in the dynamics of linguistic metaphor concretely demonstrate the emergence of metaphor in discourse interaction as an inherently social affair.

Of course, source terms such as *came, went,* and *my journey* are highly conventional instances of metaphor. The question, however, is whether these varied uses of metaphor sources, in this case revolving around the idea of *journey* are driven by the activation of some prestored conceptual metaphor, such as *life is a journey*. Cameron (2011) argued that the microlevel shifts and changes in the dynamics of linguistic metaphor, as seen in the excerpt, concretely demonstrate the emergence of metaphor in discourse interaction as an inherently social affair. Conventional metaphors do not have similar meanings in different contexts but are dynamically recreated depending on the specific histories of the participants at the very points in which their talk unfolds. There is never a neutral position to which the cognitive system retreats after each use of a metaphor source, because each word is spoken in an always changing dynamic context that constrains what words, and metaphors, will come next. For this reason, conceptual metaphors may be better characterized as emergent stabilities that become "actualized" as people solve different problems for themselves and coordinate their actions with others.

My earlier discussion of metaphor use as embodied simulation is consistent with this dynamic perspective in that metaphoric thoughts and language are created, and not retrieved, via simulation processes that are shaped by specific bodily, cognitive, and social contexts. For instance, when Jo and Pat are using different metaphoric source terms related to the idea of "journey," they are imagining that they are physically engaged in different kinds of journeys, starting at some point, moving along a path, and attempting to reach particular destinations. Yet the imaginative simulation here truly differs depending on the exact moments in their conversational interaction, including factors such as their felt experience of the journeys from their earlier discourse and the particular source terms used (e.g., journey's beginning, proceeding, the IRA movement, being catapulted into a struggle, looking back at the distance traveled, or looking back at the remarkable journey). These instances of metaphoric thinking may from a distance all seem relevant to the *life is a journey* concept, but the actual living of the conceptual metaphor is far more specific, has an embodied feel to it, and is truly created according to the social circumstances of the discourse.

CONCLUSIONS AND RECOMMENDATIONS

The long history of metaphor scholarship has evolved from claims that metaphor was only a deviant, at best ornamental, use of language to the contemporary view that metaphors are fundamental to human thought. CMT continues to be the dominant, but by no means uncontroversial, theory in metaphor studies because it provides a detailed explanation for why people use metaphors in the ways they do and how many metaphors of thought arise from recurring embodied experiences.

Yet much of the linguistic and psychological evidence on conceptual metaphor originates in contexts in which people are participating in some kind of social action. Even when individuals are alone or engaged in some solitary experimental task, there is always an implicit sociality that significantly constrains behavior. Viewing conceptual metaphors as primarily situated in thought and arising from bodily experiences misses the dynamic coupling that all cognitive acts have with communicative, social actions. This claim about the social foundation of cognition is by no means novel and has a long history in psychology going back to the work of Mead (1934) and Vygotsky (1978), who emphasized how thinking takes its form from socially shared cognitive activities. In more recent years, psychologists and others have argued for *situated* and *distributed* cognition in which knowledge is situated in activity bound to social, cultural, and physical contexts (Robbins & Aydede, 2008). My argument is that conceptual metaphors are also inherently situated and must be studied in terms of the dynamic couplings between language and social actions, not just as pure cognitive entities passively stored in individual minds.

There are several concrete recommendations that follow from this revised perspective on the social nature of conceptual metaphor. First, metaphor scholars, regardless of their disciplinary orientation, must acknowledge the multiple constraints that shape metaphoric performance. Frankly, the world of metaphor research is too sharply divided into those embracing the belief that metaphors are primarily linguistic, cognitive (and even neural), social, or cultural, respectively, with some scholars denying the influence of other factors when they privilege the dimension of metaphor they personally study. It may be impossible to study, within the context of any individual research project, experimentally or otherwise, all of the factors that constrains when and how metaphoric actions come into being. However, metaphor researchers can acknowledge the complex, dynamical nature of human metaphoric action (e.g., language, gesture, art, social behaviors), and seek out correspondences between variables that they specifically examine and those studied by other metaphor scholars (e.g., between cognitive and sociocultural factors). Doing this would point the way to critical interactions among neural, cognitive, linguistic, and social forces that truly make up any set of human behaviors, including different metaphor performances.

Second, cognitive linguists who support CMT need to study the empirical results from social psychology and integrate these findings within their own theoretical explanations of metaphor in language and thought. The social psychological literature on conceptual metaphor that has emerged in recent years should not simply be seen as confirming hypotheses on "metaphors we live by" but as highlighting the distinctive social and embodied nature of metaphor. Furthermore, as is the case within psycholinguistics, a closer reading of the social psychological research on metaphoric action suggests that there are important boundary conditions under which embodied metaphoric effects are likely to be found, many of which relate to the particular experimental task used in some specific study. Metaphors may, once more, be a major part of how we live, yet metaphoric thinking and action, including language, may only emerge in particular contexts and given different adaptive goals. Rather than simply asserting that metaphor is or is not essential for thought and social life, which is how too much of the debate in the literature goes, it may be far more realistic to explore the circumstances under which metaphoric effects arise in human experience. Having some knowledge of the experimental literature on metaphor in social life should be helpful to linguists and others in understanding the true adaptive purposes that metaphor serves.

At the same time, as much as there is a continual need for further experimental studies on metaphor in thought and social life, psychologists, linguists, and others must examine the way metaphor emerges in discourse. As noted earlier, there have been major criticisms of linguistic studies on conceptual metaphor. Still, there is increasing attention to metaphor in realistic discourse, as illustrated by the discourse dynamics approach. One lesson, as noted earlier, is that some aspects of conceptual metaphor may arise from people's exposure to metaphoric language, not just from embodied experience alone. Linking experimental effects from social psychological studies with corpus linguistic studies on metaphoric word occurrence is surely one future empirical challenge to explore possible verbal metaphor influences on metaphoric thinking and social action. However, as mentioned earlier, both linguists and psychologists need to address the remarkable variability seen in metaphoric behaviors, evidenced in both discourse studies and experimental investigations. Part of this variability involves people using multiple, sometimes contradictory, source domains in their metaphoric talk. Moreover, metaphoric social action is likely shaped by multiple metaphoric constraints not yet studied by social psychologists. For example, people's social evaluations of another person may not simply be attributed to whether they hold a warm cup of coffee beforehand but by other metaphoric related factors such as the cleanliness of the room in which these judgments are made, the weight of the clipboard held, the upward position in which they may sit or stand as they participate in the experiment, to note just a few other variables. These different embodied metaphoric influences may be partial, and not all or none, and they may interact in complex, nonlinear ways that is the hallmark of much human behavior. We need to study not just single metaphoric behaviors but complex ones as well.

Another potential lesson of discourse studies is that metaphor need not be stored in minds as passively listed entities in memory for metaphor to really be seen as conceptual. This work documents the ways that metaphor comes and goes in discourse and suggests the strong possibility that metaphoric concepts dynamically emerge from conversational interaction as much as being retrieved from conceptual memory. Fans of CMT, and psychologists more generally, too often find empirical evidence that certain metaphoric concepts seem to shape human language or behavior but then immediately assume that these conceptual metaphors must be internal, mental, cognitive (and less social) representations. Examining real-life discourse offers significant insights into the dynamics of metaphor in social life that may also lead to a more social, discursive view of metaphor, one that still sees metaphor as part of thought, but as socially emergent cognition, not just as private concepts buried inside people's heads.

REFERENCES

Barsalou, L. (2008). Situating concepts. In P. Robbins & M. Aydede (Eds.), *Cambridge handbook of situated cognition* (pp. 236–263). New York, NY: Cambridge University Press. doi:10.1017/CBO9780511816826.014

Boroditsky, L., & Ramscar, M. (2002). The roles of body and mind in abstract thought. *Psychological Science, 13,* 185–189. doi:10.1111/1467-9280.00434

Cameron, L. (2011). *Metaphor and reconciliation: The discourse dynamics of empathy in post-conflict conversations.* London, England: Routledge.

Deignan, A. (2006). *Metaphor in corpus linguistics.* Amsterdam, The Netherlands: Benjamins.

Edwards, D. (1991). Categories are for talking: On the cognitive and discursive bases of categorization. *Theory & Psychology, 1,* 515–542. doi:10.1177/0959354391014007

Forceville, C., & Urios-Aparisi, E. (Eds.). (2009). *Multimodal metaphor.* Berlin, Germany: Mouton De Gruyter. doi:10.1515/9783110215366

Fridlund, A. (1994). *Human facial expression: An evolutionary view.* San Diego, CA: Academic Press.

Gentner, D., Imai, M., & Boroditsky, L. (2002). As time goes by: Evidence for two systems in processing space. *Language and Cognitive Processes, 17,* 537–565. doi:10.1080/01690960143000317

Gibbs, R. (1994). *The poetics of mind: Figurative thought, language, and understanding.* New York, NY: Cambridge University Press.

Gibbs, R. (2006a). *Embodiment and cognitive science.* New York, NY: Cambridge University Press.

Gibbs, R. (2006b). Metaphor interpretation as embodied simulation. *Mind & Language, 21,* 434–458. doi:10.1111/j.1468-0017.2006.00285.x

Gibbs, R. (2011a). Are deliberate metaphors really deliberate? A question of human consciousness and action. *Metaphor and the Social World, 1,* 26–52. doi:10.1075/msw.1.1.03gib

Gibbs, R. (2011b). Evaluating conceptual metaphor theory. *Discourse Processes, 48,* 529–562. doi:10.1080/0163853X.2011.606103

Gibbs, R. (2012). Walking the walk while thinking about the talk: Embodied interpretation of metaphorical narratives. Advance online publication. *Journal of Psycholinguistic Research.* doi:10.1007/s10936-012-9222-6

Gibbs, R., & Cameron, L. (2008). Social-cognitive dynamics of metaphor performance. *Cognitive Systems Research, 9,* 64–75. doi:10.1016/j.cogsys.2007.06.008

Gibbs, R., & Colston, H. (2012). *Interpreting figurative meaning.* New York, NY: Cambridge University Press. doi:10.1017/CBO9781139168779

Gibbs, R., Gould, J., & Andric, M. (2005–2006). Imagining metaphorical actions: Embodied simulations make the impossible plausible. *Imagination, Cognition and Personality, 25,* 221–238. doi:10.2190/97MK-44MV-1UUF-T5CR

Gibbs, R., & Santa Cruz, M. (2012). Temporal unfolding of conceptual metaphor experience. *Metaphor and Symbol, 27,* 299–311. doi:10.1080/10926488.2012.716299

Goatly, A. (2007). *Washing the brain: Metaphor and hidden ideology.* Amsterdam, The Netherlands: Benjamins.

Grady, J. (1997). Theories are buildings revisited. *Cognitive Linguistics, 8,* 267–290.

Haser, V. (2005). *Metaphor, metonymy, and experientialist philosophy: Challenging cognitive semantics.* Berlin, Germany: Mouton de Gruyter. doi:10.1515/9783110918243

Kövecses, Z. (2006). *Language, mind and culture.* New York, NY: Oxford University Press.

Lakoff, G., & Johnson, M. (1980). *Metaphors we live by.* Chicago, IL: University of Chicago Press.

Martin, J. (1990). *A computational model of metaphor interpretation.* San Diego, CA: Academic Press.

Mason, Z. (2004). CorMet: A computational, corpus-based conventional metaphor extraction system. *Computational Linguistics, 30,* 23–44. doi:10.1162/089120104773633376

McGlone, M. (2007). What is the explanatory value of a conceptual metaphor? *Language & Communication, 27,* 109–126. doi:10.1016/j.langcom.2006.02.016

Mead, G. H. (1934). *Mind, self and society.* Chicago, IL: University of Chicago Press.

Meier, B. P., & Robinson, M. D. (2004). Why the sunny side is up. *Psychological Science, 15,* 243–247. doi:10.1111/j.0956-7976.2004.00659.x

Murphy, G. L. (1996). On metaphoric representations. *Cognition, 60,* 173–204. doi:10.1016/0010-0277(96)00711-1

Pinker, S. (2007). *The stuff of thought.* New York, NY: Basic Books.

Pragglejaz Group. (2007). MIP: A method for identifying metaphorically-used words in discourse. *Metaphor and Symbol, 22,* 1–39.

Ritchie, D. (2003). ARGUMENT IS WAR—or a game of chess? Multiple meanings in the analysis of implicit metaphors. *Metaphor and Symbol, 18,* 125–146. doi:10.1207/S15327868MS1802_4

Robbins, P., & Aydede, M. (Eds.). (2008). *Cambridge handbook of situated cognition.* New York, NY: Cambridge University Press. doi:10.1017/CBO9780511816826

Scacco, J. (2009). Shaping economic reality: A critical metaphor analysis of President Barack Obama's economic language during his first 100 days. *Gnovis, X.* Retrieved from online.http://gnovisjournal.org/2009/12/22/shaping-economic-reality-critical-metaphor-analysis-president-barack-obama-s-economic-langua/

Schnall, S., Benton, J., & Harvey, S. (2008). With a clean conscience: Cleanliness reduces the severity of moral judgments. *Psychological Science, 19,* 1219–1222. doi:10.1111/j.1467-9280.2008.02227.x

Schubert, T. W. (2005). Your highness: Vertical positions as perceptual symbols of power. *Journal of Personality and Social Psychology, 89,* 1–21. doi:10.1037/0022-3514.89.1.1

Steen, G. (2006). The paradox of metaphor: Why we need a three-dimensional model of metaphor. *Metaphor and Symbol, 23,* 213–241.

Steen, G., Dorst, A., Herrmann, B., Kaal, A., Krennmayr, T., & Pasma, T. (2010). *A method for linguistic metaphor identification.* Amsterdam, The Netherlands: Benjamins.

Stefanowitsch, A. (2011). Cognitive linguistics as cognitive science. In M. Callies, W. Keller, & A. Lohofer (Eds.), *Bi-directionality in the cognitive sciences* (pp. 295–310). Amsterdam, The Netherlands: Benjamins.

Stefanowitsch, A., & Gries, S. (Eds.). (2006). *Corpus-based approaches to metaphor and metonymy.* Berlin, Germany: Mouton de Gruyter. doi:10.1515/9783110199895

Svanlund, J. (2007). Metaphor and convention. *Cognitive Linguistics, 18,* 47–89. doi:10.1515/COG.2007.003

Thibodeau, P. H., & Boroditsky, L. (2011). Metaphors we think with: The role of metaphor in reasoning. *PLoS ONE, 6,* e16782. doi:10.1371/journal.pone.0016782

Vervaeke, J., & Kennedy, J. (1996). Metaphors in language and thought: Disproof and multiple meanings. *Metaphor and Symbolic Activity, 11,* 273–284. doi:10.1207/s15327868ms1104_3

Vygotsky, L. (1978). *Mind in society.* Cambridge, MA: Harvard University Press.

Williams, L. E., & Bargh, J. A. (2008). Experiencing physical warm influences interpersonal warmth. *Science, 322,* 606–607. doi:10.1126/science.1162548

Wilson, D. (2011). Parallels and differences in the treatment of metaphor in relevance theory and cognitive linguistics. *Intercultural Pragmatics, 8,* 177–196. doi:10.1515/iprg.2011.009

Wilson, N. L., & Gibbs, R. (2007). Real and imagined body movement primes metaphor comprehension. *Cognitive Science, 31,* 721–731. doi:10.1080/15326900701399962

Zhong, C., & Liljenquist, K. (2006). Washing away your sins: Threatened morality and physical cleansing. *Science, 313,* 1451–1452. doi:10.1126/science.1130726

II

METAPHOR'S ROLE IN SOCIAL AND PERSONALITY PSYCHOLOGY PHENOMENA

3

CONCEPTUAL METAPHOR THEORY AND PERSON PERCEPTION

BRIAN P. MEIER, ABIGAIL A. SCHOLER,
AND REBECCA FINCHER-KIEFER

Fictional characters are typically portrayed with exaggerated personal qualities. These portrayals create interest for characters that may otherwise be mundane and unappealing. For example, Homer Simpson from the TV show *The Simpsons* has particular difficulty interpreting other people's emotions, leaving him at times unsure whether his wife and boss are happy or angry with him. Furthermore, his ability to attend to the present moment and reflect on the self is easily interrupted by the presence of donuts, beer, or television. The legendary fictional detective Sherlock Holmes, in contrast, has an uncanny ability to accurately interpret people's emotions, the causes of their actions, and the truthfulness of their statements.

As real people interact with others in their social environment, their ability to accurately perceive themselves and others falls somewhere in between that of Homer Simpson and Sherlock Holmes. This is because our perception of self and others is influenced by a host of variables that can bias our thoughts,

http://dx.doi.org/10.1037/14278-003

The Power of Metaphor: Examining Its Influence on Social Life, M. J. Landau, M. D. Robinson, and
B. P. Meier (Editors)

43

feelings, and behavior. For example, upon learning that a new acquaintance is an atheist, subsequent interactions with that person might be biased by our expectations and experiences with atheism (e.g., we may expect that person to be more confrontational or dogmatic). Other variables influence our interpretation of self and others in more subtle ways. Significant research has demonstrated the powerful nature of stereotypes in guiding perceptions of others (e.g., Devine, 1989; Fiske & Neuberg, 1990). We often project on others what we see in ourselves (e.g., Waytz & Mitchell, 2011) and evaluate others on the basis of our own goals and desires (e.g., Fitzsimons & Bargh, 2003; Fitzsimons & Shah, 2009). Past relationships color new ones, even without our awareness (e.g., Andersen & Chen, 2002; Andersen, Glassman, Chen, & Cole, 1995).

The perception of people is typically examined within the area of social cognition and is sometimes more specifically labeled *person perception* (Fiske & Taylor, 2008; Kunda, 1999). Here, we use the term person perception to include the perception of both self and others. Perception involves gathering information from our senses to interpret and act on our environments (Goldstein, 2010). Such information can be acted on directly or combined with preexisting knowledge. Person perception more specifically focuses on how we perceive self and others on the basis of sensory inputs as well as our accumulated knowledge.

The purpose of this chapter is to examine how conceptual metaphor theory (CMT) can enhance our understanding of the factors that influence person perception. First, we briefly review a common theory in social cognition that is used to explain person perception in terms of schemas and concept accessibility. Next, we examine research that highlights how CMT can be used to enhance our understanding of person perception processes. Finally, we present a research agenda that more fully integrates CMT into the study of person perception.

SCHEMAS AND PERSON PERCEPTION

Social cognition research is dominated by a common theory that contends that thoughts, feelings, and behaviors in the social realm are guided by schemas (e.g., Fiske & Taylor, 2008; Kunda, 1999). A *schema* is generally considered to be a representation in memory of a particular concept, category, or situation. Schemas contain general information about something that is typically true across situations. For instance, our schema for *cats* may contain information about legs, fur, temperament, and sounds such as "meow." The components of our schemas can influence person perception. For example, the decision to vote for someone in a political election may be influenced by the fact that one candidate is a lawyer. A person's lawyer schema can guide his or her perception of that individual and subsequent voting behavior (Fiske & Taylor, 2008; Wyer & Srull, 1986). Indeed, depending on the nature of one's lawyer schema, a voter may think the candidate is logical, wealthy, and smart versus egotistical, unethical, and boring. One's previous experiences with lawyers help define the content of this schema.

Decades of research have revealed that our perception of self and others is guided by the accessibility or heightened activation of schemas and their related concepts (Bargh, 2006; Higgins, 1996), a process sometimes referred to as *priming* or *spreading activation*. In a classic study that has been cited some 1,000 times (Harzing, 2007) since it was first published in 1977, Higgins, Rholes, and Jones found that unobtrusive exposure or priming of words (as part of a study on reading comprehension) naming trait concepts such as *adventurous* or *reckless* later affected participants' interpretation of a person they read about in a descriptive essay. Higgins et al. (1977) found that participants who were first exposed to words such as *adventurous* or *independent* later perceived a fictional person described in ambiguous terms to be an adventurous and independent person as well (also see Srull & Wyer, 1979). This initial research revealed that accessible trait-related concepts can bias people's perception of the personality of an unrelated target individual by priming related traits. Such findings were extremely important because people's interpretation of the personality of others can affect how they interact with them.

Since these seminal publications, numerous research findings have revealed the multitude of ways in which concept or knowledge accessibility affects person perception processes (Bargh, 2006; Förster & Liberman, 2007) and other cognitive judgments that affect social cognition. For example, priming the concept of African Americans versus Caucasians increases people's propensity to misidentify a tool as a weapon (Correll, Park, Judd, & Wittenbrink, 2002; Payne, 2001), exposure to one's national flag increases feelings of unity because it causes people to report less extreme political views (Hassin, Ferguson, Shidlovsky, & Gross, 2007), and exposure to weapons increases people's aggressive behavior toward a provoking individual (Bartholow, Anderson, Carnagey, & Benjamin, 2005; Klinesmith, Kasser, & McAndrew, 2006).

Although the foregoing description of research on the impact of schemas on person perception is admittedly simplistic (e.g., years of research have revealed several moderating variables: Bargh, 2006), the important point is that schemas are considered to be a major influence on social cognition and person perception across social psychology areas as well as other psychological disciplines. Schemas afford us the opportunity to use our cognitive resources for more pressing concerns and to offload more basic information processing to our representation of previous experiences. We would not have survived as a species if we had to continuously relearn how to act and respond to everyday social situations. One of the hallmarks of human consciousness is that we have the ability to predict the outcome of a situation given our previous experiences. We know what to expect and how to conduct ourselves when standing in line at the grocery store, trick-or-treating with our children, or attending a wedding ceremony.

Although schemas are likely essential, the research on schemas and concept accessibility has tended to focus on social judgments that are made on the basis of accessible knowledge that is typically *directly* related to the dependent measure at hand. For example, priming the concept *elderly* leads individuals to walk more slowly across a hallway (Bargh, Chen, & Burrows, 1996) because *slow* is a central characteristic of our schema of the elderly. In other words, a schema view focuses on knowledge activation elements that are typically part of a given concept or category. Recent work related to CMT, however, has revealed that our perception of self and others can be driven by relations between categories or concepts that are subtle and more indirect than has previously been documented in social cognition research. In the next section, we contend that CMT can enrich the schema view and enhance our understanding of person perception processes.

CONCEPTUAL METAPHOR THEORY

The general contention of CMT is that people use metaphor to understand and not just talk about abstract concepts (see Gibbs, 1994, 2006; see also Chapters 1 and 2, this volume). CMT asserts that metaphors provide conceptual mappings between more concrete and common *source* concepts and more abstract and less perceptual *target* concepts (Lakoff & Johnson, 1980, 1999; Landau, Meier, & Keefer, 2010). In specific relation to person perception processes, it is clear that people use metaphors in their everyday discourse to define and explain attributes of the self and others (Lakoff & Johnson, 1999; Landau et al., 2010). Asch (1946, 1958) is frequently cited as being one of the first social psychologists to write about person perception in metaphoric terms. He stated that people use descriptors that relate to perceptual experiences to examine and understand more abstract ideas about the self and others. For example, we may label people as *warm* or *cold*, *rigid* or *flexible*, *bright* or *dull*, and *straight* or *crooked*. We likely use such metaphoric descriptions because it is difficult to conceptualize abstract person qualities without linking them to more easily understood concrete experiences familiar to beings with sensory apparatuses.

Many linguistic metaphors involving person perception likely develop from physical experiences in early childhood that consistently pair the physical and the abstract. For example, the feeling of physical warmth occurs when people hug and hold others. Typically, we hug or hold someone as a display of affection and belonging. In adulthood, such experiences are described through metaphors that pair *warmth* (the physical source concept) with *likeability* or *affection* (the abstract target concept), such as when we use metaphors that suggest *a warm person is an affectionate person*. CMT predicts that such mappings actually influence the representation of self and others through a type of scaffolding or embodiment in which early perceptual experiences are used to eventually ground conceptual knowledge (Barsalou, 1999, 2008; Williams, Huang, & Bargh, 2009). In other words, individuals use more concrete and familiar experiences (e.g., physical warmth) to later conceptualize and think about more abstract concepts and experiences (e.g., psychological warmth). Glenberg (2010) contended that past bodily interaction with the environment provides the grounding for conceptual metaphors. For example, when we are sad, we lie *down*; when we are happy, we jump *up* (often literally). Therefore, it is not surprising that we talk and think about happiness and sadness in terms of high and low positions in vertical space, respectively (see Chapter 7, this volume).

It is important to point out that CMT is not an alternative to the schema-based theory discussed earlier. Schemas are essential for understanding how people interpret and navigate their social world. CMT significantly enriches a schema view by predicting that links between physical source concepts (e.g., physical cleanliness) and abstract target concepts (e.g., moral judgments) influence person perception through metaphoric mappings even though the concepts in question can be dissimilar in a prior sense. In other words, CMT allows researchers to examine person perception processes in domains that a typical schema view (e.g., thinking of the word *doctor* primes or activates the concept of *nurse*) would simply not predict. Furthermore, a conceptual metaphor view can explain priming or accessibility findings involving dissimilar concepts because it focuses on early embodied experiences as an important impetus. In the sections that follow, we discuss a number of relevant findings that illustrate the contribution of CMT to the person perception literature.

Vertical Orientation and Person Perception

Efficient spatial perception was a crucial ability for survival as early humans evolved in a three-dimensional world replete with dangers and rewards (Chatterjee, 2001; Coslett, 1999; Mirabile, Glueck, & Stroebel, 1976; Previc, 1998). The ability to perceive space and spatial orientation often requires input from multiple sensory modalities, such as vision, audition, and touch. Spatial orientation was thus a prime candidate for eventually lending meaning to the abstract aspects of a person's social world. It is perhaps no surprise, then, that linguistic metaphors commonly link locations in space to social dimensions such as interpersonal power, evaluative behavior, and religiosity (Lakoff & Johnson, 1980; Landau et al., 2010; Tolaas, 1991). A person's action can be *low*, whereas another person can be feeling *on top of the world* or have a corporate position that places her *high in the hierarchy*. We review research that suggests that these linguistic metaphors do indeed reflect representation processes in person perception.

Meier and Robinson (2004) showed that implicit associations between good–up and bad–down exist in people's memory. They found that people are faster to determine whether a word has a positive meaning if it is shown in a higher location on a computer screen, whereas people are faster to determine whether a word has a negative meaning if it is shown in a lower location on a computer screen (see also Crawford, Margolies, Drake, & Murphy, 2006; Palma, Garrido, & Semin, 2011). Meier, Moller, Chen, and Riemer-Peltz (2011) found that this metaphoric association can affect person perception. They examined map coordinates and housing location. Maps in many countries are typically drawn so that north is on top and south is on the bottom. In their Study 3, they found that people preferred to live in the northern half of a hypothetical city, but only when the city map was presented with north on the top (i.e., this north preference disappeared when a map was presented with north on the bottom and south on the top). Their Study 4 has implications for person perception. Meier et al. (2011) randomly assigned participants to read about a high or low socioeconomic status (SES) person named "Bennett." In the low SES condition, Mr. Bennett was an unemployed high school dropout who struggled to pay the rent each month. In the high SES condition, Dr. Bennett was a wealthy businessman who inherited money. Participants were asked to choose a location on a map (see Figure 3.1) of a fictitious city where they thought Bennett lived. The map boundaries measured 11.60 centimeters in both the north–south (up–down) and west–east (left–right) directions. As shown in Figure 3.2, participants believed the low SES Bennett lived in the southern or lower half of the city, whereas they believed the high SES Bennett lived in the northern or upper half of the city.

Research has also has examined the implications of power–vertical position metaphors. Giessner and Schubert (2007) showed participants an organizational chart of a company with five "subordinate" boxes at the bottom connected by a horizontal line, with the middle box connected by a vertical line to a box on top that was labeled "Manager A." The length of this line was manipulated so that it was 2 or 7 centimeters in height, which placed "Manager A" at a higher or lower location on the paper. Participants were given information about Manager A and were asked to rate him on perceived power (e.g., "I think that Manager A is dominant"). Participants who viewed the long line gave higher power ratings than participants who viewed the short line. Thus, higher locations in vertical space were predictive of

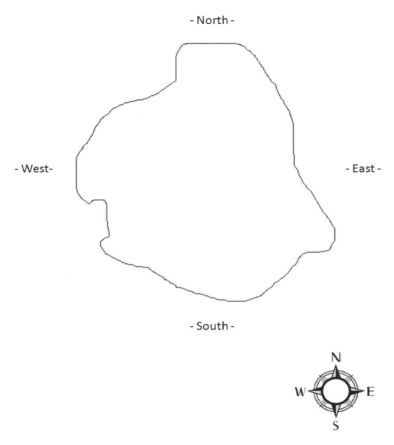

- North -

- West-

- East -

- South -

N

W   E

S

Figure 3.1. Map used in Study 4. From "Spatial Metaphor and Real Estate: North-South Location Biases Housing Preference," by B. P. Meier, A. C. Moller, J. Chen, and M. Riemer-Peltz, 2011, *Social Psychological and Personality Science, 2,* p. 551. Copyright 2011 by Sage Publishing. Reprinted with permission.

increased interpersonal power perceptions (see also Lakens, Semin, & Foroni, 2011; Meier, Hauser, Robinson, Friesen, & Schjeldahl, 2007; Schubert, 2005; Schwartz, Tesser, & Powell, 1982).

Meier and Dionne (2009) built on the findings of Giessner and Schubert (2007) in the domain of physical attraction. Evolutionary views of human mating strategy focus on the preference for dominant or powerful males and submissive or powerless females as potential mates (Buss, 1989, 1994). Meier and Dionne found that people appear to use verticality as an implicit cue to power when rating the attractiveness of opposite-sex individuals. Their male participants rated pictures of females as more attractive when their images were presented near the bottom of a computer screen, whereas their female

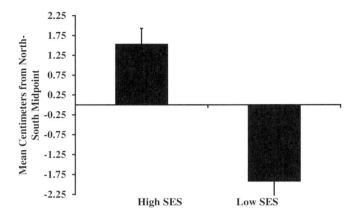

Figure 3.2. Mean location chosen in Study 4. The numbers reflect the mean distance in centimeters from the north–south map midpoint (i.e., positive numbers = northern/upper location; negative numbers = southern/lower location). From "Spatial Metaphor and Real Estate: North-South Location Biases Housing Preference," by B. P. Meier, A. C. Moller, J. Chen, and M. Riemer-Peltz, 2011, *Social Psychological and Personality Science, 2,* p. 552. Copyright 2011 by Sage Publishing. Reprinted with permission.

participants rated pictures of males as more attractive when their images were presented near the top of a computer screen.

Other research has shown that power–vertical position metaphors are implicated in more practical social settings. For example, researchers have shown that taller people have higher incomes (Frieze, Olson, & Good, 1990; Judge & Cable, 2004; Loh, 1993) and better health-related quality of life (Christensen, Djurhus, Clayton, & Christiansen, 2007) than shorter people. Individuals randomly assigned to complete a general knowledge test on a higher (eighth floor) versus lower (second floor) location in an office building had more confidence in their ability (Sun, Wang, & Li, 2011). Van Quaquebeke and Giessner (2010) conducted a fascinating series of studies on soccer fouls in actual soccer games and in a laboratory setting. Using data from German Bundesliga seasons, UEFA Champions League seasons, and FIFA World Cup tournaments, the authors found that players who were called for fouls were, on average, taller than the alleged victims. To address the fact that taller players may simply be more dominant, a laboratory study was conducted. It was found that participants expected a taller versus shorter player to be more likely to commit a foul when both players were presented in pictures chasing a soccer ball. These data confirm that height is an implicit cue to social dominance. Although these additional findings could be due to a variety of factors, they are similar to the aforementioned studies that found a consistent link between power and vertical space. In summary, power–vertical position metaphoric links play a real but subtle role in person perception.

Vertical orientation is also commonly used in metaphors that describe religious concepts. Jesus and God are considered the "most high," whereas the antithesis of God, Satan, is considered to be a "lowly" being. Such metaphors likely develop through the historical belief that God resides high in the heavens, whereas Satan resides deep in the underworld (Favazza, 2004). Even nonreligious individuals are likely to encounter such metaphors in cultures in which Christianity is prevalent (e.g., the United States). This metaphoric link between the physical and abstract has been shown to influence person perception. Meier, Hauser, et al. (2007) showed that people have implicit associations between God–Up and Devil–Down. Chasteen, Burdzy, and Pratt (2010) extended these findings by showing that thinking about God versus Satan biases people's visual attention to a higher location in space. Meier, Hauser, et al. (2007) revealed the implications such associations have for person perception as they found that people believed strangers had a stronger belief in God if their images appeared higher versus lower in visual space.

Brightness and Person Perception

Brightness is another perceptual characteristic that is invoked in metaphors to describe the social world (Lakoff & Johnson, 1999; Meier & Robinson, 2005). Brightness perception is a physical experience that developing humans engage in at birth. Young infants quickly learn that brightness is predictive of the presence of loved ones and darkness is predictive of the absence of loved ones. It is probably no surprise that brightness eventually comes to represent aspects related to the social world. Indeed, one can have a *bright day*, a *dark time*, or a *shady disposition*. In a general sense, dark things are described as bad, and light things are described as good. Terms related to brightness and darkness have been used throughout history to portray positivity and negativity, especially in religious texts (Meier & Robinson, 2005). Furthermore, common media portrayals borrow this visual characteristic to present heroes (in white) and villains (in black), such as in classic movies like *Star Wars* and *The Wizard of Oz*.

Do affect–brightness metaphors have relevance for person perception processes that move beyond language? The first step in such work is to determine whether associations between good–light and bad–dark exist in nonlinguistic tasks. Meier, Robinson, and Clore (2004) and Meier, Robinson, Crawford, and Ahlvers (2007) showed that people do indeed have strong associations in memory between brightness perception and valence in a metaphor-consistent fashion (see also related work by Banerjee, Chatterjee, & Sinha, 2012; Sherman & Clore, 2009). Other work has revealed that these metaphoric associations bias person perception. For example, in an illuminating series of studies by Frank and Gilovich (1988), sports teams in darker uniforms were rated as more malevolent and were more likely to be called for penalties than sports teams in lighter uniforms. Furthermore, participants who wore darker versus lighter uniforms in an experimental laboratory study chose more aggressive forms of game play (e.g., a fun darts duel) in an ostensible study on the psychology of competition. The studies by Frank and Gilovich reveal that brightness biases the judgments of others (i.e., teams in darker uniforms received more penalties from referees) as well as the self-concept (i.e., individuals wearing darker uniforms chose to play more aggressive games). Similar results were found in a study by Webster, Urland, and Correll (2012) with data from the National Hockey League and in a laboratory study that examined participants behavior and expectations in an online game in which their avatars wore black or white cloaks (Peña, Hancock, & Merola, 2009).

A large amount of work in social psychology has shown that people have strong automatic associations between race and valence. Specifically, African Americans are more strongly associated with negativity and Caucasians are more strongly associated with positivity (Fazio & Olson, 2003; Nosek et al., 2007). The typical study reveals that people are faster to recognize stereotypical Caucasian names when they are paired with positive words and stereotypical African American names when they are paired with negative words (the Implicit Associations Test or IAT; Greenwald, McGhee, & Schwartz, 1998). Although automatic negative stereotypes for African Americans likely have a host of causes (e.g., a history of slavery, ingroup–outgroup differences, categorization processes), it appears that at least part of the effect is due to a more basic association between affect and brightness and to the metaphors that reinforce such associations. For example, Smith-McLallen, Johnson, Dovidio, and Pearson (2006) showed that the typical IAT effect mentioned above (Greenwald et al., 1998) is significantly reduced when the extent to which people associate the colors white and black with positive and negative valence, respectively, is statistically controlled. In a related study, Ronquillo et al. (2007) examined activation in the amygdala, an area of the brain that becomes active when people are exposed to a potential threat. They found that participants had greater amygdala activation when people were shown pictures of darker versus lighter skinned Caucasians (i.e., suggesting a deeper neurological connection between affect and brightness).

The results of the research on stereotypes suggest that darker skinned individuals are at a disadvantage compared with their lighter skinned counterparts. The metaphoric association between brightness and valence may partially drive such effects. Although conceptual metaphors may be involved in inducing stereotypical thinking about race, it may also allow one to understand how to reduce it. Song, Vonasch, Meier, and Bargh (2012) used CMT to predict that smiling faces would be judged as perceptually brighter or lighter than frowning faces. They found that people perceived different colored schematic and real faces as lighter in color when the faces were presented with a smile versus a frown and the actual luminance was held constant across stimuli. Such effects were found in a two-choice forced judgment task (judging which of two faces is brighter) and when smiling and frowning faces were independently shown to different participants and the task was to select a color shade on a scale that reflected their judgment of the face's brightness. Although speculative, such findings suggest that emotional expressions could reduce automatic stereotypes based on facial brightness.

Other Source Domains Involved in Person Perception

A host of other physical factors are used in metaphors to help people make sense of social concepts in terms of more concrete experiences. Such links have been shown to have an impact on person perception. The nature of the relationships cannot be fully discussed here, but there are many examples. Meier, Moeller, Riemer-Peltz, and Robinson (2012) found that taste-related metaphors (e.g., "she's a sweetie") have implications for people's personality as well as their perception of others. They found that sweet taste preferences and experiences were associated with agreeable personalities, perceptions, and behavior. For example, in their Study 1, individuals rated strangers as more agreeable if they were said to like sweet foods (e.g., candy, chocolate cake) compared with other food types (e.g., salty peanuts, peppers).

Several researchers have found that physical warmth or high temperature stimuli affect the perception of others (Bargh & Shalev, 2012; IJzerman & Semin, 2009; Wilkowski, Meier, Robinson, Carter, & Feltman, 2009; Williams & Bargh, 2008a; Zhong & Leonardelli, 2008). For example, Williams and Bargh (2008a) found that holding a warm versus cold coffee cup caused participants to perceive another person as more psychologically warm or friendly. This research is being published at a quickening pace. Recent papers have shown metaphor-related effects on person perception in a number of diverse areas, such as physical distance and emotional closeness (Williams & Bargh, 2008b), left–right bodily sway and political attitudes (Oppenheimer & Trail, 2010), the perception of soft versus hard objects, judgments of a person's gender and personality (Ackerman, Nocera, & Bargh, 2010; Slepian, Weisbuch, Rule, & Ambady, 2011), and physical cleanliness and morality (Lee & Schwarz, 2011; Schnall, Benton, & Harvey, 2008; Zhong & Liljenquist, 2006), to name a few.

PITFALLS AND PROMISES OF CONCEPTUAL METAPHOR THEORY AND PERSON PERCEPTION

The research reviewed in this chapter represents only a portion of the conceptual metaphor work that is relevant for person perception. Even though our review of the literature is not exhaustive, the amount and breadth of the work discussed reveal that CMT should not be overlooked in the realm of person perception. Some writers have even gone as far as to suggest that a general embodiment view could be a unifying perspective in psychology because it provides a similar explanation of human behavior regardless of the psychological subdiscipline in question (Glenberg, 2010; Schubert & Semin, 2009). At the same time, however, the upsurge of research in this area has led to interesting findings that seem to be outpacing the focus on theory development. In the sections that follow, we discuss some of the pitfalls and promises that conceptual metaphor holds for understanding person perception.

Pitfalls

Our review suggests that conceptual metaphor research in person perception is in its infancy. The existing work has typically focused on demonstration effects, which are certainly essential for any new area of inquiry because they identify whether there is indeed an area worthy of empirical interest (Meier, Schnall, Schwarz, & Bargh, 2012; Rozin, 2009). The excitement generated by this area has likely led to the increasing number of studies. That excitement may also be a pitfall unless the research begins to move beyond the beginning stages. Ideally, new research would begin to examine process variables in addition to demonstration work.

Landau et al. (2010) suggested that one way research can move beyond an initial phase is for researchers to develop questions using a phenomenon-based focus, which is an approach that centers on particular behaviors (e.g., aggression, helping, loving) and then examines how CMT can be used to explain and modify the behavior in predictable ways. Such an approach builds on existing theories while examining the potential for CMT to enrich present viewpoints. For example, consider the research on physical and psychological warmth. Williams and Bargh (2008a) found that feelings of physical warmth caused people to rate a stranger as more psychologically warm or friendly. Furthermore, feelings of physical warmth caused people to act in a more agreeable manner. This initial work showed that metaphoric mappings between physical warmth and psychological warmth have implications for person perception in areas other than metaphoric language. Bargh and Shalev (2012) extended this work by revealing that individual differences in the desire for physical warmth (i.e., bath taking behavior) correlated positively with individual differences in the experience of loneliness. That is, lonelier people bathed more frequently and for longer durations. Bargh and Shalev's research moves beyond demonstration because it enriches existing theories in person perception and self-regulation. Furthermore, it invites intriguing new research questions in such diverse areas as clinical interventions for mental health, techniques for persuasive appeals, and even industrial organizational research that focuses on environmental factors in the workplace (e.g., temperature).

Another pitfall in the existing research on CMT in person perception is the absence of work that examines theoretical boundary conditions, moderators, and mediators. We know little about whether conceptual metaphors shape, constrain, or reflect the body's influence on person perception. Much of the existing work has led to fascinating findings of everyday interest. However, CMT will become less viable for new researchers unless more is known about the factors that moderate and mediate the effects. It is likely that concept accessibility processes suggested earlier (Fiske & Taylor, 2008; Kunda, 1999) are involved in many of the effects discussed in this chapter, but few researchers have examined such possibilities. Landau et al. (2011), however, provided one example of how a mediation study elucidates the factor involved. They examined self-perception in terms of physical expansion by focusing on linguistic metaphors that describe the self in terms of an expanding or contracting entity (e.g., "he needs to grow"). Landau et al. (2011) hypothesized that exposing people to an image of an expanding figure versus a static or fragmented figure would cause people to report feeling more self-actualized. They further predicted that accessibility of the concept of expansion (e.g., thoughts like "grow" or "broaden") would mediate the effect. They found that participants exposed to an expanding (vs. a static or fragmented) figure perceived themselves as more self-actualized, and this effect was mediated by accessible thoughts related to the concept of expansion.

Landau et al. (2011) provided an example of how to test for a mediating variable that relies on the explanatory process of schema theories. Sun et al. (2011) examined a moderating variable in their search for explanations of conceptual metaphors' impact on person perception. Recall that they found people believed they were better than others on a general knowledge test when presented with the test in a higher versus lower location in space (i.e., a high vs. low floor in an office building). In a follow-up study, the effect disappeared when these researchers presented the ranking question (i.e., what percentage of people would have fewer correct answers than you) in a vertical manner such that higher percentages were at the bottom rather than top of a piece of paper. Thus, verticality's influence on power or ability was eliminated when participants were presented with a "power is down" figure, which likely interrupted one's chronic "power is up" representation (for related work, see Meier et al., 2011; Chapter 7, this volume).

Process-oriented research like the studies by Landau et al. (2011) and Sun et al. (2011) are a welcome addition to this literature. Nevertheless, several additional interesting questions remain. For example, the results of the study by Sun et al. may lead one to wonder when and how contextual factors play a role in verticality's effect on person perception processes. Whereas Sun et al. found that verticality increased one's own judgment of ability compared to similar others, Meier and Dionne (2009) found that a verticality manipulation affected people's attractiveness ratings of strangers. What promotes the likelihood of a source concept like verticality prompting one metaphor-related behavior (ability) versus another (attraction)? Answers to questions like these are necessary for a more thorough understanding of the pathways that lead from metaphoric manipulations to cognitive, affective, or behavioral effects on person perception.

Promises

Existing conceptual metaphor research in person perception is associated with some potential pitfalls. These pitfalls, however, do not yet overshadow the promise CMT has for social cognition. The key promise is its potential breadth in terms of explanation and application. This potential is based on the simple fact that humans are body-based beings. As far as we can tell from contemporary scientific inquiry, our minds cannot exist apart from our bodies. Therefore, our thinking, acting, and feeling occur within the confines of our bodies. This is true regardless of whether we play a slot machine, partake in a provocative debate, or vote for a political candidate. This deep connection between body and mind suggests that propositions about the operation of schemas in ways that are devoid of the body fail to capture life as it is lived. Metaphor and embodiment research has led some to suggest that current models of artificial intelligence will never truly mimic human intelligence because they do not have the ability to consider information from sensorimotor systems (Barsalou, 1999). The mind–body connection has deep implications for the potentially widespread influence of CMT in psychology in general and person perception in particular.

Metaphoric descriptions of self and others had once been examined under the umbrella of folk theories of personality. Folk views are based on commonsense ideas of how people perceive others in everyday naturalistic settings. Such folk views, however, have been shown to have considerable merit (Gibbs & Beitel, 1995; Haas, 2002; Mehl, Gosling, & Pennebaker, 2006). CMT adds novel predictive power to folk views because it provides an underlying framework for why common perceptual-based descriptions of people often ring true. For example, consider two very different sets of studies. Meier, Moeller, et al. (2012) found that people who have a stronger liking for sweet foods were also higher in the prosocial personality trait of agreeableness. Bargh and Shalev (2012) found that people who prefer taking more and longer baths were also higher in loneliness. Thus, both sets of studies found that individual differences in source domain preferences (i.e., sweet taste and physical warmth) were associated with related personality traits in ways consistent with everyday linguistic metaphors for describing others (e.g., "sweetie" or "cold").

Work in neuroscience may eventually be able to partially explain some of the work discussed in this chapter. Gallese, Keysers, and Rizzolatti (2004), Gallese and Sinigaglia (2011), and Glenberg (2010) have suggested that the human brain, like those of primates, has developed a *mirror mechanism* that allows experiential insight into others' minds. This mirror mechanism (a collection of mirror neurons) maps a sensory representation of another's sensation, action, or emotion, onto the observer's own mental representation of that same sensation, action, or emotion. This mapping, or simulation of another's experience, allows for the perceiver to make accurate inferences and predictions of behavior. Lakoff (2008) contended that such mirror neurons are multimodal and allow us to simulate actions or behaviors without actually engaging in them. The discovery of mirror neurons provides another advance in the mechanisms that may help explain not just why language is metaphoric but also how abstract concepts in areas such as person perception are literally grounded in neural activity representing bodily experiences.

CMT, then, holds considerable promise for deriving accurate person perceptions because metaphors abound in describing self and others. Asch (1946, 1958) pointed out the extensive use of metaphor in person description decades ago, but even he would likely be surprised by the manner in which such descriptions are being used to study and understand actual social behavior.

SUMMARY AND CONCLUSION

A necessary aspect of human interaction is the perception of self and others. Person perceptions are not always accurate and are subject to internal and external influences. An influential view reveals that person perception judgments are often made on the basis of accessible knowledge related to the judgment at hand (e.g., priming hostility may lead individuals to perceive others as hostile). Common metaphors (e.g., "she's a sweetheart") suggest that person perception may be influenced by less direct, yet broader, conceptual mappings. Our chapter reveals just how widespread conceptual metaphor influences are on the perception of self and others. Indeed, evidence exists in diverse realms such as social status, evaluation, religiosity, anger, mate value, and personality characteristics such as agreeableness and psychological warmth. CMT offers considerable promise for widening the understanding of the factors that influence person perception. The current literature, however, is in its infancy, and we contend that future work should more readily focus on the identification of the mediators and moderators that cause people to be more or less likely to use conceptual metaphor to understand themselves and others. Even though there are some shortcomings in the existing literature, this burgeoning area holds considerable promise for what is likely to be a major addition to the study of person perception.

REFERENCES

Ackerman, J. M., Nocera, C. C., & Bargh, J. A. (2010). Incidental haptic sensations influence social judgments and decisions. *Science, 328,* 1712–1715. doi:10.1126/science.1189993

Andersen, S. M., & Chen, S. (2002). The relational self: An interpersonal social-cognitive theory. *Psychological Review, 109,* 619–645. doi:10.1037/0033-295X.109.4.619

Andersen, S. M., Glassman, N. S., Chen, S., & Cole, S. W. (1995). Transference in social perception: The role of chronic accessibility in significant-other representations. *Journal of Personality and Social Psychology, 69,* 41–57. doi:10.1037/0022-3514.69.1.41

Asch, S. E. (1946). Forming impressions of personality. *The Journal of Abnormal and Social Psychology, 41,* 258–290. doi:10.1037/h0055756

Asch, S. E. (1958). The metaphor: A psychological inquiry. In R. Tagiuri & L. Petrullo (Eds.), *Person perception and interpersonal behavior* (pp. 86–94). Stanford, CA: Stanford University Press.

Banerjee, P., Chatterjee, P., & Sinha, J. (2012). Is it light or dark? Recalling moral behavior changes perception of brightness. *Psychological Science, 23,* 407–409. doi:10.1177/0956797611432497

Bargh, J. A. (2006). What have we been priming all these years? On the development, mechanisms, and ecology of nonconscious social behavior. *European Journal of Social Psychology, 36,* 147–168. doi:10.1002/ejsp.336

Bargh, J. A., Chen, M., & Burrows, L. (1996). Automaticity of social behavior: Direct effects of trait construct and stereotype activation on action. *Journal of Personality and Social Psychology, 71,* 230–244. doi:10.1037/0022-3514.71.2.230

Bargh, J. A., & Shalev, I. (2012). The substitutability of physical and social warmth in everyday life. *Emotion, 12,* 154–162. doi:10.1037/a0023527

Barsalou, L. W. (1999). Perceptual symbol systems. *Behavioral and Brain Sciences, 22,* 577–660.

Barsalou, L. W. (2008). Grounded cognition. *Annual Review of Psychology, 59,* 617–645. doi:10.1146/annurev.psych.59.103006.093639

Bartholow, B. D., Anderson, C. A., Carnagey, N. L., & Benjamin, A. J., Jr. (2005). Interactive effects of life experience and situational cues on aggression: The weapons priming effect in hunters and nonhunters. *Journal of Experimental Social Psychology, 41*, 48–60. doi:10.1016/j.jesp.2004.05.005

Buss, D. M. (1989). Sex differences in human mate preferences: Evolutionary hypotheses tested in 37 cultures. *Behavioral and Brain Sciences, 12*, 1–49. doi:10.1017/S0140525X00023992

Buss, D. M. (1994). *The evolution of desire: Strategies of human mating.* New York, NY: Basic Books.

Chasteen, A. L., Burdzy, D. C., & Pratt, J. (2010). Thinking of God moves attention. *Neuropsychologia, 48*, 627–630. doi:10.1016/j.neuropsychologia.2009.09.029

Chatterjee, A. (2001). Language and space: Some interactions. *Trends in Cognitive Sciences, 5*, 55–61. doi:10.1016/S1364-6613(00)01598-9

Christensen, T. L., Djurhus, C. B., Clayton, P., & Christiansen, J. S. (2007). An evaluation of the relationship between adult height and health-related quality of life in the general UK population. *Clinical Endocrinology (Oxford), 67*, 407–412.

Correll, J., Park, B., Judd, C. M., & Wittenbrink, B. (2002). The police officer's dilemma: Using ethnicity to disambiguate potentially threatening individuals. *Journal of Personality and Social Psychology, 83*, 1314–1329. doi:10.1037/0022-3514.83.6.1314

Coslett, H. B. (1999). Spatial influences on motor and language function. *Neuropsychologia, 37*, 695–706. doi:10.1016/S0028-3932(98)00116-X

Crawford, L. E., Margolies, S. M., Drake, J. T., & Murphy, M. E. (2006). Affect biases memory of location: Evidence for the spatial representation of affect. *Cognition and Emotion, 20*, 1153–1169. doi:10.1080/02699930500347794

Devine, P. G. (1989). Stereotypes and prejudice: Their automatic and controlled components. *Journal of Personality and Social Psychology, 56*, 5–18. doi:10.1037/0022-3514.56.1.5

Favazza, A. (2004). *PsychoBible: Behavior, religion, and the holy book.* Charlottesville, VA: Pitchstone.

Fazio, R. H., & Olson, M. A. (2003). Implicit measures in social cognition: Their meaning and use. *Annual Review of Psychology, 54*, 297–327. doi:10.1146/annurev.psych.54.101601.145225

Fiske, S. T., & Neuberg, S. L. (1990). A continuum of impression formation, from category-based to individuating processes: Influences of information and motivation on attention and interpretation. *Advances in Experimental Social Psychology, 23*, 1–74. doi:10.1016/S0065-2601(08)60317-2

Fiske, S. T., & Taylor, S. E. (2008). *Social cognition: From brains to culture.* New York, NY: McGraw-Hill.

Fitzsimons, G. M., & Bargh, J. A. (2003). Thinking of you: Nonconscious pursuit of interpersonal goals associated with relationship partners. *Journal of Personality and Social Psychology, 84*, 148–164. doi:10.1037/0022-3514.84.1.148

Fitzsimons, G. M., & Shah, J. Y. (2009). Confusing one instrumental other for another: Goal effects on social categorization. *Psychological Science, 20,* 1468–1472. doi:10.1111/j.1467-9280.2009.02475.x

Förster, J., & Liberman, N. (2007). Knowledge activation. In A. W. Kruglanski & E. T. Higgins (Eds.), *Social psychology: Handbook of basic principles* (2nd ed., pp. 201–231). New York, NY: Guilford Press.

Frank, M. G., & Gilovich, T. (1988). The dark side of self- and social perception: Black uniforms and aggression in professional sports. *Journal of Personality and Social Psychology, 54,* 74–85. doi:10.1037/0022-3514.54.1.74

Frieze, I. H., Olson, J. E., & Good, D. C. (1990). Perceived and actual discrimination of male and female managers. *Journal of Applied Social Psychology, 20,* 46–67. doi:10.1111/j.1559-1816.1990.tb00377.x

Gallese, V., Keysers, C., & Rizzolatti, G. (2004). A unifying view of the basis of social cognition. *Trends in Cognitive Sciences, 8,* 396–403. doi:10.1016/j.tics.2004.07.002

Gallese, V., & Sinigaglia, C. (2011). What is so special about embodied simulation? *Trends in Cognitive Sciences, 15,* 512–519. doi:10.1016/j.tics.2011.09.003

Gibbs, R. W., & Beitel, D. (1995). What proverb understanding reveals about how people think. *Psychological Bulletin, 118,* 133–154.

Gibbs, R. W., Jr. (1994). *The poetics of mind: Figurative thought, language, and understanding.* Cambridge, England: Cambridge University Press.

Gibbs, R. W., Jr. (2006). Embodiment and cognitive science. New York, NY: Cambridge University Press.

Giessner, S. R., & Schubert, T. W. (2007). High in the hierarchy: How vertical location and judgments of leaders' power are interrelated. *Organizational Behavior and Human Decision Processes, 104,* 30–44. doi:10.1016/j.obhdp.2006.10.001

Glenberg, A. M. (2010). Embodiment as a unifying perspective for psychology. *Interdisciplinary Reviews: Cognitive Science, 1,* 586–596.

Goldstein, B. E. (2010). *Sensation and perception* (8th ed.). Belmont, CA: Wadsworth, Cengage Learning.

Greenwald, A. G., McGhee, D. E., & Schwartz, J. K. L. (1998). Measuring individual differences in implicit cognition: The Implicit Association Test. *Journal of Personality and Social Psychology, 74,* 1464–1480. doi:10.1037/0022-3514.74.6.1464

Haas, H. A. (2002). Extending the search for folk personality constructs: The dimensionality of the personality-relevant proverb domain. *Journal of Personality and Social Psychology, 82,* 594–609.

Harzing, A. W. (2007). *Publish or perish.* Retrieved from from http://www.harzing.com/pop.htm

Hassin, R. R., Ferguson, M. J., Shidlovsky, D., & Gross, T. (2007). Waved by invisible flags: The effects of subliminal exposure to flags on political thought and behavior. *Proceedings of the National Academy of Sciences of the United States of America, 104,* 19757–19761. doi:10.1073/pnas.0704679104

Higgins, E. T. (1996). Knowledge activation: Accessibility, applicability, and salience. In E. T. Higgins & A. W. Kruglanski (Eds.), *Social psychology: Handbook of basic principles* (pp. 133–168). New York, NY: Guilford Press.

Higgins, E. T., Rholes, W. S., & Jones, C. R. (1977). Category accessibility and impression formation. *Journal of Experimental Social Psychology, 13,* 141–154. doi:10.1016/S0022-1031(77)80007-3

IJzerman, H., & Semin, G. R. (2009). The thermometer of social relations: Mapping social proximity on temperature. *Psychological Science, 20,* 1214–1220. doi:10.1111/j.1467-9280.2009.02434.x

Judge, T. A., & Cable, D. M. (2004). The effect of physical height on workplace success and income: Preliminary test of a theoretical model. *Journal of Applied Psychology, 89,* 428–441. doi:10.1037/0021-9010.89.3.428

Klinesmith, J., Kasser, T., & McAndrew, F. T. (2006). Guns, testosterone, and aggression. *Psychological Science, 17,* 568–571. doi:10.1111/j.1467-9280.2006.01745.x

Kunda, Z. (1999). *Social cognition.* Cambridge, MA: MIT Press.

Lakens, D., Semin, G. R., & Foroni, F. (2011). Why your highness needs the people: Comparing the absolute and relative representation of power in vertical space. *Social Psychology, 42,* 205–213. doi:10.1027/1864-9335/a000064

Lakoff, G. (2008). The neural theory of metaphor. In R. W. Gibbs, Jr. (Ed.), *The Cambridge handbook of metaphor and thought* (pp. 17–38). New York, NY: Cambridge University Press. doi:10.1017/CBO9780511816802.003

Lakoff, G., & Johnson, M. (1980). *Metaphors we live by.* Chicago, IL: The University of Chicago Press.

Lakoff, G., & Johnson, M. (1999). *Philosophy in the flesh: The embodied mind and its challenges to western thought.* New York, NY: Basic Books.

Landau, M. J., Meier, B. P., & Keefer, L. A. (2010). A metaphor-enriched social cognition. *Psychological Bulletin, 136,* 1045–1067. doi:10.1037/a0020970

Landau, M. J., Vess, M., Arndt, J., Rothschild, Z. K., Sullivan, D., & Atchley, R. A. (2011). Embodied metaphor and the "true" self: Priming entity expansion and protection influences intrinsic self-expressions in self-perceptions and interpersonal behavior. *Journal of Experimental Social Psychology, 47,* 79–87. doi:10.1016/j.jesp.2010.08.012

Lee, S. W. S., & Schwarz, N. (2011). Wiping the slate clean: Psychological consequences of physical cleansing. *Current Directions in Psychological Science, 20,* 307–311. doi:10.1177/0963721411422694

Loh, E. S. (1993). The economic effects of physical appearance. *Social Science Quarterly, 74,* 420–438.

Mehl, M. R., Gosling, S. D., & Pennebaker, J. W. (2006). Personality in its natural habitat: Manifestations and implicit folk theories of personality in daily life. *Journal of Personality and Social Psychology, 90,* 862–877. doi:10.1037/0022-3514.90.5.862

Meier, B. P., & Dionne, S. (2009). Downright sexy: Verticality, implicit power, and perceived physical attractiveness. *Social Cognition, 27*, 883–892. doi:10.1521/soco.2009.27.6.883

Meier, B. P., Hauser, D. J., Robinson, M. D., Friesen, C. K., & Schjeldahl, K. (2007). What's "up" with God?: Vertical space as a representation of the divine. *Journal of Personality and Social Psychology, 93*, 699–710. doi:10.1037/0022-3514.93.5.699

Meier, B. P., Moeller, S. K., Riemer-Peltz, M., & Robinson, M. D. (2012). Sweet taste preferences and experiences predict pro-social inferences, personalities, and behaviors. *Journal of Personality and Social Psychology, 102*, 163–174. doi:10.1037/a0025253

Meier, B. P., Moller, A. C., Chen, J., & Riemer-Peltz, M. (2011). Spatial metaphor and real estate: North-south location biases housing preference. *Social Psychological and Personality Science, 2*, 547–553. doi:10.1177/1948550611401042

Meier, B. P., & Robinson, M. D. (2004). Why the sunny side is up: Associations between affect and vertical position. *Psychological Science, 15*, 243–247. doi:10.1111/j.0956-7976.2004.00659.x

Meier, B. P., & Robinson, M. D. (2005). The metaphorical representation of affect. *Metaphor and Symbol, 20*, 239–257. doi:10.1207/s15327868ms2004_1

Meier, B. P., Robinson, M. D., & Clore, G. L. (2004). Why good guys wear white: Automatic inferences about stimulus valence based on color. *Psychological Science, 15*, 82–87. doi:10.1111/j.0963-7214.2004.01502002.x

Meier, B. P., Robinson, M. D., Crawford, L. E., & Ahlvers, W. J. (2007). When "light" and "dark" thoughts become light and dark responses: Affect biases brightness judgments. *Emotion, 7*, 366–376. doi:10.1037/1528-3542.7.2.366

Meier, B. P., Schnall, S., Schwarz, N., & Bargh, J. A. (2012). Embodiment in social psychology. *Topics in Cognitive Science, 4*, 705–716. doi:10.1111/j.1756-8765.2012.01212.x

Mirabile, C. S., Jr., Glueck, B., & Stroebel, C. F. (1976). Spatial orientation, cognitive processes, and cerebral specialization. *Psychiatric Journal of the University of Ottawa, 1*, 99–104.

Nosek, B. A., Smyth, F. L., Hansen, J. J., Devos, T., Lindner, N. M., Ranganath, K. A., . . . Banaji, M. (2007). Pervasiveness and correlates of implicit attitudes and stereotypes. *European Review of Social Psychology, 18*, 36–88. doi:10.1080/10463280701489053

Oppenheimer, D. M., & Trail, T. E. (2010). Why leaning to the left makes you lean to the left: Effect of spatial orientation on political attitudes. *Social Cognition, 28*, 651–661. doi:10.1521/soco.2010.28.5.651

Palma, T. A., Garrido, M. V., & Semin, G. R. (2011). Grounding person memory in space: Does spatial anchoring of behaviors improve recall? *European Journal of Social Psychology, 41*, 275–280. doi:10.1002/ejsp.795

Payne, B. K. (2001). Prejudice and perception: The role of automatic and controlled processes in misperceiving a weapon. *Journal of Personality and Social Psychology, 81*, 181–192. doi:10.1037/0022-3514.81.2.181

Peña, J., Hancock, J. T., & Merola, N. A. (2009). The priming effects of avatars in virtual settings. *Communication Research, 36,* 838–856. doi:10.1177/0093650209346802

Previc, F. H. (1998). The neuropsychology of 3-D space. *Psychological Bulletin, 124,* 123–164. doi:10.1037/0033-2909.124.2.123

Ronquillo, J., Denson, T. F., Lickel, B., Zhong-Lin, L., Nandy, A., & Maddox, K. B. (2007). The effects of skin tone on race-related amygdala activity: An fMRI investigation. *Social Cognitive and Affective Neuroscience, 2,* 39–44. doi:10.1093/scan/nsl043

Rozin, P. (2009). What kind of empirical research should we publish, fund, and reward? A different perspective. *Perspectives on Psychological Science, 4,* 435–439. doi:10.1111/j.1745-6924.2009.01151.x

Schnall, S., Benton, J., & Harvey, S. (2008). With a clean conscience: Cleanliness reduces the severity of moral judgments. *Psychological Science, 19,* 1219–1222. doi:10.1111/j.1467-9280.2008.02227.x

Schubert, T. W. (2005). Your highness: Vertical positions as perceptual symbols of power. *Journal of Personality and Social Psychology, 89,* 1–21. doi:10.1037/0022-3514.89.1.1

Schubert, T. W., & Semin, G. R. (2009). Embodiment as a unifying perspective for psychology. *European Journal of Social Psychology, 39,* 1135–1141. doi:10.1002/ejsp.670

Schwartz, B., Tesser, A., & Powell, E. (1982). Dominance cues in nonverbal behavior. *Social Psychology Quarterly, 45,* 114–120. doi:10.2307/3033934

Sherman, G. D., & Clore, G. L. (2009). The color of sin: White and black are perceptual symbols of moral purity and pollution. *Psychological Science, 20,* 1019–1025.

Slepian, M. L., Weisbuch, M., Rule, N. O., & Ambady, N. (2011). Tough and tender: Embodied categorization of gender. *Psychological Science, 22,* 26–28. doi:10.1177/0956797610390388

Smith-McLallen, A., Johnson, B. T., Dovidio, J. F., & Pearson, A. R. (2006). Black and white: The role of color bias in implicit race bias. *Social Cognition, 24,* 46–73. doi:10.1521/soco.2006.24.1.46

Song, H., Vonasch, A., Meier, B. P., & Bargh, J. A. (2012). Brighten up: Smiles facilitate perceptual judgments of facial lightness. *Journal of Experimental Social Psychology, 48,* 450–452. doi:10.1016/j.jesp.2011.10.003

Srull, T. K., & Wyer, R. S., Jr. (1979). The role of category accessibility in the interpretation of information about persons: Some determinants and implications. *Journal of Personality and Social Psychology, 37,* 1660–1672. doi:10.1037/0022-3514.37.10.1660

Sun, Y., Wang, F., & Li, S. (2011). Higher height, higher ability: Judgment confidence as a function of spatial height perception. *PLoS ONE, 6,* e22125. doi:10.1145/2039239.2039248

Tolaas, J. (1991). Notes on the origin of some spatialization metaphors. *Metaphor and Symbolic Activity, 6,* 203–218. doi:10.1207/s15327868ms0603_4 van Quaquebeke, N., & Giessner, S. R. (2010). How embodied cognitions affect judgments: Height-related attribution bias in football foul calls. *Journal of Sport & Exercise Psychology, 32*, 3–22.

Waytz, A., & Mitchell, J. P. (2011). Two mechanisms for simulating other minds: Dissociable neural bases for self-projection and mirroring. *Current Directions in Psychological Science, 20*, 197–200. doi:10.1177/0963721411409007

Webster, G. D., Urland, G. R., & Correll, J. (2012). Can uniform color color aggression? Quasi-experimental evidence from professional ice hockey. *Social Psychological and Personality Science, 3*, 274–281. doi:10.1177/1948550611418535

Wilkowski, B. M., Meier, B. P., Robinson, M. D., Carter, M. S., & Feltman, R. (2009). "Hotheaded" is more than an expression: The embodied representation of anger in terms of heat. *Emotion, 9*, 464–477. doi:10.1037/a0015764

Williams, L. E., & Bargh, J. A. (2008a). Experiencing physical warmth influences interpersonal warmth. *Science, 322*, 606–607. doi:10.1126/science.1162548

Williams, L. E., & Bargh, J. A. (2008b). Keeping one's distance: The influence of spatial distance cues on affect and evaluation. *Psychological Science, 19*, 302–308. doi:10.1111/j.1467-9280.2008.02084.x

Williams, L. E., Huang, J. Y., & Bargh, J. A. (2009). The scaffolded mind: Higher mental processes are grounded in early experience of the physical world. *European Journal of Social Psychology, 39*, 1257–1267. doi:10.1002/ejsp.665

Wyer, R. S., Jr., & Srull, T. K. (1986). Human cognition in its social context. *Psychological Review, 93*, 322–359. doi:10.1037/0033-295X.93.3.322

Zhong, C. B., & Leonardelli, G. J. (2008). Cold and lonely: Does social exclusion feel literally cold? *Psychological Science, 19*, 838–842. doi:10.1111/j.1467-9280.2008.02165.x

Zhong, C. B., & Liljenquist, K. (2006). Washing away your sins: Threatened morality and physical cleansing. *Science, 313*, 1451–1452. doi:10.1126/science.1130726

4

THE ROLE OF CONCEPTUAL METAPHOR IN MEMORY

L. ELIZABETH CRAWFORD

In recent years, psychology has shifted away from viewing minds as disembodied information processors and has come to embrace the role of the body in cognition. The general labels of *embodied* or *grounded* cognition encompass several related lines of research. Some focus on the role of perceptual and motoric simulation in representation and information processing or on the ways that physical action supports thinking and remembering. Others address how cognition is situated in an environment that imposes physical and temporal constraints and that can be used to externalize information, "off loading" it from the mind to reduce demands on cognition. Another thread, and the focus of this volume, is conceptual metaphor: how we capitalize on concrete, physically embodied domains of experience to conceptualize abstractions.

This work was supported by a grant from the University of Richmond's Faculty Research Committee. I thank James Blair, Cindy Bukach, and Matthew Crawford for their helpful comments.

http://dx.doi.org/10.1037/14278-004
The Power of Metaphor: Examining Its Influence on Social Life, M. J. Landau, M. D. Robinson, and B. P. Meier (Editors)

Early work sought evidence for metaphoric representation by examining language use (Gibbs, 1994; Lakoff & Johnson, 1980), but recent investigations have applied the approaches of experimental psychology (for reviews, see Crawford, 2009; Landau, Meier, & Keefer, 2010; Meier & Robinson, 2005). These studies have provided new evidence that metaphors can structure cognition. In particular, there is growing evidence that metaphors are used to conceptualize many social constructs, such as emotion, relationships, and morality.

The majority of these experiment-based studies of metaphor focus on immediate judgments about stimuli that are currently available. There is relatively little work on the role of conceptual metaphors in memory. Here I argue that studying the impact of metaphor on memory can enrich our understanding of how metaphors structure cognition. I consider how metaphors relate to other kinds of knowledge structures, such as schemas and categories, that are known to influence remembering. Finally, I address how memory research from other areas of embodied cognition suggests new directions for the study of conceptual metaphor.

BACKGROUND: CONCEPTUAL METAPHOR

The idea of *conceptual metaphor* is that abstract concepts are represented in terms of more concrete, physically embodied ones. In their seminal work, *Metaphors We Live By*, Lakoff and Johnson (1980) argued that there are relatively few concepts that are understood directly, on their own terms. For example, containment and vertical position are primary concepts that come to be understood through direct, physical experiences. In contrast, our more abstract concepts are not understood directly; instead, they repurpose our understanding of primary domains. Thus, the notions of containment and verticality structure the way we think about emotional experience, which is reflected in expressions such as "*overflowing* with joy" or "*lifted* spirits." The conceptual metaphor view addresses the conceptualization of emotion rather than the immediate experience of it. This distinction can be seen in development, as infants experience positive and negative affect long before they can control the spatial orientation of their bodies, but they learn to communicate about *up* and *down* before they can communicate about *happy* and *sad* (Bloom, 2001; Bretherton, Fritz, Zahn-Waxler, & Ridgeway, 1986).

Lakoff and Johnson (1980) distinguished between structural metaphors and orientational metaphors. *Structural* metaphors describe one concept in terms of another concept (e.g., *love* is a *journey*), whereas *orientational* metaphors are used to organize a system of concepts with respect to one another.

The most prominent of the orientational metaphors is *good is up*, which underlies expressions such as *feeling up, down*, or *under the weather*; *climbing the corporate ladder*; *falling from grace*; and *taking the moral high ground*. As those examples illustrate, we use the vertical dimension of space to localize valenced dimensions such as happiness, health, power, success, holiness, and morality. Because this metaphor orients several positive and negative concepts in the same way, it is coherent and systematic. It is also pervasive. Because this is the metaphor that has produced the most empirical work, and the only one to be examined with respect to memory processes, it is the primary focus of this chapter.

Metaphors such as *good is up* are not arbitrary. They depend on the workings of the body and its relation to the physical environment and affective experience. For example, given that we are subject to gravity, we cannot be upright without some degree of health and vitality. Physical power often means being literally on top, and happiness and sadness are associated with upright or downturned physical posture (LaFrance & Mayo, 1978). Many such bodily experiences are universal, which may account for the similarities in this spatial ordering of valence across languages (Gibbs, 1994; Kövecses, 2000, 2002). Although the original work on conceptual metaphor examined language, the theory is not about language so much as conceptual structure. Concepts are the building blocks of cognition, and any claim about their nature has implications not only for language but also for attention, judgment, and remembering.

WHY INVESTIGATE MEMORY?

The majority of experiment-based studies of conceptual metaphor focus on immediate, online judgments about stimuli that are currently available. This focus is consistent with the current emphasis on cognition that is embedded in an immediate spatial and temporal context (Wilson, 2002). Many studies use reaction time as a dependent measure. For example, after evaluating a positive or negative word, participants are faster to shift attention to regions of space that are congruent with the *good is up* metaphor (for examples of similar reaction-time effects, see Meier, Hauser, Robinson, Friesen, & Schjeldahl, 2007; Meier & Robinson, 2004; Meier, Sellbom, & Wygant, 2007). Other studies demonstrate how various metaphors influence judgments. For example, individuals appearing high in space are judged as having stronger faith in God (congruent with the metaphor *divinity is up*; Meier, Hauser, et al., 2007), the font color of positively valenced words is judged to be brighter than that of negatively valenced words (*good is bright*; Meier, Robinson, Crawford, & Ahlvers, 2007), and a social issue is judged to be more important when participants hold a heavy rather than a light clipboard (*importance is heavy*; Jostmann, Lakens, & Schubert, 2009). These studies indicate that when making judgments about available stimuli, we refer to physically embodied experiences. It may be the case that such embodied domains are especially relevant for immediate judgments because action is tightly coupled with triggering stimuli in the environment (Noë, 2004; Norman, 1988). However, memory is, by its nature, partially dissociated from the immediate environment. When information is available in the environment, we need not bother to store it in memory, and knowing this, people often arrange information in their environments to reduce the burden on memory (Kirsh, 1995). Although environmental cues guide behavior, we are not completely subject to them. One of the hallmarks of human cognition is our ability to deliberate about, plan for, and remember that which is not immediately present (e.g., Donald, 1993). These forms of mental time travel require us to suppress information coming in from the environment in order to imagine alternatives (Glenberg, 1997). When we disengage from the immediate environment and recall things that are no longer available to be acted on, does embodiment matter?

Given what is known about memory, it makes sense that it would be influenced by embodied associations and metaphorically related content. Memory is reconstructive. When trying to retrieve an experience from memory, participants do not just rewind and play back a mental recording. Instead, they piece together a memory that includes traces of the original event along with other sources of information such as prior knowledge, expectations, and information acquired after the original memory trace was laid (Loftus, Feldman, & Dashiell, 1995; Schacter, Guerin, & St. Jacques, 2011). Given the growing evidence that some concepts are understood metaphorically, metaphorically related information may be another ingredient in reconstructive memory. If so, metaphors would be expected to influence how information is encoded into and retrieved from memory. If metaphors are as cognitively pervasive as theorists have claimed (Gibbs, 2006; Lakoff & Johnson, 1980), then they should influence offline cognition as well.

Furthermore, it is valuable to examine memory in addition to immediate stimulus processing because the conditions that are known to facilitate attention and judgment sometimes have the opposite effect on memory (e.g., Mulligan, 1996; Nairne, 1988; Stangor & McMillan, 1992). As the following review of the literature reveals, memory for spatial location and autobiographical events shows biases in favor of metaphor congruence, but memory for recently encountered stimulus content produces a less consistent pattern of findings. Without examining a range of cognitive processes, we risk drawing an overly simplistic conclusion that cognition favors metaphor-congruent information.

SPATIAL MEMORY

A few studies have examined the impact of the *good is up* metaphor on memory for the spatial locations of emotionally evocative stimuli. Crawford, Margolies, Drake, and Murphy (2006) conducted a series of studies in which positive and negative images from the International Affect Picture System (IAPS; Center for the Study of Emotion and Attention, 1999) were presented in various locations on a screen. After viewing all of the images (Experiment 1), participants saw each image again and moved it to the location where they remembered having seen it previously. Although the task was challenging and the responses rather inaccurate, there was a significant effect of image valence, with positive pictures were biased upward relative to comparably located negative images. In a subsequent experiment, participants reproduced the location of each picture immediately after viewing it. This immediate memory task creates different processing demands. Not only is the task much easier, it does not require participants to use the image content as a retrieval cue for location, and thus the emotional content of the stimuli are incidental to the task. In fact, participants can do this task by attending only to location and not even encoding the images, as they would if their vision were blurry. Despite deemphasizing the image content, this experiment showed a similar effect of valence on memory for location.

An advantage of using images such as the IAPS is that they are vivid and well known to evoke affective responses (e.g., Larsen, Norris, & Cacioppo, 2003). A disadvantage is that it is difficult to control for other features of the stimuli that could affect spatial memory, such as brightness and coloration, the direction of a pictured person's eye gaze, or the location of the main content within the picture. Because such variables could confound the effects of valence, we conducted another experiment in which we manipulated how participants felt about a set of stimuli. We presented participants with yearbook photos of high school girls who appeared in various locations. Each photograph was randomly paired with a positive or negative vignette about the pictured girl. Positive vignettes described behaviors that demonstrate kindness, loyalty to friends, leadership, or success, such as, "She was captain of her school's soccer team and was respected by all of her teammates. In the state championship game, she scored the winning goal and was voted most valuable player." Negative vignettes demonstrated disloyalty, dishonesty, failure, or meanness, such as, "She comes from a wealthy family and always wears fashionable and expensive clothes. During high school, she and her friends used to make fun of the poorer girls' outfits." In a subsequent block, each photo was shown again, and participants moved it back to its previous position and then rated how they felt about the target. Those whom they evaluated positively were biased upward in memory compared with those who were evaluated negatively. Additional studies using single-word stimuli instead of images find a similar pattern of results (Crawford & Drake, 2012). Thus, the results suggest that the *good is up* bias in memory for spatial location generalizes beyond the IAPS pictures.

Because we were interested in the general orientational metaphor *good is up*, our studies did not address more specific valenced concepts that are mapped to the vertical dimension. Meier, Hauser, and colleagues (2007) focused on the metaphoric mapping of God and the devil to *up* and *down*, respectively. This metaphor is reflected in the language and iconography of many religions and is especially salient in the Christian tradition. Meier, Hauser, et al. found that not only were people faster to recognize words related to God or the devil when they appeared in metaphor-congruent spatial locations, they also tended to bias their memory of location. Memories of picture locations were biased upward when the pictures depicted God and downward when they depicted the devil. The *God is up* metaphor is coherent with *good is up*, and this study provides additional evidence that such spatial metaphors play a role in remembering locations of objects.

Do these biases emerge during perceptual encoding or later on, when the item is retrieved from memory? The question is important because if these results reflect only biases in perception, then they tell us little about whether and how metaphors may operate in memory. The biases observed in the Crawford et al. (2006) studies cannot be attributed to perceptual encoding alone because the same stimuli were shown at initial presentation and again at test, when participants returned each to its previous position. If perception of location were biased, this bias would apply both during study and at test and so would cancel out in estimation, producing no net bias in responses. The results observed in these studies would only emerge if retaining the stimulus in memory introduced bias in addition to any that might occur in perception.

This account is in keeping with other findings from the literature on spatial memory. It is well known that when participants recall locations of objects, they reconstruct those memories by combining information about the object's specific location with other sources of information. For example, estimates of a point location integrate information about the geographic category or larger spatial region in which a stimulus appeared (Friedman & Brown, 2000; Huttenlocher, Hedges, & Duncan, 1991) as well as participants' expectations about stimulus movement (Freyd & Finke, 1984). These sources of information lead to systematic biases in memories of location, biases that become more extreme the longer the stimulus is held in memory. It may be the case that people integrate metaphor-activated spatial regions into their location memories in a similar way. That is, when people view an emotionally charged stimulus, their own affective response activates metaphorically related areas of space. When asked to retrieve the location, that spatial area is blended with memory for the particular location. Integrating these two sources of information will lead items to be biased in the direction of the metaphor—good things upward, bad things downward.

AUTOBIOGRAPHICAL MEMORY

One of the many possible physical bases for the *good is up* metaphor may be the connection between affective state and posture. As noted earlier, health and liveliness are necessary to remain upright in the face of gravity. When sad, people tend to hold a stooped posture in which the head tilts downward, whereas happy people are more erect (LaFrance & Mayo, 1978). Such bodily associations with emotional states may constrain the range of possible metaphors for affective experience, making it more felicitous to conceptualize *good* as *up* than as *down*.

Some research suggests that the posture one adopts can affect retrieval of autobiographical memories. Riskind (1983) had participants adopt the posture and facial expression commensurate with happiness or sadness and then, as they maintained this, to recall positive or negative experiences from their lives. They found that participants retrieved memories faster when their posture and the valence prompt were congruent, suggesting that the congruency produced a more efficient search. As Casasanto and Dijkstra (2010) noted, this effect could be due to the activation of the *good is up* metaphor, but it could also be attributed to the well-known phenomenon of encoding specificity (Godden & Baddeley, 1975; Tulving, 1986) through which memory is facilitated when encoding and retrieval conditions are similar. Specifically, if people were smiling and upright when the memory was originally encoded, then taking that position at retrieval is likely to have a facilitating effect. This facilitation would be expected whether or not emotions were conceptualized via spatial metaphor.

These accounts are teased apart in a study by Casasanto and Dijkstra (2010). Rather than manipulate posture, they had participants move marbles upward or downward while retrieving autobiographical memories. In one experiment, participants were asked to retrieve a memory with a positive or negative valence, such as a time when they felt proud or ashamed. The results showed that participants were faster to respond when the movement of the marbles was congruent with the valence of the memory, suggesting that retrieval was more efficient when the valence of the memory and movement of the marbles were congruent with the *good is up* metaphor. In another experiment, participants were given neutral memory prompts (e.g., something that happened yesterday) and asked to respond while moving marbles upward or downward. They retrieved a greater number of positive than negative memories in the upward condition, but the opposite occurred in the downward condition. Because it is highly unlikely that people were moving objects upward or downward during the original encoding of these memories, the results are not consistent with an encoding specificity account. Rather, it seems that upward or downward goal-directed actions activated associations of positive and negative valence, thus influencing the efficiency with which people retrieved valenced memories as well as the likelihood that they would recall metaphor-congruent as opposed to incongruent content.

Autobiographical memory and metaphor were examined using a different approach by Keefer, Landau, Sullivan, and Rothschild (2011). Rather than examine how spatial behavior affects what is retrieved, they examined how spatial behavior during retrieval affects judgments about the present. In one condition, college students were asked to focus on uncertainties they felt about their lives and then asked to remember and list the factors that influenced their decision to attend their university in order from earliest to most recent. Finally, they rated their satisfaction with their decision. The key spatial manipulation was that they ordered their reasons in an upward direction (i.e., entering text starting at the bottom and moving upward with each item) or in the opposite direction. As predicted, those who listed the reasons for their choice in the upward direction rated themselves as more satisfied with their university decision than those that listed them in the downward direction. Most important, this metaphor effect only emerged when participants initially focused on uncertainty and not when they instead focused on pain or the shelving of books. As Keefer et al. noted, the results support the idea that metaphors serve the epistemic function of managing uncertainty (see also Landau et al., 2010).

MEMORY FOR STIMULUS CONTENT

An alternative approach to the study of metaphor and memory is to examine memory for the content of recently encountered stimuli. Palma, Garrido, and Semin (2011) did this in a study of impression formation and memory. They gave participants a description of someone who belonged to a positively stereotyped group (a child-care worker) or a negatively stereotyped group (a skinhead). Participants then read behavioral descriptions, some of which were consistent with the valence of the group membership and some of which were neutral. The critical variable was the spatial location in which these behavioral descriptions were shown: Some appeared at the top and others at the bottom of a screen. After doing a filler task and then rating how they felt about the target, participants were given a surprise free-recall task in which they were asked to remember as many of the behaviors as possible. Participants recalled more behaviors that had been presented in the metaphor-compatible positions (for the child-care worker, positive in the upper region of space; for the skinhead, negative in the lower region) than in the opposite pairing of valence and location. The same pattern of results was found in an experiment that manipulated location by printing the behavioral descriptions on cards that participants placed on either high or low shelves. These results are in keeping with other studies of physical compatibility and memory. For example, Förster and Strack (1996) had people hear a list of positive and negative words while doing a nodding or head-shaking motion (ostensibly as a marketing test for the headphones they were wearing) and found an interaction between action and valence such that positive words were better remembered when nodding than when shaking and the opposite was true for negative words. Metaphor compatibility with respect to valenced stimuli may operate like other kinds of action compatibility, benefiting memory performance.

Crawford and Cohn (2012) reached a different conclusion in their study of spatial location and memory for text. In these experiments, stimuli were individual positive and negative words, each of which was randomly assigned to appear at the top or bottom of a screen. In a subsequent free-recall task, participants remembered more of the words that had been presented in metaphor incongruent locations than in congruent ones, an effect that was mostly driven by responses to negative words. In another study, they used a recognition test in which the vertical position of words varied during initial stimulus presentation but was constant and centered at the testing stage. As with the free-recall results, negative words were better recognized when they had previously appeared at the top of the screen than at the bottom. This study suggests that at least under certain conditions, there is a memory advantage for material that was studied in metaphor-incongruent locations.

The results of the Crawford and Cohn (2012) study are in keeping with previous work showing a memory advantage for information that violates expectation (e.g., Graesser, 1981; Stangor & McMillan, 1992), but they conflict with the congruency advantage that Palma et al. (2011) found. The reason for these disparate outcomes cannot be discerned because there were many methodological differences between the studies. Palma et al.'s participants read behavioral descriptions, were instructed to form an impression of a stereotyped person, and viewed stimuli drawn from half of the valence continuum (i.e., neutral to positive or neutral to negative). Crawford and Cohn's (2012) participants read individually presented words, were not told to think of them as person descriptions, and encountered a wider range of valence. Compared with Crawford and Cohn's procedures, it seems likely that Palma et al.'s (2011) would lead participants to form a more cohesive, entitative representation of the presented material. It is possible that this produces a strong expectation of, and preference for, stimulus compatibility that extends to spatial location. Crawford and Cohn's results suggest that the effects of metaphors on memory may be complex. They also suggest ways in which metaphors may relate to other kinds of knowledge structures, as discussed in what follows.

METAPHORS AND SCHEMAS

In a review article, Landau et al. (2010) called for researchers to consider how conceptual metaphors can enrich our understanding of social cognition. They acknowledged that we already have a powerful account of how people make sense of social stimuli: *schemas*. According to the extensive literature on schemas, people interpret individual stimuli by relating them to what is already known about stimuli of the same kind. Conceptual metaphor is similar in that previously existing knowledge structures are used to understand newly encountered stimuli, but it differs in that this knowledge is pulled from an alternate domain rather than from similar instances within the same domain.[1] Conceptual metaphor theory makes the additional claim that we tend to do this when trying to interpret, reason, or remember things that are relatively abstract. On the basis of these differences, Landau et al. (2010) proposed that metaphor should be viewed as a unique mechanism that operates in addition to schemas.

An important difference between metaphor theory and schemas is that schemas are traditionally assumed to be abstracted, amodally represented knowledge that is dissociated from sensory systems (IJzerman & Koole, 2011; Landau, Keefer, & Meier, 2011; Landau et al., 2010). The growing evidence for conceptual metaphor indicates that the schema account of social cognition is incomplete. It may be the case that we need to treat metaphor as an additional, unique mechanism that operates in addition to schemas. Alternatively, we may need to expand our notion of schema so that it includes metaphor-based components. That is, rather than posit two separate kinds of knowledge structures, we assume one that has embodied, metaphor-based aspects. This is happening in the study of concepts. Like schemas, concepts were traditionally viewed as abstracted and disembodied, but recent work argues that concepts include modality-specific, embodied elements (Barsalou, 1999; Barsalou, Simmons, Barbey, & Wilson, 2003). Expanding schemas to

---

[1]Both schemas and metaphors exert what psychology has traditionally referred to as *top-down* effects in which prior knowledge influences how we process information coming in through the senses. The *top-down/bottom-up* terminology reflects the underlying conceptual metaphor *abstract is up, concrete is down*. The terms are awkwardly incoherent when applied to conceptual metaphor theory, according to which cognitive structures (i.e., the *top*) are structured by concrete, physical experience.

encompass metaphors might provide a parsimonious way to account for the commonalities in how schemas and metaphors affect cognition.

One hallmark of schemas and categories is that whereas facilitation is seen for initial processing of information that fits the schema, the effects in memory are more variable. Although memory is sometimes better for information that is congruent with prior knowledge (e.g., Cantor & Mischel, 1979; Rothbart, Evans, & Fulero, 1979), many studies find the opposite effect. In their meta-analysis of studies that examined memory for expectancy-congruent and expectancy-incongruent social information, Stangor and McMillan (1992) concluded that recall and recognition measures that are corrected for response bias show an overall advantage for incongruent over congruent information. This conclusion is consistent with Srull and Wyer's (1989) associative network model, which proposed that when information about a person violates expectations, it prompts people to think more elaborately to resolve the incongruency, leaving a stronger memory trace. It is also consistent with Graesser's (1981) *schema-pointer plus tag* model, which posits that incongruent information is stored separately from congruent information, supporting memory for the discrepancies (see also Sakamoto & Love, 2004, for a similar account in nonsocial categorization).

It is also possible that metaphor incongruency garners memory advantages during encoding, regardless of deliberate attempts to reconcile incongruent information after encoding. Previous studies have shown that making perceptual encoding of items more difficult can lead to better memory for the studied material. For example, words that are immediately followed by an interfering perceptual mask are harder to read but better remembered than unmasked words (Mulligan, 1996; Nairne, 1988). When perceptual disfluency is increased by showing words printed in difficult-to-read fonts, memory for those items is enhanced (Diemand-Yauman, Oppenheimer, & Vaughan, 2011). The fact that metaphor incongruent information takes longer to process initially (as in Meier, Robinson, & Clore, 2004) suggests that metaphor incongruency may pose the kind of encoding challenge that leads to enhanced memory.

COGNITIVE FUNCTIONS OF METAPHORS

A functional approach to cognition suggests that we use mechanisms such as metaphor because they confer some cognitive benefit. Landau et al. (2010) suggested that we are averse to abstraction, presumably because we are cognitive misers and abstractions require more cognitive effort. In general terms, metaphors may operate like other kinds of cognitive structures in that they enable us to draw inferences, reconstruct memories, and make sense of what would otherwise be the "blooming and buzzing confusion" of sensory input (James, 1890, p. 462). Thus, they enable us to reduce uncertainty not only about major life events (Keefer et al., 2011) but also about basic cognitive operations. However, is there reason to believe that cognitive structures that are metaphorical are particularly useful in ways that are not addressed by traditional accounts of categories and schemas?

Studies of recoding (or re-representation) suggest that there is. There is good evidence that memory is improved when information can be represented in formats that have a spatial component. For example, Paivio's (1971) work on dual coding shows that words are better remembered when presented along with visual representations and that words referring to concrete objects are better remembered than abstract ones because they can be visualized. Watson and Rubin (1996) showed that memory for a sequence of events was enhanced when those events were presented in consecutive locations rather than in a single central location, indicating that mapping the nonspatial dimension of sequential order to space is beneficial for memory. Relatedly, Casasanto and Boroditzky (2008) showed that people integrate information about the spatial extent of an object when reproducing the object's duration but do not use duration to reproduce spatial extent. They concluded that we build representations of "things we can never see or touch" out of experience with perception and action (p. 591).

In addition, a number of studies have shown that physical actions, which are both spatial and motoric, support memory. For example, memory for a string of digits is enhanced when participants are taught to rehearse them both verbally and with a sequence of corresponding finger movements (Reisberg, Rappaport, & O'Shaughnessy, 1984). Memory for verbal material is enhanced when people enact the studied content than when they do not (Engelkamp, 1998; Hornstein & Mulligan, 2001). In addition, gesturing while verbally describing video vignettes leads to better subsequent recall of the presented events than not gesturing (Cook, Yip, & Goldin-Meadow, 2010). Physical action produces detailed sensory information, including spatial information, that may provide for more detailed encoding as well as a richer set of retrieval cues.

Conceptual metaphors may be beneficial because they allow for information to be re-represented into domains that our brains handle especially well. This is especially plausible with respect to spatial metaphors. Spatial location is encoded relatively automatically, regardless of task instructions or cognitive load (Hasher & Zacks, 1979). Mnemonic devices such as the *method of loci* work by recruiting spatial memory to support memory for other kinds of information that is not easily retained (Yates, 1966/2001). In addition, space is inherently relational, which makes it an especially useful representational format for relational concepts. When two objects are shown simultaneously, the spatial relations are available in the world and do not need to be computed and maintained in memory, as they would be if the same information were presented verbally. Thus, serial logic and class-inclusion problems are made easier when they can be recoded in a spatial format, such as a Venn diagram (Bryant & Squire, 2001; Gattis, 2001). By locating abstract concepts in space, orientational metaphors such as *good is up* may take advantage of a representational format that reduces computational complexity.

So far, the *good is up* metaphor has received the most attention, but metaphors involving other spatial dimensions may function similarly. For example, one way to conceptualize time is in terms of movement through space (e.g., Boroditsky & Ramscar, 2002; Margolies & Crawford, 2008; Miles, Nind, & Macrae, 2010), and one way to conceptualize social relationships is through distance (e.g., Williams & Bargh, 2008). By examining a greater variety of metaphors, researchers will build a more complete understanding of the role of metaphors in memory.

FUTURE DIRECTIONS

As this volume shows, we now have a convincing body of evidence that when evaluating, interpreting, or remembering information, people make use of knowledge from metaphorically related domains. Having established that, we are now poised to test hypotheses generated by theoretical accounts of how metaphors are used and what functions they serve. To do so, future studies will need to examine variability in metaphor use. If we can manipulate people's reliance on metaphors or take advantage of natural variation in it, we can examine the consequences of their use.

Keefer et al. (2011) argued that metaphor may serve the epistemic function of reducing uncertainty. As evidence for this, they found that people relied more on metaphor when they were primed with uncertainties about significant aspects of their lives (e.g., the value of their college experience). It may also be the case that metaphors are integrated into memories because they reduce uncertainty about the past. If so, then we would expect that conditions under which people are less certain about previously experienced stimuli or events would produce greater reliance on metaphor. One way to examine this would be to manipulate conditions that are known to affect memory performance, such as the quantity of information to be remembered, the amount of delay or interference after the information has been encoded, or the correspondence between encoding and retrieval context. An alternative approach, akin to Keefer et al.'s, would be to manipulate subjects' confidence in their own memory ability. In addition, we might expect that natural variation in memory ability (or memory self-efficacy) would correlate with metaphor use. That is, if we assume that access to conceptual metaphors is more or less constant but that memory competence varies, then those with worse memory may rely more heavily on metaphor. Such findings would provide strong additional support that metaphors serve the epistemic function of reducing uncertainty.

The function of reducing uncertainty is not essentially different from the function of other knowledge structures, such as categories, stereotypes, traits, and schemas. We know that these conceptual structures can be activated, even outside of conscious awareness, and lead to changes in subsequent judgments and behavior (reviewed in Bargh, 1997). It seems likely that metaphors can be differentially activated as well. There is evidence that spatial experience can achieve this. For example, Boroditsky and Ramscar (2002) showed that traversing a spatial distance can make people more likely to think of themselves as moving through time rather than as being stationary as time passes by. Keefer et al. (2011) showed that having participants spatially arrange textual descriptions of life events as if along a path increases the salience of the metaphor *life course* is a *path*. There are likely to be many ways that metaphors can be activated, and more work is needed to establish the most effective approaches.

Manipulating the application of metaphors is a potentially powerful tool for understanding their role in cognition. As work in this area progresses, it will allow us to investigate the consequences of using metaphors, informing our understanding of what functions they serve. For example, if using the *good is up* metaphor supports reasoning and memory about affective experiences, then making that metaphor less available could have several effects. A simple prediction would be that it would decrease performance on tasks that depend on reasoning and memory about emotional content. A more nuanced prediction would be that it would increase reliance on other cognitive structures with which metaphor probably works in concert.

As noted earlier (see also IJzerman & Koole, 2011; Landau et al., 2010), metaphors are similar to schemas but differ in that they cross knowledge domains. Interestingly, many metaphors cross domains that are thought to be cognitively and neurologically separable, such as emotion, language, and spatial cognition. Thus, although metaphors may operate like schemas in many respects, conceptual metaphor theory also generates new hypotheses that traditional schema theory does not. For example, if we use spatial representations to support conceptualization of nonspatial content, then we might be able to decrease metaphor effects by selectively interfering with spatial (but not verbal) working memory. Using a similar logic, patients who have selective deficits in spatial cognition would be expected to show less reliance on spatial metaphors. For example, due to damage in the parietal lobes, patients with Balint's syndrome can identify individual objects without being able to locate them in space and, in some cases, can perceive only one object at a time (Robertson, 2004). Although such patients may still speak using common, practiced spatial metaphors, they may not use spatial representations to conceptualize emotion, time, or other abstractions.

Another topic for future research is to consider differences between types of metaphors. This chapter focused on spatialization metaphors, which are among the most prevalent, but these may operate differently from other kinds of metaphors. Some metaphors, such as *good is up*, may be more automatic and obligatory; others may depend on deliberate, optional strategy. For example, we may have some control over whether we think of love as a journey, a battlefield, or a collaborative work of art. In such cases, the choice of metaphor is important because it does not leave unaltered the experience that we view through it. The character of love itself changes when we adopt different metaphors, and it seems likely that our memories of past love would change as well.

CONCLUSION

The findings that metaphors affect memory suggest that conceptual metaphors play a role in offline cognition, when a stimulus is no longer available to elicit direct action. This work complements studies that focus on immediate judgments of perceptible items. In keeping with studies of schemas, stereotypes, and categories, the findings reviewed here illustrate that metaphors can influence cognition in complex ways, producing variable outcomes across different tasks.

REFERENCES

Bargh, J. A. (1997). The automaticity of everyday life. In R. S. Wyer, Jr. (Ed.), *The automaticity of everyday life: Advances in social cognition* (Vol. 10, pp. 1–61). Mahwah, NJ: Erlbaum.

Barsalou, L. W. (1999). Perceptual symbol systems. *Behavioral and Brain Sciences, 22,* 577–660.

Barsalou, L. W., Simmons, W. K., Barbey, A. K., & Wilson, C. D. (2003). Grounding conceptual knowledge in modality-specific systems. *Trends in Cognitive Sciences, 7,* 84–91. doi:10.1016/S1364-6613(02)00029-3

Bloom, P. (2001). Précis of how children learn the meaning of words. *Behavioral and Brain Sciences, 24,* 1095–1134. doi:10.1017/S0140525X01000139

Boroditsky, L., & Ramscar, M. (2002). The roles of mind and body in abstract thought. *Psychological Science, 13,* 185–189. doi:10.1111/1467-9280.00434

Bretherton, I., Fritz, J., Zahn-Waxler, C., & Ridgeway, D. (1986). Learning to talk about emotions: A functionalist perspective. *Child Development, 57,* 529–548. doi:10.2307/1130334

Bryant, P., & Squire, S. (2001). Children's mathematics: Lost and found in space. In M. Gattis (Ed.), *Spatial schemas and abstract thought* (pp. 175–200). Cambridge, MA: MIT Press.

Cantor, N., & Mischel, W. (1979). Prototypicality and personality: Effects on free recall and personality impressions. *Journal of Research in Personality, 13*, 187–205. doi:10.1016/0092-6566(79)90030-8

Casasanto, D., & Boroditsky, L. (2008). Time in the mind: Using space to think about time. *Cognition, 106*, 579–593. doi:10.1016/j.cognition.2007.03.004

Casasanto, D., & Dijkstra, K. (2010). Motor action and emotional memory. *Cognition, 115*, 179–185. doi:10.1016/j.cognition.2009.11.002

Center for the Study of Emotion and Attention. (1999). *The International Affective Picture System* [IAPS: Photographic slides]. Gainesville: The Center for Research in Psychophysiology, University of Florida.

Cook, S. W., Yip, T. K., & Goldin-Meadow, S. (2010). Gesturing makes memories that last. *Journal of Memory and Language, 63*, 465–475. doi:10.1016/j.jml.2010.07.002

Crawford, L. E. (2009). Conceptual metaphors of affect. *Emotion Review, 1*, 129–139. doi:10.1177/1754073908100438

Crawford, L. E., & Cohn, S. (2012). *"Good is up" is not always better: A memory advantage for words in metaphor incompatible locations*. Manuscript submitted for publication.

Crawford, L.E., & Drake, J. T. (2012). *Using stimulus valence to form inductive spatial categories*. Manuscript submitted for publication.

Crawford, L. E., Margolies, S. M., Drake, J. T., & Murphy, M. E. (2006). Affect biases memory of location: Evidence for the spatial representation of affect. *Cognition and Emotion, 20*, 1153–1169. doi:10.1080/02699930500347794

Diemand-Yauman, C., Oppenheimer, D. M., & Vaughan, E. B. (2011). Fortune favors the bold (and the italicized): Effects of disfluency on educational outcomes. *Cognition, 118*, 111–115. doi:10.1016/j.cognition.2010.09.012

Donald, M. W. (1993). Human cognitive evolution: What we were, what we are becoming. *Social Research, 60*, 143–170.

Engelkamp, J. (1998). *Memory for actions*. Hove, England: Psychology Press/Taylor & Francis.

Förster, J., & Strack, F. (1996). Influence of overt head movements on memory for valenced words: A case of conceptual-motor compatibility. *Journal of Personality and Social Psychology, 71*, 421–430. doi:10.1037/0022-3514.71.3.421

Freyd, J. J., & Finke, R. A. (1984). Representational momentum. *Journal of Experimental Psychology: Learning, Memory, and Cognition, 10*, 126–132. doi:10.1037/0278-7393.10.1.126

Friedman, A., & Brown, N. R. (2000). Updating geographical knowledge: Principles of coherence and inertia. *Journal of Experimental Psychology: Learning, Memory, and Cognition, 26*, 900–914. doi:10.1037/0278-7393.26.4.900

Gattis, M. (2001). *Spatial schemas and abstract thought*. Cambridge, MA: MIT Press.

Gibbs, R. W. (1994). *The poetics of mind: Figurative thought, language, and understanding*. Cambridge, England: Cambridge University Press.

Gibbs, R. W. (2006). *Embodiment and cognitive science*. Cambridge, England: Cambridge University Press.

Glenberg, A. M. (1997). What memory is for. *Behavioral and Brain Sciences, 20*, 1–55.

Godden, D. R., & Baddeley, A. D. (1975). Context-dependent memory in two natural environments: On land and underwater. *British Journal of Psychology, 66*, 325–331. doi:10.1111/j.2044-8295.1975.tb01468.x

Graesser, A. C. (1981). *Prose comprehension: Beyond the word*. New York, NY: Springer. doi:10.1007/978-1-4612-5880-3

Hasher, L., & Zacks, R. T. (1979). Automatic and effortful processes in memory. *Journal of Experimental Psychology: General, 108*, 356–388. doi:10.1037/0096-3445.108.3.356

Hornstein, S. L., & Mulligan, N. W. (2001). Memory of action events: The role of objects in memory of self- and other-performed tasks. *The American Journal of Psychology, 114*, 199–217. doi:10.2307/1423515

Huttenlocher, J., Hedges, L. V., & Duncan, S. (1991). Categories and particulars: Prototype effects in estimating spatial location. *Psychological Review, 98*, 352–376. doi:10.1037/0033-295X.98.3.352

IJzerman, H., & Koole, S. L. (2011). From perceptual rags to metaphoric riches—Bodily, social, and cultural constraints on sociocognitive metaphors: Comment on Landau, Meier, and Keefer (2010). *Psychological Bulletin, 137*, 355–361. doi:10.1037/a0022373

James, W. (1890). *The principles of psychology*. New York, NY: Holt. doi:10.1037/11059-000

Jostmann, N. B., Lakens, D., & Schubert, T. W. (2009). Weight as an embodiment of importance. *Psychological Science, 20*, 1169–1174. doi:10.1111/j.1467-9280.2009.02426.x

Keefer, L. A., Landau, M. J., Sullivan, D., & Rothschild, Z. K. (2011). Exploring metaphor's epistemic function: Uncertainty moderates metaphor-consistent priming effects on social perceptions. *Journal of Experimental Social Psychology, 47*, 657–660. doi:10.1016/j.jesp.2011.02.002

Kirsh, D. (1995). The intelligent use of space. *Artificial Intelligence, 73*, 31–68. doi:10.1016/0004-3702(94)00017-U

Kövecses, Z. (2000). *Metaphor and emotion: Language, culture, and body in human feeling*. Cambridge, England: Cambridge University Press.

Kövecses, Z. (2002). *Metaphor: A practical introduction*. Oxford, England: Oxford University Press.

LaFrance, M., & Mayo, C. (1978). Cultural aspects of nonverbal communication. *International Journal of Intercultural Relations, 2*, 71–89. doi:10.1016/0147-1767(78)90029-9

Lakoff, G., & Johnson, M. (1980). *Metaphors we live by*. Chicago, IL: University of Chicago Press.

Landau, M. J., Keefer, L. A., & Meier, B. P. (2011). Wringing the perceptual rags: Reply to IJzerman and Koole (2011). *Psychological Bulletin, 137*, 362–365. doi:10.1037/a0022457

Landau, M. J., Meier, B. P., & Keefer, L. A. (2010). A metaphor-enriched social cognition. *Psychological Bulletin, 136*, 1045–1067. doi:10.1037/a0020970

Larsen, J. T., Norris, C. J., & Cacioppo, J. T. (2003). Effects of positive and negative affect on electromyographic activity over *zygomaticus major* and *corrugator supercilii*. *Psychophysiology, 40*, 776–785. doi:10.1111/1469-8986.00078

Loftus, E. F., Feldman, J., & Dashiell, R. (1995). The reality of illusory memories. In J. T. Coyle (Ed.), *Memory distortions: How minds, brains, and societies reconstruct the past* (pp. 47–68). Cambridge, MA: Harvard University Press.

Margolies, S. O., & Crawford, L. E. (2008). Event valence and spatial metaphors of time. *Cognition and Emotion, 22*, 1401–1414. doi:10.1080/02699930701810335

Meier, B. P., Hauser, D. J., Robinson, M. D., Friesen, C. K., & Schjeldahl, K. (2007). What's "up" with God? Vertical space as a representation of the divine. *Journal of Personality and Social Psychology, 93*, 699–710. doi:10.1037/0022-3514.93.5.699

Meier, B. P., & Robinson, M. D. (2004). Why the sunny side is up: Associations between affect and vertical position. *Psychological Science, 15*, 243–247.

Meier, B. P., & Robinson, M. D. (2005). The metaphorical representation of affect. *Metaphor and Symbol, 20*, 239–257. doi:10.1207/s15327868ms2004_1

Meier, B. P., Robinson, M. D., & Clore, G. L. (2004). Why good guys wear white: Automatic inferences about stimulus valence based on brightness. *Psychological Science, 15*, 82–87. doi:10.1111/j.0963-7214.2004.01502002.x

Meier, B. P., Robinson, M. D., Crawford, L. E., & Ahlvers, W. J. (2007). When "light" and "dark" thoughts become light and dark responses: Affect biases brightness judgments. *Emotion, 7*, 366–376. doi:10.1037/1528-3542.7.2.366

Meier, B. P., Sellbom, M., & Wygant, D. B. (2007). Failing to take the moral high ground: Psychopathy and the vertical representation of morality. *Personality and Individual Differences, 43*, 757–767. doi:10.1016/j.paid.2007.02.001

Miles, L. K., Nind, L. K., & Macrae, N. C. (2010). Moving through time. *Psychological Science, 21*, 222–223. doi:10.1177/0956797609359333

Mulligan, N. W. (1996). The effects of perceptual interference at encoding on implicit memory, explicit memory, and memory for source. *Journal of Experimental Psychology: Learning, Memory, and Cognition, 22*, 1067–1087. doi:10.1037/0278-7393.22.5.1067

Nairne, J. S. (1988). The mnemonic value of perceptual identification. *Journal of Experimental Psychology: Learning, Memory, and Cognition, 14*, 248–255. doi:10.1037/0278-7393.14.2.248

Noë, A. (2004). *Action in perception*. Cambridge, MA: MIT Press.

Norman, D. A. (1988). *The design of everyday things*. New York, NY: Basic Books.

Paivio, A. (1971). *Imagery and verbal processes*. Oxford, England: Holt, Rinehart & Winston.

Palma, T. A., Garrido, M. V., & Semin, G. R. (2011). Grounding person memory in space: Does spatial anchoring of behaviors improve recall? *European Journal of Social Psychology, 41*, 275–280. doi:10.1002/ejsp.795

Reisberg, D., Rappaport, I., & O'Shaughnessy, M. (1984). Limits of working memory: The digit digit-span. *Journal of Experimental Psychology: Learning, Memory, and Cognition, 10*, 203–221. doi:10.1037/0278-7393.10.2.203

Riskind, J. H. (1983). Nonverbal expressions and the accessibility of life experience memories: A congruence hypothesis. *Social Cognition, 2*, 62–86. doi:10.1521/soco.1983.2.1.62

Robertson, L. C. (2004). *Space, objects, minds and brains*. New York, NY: Psychology Press.

Rothbart, M., Evans, M., & Fulero, S. (1979). Recall for confirming events: Memory processes and the maintenance of social stereotypes. *Journal of Experimental Social Psychology, 15*, 343–355. doi:10.1016/0022-1031(79)90043-X

Sakamoto, Y., & Love, B. C. (2004). Schematic influences on category learning and recognition memory. *Journal of Experimental Psychology: General, 133*, 534–553. doi:10.1037/0096-3445.133.4.534

Schacter, D. L., Guerin, S. A., & St. Jacques, P. L. (2011). Memory distortion: An adaptive perspective. *Trends in Cognitive Sciences, 15*, 467–474. doi:10.1016/j.tics.2011.08.004

Srull, T. K., & Wyer, R. S. (1989). Person memory and judgment. *Psychological Review, 96*, 58–83. doi:10.1037/0033-295X.96.1.58

Stangor, C., & McMillan, D. (1992). Memory for expectancy-congruent and expectancy-incongruent information: A review of the social and social developmental literatures. *Psychological Bulletin, 111*, 42–61. doi:10.1037/0033-2909.111.1.42

Tulving, E. (1986). What kind of a hypothesis is the distinction between episodic and semantic memory? *Journal of Experimental Psychology: Learning, Memory, and Cognition, 12*, 307–311. doi:10.1037/0278-7393.12.2.307

Watson, M. E., & Rubin, D. C. (1996). Spatial imagery preserves temporal order. *Memory (Hove, England), 4*, 515–534. doi:10.1080/741940777

Williams, L. E., & Bargh, J. A. (2008). Keeping one's distance: The influence of spatial distance cues on affect and evaluation. *Psychological Science, 19*, 302–308. doi:10.1111/j.1467-9280.2008.02084.x

Wilson, M. (2002). Six views of embodied cognition. *Psychonomic Bulletin & Review, 9*, 625–636. doi:10.3758/BF03196322

Yates, F. A. (2001). *The art of memory*. Chicago, IL: University of Chicago Press. (Original work published 1966)

5

METAPHOR IN JUDGMENT AND DECISION MAKING

SPIKE W. S. LEE AND NORBERT SCHWARZ

"I say, block those metaphors. America's economy isn't a stalled car, nor is it an invalid who will soon return to health if he gets a bit more rest. Our problems are longer-term than either metaphor implies. And bad metaphors make for bad policy," wrote Nobel-winning economist Paul Krugman in his *New York Times* column (2010, p. A25). Why would bad metaphors make for bad policy? Can metaphors shape how people think about the issues at hand and how they decide to fix them?

Neither traditional theories of metaphoric thought nor standard approaches to decision making would suggest so. However, key assumptions underlying both of these perspectives have been challenged by recent experimental findings. We begin this chapter by briefly outlining the traditional perspectives and the recent challenges. We propose why metaphors should

We thank the editors for helpful and insightful comments and the R C Lee Charitable Foundation for generous support.

http://dx.doi.org/10.1037/14278-005
The Power of Metaphor: Examining Its Influence on Social Life, M. J. Landau, M. D. Robinson, and B. P. Meier (Editors)

affect decision making in predictable ways. We then review experimental findings that document profound effects of metaphors on decision making across a variety of economic, consumer, and social domains. We conclude by discussing their theoretical implications and identifying promising directions for future research.

TRADITIONAL AND CURRENT PERSPECTIVES ON METAPHOR IN THINKING AND DECISION MAKING

Does Metaphor Matter for Thinking?

Traditional Western philosophy, linguistics, and related cognitive sciences viewed metaphoric language as something of imaginative and extraordinary use. Poets and playwrights (and perhaps some columnists) may use it for decorative and artistic purposes, but it bears little if any relation to ordinary thinking. From this perspective, metaphoric language is peripheral rather than central to thought (see Chapter 2, this volume).

Lakoff and Johnson (1980) challenged this view by highlighting the systematic patterns underlying metaphoric expressions and their pervasive, mostly unconscious, use in everyday language. Such systematicity and pervasiveness, they argued, would be unlikely if metaphoric language was nothing more than fancy talk invoked idiosyncratically on limited occasions. Their cognitive linguistics analysis assumed that "since communication is based on the same conceptual system that we use in thinking and acting, language is an important source of evidence for what that system is like" (p. 3). Through the window of linguistic patterns, their view of the conceptual system was strikingly different from tradition. They proposed that the conceptual system itself is metaphorical. Thought about abstract concepts (e.g., morality, love) is guided by the schematic and inferential structures of relatively concrete concepts (e.g., cleanliness, journey) that involve more direct bodily experience with the physical world. Although the linguistic evidence supporting this argument is sizeable and provocative, others warned that linguistic patterns only indirectly bear on mental processes—language and thought are different things (e.g., Murphy, 1996, 1997; see also Chapter 2, this volume).

Going beyond the limits of linguistic analyses, a rapidly growing body of experimental research provides persuasive evidence for the role of metaphors in human thought. It shows that even subtle, incidental bodily experiences can unconsciously affect thought about metaphorically related targets (for recent reviews, see Barsalou, 2008; Landau, Meier, & Keefer, 2010; Williams, Huang, & Bargh, 2009). This work produced many surprising and memorable effects that would not have been predicted a few years ago. What is more important, the findings highlight the role of bodily experiences in a variety of psychological processes, from basic attention and memory to social perception, attitude, inference, and judgment. How a given bodily experience affects a psychological outcome can typically be predicted on the basis of metaphoric associations, although the specific mechanisms remain a matter of debate (cf. Anderson, 2008; Barsalou, 2008; Lakoff & Johnson, 1999).

Does Metaphor Matter for Decision Making?

That incidental bodily experiences affect how people think about metaphorically associated targets does not necessarily imply that they also affect how people act and decide. In classic rational choice approaches and their derivatives, actions and decisions are based on the expected utility of an outcome (e.g., Becker, 1976; Elster, 2006; Fishbein & Ajzen, 1975). Some bodily experiences are directly relevant to the expected utility of a choice alternative, as when hunger and thirst increase the utility of food and drink. Bodily experiences that are merely metaphorically relevant to the choice alternatives should exert no influence.

But as numerous studies have demonstrated, how people think and how they behave are strongly driven by their mental construal of the choice alternatives and the situation in which they are embedded (e.g., Lichtenstein & Slovic, 2006; Schwarz, 2007, 2009; Smith & Conrey, 2007; Smith & Semin, 2004). In many contexts of judgment and decision making, social and moral concerns like fairness and altruism (e.g., Fehr & Gächter, 2005; Fehr & Schmidt, 1999; Rabin, 1993) play a more influential role than has long been assumed, as do motivation, self-regulation, and actual or illusory control (e.g., Higgins, 2012). Importantly, these notions tend to be constructed and comprehended metaphorically in terms of bodily experiences, from morality (dirty behavior) and sociability (warm person) to fairness (evenhanded) and self-control (see Chapters 6 and 11, this volume). Furthermore, the language of evaluative judgment brims with metaphors, as shown by the impartiality of balanced judgments and the importance of weighty matters. Such observations suggest that metaphors may play an important role in how people mentally construe the decision task, from their perception of the choice alternatives and the outcomes they afford to the social context in which the decision is situated.

From this perspective, incidental bodily experiences may activate metaphorically associated thoughts, goals, and feelings that pervade the construal of a decision: How attractive are the choice alternatives? Are the benefits worth the costs? Is my negotiation partner trustworthy? Is luck on my side? Do I have what it takes to pull this off? The underlying processes of mental construal are familiar from research on knowledge and goal accessibility (for reviews, see Bless & Schwarz, 2010; Förster & Liberman, 2007; Higgins, 1996; Schwarz, 2009). An embodied and metaphoric approach adds that mental representations are multimodal instead of amodal (Barsalou, 1999, 2008) and hence can be activated through diverse sensory experiences; moreover, knowledge associations can be not only literal but also metaphoric. To date, most demonstrations of metaphoric effects on judgment and decision making seem to occur through this process—bodily experiences activating metaphorically associated thoughts, goals, and feelings—but other processes are likely to exist as well. We will revisit this issue of multiple processes and elaborate its implications after reviewing some illustrative evidence.

EMBODIED METAPHORS AFFECT MENTAL CONSTRUAL

People are social (Fiske, 2004) and moral beings (Haidt & Kesebir, 2010), and both aspects figure prominently in how people make decisions. Human thought about sociality and morality is highly metaphoric, with many attributes conceptualized in terms of bodily interactions with the physical world (see Chapter 11, this volume). As such, incidental bodily experiences that cue metaphorically associated meanings should be able to change how people make decisions. Empirically, it is true across economic, consumer, and social domains.

Metaphorical Cues With Social Meanings

Fishy and Suspicious

Linguistic analyses (Soriano & Valenzuela, 2008) indicate that social suspicion is metaphorically associated with the sensory experience of smell in at least 18 languages, including Arabic, Chinese, English, French, German, and Spanish. However, the specific odor differs by language, suggesting a universal conceptual metaphor with culture-specific instantiations. In English, the relevant odor is fishy. Can smelling something fishy make people suspicious and unwilling to engage in trust-based investment in a joint venture or in a common cause?

To test this possibility, we (Lee & Schwarz, 2012a, Study 1) had an experimenter spray fish oil, fart spray, or odorless water at a corner area in a campus building. Another experimenter, blind to the smell condition, approached students in a different area and invited them to participate in a one-shot trust game (Berg, Dickhaut, & McCabe, 1995) with another "participant," who was actually a confederate. They walked over to the smell-manipulated corner area, where each received 20 quarters ($5) and an investment form with instructions and response space. The true participant was always approached first and thus designated as decision maker A (the sender), who could freely decide how much money to send to decision maker B. Any amount sent would be quadrupled in value, and decision maker B could then decide how much to send back to decision maker A. Hence, if A trusts B to reciprocate the favor, A should send more money, thus quadrupling what is available for later distribution. If A suspects, however, that B may not be trustworthy, A is better off by sending less. As expected, participants exposed to incidental fishy smells sent significantly less money ($2.53 of their $5 endowment) than those exposed to fart spray ($3.38) or odorless water ($3.34). The amount sent did not differ significantly between the last two conditions, indicating that the metaphoric effect was not driven by generic valence. This "fishy effect" was replicated in a second study using a one-shot public goods game (Ledyard, 1995) in which people should be less likely to invest in a pool of shared resources if they suspect their partners might not carry their share of responsibility. Again, smelling something fishy rather than farty or odorless led participants to contribute less money to the public good.

These studies highlight that incidental exposure to a subtle smell with metaphoric meaning is sufficient to elicit suspicion about the motives and trustworthiness of one's partners, with adverse effects on cooperative behavior. The effect is driven not by the generic valence of the sensory experience but by its specific metaphoric associations, as the comparison between fishy and farty smells suggested. Participants' debriefing reports revealed no conscious awareness of the smell and its influence.

We also tested for the reverse direction of influence: Would feeling suspicious influence participants' perception of incidental fishy smells? As expected, inducing social suspicion improved participants' ability to correctly identify fishy smells (Lee & Schwarz, 2012a, Study 3) and heightened their sensitivity to the presence of faint fishy smells in a signal detection paradigm (Study 7). Both of these effects were specific to the metaphorically related fishy smell and not observed for other smells, which lacked a metaphoric relationship with suspicion. Additional experiments indicated that social suspicion exerts its influence on the perception of fishy smells by activating metaphorically associated concepts related to fishy (Studies 4–6). Next, we consider embodied metaphors that can increase trust.

Warm and Trustworthy

People who are "warm and caring" are those we can trust. Surprisingly, the impression that someone has a warm personality can be induced by incidental experiences of physical warmth. Merely holding a warm rather than cold object (e.g., a cup of warm vs. iced coffee) can lead one to perceive another's personality as warmer (Williams & Bargh, 2008, Study 1) and to act in socially warm and caring ways (e.g., choosing a reward for a friend rather than for oneself; Study 2). Consistent with this metaphoric association between physical and social warmth, Kang, Williams, Clark, Gray, and Bargh (2011) found that incidental physical warmth can also increase trust in cooperation games. Their participants first held and evaluated either a warm or cold temperature pack and then played 15 rounds of a trust game (Berg et al., 1995). Each round ostensibly involved a different partner, but in fact all "partner" responses were computer-generated. As predicted, participants who had held a warm rather than cold pack invested more money in the trust game (Kang et al., 2011, Study 1). The size of this effect depends on the constraints imposed by the choice alternatives (Study 2), highlighting the need to test for the robustness of metaphoric effects on decisions with varying degrees of constraint in natural contexts.

Hard and Unyielding; Rough and Adversarial

Whereas warm people are trustworthy, people who are rough or hard seem less inviting, and interacting with them elicits corresponding behaviors on the perceiver's side. The incidental experience of tactile hardness or roughness turns out to be sufficient to elicit the same behaviors. Exploring the metaphoric meaning of hardness, Ackerman, Nocera, and Bargh (2010, Study 6) had participants imagine shopping for a new car, making an offer to the dealer, being rejected, and having to make a second offer. Depending on condition, participants were sitting in a hard wooden chair or a soft cushioned chair. As predicted, those sitting in a hard chair receded less from the first to the second offer. Apparently, they held a harder line in negotiation. Follow-up work (Cherkasskiy, Song, Malahy, & Bargh, 2012) also found that sitting in a hard rather than soft chair while reading criminal scenarios led people to recommend harsher sentences.

In a conceptually similar study, Ackerman et al. (2010, Study 3) observed that touching rough materials increased the perception that a social interaction is rough and adversarial. Building on this finding, they asked participants in a decision experiment (Study 4) to complete a puzzle with pieces that were either smooth or covered in rough sandpaper. Next, participants played an ultimatum game (Güth, Schmittberger, & Schwarze, 1982). They received 10 tickets for a $50 lottery and decided how many to give to an anonymous (bogus) participant, who supposedly would decide whether to accept the offer (allowing both decision makers to keep their respective allocations) or to reject it (in which case both decision makers would get nothing). As predicted, participants who had played with a rough rather than smooth puzzle offered more tickets in the ultimatum game, presumably to ensure acceptance of their offer in the context of a potentially rough interaction.

Metaphoric Cues With Moral Meanings

Morality is a central domain of social thought, and a variety of metaphors have been found to ground moral thought in embodied experience (Lakoff & Johnson, 1999; see also Chapter 6, this volume). For example, virtuous people have a clean conscience and walk in the light. Can these bodily experiences—feeling clean or seeing light—serve as metaphoric cues that promote honorable decision making against self-interest?

Moral and Physical Purity

People respond to moral transgressions with disgust, an emotion otherwise associated with exposure to physical contaminants from open wounds to spoiled food (e.g., Curtis, Aunger, & Rabie, 2004; Lee & Ellsworth, in press). In fact, moral and physical disgust involve similar subjective feelings, facial expressions, and overlapping neural network activities. Their overlap is also apparent in language use, from the Psalms' (24:4) notion of "clean hands and a pure heart" to everyday references to "dirty hands" or a "dirty mouth" (for a review, see Lee & Schwarz, 2011). Testing the behavioral consequences of these metaphoric associations, Zhong and Liljenquist (2006) found that immoral thoughts increased the appeal of cleaning products. Merely copying a story about someone else's unethical rather than ethical behavior was sufficient to make cleaning products more desirable (Study 2), and participants who had to recall their own immoral rather than moral acts were more likely to choose an antiseptic wipe as a gift (Study 3). As in the physical domain, the desire to cleanse is specific to the contaminated body part. Participants who were induced to sin with their mouth by conveying a lie on voicemail preferred mouthwash over hand sanitizer; conversely, those induced to sin with their hands by conveying the same lie on e-mail preferred hand sanitizer over mouthwash (Lee & Schwarz, 2010a). Just as rinsing your mouth would not help after getting your hands dirty, rinsing your mouth also does not help after doing something unethical with your hands. These parallel responses to moral and physical contamination illustrate the extent to which moral thought draws on mechanisms of disgust that evolved to keep us away from sources of physical contamination (Lee & Schwarz, 2011; see also Chapter 11, this volume).

Applying these insights to the legal domain, Bilz (2012, Study 3) found that law students who did rather than did not have to use "dirty evidence" in a mock trial were more likely to choose a bottle of hand sanitizer over a pen as a free gift. Going beyond the effect of disgust on preference and choice, Zhong and Liljenquist (2006, Study 4) further demonstrated that using a cleaning product can reduce feelings of guilt and the need to make amends.

After recalling a moral transgression, 74% of their participants volunteered time to help another researcher, yet simply cleaning their hands with an antiseptic wipe reduced volunteerism to a mere 41%.

Whereas these studies illustrate that immoral acts are experienced as "dirty" and elicit a desire to cleanse, other studies show that cleanliness can facilitate adherence to moral standards. For example, Liljenquist, Zhong, and Galinsky (2010) hypothesized that clean scents might promote adherence to moral codes such as reciprocity and charity in the context of economic decisions. Each participant played a one-shot trust game (modeled after Berg et al., 1995) with a (bogus) partner in a room that either was or was not sprayed with citrus-scented Windex. The participant was told that she was randomly assigned to be the receiver and that her partner (the sender) had decided to send her the full amount of $4, now tripled to $12. As it turns out, participants in the clean-scented room returned more money to the partner, exhibiting greater reciprocity (Study 1). Participants in the clean-scented room were also more likely to volunteer for and donate money to a nonprofit organization, acting more charitably (Study 2).

Walking in the Light

Zhong, Bohns, and Gino (2010, Study 2) explored the metaphoric association between having a dark view and making a morally questionable decision. Under the disguise of a product test, participants received either a pair of sunglasses or clear glasses to test-wear while completing a supposedly unrelated task—namely, a one-shot dictator game (modeled after Kahneman, Knetsch, & Thaler, 1986). In the dictator game, participants were given $6 to freely allocate between themselves and the recipient and were told that they could keep any money they did not offer to the recipient for themselves. All interactions were computer-mediated and, unbeknownst to the participants, the experimenter played the recipient. As predicted, participants wearing sunglasses rather than clear glasses offered less money, and their offers fell below the point of fair division ($3). Thus, the subjective experience of darkness, induced by wearing sunglasses, created an illusory sense of anonymity (Study 3) and set the stage for shady economic decisions.

Other Metaphors

The examples so far reveal how incidental bodily experiences can affect judgment and decision making in line with widely shared metaphors about sociality and morality. Of course, metaphors are not limited to these domains of human experience. The next few examples, on what feels important and how people exert control over their lives, illustrate how wide-ranging metaphoric effects can be.

Heavy and Important

When describing a decision process, we may note that some considerations carry more weight than others, reflecting a metaphoric association between physical weight and conceptual importance or impact. A number of studies highlight the power of this metaphor by showing that things seem more important, and exert more influence, the heavier they weigh in our hands (Jostmann, Lakens, & Schubert, 2009; Schneider, Rutjens, Jostmann, & Lakens, 2011; Zhang & Li, 2012). For example, Ackerman et al. (2010, Study 2) asked participants by how much the government should increase or decrease funding for various social issues. When the questionnaire was presented on a heavy clipboard, participants chose to allocate more money than when it was presented on a light clipboard. However, this effect was limited to issues that participants were likely to know about (e.g., air pollution) and not found for less familiar issues (e.g., regulation of the frequency bands for radio broadcast). This boundary condition seems surprising because one might expect incidental cues to exert more influence the less other information people have about the issue; if this were true, decisions about unfamiliar (rather than familiar) issues should have been more affected by incidental cues.

Subsequent research by Chandler, Reinhard, and Schwarz (2012) shed light on the underlying reason by revealing a possible process. In three studies, they observed that a book was evaluated as more important and influential when its heft was increased by a concealed weight. However, this metaphoric effect of weight was observed only for participants who knew something about the book, either because they had read it (Studies 1 and 2) or because they could peruse a short synopsis (Study 3). Apparently, the metaphorically relevant weight cue provided an initial hypothesis ("this seems important"), which participants subsequently tested against other information. Only when they could muster supporting evidence did they endorse the book's importance. Hence, factual knowledge does not necessarily protect us against the effect of incidental cues; it may increase our susceptibility. From this perspective, in Ackerman et al.'s (2010) study, the clipboard's weight may have increased fund allocation when participants could muster some supporting information but not otherwise, giving an advantage to issues they knew something about. An important future direction is to test whether this logic applies to other metaphoric effects. For example, would fishy smells (Lee & Schwarz, 2012a) be more likely to undermine trust and cooperation when decision makers can recruit some information about their partner or the situation to support their suspicion? Would physical warmth (Williams & Bargh, 2008) only render another person socially warmer when the perceiver can find some information that is compatible with this first impression?

Firming Willpower (Self-Control)

To many people, decisions about what kinds and amounts of food to consume pose an everyday self-control challenge: gustatory pleasure at the table and weight gain on the scale, or bland food now and better health later? Forgoing the immediate pleasure for the long-term health goal often requires firming one's willpower.

Hung and Labroo (2011) tested whether, why, when, and for whom the bodily experience of firming muscles has the metaphoric benefit of firming willpower and promoting healthier food choices. In a lab study (Study 3), participants first completed a sentence-unscrambling task that either did or did not prime health goals. Then they were given a nasty, sour-tasting health tonic to test-drink and were asked to report their online thoughts between sips. Meanwhile, under the pretense of motor skills assessment, they had to maintain a given posture that required either lifting the heels off the floor by contracting the calf muscles or simply keeping the feet on the ground. As expected, firming one's muscles increased tonic consumption (by a surprising 67%) relative to not firming one's muscles, and this effect was partially mediated by more willpower-related thoughts. These effects were observable only if health goals had been primed, suggesting that firm muscles facilitate self-control in goal pursuit and exert no influence in the absence of a relevant goal.

Moving to a field setting (Study 4), Hung and Labroo (2011) also found that simply holding a pen between stretched fingers (rather than holding it loosely between index and middle fingers) increased the purchase of healthy food and drinks at a snack bar. This effect was observable only for participants with chronic health goals but not for participants with chronic indulgence goals, again indicating that firmed muscles facilitate the pursuit of active goals. In a final lab study (Study 5), participants who contracted their biceps showed more disapproval of a scenario character's unhealthy food choice (chocolate cake) and were more likely to make a healthy food choice for themselves, picking an apple rather than chocolate to consume. These effects on vicarious and own food choices were observable only if muscle-firming occurred during a self-control scenario related to food choice, not if muscle firming occurred during a previous self-control scenario unrelated to food choice (the scenario was about resisting boredom). This set of studies shows that as long as health goals are temporarily or chronically accessible, firming muscles while making food choices can firm willpower and promote healthy eating.

Washing Away Past Good or Bad Luck and Other Residue (Illusory Control)

Good or bad luck is the target of many superstitious behaviors (Vyse, 1997). People believe that luck can "rub off" when they touch lucky individuals or objects (Radford & Radford, 1949). Athletes and gamblers on a winning streak keep wearing their "lucky" shirts and socks but prefer changing their clothes when they are on a losing streak (Bleak & Frederick, 1998; Gmelch, 1974). Such superstitions suggest that people think about luck as a contagious substance (Rozin & Nemeroff, 1990) that can be transferred through physical contact and removed through physical cleansing.

To test this possibility, Xu, Schwarz, and Zwick (2012, Study 1) had participants recall either a lucky or unlucky financial decision and asked them to describe what happened and how they felt. Next, participants were handed an antiseptic wipe as part of an allegedly unrelated product evaluation task. Depending on condition, they either examined it only or tested it by wiping their hands before providing a product evaluation. Finally, participants assumed the role of a CEO as part of a third task and decided between a high-risk and a no-risk business option. As expected, those who had initially been assigned to recall a lucky financial decision took more risk in the business context than those who had to recall an unlucky financial decision. However, this effect was observed only for participants who merely examined the antiseptic wipe; the effect was fully eliminated for participants who actually used the wipe. Apparently, wiping hands removed the residues of previous luck, making the previously lucky participants more cautious and the previously unlucky ones more adventurous.

The same effect was observed when participants gambled with their own money (Xu et al., 2012, Study 2). Specifically, participants initially gambled for several rounds before they were asked to participate in a product test involving an organic soap. Some participants merely examined the soap before evaluating it; others tested it by washing their hands. Subsequently, participants played a final round of the gamble during which they could bet as much as they wanted. As expected, those who had been on a winning streak in the first few rounds of gambling bet the most in the final round, whereas those who had been on a losing streak bet the least. Participants who had experienced some wins and some losses fell in between these extremes, although their losses loomed larger than their gains (consistent with prospect theory; Kahneman & Tversky, 1979). More important, this influence of previous good or bad luck was observed only among participants who merely examined the soap but was eliminated among those who washed their hands (see Figure 5.1). In both studies, physical cleansing metaphorically removed the residues of one's previous good or bad luck and its impact on subsequent risk-taking behavior.

Taking this reasoning to the domain of academic performance, Kaspar (2012) found that participants who washed their hands after failing a test became more optimistic about their future performance on a related task. Unfortunately, this optimism undermined their motivation to exert effort

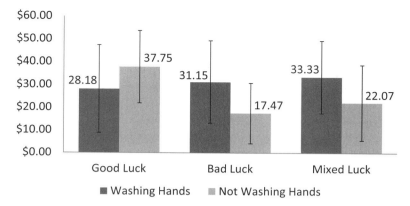

Figure 5.1. Amount of bet as a function of previous luck and hand washing. Error bars represent standard errors. From "Washing Away Your (Good or Bad) Luck: Physical Cleansing Affects Risk-Taking Behavior," by A. J. Xu, R. Zwick, and N. Schwarz, 2012, *Journal of Experimental Psychology: General, 141*, pp. 26–30, Study 2. Copyright 2012 by the American Psychological Association.

and thus impaired their subsequent actual performance—wiping off a bad past is not always a good thing.

In combination, these studies highlight that physical cleansing can remove more than one's sins. It can remove many other residues of the past, from good or bad luck to doubts and bad feelings, metaphorically wiping the slate clean (Lee & Schwarz, 2011). We return to this issue in the next section. Moreover, the psychological impact of physical cleansing is not limited to things that people want to wash away. When given a choice, people want to remove the residues of negative experiences and avoid removing the residues of positive ones (Lee & Schwarz, 2010a), but once they do cleanse, it also removes residues they would rather keep, including the glow of good luck (Xu et al., 2012) and positive life events (Lee, Schwarz, & Shaw, 2011).

EMBODIED METAPHORS AFFECT DECISION PROCESSES

The metaphoric effects reviewed so far can be conceptualized by assuming that incidental bodily experiences activate metaphorically associated thoughts, goals, and feelings, which enter the mental construal of the situation at hand, from the nature of one's choice alternatives and the trustworthiness of one's interaction partner to the assessment of one's mental resources and concerns about one's luck. To date, research has mostly focused on establishing the existence of such metaphoric effects and has paid limited attention to the underlying processes (Meier, Schnall, Schwarz, & Bargh, 2012). The available evidence is even more limited for another category of metaphoric effects: Incidental bodily experiences may trigger metaphorically associated procedures that influence how people go about making a decision. Next, we review the preliminary evidence for this type of effect.

Washing Away Postdecisional Dissonance

As noted earlier, physical cleansing has powerful and surprising metaphoric effects, allowing people to wash away their sins (Zhong & Liljenquist, 2006) and remove other residues of past experience such as good or bad luck (Xu et al., 2012) and failure on a test (Kaspar, 2012). Indeed, metaphoric expressions about cleansing are not limited to issues of moral purity. If songs and sayings are any guide to lay thinking, phrases such as wiping the slate clean and "wash away my trouble, wash away my pain" (in the song "Shambala") suggest that the psychological effects of physical cleansing may not be limited to the domain of moral purity. Instead, physical cleansing may wipe the slate clean in a more general sense, allowing people to metaphorically remove residues of past experience (Lee & Schwarz, 2011).

If so, decision makers may be able to remove concerns about their previous choices with the help of a little soap. As seen in numerous cognitive dissonance studies (Festinger, 1957; for recent developments, see Cooper, 2007), the choices we make can profoundly affect later judgment and behavior. To test whether dissonance effects can be eliminated through physical cleansing, we (Lee & Schwarz, 2010b, Study 1) asked participants to rank 10 CDs in order of preference. Next, they were offered a free choice between two CDs that they had ranked as similarly and moderately attractive. Immediately after choosing which of the two CDs they wanted to take home, participant were asked to help with an unrelated product test; depending on condition, they evaluated a bottle of hand soap by merely examining or actually using it. Finally, participants provided another ranking of the 10 CDs based on their current feelings.

In this free-choice paradigm (Brehm, 1956), people tend to justify their choice by changing their perception of the choice alternatives: After having made a choice, they perceive the chosen alternative as more attractive than they did before and the rejected alternative as less attractive than they did before. This increases the perceived difference between the alternatives, putting any doubt about one's choice to rest. As expected, this classic postdecisional dissonance effect replicated when participants merely examined the soap without washing their hands, but it was eliminated when participants did wash their hands (see Figure 5.2). Apparently, they had washed away their postdecisional dissonance and had no further need to justify their choice. In a conceptual replication (Study 2), participants who merely examined an antiseptic wipe after choosing between two fruit jams expected their

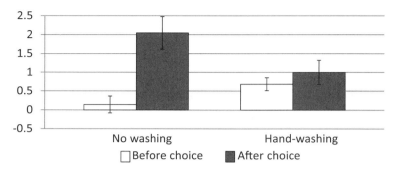

Difference between choice alternatives

Figure 5.2. Postdecisional dissonance after hand washing or no hand washing. Higher values indicate higher preferences for the chosen alternative. Error bars represent standard errors. From "Washing Away Postdecisional Dissonance," by S. W. S. Lee and N. Schwarz, 2010, *Science, 328*, p. 709. Copyright 2010 S. W. S. Lee and N. Schwarz. Reprinted with permission from the authors.

chosen jam to taste better than the rejected one; actually using the wipe again eliminated this dissonance effect.

De Los Reyes, Aldao, Kundey, Lee, and Molina (2012) replicated the clean slate effect on postdecisional dissonance, using confidence in the quality of chosen and rejected pens as dependent measures. They also explored individual differences and found that wiping hands eliminated postdecisional dissonance only for participants who scored low on a composite measure of intolerance of uncertainty, rumination, and generalized anxiety, but not for participants who scored high on this measure. They noted that such individual differences in clean slate effects might hold promise for identifying impulsive decision makers and for differential diagnosis. We see a broader need for research on personal and situational variables such as rational versus experiential thinking (Epstein, Pacini, Denes-Raj, & Heier, 1996) and abstract versus concrete construal (Trope & Liberman, 2010) that may facilitate or impair people's ability to distance themselves from past decisions with the aid of physical cleansing. Identifying these variables may illuminate some of the potential complexity of metaphoric effects and the underlying mental processes.

Attaining Balance Through Compromise Choice

Another classic phenomenon in the decision-making literature is compromise choice (e.g., Simonson, 1989). In a simple choice set involving three options that vary on two attributes, such as price and quality, the choice share of the compromise option (medium price and medium quality) should increase when people find both attributes important. Attributes are ideas, and ideas are metaphorically referred to as objects that one can give, take, or hold (e.g., let me give you a better idea, don't steal my idea, I can't quite grasp it, catch this; Lakoff & Johnson, 1980). Objects have weight, and weight is used metaphorically to conceptualize importance (e.g., that's a heavy topic, his opinion carries weight). Therefore, giving weight to an idea renders it important—not just as a metaphoric statement but also with behavioral consequences, as reviewed earlier. If giving weight to one idea renders it important, giving weight to two ideas should render both important. Accordingly, a bodily state that involves holding two ideas in hand and giving weight to both may have such a procedural effect as assigning similar weights to two attributes, thereby increasing compromise choice.

What might this bodily state look like? The balancing gesture is a prime candidate. It has two aspects: (a) With the palms facing up, objects or ideas can sit on the hands; (b) with the two hands moving alternately up and down, the two objects or ideas are given similar weights ("on the one hand, this attribute matters; on the other hand, that attribute matters too"). This analysis also suggests that deviations from either aspect would rob the gesture of its balancing meaning. If the palms are facing down, objects or ideas cannot sit on the hands. If the two hands are stationary, the two objects or ideas are not given similar weights. Does the balancing gesture really encourage compromise choice? If so, does either deviation eliminate its effect?

To answer these questions, we (Lee & Schwarz, 2012b, Study 3) conducted a study allegedly about multitasking in which participants were asked to maintain a specific gesture for 20 seconds while reading two sets of product descriptions (adapted from Drolet, Luce, & Simonson, 2009). Depending on condition, the experimenter demonstrated one of three gestures: (a) moving both hands alternately up and down with palms facing up or (b) facing down, or (c) holding both hands palms up and stationary. The first product set included three barbeque grills: one large size/heavy weight, one small size/light weight, and one medium size/medium weight (compromise option). The second set included three stereo speakers: one high power/high price, one low power/low price, and one medium power/medium price (compromise option). Right after the "multitasking" phase, participants marked which grill and speaker they would like to buy. As expected, participants who moved their hands palms up made more compromise choices than those who moved their hands palms down or those who held their hands palms up and stationary, with no significant difference between the last two groups. Other studies using the same manipulations also found that the balancing gesture resulted in more balanced time allocations to work and leisure activities (Study 2) and heightened the perceived importance of having "balance in life" (Study 1).

In summary, a gesture that metaphorically weighs what is on one hand against what is on the other hand can increase compromise choice and balanced time budgeting, probably due to the activation of a balancing procedure. Both of the metaphoric bases of this gesture, palms up and hands moving, are necessary for the metaphoric effect to occur.

IMPLICATIONS AND FUTURE DIRECTIONS

Just a few years ago, it would have been absurd to predict that smelling something fishy could reduce monetary investment in trust-based exchanges, that sitting in a hard chair could lead one to hold a harder line in negotiations, or that firming one's muscles could firm one's willpower in making healthier food choices. However, the past few years have seen a rapidly growing list of such metaphoric effects, cutting across economic, consumer, and social domains of judgment and decision making. These effects are often counterintuitive and surprising, ensuring considerable attention. They are also theoretically significant by shedding new light on the embodied and situated nature of human cognition and by adding to the multitude of ways in which human decision making deviates from normative models of rational choice.

Having established that incidental bodily experiences can reliably affect judgment and decision making in ways that are consistent with their metaphoric meanings, it is time to go beyond mere demonstration and begin unpacking the processes. In doing so, we will most likely learn that multiple processes contribute to the growing list of bodily influences; below are four examples.

- *Issue 1: Direct, nonmetaphoric effects.* Incidental bodily experiences can directly serve as information that people use like any other experiential information (Schwarz, 2012). Familiar examples are the informative functions of physiologic arousal (Zillman, 1978), head movement (Wells & Petty, 1980), and proprioceptive feedback from facial expressions (Strack, Martin, & Stepper, 1988). These effects require no metaphoric meanings. They occur presumably because in daily life nodding tends to correlate with agreement and smiling with amusement, so over time the sensorimotor experiences pick up the ability to produce the same effects in their own right.
- *Issue 2: Metaphoric effects on mental construal of the decision situation.* Incidental bodily experiences can activate metaphorically associated thoughts, goals, and feelings to affect how people construe the situation at hand. Most of the findings we reviewed can be conceptualized as reflecting differences in the mental construal of various aspects of the decision situation, such as

the task's nature, the choice alternatives, one's resources, and the likely behavior of one's partner. This conceptualization integrates metaphors research with traditional themes of social cognition such as knowledge and goal activation (e.g., Förster & Liberman, 2007; Higgins, 1996) and mental correction (Bless & Schwarz, 2010; Wilson & Brekke, 1994). Much can be learned from exploring the links between metaphor effects and robust phenomena of social cognition research. For example, basic principles of knowledge activation and use (Higgins, 1996) predict that metaphoric effects are mediated by the accessibility of metaphoric knowledge and moderated by its applicability to the target; both predictions receive empirical support (Lee & Schwarz, 2012a). Furthermore, metaphoric cues seem to affect judgment only if one can recruit some pertinent knowledge about the target (Chandler et al., 2012), again consistent with familiar phenomena of confirmatory hypothesis testing.

A theoretical cross-fertilization with social cognition theorizing does not diminish the novelty and significance of metaphorical effects. To illustrate, consider that actual cleansing (Zhong & Liljenquist, 2006) or visualizing oneself as cleansed (Zhong, Strejcek, & Sivanathan, 2011) has been shown to attenuate one's guilt and make one feel morally pure and righteous, whereas simply being primed with purity concepts without cleansing does not produce the same effects (Lee & Schwarz, 2011). Apparently, for some metaphoric effects, merely making the concepts accessible may be insufficient; the action requirements need to be fulfilled. In fact, merely making the concepts accessible may even backfire because thinking about purity without a chance to cleanse may increase one's sense of impurity, a possibility that awaits testing. Contrast this with the fishy findings (Lee & Schwarz, 2012a) in which the presence of fishy smells is sufficient to produce metaphoric effects on social suspicion, much as the accessibility of trait concepts is sufficient to affect the encoding of person descriptions (e.g., Higgins, Rholes, & Jones, 1976; Srull & Wyer, 1979). The critical factor to explore may be what sensation or motor action is implied by the metaphor of interest. To be clean, one typically needs to cleanse. To smell something fishy, one simply needs to smell. An exploration of such bodily nuances may advance our understanding of metaphoric effects as well as knowledge accessibility.

■ *Issue 3. Metaphoric effects on mental procedures in the decisional process.* Incidental bodily experiences may activate metaphorically associated mental procedures that initiate, terminate, or change the decision process itself. For example, physical cleansing allows people to metaphorically wipe the slate clean and frees them from residual concerns about their recent decisions, thereby eliminating postdecisional dissonance (Lee & Schwarz, 2010b). Moving one's hands up and down with palms facing up elicits more "balanced" judgments and decisions, presumably by assigning more equal weights to the two attributes in the decision task (Lee & Schwarz, 2012b). To date, experimental support for this type of effects is limited, but we find it promising. It allows researchers to leverage numerous well-understood paradigms in behavioral decision making to explore the potentially broad impact of embodied metaphors.

- *Issue 4: Metaphoric effects without awareness.* We expect that both the direct and metaphoric effects of incidental bodily experiences will be eliminated when people become aware of their incidental nature, consistent with feelings-as-information theory (Schwarz, 2012) and models of mental correction (Strack & Hannover, 1996; Wilson & Brekke,1994). Just as awareness undermines the influence of moods (e.g., Schwarz & Clore, 1983), arousal (e.g., Schwarz, Servay, & Kumpf, 1985), metacognitive experience (e.g., Schwarz et al., 1991), and semantic primes (e.g., Strack, Schwarz, Bless, Kübler, & Wänke, 1993), awareness that a weight has been inserted in a book eliminates its metaphoric effect on judgments of the book's importance (Reinhard, Chandler, & Schwarz, 2012). This suggests that bodily experiences are most influential when they are subtle and escape direct attention, paralleling the influence of other experiential information.

In some decision situations, the processes just described may be pitted against each other. For example, would physical cleansing eliminate postdecisional dissonance in a choice between guilty pleasure and virtuous restraint? If cleansing simply wipes the slate clean (Issue 3), it should matter little what the content is and postdecisional dissonance should be eliminated. However, if cleansing activates moral meanings (Issue 2), it should affect how moral one feels about the choice alternatives or oneself, and the downstream consequences may be more complicated. Which of these processes occur may depend on whether people are aware or not (Issue 4) of the metaphoric effects of physical cleansing on thoughts, feelings, goals, and procedures. Divergent outcomes of these processes are promising avenues for future research.

Finally, we emphasize that this chapter's focus on incidental bodily experiences with metaphoric meanings does not imply that metaphors require bodily experience in situ to exert an influence. As numerous studies illustrate, linguistic or graphical priming of different metaphoric frames can affect people's thinking and inferences (e.g., Boroditsky, 2000; Morris, Sheldon, Ames, & Young, 2007) without requiring a concurrent bodily input. Hence, simply presenting tasks in different metaphoric frames can have powerful effects on judgments and choices, and such framing effects may themselves interact with whatever bodily experience the decision maker has at the time. The exploration of such possibilities promises to extend the long list of insights provided by recent work on the role of embodied metaphors in judgment and decision making.

REFERENCES

Ackerman, J. M., Nocera, C. C., & Bargh, J. A. (2010). Incidental haptic sensations influence social judgments and decisions. *Science, 328,* 1712–1715. doi:10.1126/science.1189993

Anderson, M. L. (2008). On the grounds of x-grounded cognition. In P. Calvo & T. Gomila (Eds.), *The Elsevier handbook of cognitive science: An embodied approach* (pp. 423–435). Amsterdam, The Netherlands: Elsevier. doi:10.1016/B978-0-08-046616-3.00021-9

Barsalou, L. W. (1999). Perceptual symbol systems. *Behavioral and Brain Sciences, 22,* 577–660.

Barsalou, L. W. (2008). Grounded cognition. *Annual Review of Psychology, 59,* 617–645. doi:10.1146/annurev.psych.59.103006.093639

Becker, G. (1976). *The economic approach to human behavior.* Chicago, IL: The University of Chicago Press.

Berg, J., Dickhaut, J., & McCabe, K. (1995). Trust, reciprocity, and social history. *Games and Economic Behavior, 10,* 122–142. doi:10.1006/game.1995.1027

Bilz, K. (2012). Dirty hands or deterrence? An experimental examination of the exclusionary rule. *Journal of Empirical Legal Studies, 9,* 149–171. doi:10.1111/j.1740-1461.2011.01250.x

Bleak, J. L., & Frederick, C. M. (1998). Superstitious behavior in sport: Levels of effectiveness and determinants of use in three collegiate sports. *Journal of Sport Behavior, 21,* 1–15.

Bless, H., & Schwarz, N. (2010). Mental construal and the emergence of assimilation and contrast effects: The inclusion/exclusion model. *Advances in Experimental Social Psychology, 42,* 319–373.

Boroditsky, L. (2000). Metaphoric structuring: Understanding time through spatial metaphors. *Cognition, 75,* 1–28. doi:10.1016/S0010-0277(99)00073-6

Brehm, J. W. (1956). Postdecision changes in the desirability of alternatives. *The Journal of Abnormal and Social Psychology, 52,* 384–389.

Chandler, J., Reinhard, D., & Schwarz, N. (2012). To judge a book by its weight you need to know its content: Knowledge moderates the use of embodied cues. *Journal of Experimental Social Psychology, 48,* 948–952. doi:10.1016/j.jesp.2012.03.003

Cherkasskiy, L., Song, H., Malahy, S., & Bargh, J. A. (2012, January). *Soft on crime: Sitting in soft versus hard chairs produces more lenient recommended sentences.* Hot topic talk at the embodiment preconference of the Society for Personality and Social Psychology, San Diego, CA.

Cooper, J. (2007). *Cognitive dissonance: 50 years of a classic theory.* London, England: Sage.

Curtis, V., Aunger, R., & Rabie, T. (2004). Evidence that disgust evolved to protect from risk of disease. *Proceedings of the Royal Society B: Biological Sciences, 271*(Suppl. 4), S131–S133. doi:10.1098/rsbl.2003.0144

De Los Reyes, A., Aldao, A., Kundey, S. M. A., Lee, B. G., & Molina, S. (2012). Compromised decision making and the effects of manipulating physical states on human judgments. *Journal of Clinical Psychology, 68,* 1–7. doi:10.1002/jclp.20851

Drolet, A., Luce, M. F., & Simonson, I. (2009). When does choice reveal preference? Moderators of heuristic versus goal-based choice. *Journal of Consumer Research, 36,* 137–147. doi:10.1086/596305

Elster, J. (2006). *Explaining social behavior: More nuts and bolts for the social sciences.* New York, NY: Cambridge University Press.

Epstein, S., Pacini, R., Denes-Raj, V., & Heier, H. (1996). Individual differences in intuitive–experiential and analytical–rational thinking styles. *Journal of Personality and Social Psychology, 71,* 390–405. doi:10.1037/0022-3514.71.2.390

Fehr, E., & Gächter, S. (2005). Human behaviour: Egalitarian motive and altruistic punishment (reply). *Nature, 433,* E1–E2.

Fehr, E., & Schmidt, K. M. (1999). A theory of fairness, competition, and cooperation. *The Quarterly Journal of Economics, 114,* 817–868. doi:10.1162/003355399556151

Festinger, L. (1957). *A theory of cognitive dissonance.* Stanford, CA: Stanford University Press.

Fishbein, M., & Ajzen, I. (1975). *Belief, attitude, intention, and behavior: An introduction to theory and research.* Reading, MA: Addison-Wesley.

Fiske, S. T. (2004). *Social beings: Core motives in social psychology.* New York, NY: Wiley.

Förster, J., & Liberman, N. (2007). Knowledge activation. In A. W. Kruglanski & E. T. Higgins (Eds.), *Social psychology: Handbook of basic principles* (2nd ed., pp. 201–231). New York, NY: Guilford Press.

Gmelch, G. (1974). Baseball magic. In J. Spradley & D. McCurdy (Eds.), *Conformity and conflict* (pp. 346–352). Boston, MA: Little, Brown.

Güth, W., Schmittberger, R., & Schwarze, B. (1982). An experimental analysis of ultimatum bargaining. *Journal of Economic Behavior & Organization, 3,* 367–388. doi:10.1016/0167-2681(82)90011-7

Haidt, J., & Kesebir, S. (2010). Morality. In S. T. Fiske, D. T. Gilbert, & G. Lindezey (Eds.), *Handbook of social psychology* (5th ed., Vol. 2, pp. 797–832). Hoboken, NJ: Wiley.

Higgins, E. T. (1996). Knowledge activation: Accessibility, applicability, and salience. In E. T. Higgins & A. W. Kruglanski (Eds.), *Social psychology: Handbook of basic principles* (pp. 133–168). New York, NY: Guilford Press.

Higgins, E. T. (2012). *Beyond pleasure and pain: How motivation works*. New York, NY: Oxford University Press.

Higgins, E. T., Rholes, W. S., & Jones, C. R. (1977). Category accessibility and impression formation. *Journal of Experimental Social Psychology, 13*, 141–154. doi:10.1016/S0022-1031(77)80007-3

Hung, I. W., & Labroo, A. A. (2011). From firm muscles to firm willpower: Understanding the role of embodied cognition in self-regulation. *Journal of Consumer Research, 37*, 1046–1064. doi:10.1086/657240

Jostmann, N. B., Lakens, D., & Schubert, T. W. (2009). Weight as an embodiment of importance. *Psychological Science, 20*, 1169–1174. doi:10.1111/j.1467-9280.2009.02426.x

Kahneman, D., Knetsch, J. L., & Thaler, R. (1986). Fairness as a constraint on profit seeking: Entitlements in the market. *The American Economic Review, 76*, 728–741.

Kahneman, D., & Tversky, A. (1979). Prospect theory: An analysis of decision under risk. *Econometrica, 47*, 263–291. doi:10.2307/1914185

Kang, Y., Williams, L. E., Clark, M. S., Gray, J. R., & Bargh, J. A. (2011). Physical temperature effects on trust behavior: The role of insula. *Social Cognitive and Affective Neuroscience, 6*, 507–515. doi:10.1093/scan/nsq077

Kaspar, K. (2013). Washing one's hands after failure enhances optimism but hampers future performance. *Social Psychological and Personality Science, 4*, 69–73.

Krugman, P. (2010, December 13). Block those metaphors. *The New York Times*, A25.

Lakoff, G., & Johnson, M. (1980). *Metaphors we live by*. Chicago, IL: The University of Chicago Press.

Lakoff, G., & Johnson, M. (1999). *Philosophy in the flesh: The embodied mind and its challenge to Western thought*. New York, NY: Basic Books.

Landau, M. J., Meier, B. P., & Keefer, L. A. (2010). A metaphor-enriched social cognition. *Psychological Bulletin, 136*, 1045–1067. doi:10.1037/a0020970

Ledyard, J. O. (1995). Public goods: A survey of experimental research. In J. H. Kagel & A. E. Roth (Eds.), *The handbook of experimental economics* (pp. 111–194). Princeton, NJ: Princeton University Press.

Lee, S. W. S., & Ellsworth, P. C. (in press). Maggots and morals: Physical disgust is to fear as moral disgust is to anger. In J. R. J. Fontaine, K. R. Scherer, & C. Soriano (Eds.), *Components of emotional meaning: A sourcebook*. Oxford, England: Oxford University Press.

Lee, S. W. S., & Schwarz, N. (2010a). Dirty hands and dirty mouths: Embodiment of the moral-purity metaphor is specific to the motor modality involved in moral transgression. *Psychological Science, 21,* 1423–1425. doi:10.1177/0956797 610382788

Lee, S. W. S., & Schwarz, N. (2010b). Washing away postdecisional dissonance. *Science, 328,* 709. doi:10.1126/science.1186799

Lee, S. W. S., & Schwarz, N. (2011). Wiping the slate clean: Psychological consequences of physical cleansing. *Current Directions in Psychological Science, 20,* 307–311. doi:10.1177/0963721411422694

Lee, S. W. S., & Schwarz, N. (2012a). Bidirectionality, mediation, and moderation of metaphorical effects: The embodiment of social suspicion and fishy smells. *Journal of Personality and Social Psychology, 103,* 737–749.

Lee, S. W. S., & Schwarz, N. (2012b). *On the one hand, on the other hand: How a gesture of balance influences judgment and choice.* Unpublished manuscript.

Lee, S. W. S., Schwarz, N., & Shaw, E. (2011, January). *Wipe away your past: Clean slate effects.* Hot topic talk at the embodiment preconference of the Society for Personality and Social Psychology, San Antonio, TX.

Lichtenstein, S., & Slovic, P. (Eds.). (2006). *The construction of preference.* New York, NY: Cambridge University Press. doi:10.1017/CBO9780511618031

Liljenquist, K., Zhong, C.-B., & Galinsky, A. D. (2010). The smell of virtue: Clean scents promote reciprocity and charity. *Psychological Science, 21,* 381–383. doi:10.1177/0956797610361426

Meier, B. P., Schnall, S., Schwarz, N., & Bargh, J. A. (2012). Embodiment in social psychology. *Topics in Cognitive Science, 4,* 705–716.

Morris, M. W., Sheldon, O. J., Ames, D. R., & Young, M. J. (2007). Metaphors and the market: Consequences and preconditions of agent and object metaphors in stock market commentary. *Organizational Behavior and Human Decision Processes, 102,* 174–192. doi:10.1016/j.obhdp.2006.03.001

Murphy, G. L. (1996). On metaphoric representation. *Cognition, 60,* 173–204. doi:10.1016/0010-0277(96)00711-1

Murphy, G. L. (1997). Reasons to doubt the present evidence for metaphoric representation. *Cognition, 62,* 99–108. doi:10.1016/S0010-0277(96)00725-1

Rabin, M. (1993). Incorporating fairness into game theory and economics. *The American Economic Review, 83,* 1281–1302.

Radford, E., & Radford, M. A. (1949). *Encyclopedia of superstitions.* New York, NY: Philosophical Library.

Reinhard, D., Chandler, J., & Schwarz, N. (2012, January). *Knowing what's inside counts: Prime awareness diminishes effects of embodied metaphors.* Hot topic talk at the embodiment preconference of the Society for Personality and Social Psychology, San Diego, CA.

Rozin, P., & Nemeroff, C. (1990). The laws of sympathetic magic: A psychological analysis of similarity and contagion. In J. W. Sitgler, R. A. Shweder, & G. Herdt (Eds.), *Cultural psychology: Essays on comparative human judgment* (pp. 205–232). Cambridge, England: Cambridge University Press. doi:10.1017/CBO9781139173728.006

Schneider, I. K., Rutjens, B. T., Jostmann, N. B., & Lakens, D. (2011). Weighty matters: Importance literally feels heavy. *Social Psychological and Personality Science, 2,* 474–478. doi:10.1177/1948550610397895

Schwarz, N. (2007). Attitude construction: Evaluation in context. *Social Cognition, 25,* 638–656. doi:10.1521/soco.2007.25.5.638

Schwarz, N. (2009). Mental construal in social judgment. In F. Strack & J. Förster (Eds.), *Social cognition: The basis of human interaction* (pp. 121–137). Philadelphia, PA: Psychology.

Schwarz, N. (2012). Feelings-as-information theory. In P. A. M. Van Lange, A. W. Kruglanski, & E. T. Higgins (Eds.), *Handbook of theories of social psychology* (pp. 289–308). Thousand Oaks, CA: Sage.

Schwarz, N., Bless, H., Strack, F., Klumpp, G., Rittenauer-Schatka, H., & Simons, A. (1991). Ease of retrieval as information: Another look at the availability heuristic. *Journal of Personality and Social Psychology, 61,* 195–202. doi:10.1037/0022-3514.61.2.195

Schwarz, N., & Clore, G. L. (1983). Mood, misattribution, and judgments of well-being: Informative and directive functions of affective states. *Journal of Personality and Social Psychology, 45,* 513–523. doi:10.1037/0022-3514.45.3.513

Schwarz, N., Servay, W., & Kumpf, M. (1985). Attribution of arousal as a mediator of the effectiveness of fear-arousing communications. *Journal of Applied Social Psychology, 15,* 178–188. doi:10.1111/j.1559-1816.1985.tb02343.x

Simonson, I. (1989). Choice based on reasons: The case of attraction and compromise effects. *Journal of Consumer Research, 16,* 158–174. doi:10.1086/209205

Smith, E. R., & Conrey, F. R. (2007). Mental representations are states not things: Implications for implicit and explicit measurement. In B. Wittenbrink & N. Schwarz (Eds.), *Implicit measures of attitudes: Progress and controversies* (pp. 247–264). New York, NY: Guilford Press.

Smith, E. R., & Semin, G. R. (2004). Socially situated cognition: Cognition in its social context. *Advances in Experimental Social Psychology, 36,* 53–117. doi:10.1016/S0065-2601(04)36002-8

Soriano, C., & Valenzuela, J. (2008, May 31). *Sensorial perception as a source domain: A cross-linguistic study.* Paper presented at the Seventh International Conference on Researching and Applying Metaphor (RaAM 7), Cáceres, Spain.

Srull, T. K., & Wyer, R. S. Jr. (1979). The role of category accessibility in the interpretation of information about persons: Some determinants and implications. *Journal of Personality and Social Psychology, 37,* 1660–1667.

Strack, F., & Hannover, B. (1996). Awareness of the influence as a precondition for implementing correctional goals. In P. M. Gollwitzer & J. A. Bargh (Eds.), *The psychology of action: Linking cognition and motivation to behavior* (pp. 579–596). New York, NY: Guilford Press.

Strack, F., Martin, L. L., & Stepper, S. (1988). Inhibiting and facilitating conditions of the human smile: A non-obtrusive test of the facial feedback hypothesis. *Journal of Personality and Social Psychology, 54*, 768–777. doi:10.1037/0022-3514.54.5.768

Strack, F., Schwarz, N., Bless, H., Kübler, A., & Wänke, M. (1993). Awareness of the influence as a determinant of assimilation versus contrast. *European Journal of Social Psychology, 23*, 53–62. doi:10.1002/ejsp.2420230105

Trope, Y., & Liberman, N. (2010). Construal-level theory of psychological distance. *Psychological Review, 117*, 440–463. doi:10.1037/a0018963

Vyse, S. A. (1997). *Believing in magic: The psychology of superstition*. New York, NY: Oxford University Press.

Wells, G. L., & Petty, R. E. (1980). The effects of overt head movements on persuasion: Compatibility and incompatibility of responses. *Basic and Applied Social Psychology, 1*, 219–230. doi:10.1207/s15324834basp0103_2

Williams, L. E., & Bargh, J. A. (2008). Experiencing physical warmth promotes interpersonal warmth. *Science, 322*, 606–607. doi:10.1126/science.1162548

Williams, L. E., Huang, J. Y., & Bargh, J. A. (2009). The scaffolded mind: Higher mental processes are grounded in early experience of the physical world. *European Journal of Social Psychology, 39*, 1257–1267. doi:10.1002/ejsp.665

Wilson, T. D., & Brekke, N. (1994). Mental contamination and mental correction: Unwanted influences on judgments and evaluations. *Psychological Bulletin, 116*, 117–142. doi:10.1037/0033-2909.116.1.117

Xu, A. J., Zwick, R., & Schwarz, N. (2012). Washing away your (good or bad) luck: Physical cleansing affects risk-taking behavior. *Journal of Experimental Psychology: General, 141*, 26–30. doi:10.1037/a0023997

Zhang, M., & Li, X. (2012). From physical weight to psychological significance: The contribution of semantic activations. *Journal of Consumer Research, 38*, 1063–1075. doi:10.1086/661768

Zhong, C.-B., Bohns, V. K., & Gino, F. (2010). Good lamps are the best police: Darkness increases dishonesty and self-interested behavior. *Psychological Science, 21*, 311–314. doi:10.1177/0956797609360754

Zhong, C.-B., & Liljenquist, K. (2006). Washing away your sins: Threatened morality and physical cleansing. *Science, 313*, 1451–1452. doi:10.1126/science.1130726

Zhong, C.-B., Strejcek, B., & Sivanathan, N. (2010). A clean self can render harsh moral judgment. *Journal of Experimental Social Psychology, 46*, 859–862. doi:10.1016/j.jesp.2010.04.003

Zillman, D. (1978). Attribution and misattribution of excitatory reactions. In J. H. Harvey, W. I. Ickes, & R. F. Kidd (Eds.), *New directions in attribution research* (Vol. 2, pp. 335–368). Hillsdale, NJ: Erlbaum.

6

DIRT, POLLUTION, AND PURITY: A METAPHORIC PERSPECTIVE ON MORALITY

CHEN-BO ZHONG AND JULIAN HOUSE

Where does morality come from? How do people make judgments and decisions that distinguish right from wrong? Such questions have captivated scholarly minds for centuries. Whether it is the Ten Commandments or categorical imperatives, Western philosophical tradition largely sees morality as objective and external to human experience, either as divine codes of conduct or universal principles that can be derived and discovered through an independent process of reason. Drawing from a diverse body of work from linguistics, anthropology, and psychology, however, this chapter attempts to depict a view of morality that is embodied in human experience. Morality evolved out of our struggle and interaction with the mundane material world, and hence it cannot be totally separated from our concrete experiences such as fear of pollution and desire for order. In this sense, morality is not the product of neat, abstract reasoning based on universal principles but springs from our emotional reactions and embodied realities. In this chapter, we explore

http://dx.doi.org/10.1037/14278-006
The Power of Metaphor: Examining Its Influence on Social Life, M. J. Landau, M. D. Robinson, and B. P. Meier (Editors)

how the metaphoric mapping between the concepts of purity and morality may reflect a deeper conceptual overlap in how we conceive of morality in terms of our embodied experiences with cleanliness, dirt, and pollution.

NEAT MORAL REASONING

Is it OK to lie? There are typically two approaches to this question. The first would say that it depends on the consequences of the lie: Lies that harm others are morally reprehensible unless they produce good ends in aggregate. Although such consequentialist reasoning includes many fine-grained distinctions regarding which goods should be maximized and for the benefit of whom, it generally prioritizes the "good" of an action over the "right" of an action. What is morally right is thus defined as that which has the best consequences (Bentham, 1776/1948; Mill, 1861/1957). Alternatively, a deontological approach to ethics, which emphasizes duties and rights, would say that lying is wrong regardless of its consequences because deceiving someone, even for the greater good, treats that person as a means to an end rather than as someone with intrinsic value (Kant, 1785/2002). The "right" precedes the "good"; what is right can be defined completely independent of what is good.

Both approaches use impersonal, universally applicable principles. For example, the same consequentialist principle could be applied to evaluating whether it is OK to kill two species of fish to save 10 other species, or whether to kill two humans to save 10 others, or when the people you contemplate sacrificing and saving are strangers, close friends, or relatives. Similarly, the Kantian perspective might consider lying to conceal a personal misdeed to be as wrong as lying to Nazi officers to save Jews hiding in your attic because "one ought only to act such that the principle of one's act could become a universal law of human action in a world in which one would hope to live" (Donaldson & Werhane, 2002, p. 7). Although these impersonal moral rules can at times counter our moral intuitions and arrive at sharply conflicting ethical judgment of the same action, our ability to reason freely based on universal principles, without being confined by particular context, is often celebrated as the defining characteristic of ethics (see Bloom, 2011).

Kohlberg's (1963) moral development model, for instance, suggests that the inclinations and intuitions we acquire during early childhood, many of which originate from bodily experience and needs, such as the fear of punishment, are immature forms of moral reasoning constrained by the lack of more sophisticated cognitive capabilities. When people grow cognitively mature, they should outgrow this so called preconventional level of moral reasoning and develop conventional level, and eventually postconventional level, abstract moral reasoning based on universal principles such as reciprocity and fairness. Granted that not everyone advances to the postconventional level of reasoning, and that the same individual may switch back and forth between the levels across time and context, the model considers abstract moral reasoning the aspirational high ground. Underlying all theories of "neat" moral reasoning is the assumption that the moral laws that inform ethical behavior can be deduced from a set of basic principles in a quasi-mathematic fashion, such that reason and logic form the basis of moral functioning (Haidt, 2001; Monin, Pizarro, & Beer, 2007).

MESSY MORAL JUDGMENT

Neat moral rules do not always predict people's moral judgment, however, even in the artificially constructed thought experiments that philosophers often use to illustrate their arguments. One intriguing thought experiment involves two structurally equivalent dilemmas in which a runaway trolley is headed toward five track workers and will kill them if nothing is done. In the switch dilemma, the only way to save the five is to flip a switch that will turn the trolley onto an alternate set of tracks, where it will kill one person instead of five; in the footbridge dilemma, the five can only be saved if someone pushes another individual off a footbridge and onto the tracks. This person will die, but his or her body will stop the trolley before it reaches the others. In both cases, people must decide whether it is right to kill one person to save five others. A consequentialist might say that in both cases, people should save the five by sacrificing the one, whereas a deontologist might say that sacrificing the one individual is never morally justifiable because we should not treat others as means to an end. Thus, different moral principles may dictate different actions but should predict consistent actions in both scenarios: The method by which the one individual is to be sacrificed should have no bearing on the decision. Yet most people indicate that they would flip the switch but are reluctant to push a stranger to his or her death.

In a series of influential studies, Greene, Sommerville, Nystrom, Darley, and Cohen (2001) argued that people's inconsistent responses to the trolley dilemmas might be due to the nature of their emotional reactions to these scenarios. In a functional magnetic resonance imaging study, they found that the regions of participants' brains that are associated with emotional functions (e.g., medial frontal gyrus, posterior cingulated gyrus, bilateral angular gyrus) were significantly more active when they were contemplating the footbridge dilemma than when they were contemplating the switch dilemma. The visceral thought of pushing someone to his or her death was more emotionally evocative than the thought of pulling an inanimate switch, even though the actions produced the same consequences, and these emotional reactions correlate with people's choices in the two situations (Greene et al., 2001). Thus, people do not always play the role of a dispassionate judge applying universally applicable principles when making moral judgments. Although we are certainly capable of engaging in cold, impersonal calculations when we can stand at distance flipping a switch, when we have to decide whether to stain our hands with another person's blood, moral reasoning becomes messier. It is possible that morality is more than impersonal calculation of total good or the logical discovery of categorical imperatives and is instead deeply connected to the self and the important relationships and communities that are vital to our development and survival (Bloom, 2011).

This view is best articulated in Jonathan Haidt's social intuitionist model of moral judgment (Haidt, 2001) and moral foundations theory (Haidt & Joseph, 2004). In his early research, Haidt asked people to make moral judgments on a set of intriguing scenarios. One example involved kissing on the mouth between adult siblings and another involved masturbating using the carcass of a chicken before cooking and eating it. People were typically quick to judge that these actions were wrong but were unable to articulate the reasons why they were wrong when pressed (Haidt, Koller, & Dias, 1993). This moral dumbfounding seems to be driven heavily by the emotion of disgust. Not only do disgusting activities feel wrong, but incidentally induced disgust can also sway moral judgment. Wheatley and Haidt (2005), for example, hypnotized participants to experience disgust upon hearing a cue word but to have no memory of this instruction. After coming out of hypnosis, participants read a few scenarios of actions that either did or did not contain the cue word and were asked to judge the extent to which those actions were wrong. They found that participants judged actions to be more morally wrong when the description contained the disgust-inducing cue word than when it did not. Likewise, Schnall, Benton, and Harvey (2008) showed that the presence of a disgusting smell increased the severity of moral judgment and that this effect disappeared among participants who washed their hands before they made their moral judgments. Similar results have been found with gustatory disgust, such that a bad taste in one's mouth can lead to harsher moral judgment (Eskine, Kacinik, & Prinz, 2011). Finally, individuals who are more disgust sensitive—those who are easily disgusted by potential contaminants such as the smell of urine or sharing a cup—tend to pass harsher moral judgment (Jones & Fitness, 2008).

On the basis of these findings, Haidt (2001) suggested that moral judgment is often not a product of deliberative reflection but instead is determined by a quick flux of intuitions about right and wrong that requires little contemplation or reason. These intuitions are innate, evaluative feelings that are evolutionarily selected and shaped by culture, custom, and socialization processes. Haidt (2007) further outlined five domains of vital challenges faced by early humans and their ancestors that might have shaped moral intuitions: harm–care (protecting offspring), fairness–reciprocity (interaction with nonkin), ingroup–loyalty (group cooperation), authority–respect (hierarchy and control), and purity–sanctity (infection avoidance). Violations in these domains induce different emotions (e.g., anger from harm, contempt from disloyalty, and disgust from purity violations; see Rozin, Lowery, Imada, & Haidt, 1999), which translate into flashes of approval and disapproval that influence moral judgments.

Among these domains, purity is perhaps the most intriguing. The other four moral domains each serve important social functions that are of direct evolutionary advantage. For instance, caring for vulnerable offspring and protecting them from harm is essential for the propagation of human genes. Similarly, fostering an internally cohesive group through loyalty and authority, and knowing whether other groups are behaving unfairly, can promote group selection. It is not surprising, then, that our moral intuitions are founded in these domains, and in these cases intuitions and reason do not diverge drastically. Perhaps it is for this reason that some legal scholars suggest that some laws should be founded on emotions such as anger. After all, what provokes anger is injustice and threats against safety and survival. John Stuart Mill went as far as to argue that in this way, all of a society's ideas about law and justice can be seen as built on anger and fear (Nussbaum, 2004).

The same cannot be said about purity and its primary emotion, disgust. In contrast to notions of care, justice, loyalty, and authority, purity is not an inherently social concept. Although all of the other moral domains patently support social order, it is not immediately clear how concerns of contamination serve a social function beyond health and hygiene (Haidt & Joseph, 2007). Instead, scholars have connected purity and the maintenance of moral order by considering purity's symbolic meanings. In her analyses of the emotion disgust, Nussbaum (2004) argued that disgust is different from anger in that it does not reflect real threat or harm but is instead rooted in our existential desire to be separated from our animal nature and to transcend mere flesh and bones. Shweder, Much, Park, and Mahapatra (1997) similarly maintained that practices related to purity and pollution extend beyond mere hygienic needs to serve symbolic, social functions, including the demarcation of cultural boundaries (Soler, 1973/1979) and suppressing the selfishness often associated with humanity's carnal nature (e.g., lust, hunger, material greed) by cultivating a more spiritual mind-set (see also Schnall, 2011). It thus seems that purity, compared with other moral foundations, is the most distant to neat moral reasoning and that its connection to morality is primarily symbolic and metaphoric.

In the following section of this chapter, we argue that the purity foundation of morality constitutes the "messy" and embodied element of moral thinking. The construct of morality evolves out of our continuous interaction with the physical and social world and ultimately reflects our desire to establish order. To do so, people reference and borrow from the tools and mechanisms that they have developed to establish order in the physical world. This results in overlapping conceptual frameworks that we use to deal with and fence off physical (e.g., disease and pollution) and social threats (e.g., betrayal and deception). Thus, we hope to expand on the aforementioned findings that moral judgments are messy and involve older systems (e.g., emotions) by suggesting that moral judgment not only involves an intuitive element but more importantly is intimately connected with and emerges out of our concrete and embodied experiences that deal with purity and pollution. On the basis of the conceptual metaphor theory (CMT) from the linguistic literature (Lakoff & Johnson, 1999), we argue that the concept of morality may be partly built on our conceptual frameworks of dirt and cleanliness and hence have acquired properties of how we think about dirt, pollution, and purity.

METAPHORIC BASIS OF MORALITY

Concrete experiences, such as physical cleanliness, and abstract concepts, such as morality, are typically considered orthogonal to each other. In fact, the separation of bodily experience and psychological constructs is at the core of the idea of mind–body separation that dates back to Plato and Descartes. The cognitive revolution in psychology renewed this ancient idea and started a field of research that modeled human information processing after computer systems (Gigerenzer & Goldstein, 1996). The human mind was seen as the computer operating system that is directly responsible for cognitive activities, whereas the body was the hardware that provides crucial support to, but does not participate directly in, thinking and reasoning.

Purely cognitive models, however, do not seem to fully account for anomalous findings from a growing body of research showing that thinking is not independent of the body. For example, Strack, Martin, and Stepper (1988) had individuals hold a pencil in their mouth using either their lips (smile inhibiting) or teeth (smile facilitating) while reading humorous cartoons. They found that those who held the pencil between their teeth had more intense humor reactions to the cartoons than those held the pencil between their lips. In a recent study, Neal and Chartrand (2011) found that people who had received a cosmetic procedure that reduces muscular feedback from the face (Botox) had more trouble identifying emotional facial expressions compared with those who received a procedure that does not reduce feedback (a dermal filler). Thus, facial muscular feedback seems to play an important role in identifying and labeling emotions both in the self and others. These are just a few examples of a host of research that demonstrates the importance of concrete bodily experience in anchoring perception, attitudes, and behavior (see Varela, Thompson, & Rosch, 1991).

To explain these anomalies, Barsalou (1999) proposed modifications to traditional models of cognition and mental representation and suggested that cognition includes not only abstract and amodal mental representations but also modal perceptual content from various sensors (see also Varela, Thompson, & Rosch, 1991, p. 172). These perceptual inputs are recorded by systems of neurons in sensory-motor regions of the brain that capture information about perceived events in the environment and in the body (Barsalou, 1999). They are then used in perception, categorization, and judgment to construct and run simulations, similar to mental models. In other words, thinking is argued to involve perceptual simulation (Schubert, 2005). As William James (1890/1950) explained, "every representation of a movement awakens in some degree the actual movement" (p. 526). Once enacted, these perceptual symbols can in turn influence thoughts and perceptions. For example, the activation of an elderly stereotype has been shown to automatically induce behavioral changes consistent with the stereotype, leading people to actually walk slower (Bargh, Chen, & Burrows, 1996). Damasio (1994) similarly illustrated this using the scenario of expecting to see an old friend. The mental simulation of meeting an old friend not only includes mental images and representations but is also accompanied by physiological changes such as increased heart rate and blushing. Independent of thoughts and mental images, these physiological changes may inform and reinforce the extent to which we look forward to meeting the friend. Contrary to the computer model, these findings highlight the interdependence of higher level cognitive processes and lower level bodily sensations and experiences.

Barsalou's (1999) model, however, does not specify which concrete experiences are incorporated into what abstract processes, nor does it elaborate a mechanism beyond simple associative conditioning. Unlike Barsalou, Lakoff and Johnson (1999) suggested that concrete experiences are not just an input into abstract thinking but directly shape the formation and evolution of abstract thought. With their CMT, they argued that the human mind operates metaphorically. During conceptual development, human beings first acquire lower level, concrete knowledge through direct experience with the environment before later grasping more complex and abstract concepts. The concrete concepts learned early on can then serve as a metaphoric scaffolding to aid the comprehension of abstract concepts. For example, children first learn concrete concepts such as distance (close vs. far) and spatial orientation (up vs. down) through direct sensory experience before they attempt to comprehend abstract constructs such as time. CMT suggests that people may rely on the metaphor of spatial relations to make sense of time. Thus, in phrases such as

"I look forward to meeting you" or "the meeting has been moved back," time is metaphorically modeled after physical relations, and time passing is pictured as objects moving along a physical dimension. Conceptualizing time in terms of spatial relations allows people to form mental pictures of time and facilitates the understanding and communication of an otherwise ethereal concept. Many other abstract and higher order constructs are similarly conceptualized through lower level, concrete constructs such as importance and physical weight (Jostmann, Lakens, & Schubert, 2009), social exclusion and coldness (IJzerman & Semin, 2009; Williams & Bargh, 2008; Zhong & Leonardelli, 2008), and prosociality and sweetness (Meier, Moeller, Riemer-Peltz, & Robinson, 2012). Thus, abstract constructs and processes do not emerge out of the blue but evolve from our concrete experiences of interacting with the physical world.

CMT offers a unique perspective on morality: Morality may be modeled after our understanding of concrete concepts, such as dirt and cleanliness, so that moral transgression is mentally represented as dirt and virtue as cleanliness. As an abstract construct, morality develops much later than lower level concepts such as dirt and cleanliness (but see the ongoing debate surrounding moral nativism, e.g., Hamlin, Wynn, & Bloom, 2007; Scarf, Imuta, Colombo, & Hayne, 2012). Therefore, it is possible that when people start to develop an understanding of moral and social threats, they use emotional and conceptual tools that they have already grasped through dealing with physical threats, such as contamination and pollution. Indeed, disgust has been found to be an emotional reaction to both physical purity violations and moral violations. Even though disgust is originally rooted in our evolutionary past as a mechanism for avoiding the ingestion of noxious substances, such as rotten food and feces, over time, it has expanded to communicate a sense of wrongness in social and cultural domains, including moral violations such as adultery and deception (Schaller & Duncan, 2007). Physical and moral disgust not only are expressed by similar facial expressions and physiological activation (Chapman, Kim, Susskind, & Anderson, 2009; Rozin, Lowery, & Ebert, 1994) but also use partially overlapping brain regions of the frontal and temporal lobes (Borg, Lieberman, & Kiehl, 2008; Moll et al., 2002). Rather than creating new neural circuitry to process morality, individuals may have adapted existing circuitries that are used to process contaminations and pollutions (Rozin, 1999).

Similarly, concepts related to cleanliness and dirt are frequently referenced in descriptions of moral issues. In English, for example, the phrase *money laundering* implies that the proceeds of crime are "tainted" and need to be "cleaned" to pass as legitimate; a *tarnished reputation* can indicate that previous immoral acts are perceived to foretell future immoral acts, and the phrase *blood on your hands* signifies involvement in nefarious activities. In Judeo-Christian religion, the book of Leviticus repeatedly links impurity with sin and cleanliness with holiness, describing various foods, actions, and states that are abominations (Klawans, 2000).

Moreover, in less technologically advanced civilizations, people actually confound moral transgression and physical pollution (Douglas, 1966). The Nuer (also known as the Nei Ti Naath, roughly meaning *original people*) society, for example, is a confederation of tribes located in south Sudan and western Ethiopia. To Nuers, physical pollution and moral transgression are psychologically indistinguishable. Common beliefs among Nuers include that if a wife engages in adultery, her husband will experience back pain, or if incest occurs in the tribe, contagious skin diseases will spread among its members. To stop these negative consequences, the victims (and sometimes the offenders) need to perform cleansing rituals. The Nuers have such confidence in the conflation between pollution and transgression that they use signs of pollution as an evidence for transgression. Thus, the husband's back pain may be used as evidence that the wife has committed adultery.

The Nuers are not the only culture to conflate physical cleanliness with morality. Although medical advances have dispelled many superstitions so that most people today recognize that moral transgressions do not directly cause physical pollution, at some level the psychological overlap between physical cleanliness and morality remains. Recent research reveals that moral transgressions literally feel dirty, such that reminding people of their past unsavory acts induced greater desire for cleansing products such as shampoos and bars of soap (Zhong & Liljenquist, 2006). Moreover, the metaphoric link between morality and cleanliness can have quite specific effects unique to a given modality. A subsequent study found that those who lied through voice mail desired mouthwash over other things, whereas those who lied via e-mail desired antiseptic hand wipes (Lee & Schwarz, 2010). Conversely, cleanliness has been found to signal moral purity (e.g., Helzer & Pizarro, 2011; Xu, Bègue, & Bushman, 2012; Yan, Ding, & Yan, 2011; Zhong, Strejcek, & Sivanathan, 2010). Zhong et al. (2010) found that participants who felt physically clean (as opposed to the ones who were led to feel physically dirty) tended to make more severe moral judgments on a variety of social issues such as obesity, homosexuality, and using profane language. This finding seems to be driven by an enhanced moral self-image after the cleanliness induction. Other studies yielded similar results. Helzer and Pizarro (2011), for example, found that individuals standing near a hand-sanitizer dispenser tended to make harsher moral judgments than those not reminded of cleanliness. Thus, in addition to sins feeling filthy, cleanliness is psychologically next to godliness.

Together, these observations depict a picture of morality as being psychologically embodied in physical dirt and cleanliness, and demonstrate a level of psychological equivalence between the concrete experience of contamination and purity, on the one hand, and the abstract notions of vice and virtue on the other. If this is indeed the case, then we might expect more than mere spreading of activation from concrete experiences of dirt and cleanliness to abstract constructs of morality. We might also expect that how we think about morality reflects the ways in which we think about dirt and cleanliness. The following section outlines three dimensions of dirt and cleanliness that might have shaped the way people conceptualize morality.

THE METAPHORIC STRUCTURE OF MORAL MIND

One important characteristic of metaphors is property transfer. In the metaphor "Juliet is the sun," for example, the source concept of the sun is used to describe the target concept, Juliet. When Shakespeare says that Juliet is the sun, many properties associated with the source concept, such as warmth, illumination, and the center of the known universe, become automatically activated and transferred to form a mental picture of the target concept. Thus, there is no need to describe explicitly that Juliet is warm, radiant, and the center of a certain young man's life; the metaphor automatically evokes all of these concepts (see Landau, Meier, & Keefer, 2010, for a review). Thus, if the concept of morality is metaphorically built on the conceptual framework of dirt and pollution, we would expect properties associated with dirt to shape how people think about morality.

Being able to identify a potential source of pollution is undoubtedly important for increasing the chance of survival. Mere categorization of dirt from nondirt, however, is often insufficient because dirt comes in different forms with varying properties. For example, if a pond that tribe members rely on as a water source becomes polluted, it is important to know how long that pollution will persist and whether anything can be done to clean it up; it may be equally important to know whether the pollution may spread to nearby water sources; finally, what is the severity of pollution? Does it simply produce an unpleasant taste, or does it pose real health hazards? These three dimensions of dirt and pollution—permanence, contagion, and harm—may carry significant adaptive implications that shape not only how we assess physical pollution threats but also social threats from moral transgressions. Specifically, these properties of dirt may influence how we think about moral reputations, the likelihood of copycat unethical behavior, and how we assess the morality of harmless deviant behaviors, respectively. This is not a claim that permanence, contagion, and harm are the only properties of dirt and pollution relevant to morality, or even the most important ones; rather, these dimensions serve as a starting point for our analyses of the metaphoric structure of embodied morality.

Permanence

> You and your partner are in a long-term relationship. Things are going well until one day your partner confesses that he (or she) slept with someone else a couple of weeks ago. Your partner says that this was a one-time thing and asks for your forgiveness.

In a moral psychology class, a scenario such as this would typically end with the question "How wrong was your partner's behavior?" In the real world, however, moral judgment and condemnation rarely end our moral evaluation process because of ongoing social relationships. Instead, what people do in situations like this is determined not only by their judgment of the act itself, but also by the assessment of the likelihood of future transgressions. If we believe that our partner's dalliance is truly a one-time affair, the likelihood of saving the relationship and forgiving the partner is much higher than if we think that the partner may cheat again in the future. Assessments like this are not unique to intimate relationships but applicable to many other forms of transgression without the involvement of personal relationships. In the case of crime, for example, even though an individual can terminate his or her interaction with a particular criminal, as a society, we need to decide whether and how we can rehabilitate criminals and reduce the likelihood of recidivism.

According to the U.S. Bureau of Justice Statistics, 2,266,800 adults were incarcerated in U.S. federal and state prisons and county jails at year-end 2010 (Glaze, 2011). Additionally, 4,887,900 adults were on probation or on parole. In total, approximately 7,100,000 adults were under correctional supervision (probation, parole, jail, or prison) in 2010, which is slightly more than three out of every 100 resident adults in the United States. Given the large population and the stakes involved, we would expect people to follow a rational process to predict recidivism rates. Criminologists, for instance, use statistical modeling to predict recidivism (e.g., Collins, 2010; Cottle, Lee, & Heilbrun, 2001). An average person, however, often thinks of transgression and crime as permanently polluting. A person who transgresses is thought of as having been *tainted* and it is difficult to *come clean* again. This is best communicated in the aphorism *once a criminal, always a criminal.* When assessing transgressions and crimes we often conceive of stains, such as blood, that are difficult to wash away. Lady Macbeth's futile attempt to wash the blood from her hands is a dramatic example of this metaphoric thinking written into our collective conscience.

Thinking of transgressions and crimes as staining dirt and pollution may enable us to use our fear of permanent pollution to regulate social behaviors. If we believe that transgressions are going to leave a permanent "taint" on our character and reputation, we might be less willing to transgress in the first place. However, just as any heuristics in judgment and decision making, it could also have maladaptive effects. First, thinking of transgressions and crimes as staining permanently may lead us to be much less forgiving and tolerant of others' misdeeds than otherwise. One of the cornerstones of psychology is the realization that behaviors are jointly determined by character and situational factors; thus, honest people can engage in dishonest behaviors in particular circumstances (Maûar, Amir, & Ariely, 2008). If we believe "once a cheater, always a cheater," we are likely to distance ourselves from those who have made the mistake of transgressing. Given another chance, those individuals may actually be able to stay "clean," but stigma and social isolation may push them to relapse into transgression again, producing a self-fulfilling prophecy. The United States currently has the highest rate of incarceration in human history; it is interesting to think about whether this has anything to do with how Americans treat and react to dirt and pollution. The United States has hygiene standards that are unmatched in history (Smith, 2007) and this hypervigilance for germs and dirt may be reflected in the desire to expunge "pollutants" from society. A metaphoric perspective of moral judgment may thus enhance understanding of the critically understudied process of reintegration as a means of recidivism reduction (e.g., O'Donnell, Baumer, & Hughes, 2008; Shinkfield & Graffam, 2009).

Second, the permanence of stains is also dependent on the power of cleansing. Oil stains on clothing may be difficult to wash off with water alone, but powerful cleansers can often do the trick. Ironically, if we know that stains can be easily washed off, we are less likely to be as careful avoiding dirt and pollution to begin with. It turns out that such licensing effect of washing is not limited to dealing with dirt and pollution but also social transgressions. Many cultures, such as the Nuers and the Bemba (an ethnic group of central Africa), believe that moral vices, including adultery and incest, come with lethal dangers. The Bemba, however, have confidence in their purification rituals for adultery, so they frequently give in to their desires (Douglas, 1966). Many world religions, including but not limited to Christianity and Islam, embrace the idea that washing can purify body and soul, purging sins and granting new beginnings. Cleansing and purification, whether literal or symbolic, may serve as a safety net that allows people to engage in unsavory and dangerous activities that are otherwise barred by their social systems.

Moral evaluations should not be limited to episodic judgments isolated in time and space (i.e., a solitary act as good or bad) but should involve context-specific projections and assessments of future behavior. Such projections are important not only because of the personal relationships we may have with the person being judged but also because of the more general connections and mutual responsibilities we share with each other due to the social contract that binds us together as a society. Similar to the influence that the emotion disgust has on moral judgment (Haidt, 2001), moral evaluations regarding the permanence of moral record may be guided by our intuitions about the stains of dirt and pollution. Yet although a "better-safe-than-sorry" strategy may help individuals avoid those most likely to (re)offend, emphasizing the dispositional nature of moral behavior may have perverse societal consequences by further delaying an evidence-based approach to recidivism prevention policies.

Contagion

What would happen if we drop a dead cockroach into a bowl of soup? The whole pot would be spoiled because of the spreading of germs and goo that the dead cockroach oozes throughout the liquid. What about putting a dead cockroach on top of a pile of chocolates? Most people recognize that although the chocolates that come in direct contact with the dead cockroach may be contaminated, those that remain untouched are not. However, when asked whether they would like to eat pieces of chocolate near, but untouched, by the dead cockroach, many would refuse or hesitate. When it comes to dealing with contagion and contamination in the physical world, our intuitions often fail to distinguish between contamination through contact and a type of magical thinking in which contamination occurs through mere association. For example, Rozin, Millman, and Nemeroff (1986) found that people are reluctant to eat feces-shaped fudge, and Morales and Fitzsimons (2007) demonstrated that contact with an unopened package of sanitary napkins is enough to make another packaged product less desirable; mere mental association with filth seems to signal the corruption of what is otherwise perfectly clean.

Magical thinking characterizes how people deal with social pollutants as well. In traditional cultures, for example, social systems and structures often evolve alongside fear of contagion from the impure. The most cited case is probably India's caste system. Within the system, a member's defining aspect is their purity: Brahmans, considered the purest, are afforded the highest positions in society, whereas Dalits are considered both physically dirty and morally corrupted. These "untouchables" are not allowed to marry into families of higher caste, participate in religious activities, or even share physical proximity with the upper class for fear of contagion (Deliège, 1999). Although to a much lesser extent, such magical thinking can also be observed in racial tensions between Whites and Blacks in the United States. "Whites only" drinking fountains and separate seating areas, among other segregation practices, vividly demonstrate the illusory fear that Blacks would pollute communal property. Thus, fear of contagion that originates from interacting with the physical world can spill over into social segregation and discrimination. If social impurities are conceived as contaminating dirt and the mere presence of them could corrupt the otherwise pure and righteous, then separating them from the rest of the society both physically and socially seems a logical remedy. Indeed, in a recent example, a North Carolina pastor, Charles L. Worley, ranted that people should round up all "queers and homosexuals" and quarantine them inside an electric fence (Eng, 2012).

Magical contagion not only guides how we fear that a social pollutant may contaminate ourselves but also shapes our perception of the extent to which it may corrupt the behavior of others. It is impossible nowadays not to turn on the television without hearing about reports of unethical behaviors or crimes. Books, movies, and video games are filled with profane language, nudity, sex, and violence. It is thus of paramount importance that we understand how exposure to transgressions and unsavory content may affect the behaviors of others, particularly the young. Are certain unethical behaviors seen as more contagious than others? Such judgment is likely to have important consequences because the damage of a transgression depends not only on its severity but also the likelihood that it may influence others and spread through society.

The perceived contagiousness of different behaviors may depend on the extent to which they involve and resemble purity violations. Although people may generally conceive of transgressions as dirt and pollution, there may still be variations in terms of the extent to which a transgression resembles dirt and pollution. Compared with violence and corruption, for example, which also involve harm and justice concerns, nonviolent sexual transgressions are exclusively purity violations, and as such they often evoke particularly strong feelings of disgust (Haidt, 2001) and may be more likely to trigger the kind of magical thinking often associated with physical pollution. This may partly explain why sexual content provokes more media censorship than does violent content, at least in the United States. Nudity and sex, even consensual, are treated as contagiously influential for children and adolescents' behaviors. The Motion Picture Association of America's film rating system, for example, imposes harsher regulation on sex than violence, and in fact issued four times as many NC-17 ratings (no children or under 17 admitted) for sexual content than for violent content (Bourke & Dick, 2006), despite decades of research showing that children model violence in movies and computer games (e.g., Bandura, Ross, & Ross, 1961; Engelhardt, Bartholow, Kerr, & Bushman, 2011).

Thus, seeing morality through the lens of dirt and pollution may instigate an unwarranted fear of contagion in our interactions with others who are outside of our systems of social or moral order. However, the mere existence of differences in looks, opinions, values, and preferences need not automatically lead to strife; differences can coexist and be celebrated. By better understanding our deep seated fear of contagion, we may be poised to learn more about the psychological underpinnings of our tendencies toward segregation on the one hand and our strides toward integration on the other.

Harm

From the evolutionary perspective, our aversion to dirt and pollution has the adaptive advantage of promoting pathogen avoidance. There are certainly dirt and pollutants that are dangerous and harmful: deadly contagious disease, rotten flesh, and excrement, to name just a few. A big part of what we categorize as dirt and pollution, however, poses no apparent threat to our health and survival. Soil on the kitchen floor is typically seen as dirt, but there is no obvious health hazard associated with it. Mary Douglas (1966) eloquently argued that our categorization of dirt diverges from an absolute standard of what is harmful to something relative and symbolic, defined in terms of trespass within a particular system of order. In other words, there is no absolute dirt; dirt is something that falls outside of a system of order. Soil in the garden is not dirt; it only becomes dirt when it is brought into the kitchen. Likewise, for farmers that literally make their livelihoods from the land they work, soil is not dirt but a valuable resource. This relative nature of dirt is nicely demonstrated in Thomas Hardy's novel *Far From the Madding Crowd* (1874/2000) when farm laborers commend the shepherd who refuses a clean mug for his cider as a "nice unparticular man." By being "unparticular" about "dirt in its pure state," the shepherd signals that he is equal with the farmers and shares their systems of values and beliefs.

This decoupling between dirt and harm might have shaped how we think about morality, where moral judgments are often decoupled from harm. Previous research has found that although people are capable of conducting formal analysis of harm and using that as the basis of judgment, they do not always do so when making moral judgments (see Haidt, 2001). In the aforementioned phenomenon of moral dumbfounding, for example, people insisted that scenarios, such as the one involving consensual kisses between brothers and sisters, were morally wrong even though they could not articulate any harm caused by such action (Haidt, Koller, & Dias, 1993). A consensual kiss, even if it is between a brother and sister, probably does not cause much harm; however, it does make people feel uncomfortable because it is not what people normally do. It thus seems that the basis of moral judgment is broader than merely harm and justice, as philosophers speculate, but instead encompasses boundary trespassing as well. Much like soil in the kitchen is considered dirt, behaviors and values that cause no harm, but nevertheless trespass value system boundaries, are likely to be deemed wrong. Indeed, exposure to worldviews that contradict our own, and thus are considered to be morally wrong, can elicit the same gustatory disgust perceptions that prevent us from ingesting filth (Ritter & Preston, 2011).

Such moral overreaction is not without its cultural advantages: By meticulously labeling and rooting out impurities, groups are able to protect their boundaries, strengthen their core belief systems, and ultimately bind group members into tribelike communities. Basing moral judgments on boundary trespassing, however, could also induce a "groupish righteousness" (see Haidt, 2012) that intensifies culture wars and leads to the persecution of cultural minorities. Importantly, however, boundary trespassing and the uncomfortable sensations (e.g., disgust) it induces, can often be perceived as harm, thus justifying blatantly prejudicial or even violent behaviors. Vilification of ethnic and cultural minorities is a common occurrence throughout history. Even in recent years, much of the condemnation of homosexuality has been couched in illusory harm to the institution of marriage and children, not to mention natural disasters and terrorist attacks portrayed as divine retribution.

To summarize, previous research has established purity as a moral domain and has shown that manipulating physical dirt and pollution through visual or olfactory means can alter moral judgment. The current analysis suggests that the relationship among dirt, pollution, and purity on the one hand and morality on the other may be much more complex because of the many ways that we think about dirt. Rather than perceiving and categorizing dirt monolithically, people form subjective impressions of dirt along dimensions including permanence, contagion, and harm, and this in turn shapes how we think about morality.

DISCUSSION AND CONCLUSION

In her book *Chasing Dirt: The American Pursuit of Cleanliness*, Suellen Hoy (1995) described the historic transformation of the United States from a dreadfully dirty state in the 19th century to the meticulously clean society it is today. During mid-19th century, sanitation was not unknown to Americans, but people seemed to have felt no urgency to clean up. For the most part, people still lived in preindustrial, hygienically primitive situations on small farms or country villages where dirt was part of everyday work. Today, people doing dirty jobs are frowned on and stigmatized, as if they themselves were sources of pollution and contamination (Ashforth & Kreiner, 1999). Hygiene standards and sanitation in both private and public spheres have far exceeded what is necessary for health and safety reasons. From antibacterial soap, to antiperspirant, to colon cleansing, it is as if Americans have become obsessed with cleanliness. Ironically, this hypersanitation may be so extreme that it is actually making us sick by inhibiting the proper development of the immune system, which increases the risk of developing allergies and autoimmune disorders (Hampton, 2011), and by creating antibiotic-resistant superbugs (e.g., Nordmann, Naas, Fortineau, & Poirel, 2007).

From within a bubble of cleanliness, people may form misconceived ideas about dirt and pollution. Dirt, mud, dust, grease, sweat, and the like, things that are otherwise perfectly normal derivatives of everyday life, now seem tainting, contagious, and harmful. The perceived threat of dirt is no longer only that it might undermine health but also that it might breach our hypersanitation. In other words, cleanliness might have acquired value and meaning independent of health, fitness, and survival. Unbeknownst to many of us, however, is the possibility that the misconceptions we have about dirt may subtly work its way into influencing our perception and judgment in social domains. On the basis of previous work in embodied cognition and CMT, we propose that the concept of morality may be built on the conceptual framework of dirt and pollution, and hence how people think about social and moral deviants parallels how they think about dirt. Thus, just as people typically think of dirt as tainting, contagious, and harmful, they judge social deviants along the same dimensions. People who have transgressed are typically seen as being permanently tainted and can never come clean (e.g., once a criminal, always a criminal); social deviations are seen as magically contaminating and require physical and social segregation; and otherwise harmless behaviors may be seen as dangerous because they provoke the feeling of disgust. These heuristics in moral judgments can have serious consequences, leading to less tolerance of mistakes and differences. If people are eager to purge the dirt from their physical world, will they be equally passionate about eliminating deviation and diversity from their social order?

Understanding these intricacies in the metaphoric mapping between dirt and morality may thus help correct biases in our moral judgment. For example, reminders that dirt can often be removed without leaving a stain may promote forgiveness of mistakes and support for rehabilitation programs; similarly, reminding people that many stains do not rub off and that not all disease is contagious may reduce our imaginary fear that the mere presence of differences may contaminate and corrupt us and others; finally, exposing people to harmless dirt, such as soil and mud, may increase the likelihood that they will see the distinction between being different and dangerous (and wrong). These are just a few examples of how changing conceptions of a concrete construct, such as dirt, may influence or improve how we think about abstract constructs, such as moral systems.

Independent of that, the current chapter also highlights the need to study moral dimensions such as permanence and contagion that have not received much attention in moral psychology and philosophy, largely because of the emphasis on impersonal, abstract aspect of moral reasoning. The scenarios and dilemmas researchers craft to study moral reasoning processes tend to be devoid of context and relationships. The vignettes that people ponder usually happen in one-shot situations in which the individuals involved have no meaningful connections or relationships (Bloom, 2011). Thus, it makes no sense to think about whether the action may happen again or how it may affect an observer. This is obviously not the case in the real world, where actions and behaviors happen in social context, embedded in meaningful relationships. It is usually not the end of the story when we deem a lie unethical; in most cases, we need to assess whether the individual will lie again to determine our attitude toward that person, and we often must judge whether the lie will influence others to be deceitful. In the case of crimes, recidivism is one of the most important judgments to make when making decisions about sentencing. Another important concern for the correctional system is sending the right message to others so that the crime is not copied. A metaphor-based view of morality helps us to recognize that moral judgment is not simply the product of abstract reasoning but rather is modeled after our experience with the physical and social world. These deep-rooted aspects of morality constitute a blind spot in traditional moral psychology and philosophy and offer important and promising avenues for future research into embodied moral judgment.

REFERENCES

Ashforth, B. E., & Kreiner, G. E. (1999). "How can you do it?": Of dirty work and the challenge constructing a positive identity. *Academy of Management Journal, 24*, 413–434.

Bandura, A., Ross, D., & Ross, S. A. (1961). Transmission of aggression through imitation of aggressive models. *The Journal of Abnormal and Social Psychology, 63*, 575–582. doi:10.1037/h0045925

Bargh, J. A., Chen, M., & Burrows, L. (1996). Automaticity of social behavior: Direct effects of trait construct and stereotype activation on action. *Journal of Personality and Social Psychology, 71*, 230–244. doi:10.1037/0022-3514.71.2.230

Barsalou, L. W. (1999). Perceptual symbol systems. *Behavioral and Brain Sciences, 22*, 577–660.

Bentham, J. (1948). *A fragment on government and an introduction to the principles of morals and legislation* (W. Harrison, Ed.). Oxford, England: Blackwell. (Original work published 1776)

Bloom, P. (2011). Family, community, trolley problems, and the crisis in moral psychology. *The Yale Review, 99*, 26–43. doi:10.1111/j.1467-9736.2011.00701.x

Borg, J. S., Lieberman, D., & Kiehl, K. A. (2008). Infection, incest, and iniquity: Investigating the neural correlates of disgust and morality. *Journal of Cognitive Neuroscience, 20*, 1529–1546. doi:10.1162/jocn.2008.20109

Bourke, A. P. (Producer), & Dick, K. (Director). (2006). *This film is not yet rated* [Motion picture]. United States: IFC.

Chapman, H. A., Kim, D. A., Susskind, J. M., & Anderson, A. K. (2009). In bad taste: Evidence for the oral origins of moral disgust. *Science, 323,* 1222–1226. doi:10.1126/science.1165565

Collins, R. E. (2010). The effect of gender on violent and nonviolent recidivism: A meta-analysis. *Journal of Criminal Justice, 38,* 675–684. doi:10.1016/j.jcrimjus.2010.04.041

Cottle, C. C., Lee, R. J., & Heilbrun, K. (2001). The prediction of criminal recidivism in juveniles—A meta-analysis. *Criminal Justice and Behavior, 28,* 367–394. doi:10.1177/0093854801028003005

Damasio, A. R. (1994). *Descartes error: Emotion, reason, and the human brain.* New York, NY: Quill.

Deliège, R. (1999). *The untouchables of India* (N. Scott, Trans.). Oxford, England: Berg.

Donaldson, T., & Werhane, P. H. (2002). Introduction to ethical reasoning. In T. Donaldson, P. H. Werhane, & M. Cording (Eds.), *Ethical issues in business: A philosophical approach* (7th ed., pp. 1–12). Upper Saddle River, NJ: Prentice Hall.

Douglas, M. (1966). *Purity and danger: An analysis of concepts of pollution and taboo.* New York, NY: Routledge. doi:10.4324/9780203361832

Eng, J. (2012, May 22). Charles Worley, North Carolina pastor, faces backlash, outrage over call for gays to be put behind electric fence. *msnbc.com.* Retrieved from http://usnews.msnbc.msn.com/_news/2012/05/22/11813973-charles-worley-north-carolina-pastor-faces-backlash-outrage-over-call-for-gays-to-be-put-behind-electric-fence?lite

Engelhardt, C. R., Bartholow, B. D., Kerr, G. T., & Bushman, B. J. (2011). This is your brain on violent video games: Neural desensitization to violence predicts increased aggression following violent video game exposure. *Journal of Experimental Social Psychology, 47,* 1033–1036. doi:10.1016/j.jesp.2011.03.027

Eskine, K. J., Kacinik, N. A., & Prinz, J. J. (2011). A bad taste in the mouth: Gustatory disgust influences moral judgment. *Psychological Science, 22,* 295–299. doi:10.1177/0956797611398497

Gigerenzer, G., & Goldstein, D. G. (1996). Mind as computer: Birth of a metaphor. *Creativity Research Journal, 9,* 131–144.

Glaze, L. E. (2011, December 15). *Correctional populations in the United States, 2010.* Retrieved from http://bjs.ojp.usdoj.gov/index.cfm?ty=pbdetail&iid=2237

Greene, J. D., Sommerville, R. B., Nystrom, L. E., Darley, J. M., & Cohen, J. D. (2001). An fMRI investigation of emotional engagement in moral judgment. *Science, 293,* 2105–2108. doi:10.1126/science.1062872

Haidt, J. (2001). The emotional dog and its rational tail: A social intuitionist approach to moral judgment. *Psychological Review, 108,* 814–834. doi:10.1037/0033-295X.108.4.814

Haidt, J. (2007). The new synthesis in moral psychology. *Science, 316,* 998–1002. doi:10.1126/science.1137651

Haidt, J. (2012). *The righteous mind: Why good people are divided by politics and religion*. New York, NY: Pantheon.

Haidt, J., & Joseph, C. (2004). Intuitive ethics: How innately prepared intuitions generate culturally variable virtues. *Daedalus, 133*, 55–66. doi:10.1162/0011526042365555

Haidt, J., & Joseph, C. (2007). The moral mind: How 5 sets of innate moral intuitions guide the development of many culture-specific virtues, and perhaps even modules. In P. Carruthers, S. Laurence, & S. Stich (Eds.), *The innate mind* (Vol. 3, pp. 367–391). New York, NY: Oxford.

Haidt, J., Koller, S. H., & Dias, M. G. (1993). Affect, culture, and morality, or is it wrong to eat your dog? *Journal of Personality and Social Psychology, 65*, 613–628. doi:10.1037/0022-3514.65.4.613

Hamlin, J. K., Wynn, K., & Bloom, P. (2007). Social evaluation by preverbal infants. *Nature, 450*, 557–559. doi:10.1038/nature06288

Hampton, T. (2011). Research provides new insights on how hygiene affects asthma and allergies. *JAMA, 305*, 1400–1401. doi:10.1001/jama.2011.434

Hardy, T. (2000). *Far from the madding crowd*. London, England: Penguin. (Original work published 1874)

Helzer, E. G., & Pizarro, D. A. (2011). Dirty liberals! Reminders of physical cleanliness influence moral and political attitudes. *Psychological Science, 22*, 517–522. doi:10.1177/0956797611402514

Hoy, S. (1995). *Chasing dirt: The American pursuit of cleanliness*. New York, NY: Oxford University Press.

IJzerman, H., & Semin, G. R. (2009). The thermometer of social relations: Mapping social proximity on temperature. *Psychological Science, 20*, 1214–1220. doi:10.1111/j.1467-9280.2009.02434.x

James, W. (1950). *The principles of psychology*. New York, NY: Dover. (Original work published 1890)

Jones, A., & Fitness, J. (2008). Moral hypervigilance: The influence of disgust sensitivity in the moral domain. *Emotion, 8*, 613–627. doi:10.1037/a0013435

Jostmann, N. B., Lakens, D., & Schubert, T. W. (2009). Weight as an embodiment of importance. *Psychological Science, 20*, 1169–1174. doi:10.1111/j.1467-9280.2009.02426.x

Kant, I. (2002). *Groundwork for the metaphysics of morals* (A. W. Wood, Trans.). Binghampton, NY: Vail-Ballou Press. (Original work published 1785)

Klawans, J. (2000). *Impurity and sin in ancient Judaism*. New York, NY: Oxford University Press. doi:10.1093/acprof:oso/9780195132908.001.0001

Kohlberg, L. (1963). Development of children's orientations toward a moral order: Sequence in development of moral thought. *Vita Humana, 6*, 11–33.

Lakoff, G., & Johnson, M. (1999). *Philosophy in the flesh: The embodied mind and its challenge to western thought*. New York, NY: Basic Books.

Landau, M. J., Meier, B. P., & Keefer, L. A. (2010). A metaphor-enriched social cognition. *Psychological Bulletin, 136*, 1045–1067. doi:10.1037/a0020970

Lee, S. W., & Schwarz, N. (2010). Dirty hands and dirty mouths: Embodiment of the moral-purity metaphor is specific to the motor modality involved in the moral transgression. *Psychological Science, 21,* 1423–1425. doi:10.1177/0956797610382788

Mažar, N., Amir, O., & Ariely, D. (2008). The dishonesty of honest people: A theory of self-concept maintenance. *Journal of Marketing Research, 45,* 633–644. doi:10.1509/jmkr.45.6.633

Meier, B. P., Moeller, S. K., Riemer-Peltz, M., & Robinson, M. D. (2012). Sweet taste preferences and experience predict prosocial inferences, personalities and behaviors. *Journal of Personality and Social Psychology, 102,* 163–174. doi:10.1037/a0025253

Mill, J. S. (1957). *Utilitarianism* (O. Piest, Ed.). New York, NY: Macmillan. (Original work published 1861)

Moll, J., de Oliveira-Souza, R., Eslinger, P. J., Bramati, I. E., Mourao-Miranda, J., Andreiuolo, P. A., & Pessoa, L. (2002). The neural correlates of moral sensitivity: A functional magnetic resonance imaging investigation of basic and moral emotions. *The Journal of Neuroscience, 22,* 2730–2736.

Monin, B., Pizarro, D. A., & Beer, J. S. (2007). Deciding versus reacting: Conceptions of moral judgment and the reason-affect debate. *Review of General Psychology, 11,* 99–111. doi:10.1037/1089-2680.11.2.99

Morales, A. C., & Fitzsimons, G. F. (2007). Product contagion: Changing consumer evaluations through physical contact with "disgusting" products. *Journal of Marketing Research, 44,* 272–283. doi:10.1509/jmkr.44.2.272

Neal, D. T., & Chartrand, T. L. (2011). Embodied emotion perception: Amplifying and dampening facial feedback modulates emotion perception accuracy. *Social Psychological and Personality Science, 2,* 673–678. doi:10.1177/1948550611406138

Nordmann, P., Naas, T., Fortineau, N., & Poirel, L. (2007). Superbugs in the coming new decade; multidrug resistance and prospects for treatment of *Staphylococcus aureus, Enterococcus Spp.* and *Pseudomonas aeruginosa* in 2010. *Current Opinion in Microbiology, 10,* 436–440. doi:10.1016/j.mib.2007.07.004

Nussbaum, M. C. (2004). *Hiding from humanity: Disgust, shame and the law.* Princeton, NJ: Princeton University Press.

O'Donnell, I., Baumer, E. P., & Hughes, N. (2008). Recidivism in the Republic of Ireland. *Criminology & Criminal Justice: An International Journal, 8,* 123–146. doi:10.1177/1748895808088991

Ritter, R., & Preston, J. L. (2011). Gross gods and icky atheism: Disgust responses to rejected religious beliefs. *Journal of Experimental Social Psychology, 47,* 1225–1230. doi:10.1016/j.jesp.2011.05.006

Rozin, P. (1999). Preadaptation and the puzzles and properties of pleasure. In D. Kahneman, E. Diener, & N. Schwarz (Eds.), *Well being: The foundations of hedonic psychology* (pp. 109–133). New York, NY: Russell Sage.

Rozin, P., Lowery, L., & Ebert, R. (1994). Varieties of disgust faces and the structure of disgust. *Journal of Personality and Social Psychology, 66*, 870–881. doi:10.1037/0022-3514.66.5.870

Rozin, P., Lowery, L., Imada, S., & Haidt, J. (1999). The CAD triad hypothesis: A mapping between three moral emotions (contempt, anger, disgust) and three moral codes (community, autonomy, divinity). *Journal of Personality and Social Psychology, 76*, 574–586. doi:10.1037/0022-3514.76.4.574

Rozin, P., Millman, L., & Nemeroff, C. (1986). Operation of the laws of sympathetic magic in disgust and other domains. *Journal of Personality and Social Psychology, 50*, 703–712. doi:10.1037/0022-3514.50.4.703

Scarf, D., Imuta, K., Colombo, M., & Hayne, H. (2012). Social evaluation or simple association? Simple associations may explain moral reasoning in infants. *PLoS ONE, 7*(8), e42698. doi:10.1371/journal.pone.0042698

Schaller, M., & Duncan, L. A. (2007). The behavioral immune system: Its evolution and social psychological implications. In J. P. Forgas, M. G. Haselton, & W. von Hippel (Eds.), *Evolution and the social mind: Evolutionary psychology and social cognition* (pp. 293–307). New York, NY: Psychology Press.

Schnall, S. (2011). Clean, proper and tidy are more than the absence of dirty, disgusting and wrong. *Emotion Review, 3*, 264–266. doi:10.1177/1754073911402397

Schnall, S., Benton, J., & Harvey, S. (2008). With a clean conscience: Cleanliness reduces the severity of moral judgments. *Psychological Science, 19*, 1219–1222. doi:10.1111/j.1467-9280.2008.02227.x

Schubert, T. W. (2005). Your highness: Vertical positions as perceptual symbols of power. *Journal of Personality and Social Psychology, 89*, 1–21. doi:10.1037/0022-3514.89.1.1

Shinkfield, A. J., & Graffam, J. (2009). Community reintegration of ex-prisoners: Type and degree of change in variables influencing successful reintegration. *International Journal of Offender Therapy and Comparative Criminology, 53*, 29–42. doi:10.1177/0306624X07309757

Shweder, R. A., Much, N., Park, L., & Mahapatra, M. M. (1997). The "big three" of morality (autonomy, community, divinity) and the "big three" explanations of suffering. In A. Brandt & P. Rozin (Eds.), *Morality and health* (pp. 74–133). New York, NY: Routledge.

Smith, V. (2007). *Clean: A history of personal hygiene and purity*. Oxford, England: Oxford University Press.

Soler, J. (1979). The semiotics of food in the Bible. In R. Forster & O. Ranum (Trans. & Eds.) *Food and drinking history* (pp. 126–138). Baltimore, MD: Johns Hopkins University Press. (Original work published 1973)

Strack, F., Martin, L. L., & Stepper, S. (1988). Inhibiting and facilitating conditions of the human smile—a nonobtrusive test of the facial feedback hypothesis. *Journal of Personality and Social Psychology, 54*, 768–777. doi:10.1037/0022-3514.54.5.768

Varela, F., Thompson, E., & Rosch, E. (1991). *The embodied mind: Cognitive science and human experience*. Cambridge, MA: MIT Press.

Wheatley, T., & Haidt, J. (2005). Hypnotically induced disgust makes moral judgments more severe. *Psychological Science, 16*, 780–784. doi:10.1111/j.1467-9280.2005.01614.x

Williams, L. E., & Bargh, J. A. (2008). Experiencing physical warmth promotes interpersonal warmth. *Science, 322*, 606–607. doi:10.1126/science.1162548

Xu, H., Bègue, L., & Bushman, D. (2012). Too fatigued to care: Ego depletion, guilt, and prosocial behavior. *Journal of Experimental Social Psychology, 48*, 1183–1186

Yan, Z., Ding, D., & Yan, L. (2011). To wash your body, or purify your soul: Physical cleansing would strengthen the sense of high moral character. *Psychology (Savannah, GA), 2*, 992–997. doi:10.4236/psych.2011.29149

Zhong, C. B., & Leonardelli, G. J. (2008). Cold and lonely: Does social exclusion literally feel cold? *Psychological Science, 19*, 838–842. doi:10.1111/j.1467-9280.2008.02165.x

Zhong, C. B., & Liljenquist, K. (2006). Washing away your sins: Threatened morality and physical cleansing. *Science, 313*, 1451–1452. doi:10.1126/science.1130726

Zhong, C. B., Strejcek, B., & Sivanathan, N. (2010). A clean self can render harsh moral judgment. *Journal of Experimental Social Psychology, 46*, 859–862. doi:10.1016/j.jesp.2010.04.003

7

TOWARD A METAPHOR-ENRICHED PERSONALITY PSYCHOLOGY

MICHAEL D. ROBINSON AND ADAM K. FETTERMAN

Conventional wisdom on metaphor suggests that it is the province of poets, metaphor is an optional way of thinking, or that metaphor merely serves communication purposes. In this chapter, we show that such wisdom is at variance with how human beings actually think and function. We first provide a brief overview of the metaphor representation perspective. We then make a case for the utility of this perspective in understanding how people differ from each other and do so within a broader context of how personality has traditionally been assessed. We then present four lines of personality research inspired by the metaphor representation perspective. We conclude with a discussion of the challenges and unanswered questions involved in translating the metaphor representation perspective to personality psychology.

This publication was made possible by COBRE Grant P20 RR020151 from the National Center for Research Resources (NCRR), a component of the National Institutes of Health (NIH). Its contents are the sole responsibility of the authors and do not necessarily represent the official views of NCRR or NIH.

http://dx.doi.org/10.1037/14278-007
The Power of Metaphor: Examining Its Influence on Social Life, M. J. Landau, M. D. Robinson, and B. P. Meier (Editors)

A BRIEF OVERVIEW OF THE METAPHOR
REPRESENTATION PERSPECTIVE

Our view of metaphor is heavily influenced by the writings of Lakoff and Johnson (1980, 1999), a linguist and philosopher, respectively. We term their set of ideas the *metaphor representation perspective* (Meier & Robinson, 2005) and contrast it with three more conventional perspectives of metaphor. First, it might be thought that metaphor is the particular province of poets, lyricists, or expressive writers. However, this is simply not the case as linguistic metaphors appear to be commonly used by virtually everyone (Gibbs, 1994). Second, it might be thought that there are as many metaphors as there are figures of speech that are metaphoric. This is not the case in that the same conceptual metaphors (e.g., *life is a journey, the self is a container*) seem to motivate multiple specific linguistic expressions (Lakoff & Johnson, 1999). For example, the phrases "I'm feeling up," "things are looking up," and "that was an uplifting movie" are not unrelated, but rather all capitalize on the same conceptual metaphor, mostly generally *good is up*.

Third, it might be thought that metaphors are only about communication. Lakoff and Johnson (1980), however, made the novel and fundamentally interesting suggestion that we use metaphors in speech because we often *think* metaphorically. That is, language use follows from the manner in which our minds work. From this perspective, the phrase "I'm feeling up" captures how people think about their happiness, even in the absence of a communication context. A rationale for this idea is that many of our most important feelings and concepts—such as peace, love, or anger—lack a clear perceptual referent, which creates epistemic problems (Searle, 1998). People resolve such difficulties by scaffolding (Williams, Huang, & Bargh, 2009) abstract feelings and thoughts on perceptual dimensions—such as up–down, warm–cold, close–far, and dirty–clean—that are more concrete, immediate, and visceral, which in turn facilitates their intuitive understanding (Landau, Meier, & Keefer, 2010).

Lakoff and Johnson (1999) further suggested that metaphor representation processes guide our thoughts like "a hidden hand." An important body of social psychology research has supported this idea (Landau et al., 2010). These studies have manipulated perceptual cues associated with prominent metaphors and shown that they result in metaphor-consistent outcomes. For example, Meier and Robinson (2004) showed that positive words were evaluated faster when presented higher on the computer screen and negative words were evaluated faster when presented lower on the computer screen, consistent with a *good is up* conceptual metaphor. IJzerman and Semin (2009) showed that incidental manipulations of warmth influenced subsequent perceptions of interpersonal proximity, consistent with a *closeness is warmth* conceptual metaphor. We could cite multiple other important studies here, but they will be cited in other chapters in the present volume. Also, for a fuller discussion of conceptual metaphors, see Gibbs (Chapter 2, this volume) or Landau, Robinson, and Meier (Chapter 1, this volume). Of more importance for our chapter is the potential of the metaphor representation perspective to provide novel insights into personality functioning.

TOWARD A METAPHOR-ENRICHED PERSONALITY PSYCHOLOGY

In understanding how and why people differ from each other, midcentury personality psychologists had an admirably broad view of assessment. Self-reports of personality were commonly used, but the same researchers used many implicit experimental tasks as well. For example, Allport's (1937) personality text contended that expressive style (e.g., in handwriting) was informative of personality, McClelland's (1951) text contended that projective measures were crucial in discerning the social motives of individuals, and Bruner (1951) provided evidence for the idea that personal values were evident in basic perceptual tendencies.

Subsequently, Mischel (1968) published an important book in which individual differences were questioned in terms of their predictive validity. Although not desired (Mischel, 2009), this book was interpreted to suggest that behavior is a function of situations not personalities (Ross & Nisbett, 1991). A schism between social and personality psychology occurred as a result of this controversy (Kenrick & Funder, 1988). Personality psychology largely abandoned outcome predictions to focus on issues of taxonomy among self-reported traits. After many years of refining their measures, personality psychology rebounded by showing that individual differences are of substantial value in outcome prediction (e.g., Ozer & Benet-Martinez, 2006). The person–situation controversy is therefore a nonissue at present, and it is now possible to revisit the wisdom of earlier personality psychologists, such as Bruner (1951) and McClelland (1951), who insisted that personality psychology can only be complete to the extent that it focuses on implicit as well as self-reported assessments.

Implicit approaches to personality assessment have multiple benefits. Practically speaking, explicit and implicit assessments tend to be uncorrelated or only weakly correlated with each other (Robinson & Neighbors, 2006). Thus, implicit assessments of the person can reveal important insights concerning the individual that cannot be adequately captured by an exclusive reliance on self-reported traits. In addition, implicit personality variables moderate the manner in which self-reported traits function (Robinson & Gordon, 2011). Finally, and perhaps most fundamentally, implicit assessments are process-based in nature. They are not reliant on beliefs about the self (Robinson & Clore, 2002) and therefore provide insights into mechanisms that self-reported traits cannot (Robinson & Gordon, 2011). For such reasons and others, we have suggested that personality psychology needs to embrace implicit assessments of the individual to a greater extent than it currently does (Robinson & Compton, 2008).

We think that the metaphor representation perspective, which can model personality processes in an implicit manner, possesses considerable value in understanding personality and individual differences. There is an important nuance to this work that should be mentioned up front, however. Manipulations of vertical position (Meier & Robinson, 2004), warmth (IJzerman & Semin, 2009), or visual backgrounds (Wilkowski, Meier, Robinson, Carter, & Feltman, 2009) might be quite irrelevant in understanding individual differences. Individuals, for example, do not have visual backgrounds (Wilkowski et al., 2009). Considerable creativity is therefore necessary to translate this perspective to the individual difference realm.

We have now presented a theoretical and historical background for our research on metaphor-related processes in personality. Four lines of research are reviewed, two of which use reaction times to probe the vertical dimension of space. Following these earlier lines of research, we show how prominent metaphors can be translated into preference or forced choice judgments in a way that implicitly probes variations in personality.

EVIDENCE FOR A METAPHORIC VIEW OF PERSONALITY

Depression and Vertical Attention

There are two dictionary definitions for *depression*. The first refers to a downward indentation. The second refers to a condition marked by sadness, lethargy, and hopelessness. From a metaphor representation perspective, it is not likely a coincidence that we use the same word to characterize both states. Rather, the latter dictionary meaning likely borrows from the former and does so in relation to the conceptual metaphor *sadness is down*. Indeed, the adjective "down" is often used to refer to sad feelings. From an embodied perspective, the body droops when it is tired and lays supine when this is especially so, and such covariations in experience are likely responsible, in part, for the genesis of thinking of depression as a downward vertical state (Tolaas, 1991).

Taking the metaphor representation perspective (Lakoff & Johnson, 1999) seriously, individual differences in depression might constrain and entrain attention in a downward vertical direction, independent of any communication context. This prediction was examined in two studies by

Meier and Robinson (2006). In both studies, people were asked to respond as quickly as possible to spatial probes higher or lower on a computer screen, and the location of these probes was varied in a fully randomized manner. In addition, we measured levels of depression using the well-validated Beck Depression Inventory. As hypothesized, individuals higher in depression were faster to respond to low spatial probes, and individuals lower in depression were faster to respond to high spatial probes. There was thus a significant and consequential relationship between levels of depression and whether attention favors lower or higher areas of visual space, implicitly and cognitively so.

As to whether activated negative thoughts bias attention downward, they do according to the experimental results of Meier and Robinson (2004), which involved negative word evaluations. However, the results of Meier and Robinson (2006) are perhaps more profound in that they suggest that relatively chronic states of depression bias attention downward irrespective of positive or negative affective primes. In other words, vertical biases in selective attention may track levels of depression and in turn serve as a useful probe of depression levels. This idea warrants further research because probes of depressogenic cognition are considered valuable to the depression literature (Segal & Swallow, 1994), ours is a novel probe of depression levels, and there are now numerous results showing that manipulations of spatial attention (typically disfavoring threatening stimuli) are efficacious in reducing levels of psychopathology (MacLeod, Koster, & Fox, 2009). Accordingly, it would be valuable to examine whether training attention upward mitigates depression levels.

Dominance–Submission and Vertical Attention

Prominent linguistic expressions suggest that states of dominance and submission are conceptualized in terms of high and low vertical positions, respectively. For example, we refer to increasingly dominant individuals as *upwardly mobile*, *social climbers*, or *rising stars*. In contrast, we refer to individuals who are losing their social status as *headed for a fall* or on a *downward spiral*. Such metaphoric associations can explain why bosses in corporate buildings have offices that are typically on higher floors, why graphics for organizational structures typically place workers "under" their supervisors, and why standing (relative to seated) individuals are judged to be more dominant (Schwartz, 1981). Consistent with verticality metaphors, Schubert (2005) found that dominant animals (i.e., those "high" in the food chain) were categorized more quickly when presented higher on a computer screen, whereas submissive animals (i.e., those "low" in the food chain) were categorized more quickly when presented lower on a computer screen.

In two studies, Robinson, Zabelina, Ode, and Moeller (2008) sought to examine whether personality variations in dominance can be understood from a verticality perspective. They assessed personality tendencies toward dominance using the adjective markers of Wiggins, Trapnell, and Phillips (1988). In these same studies, individuals also completed a vertical attention task. Consistent with metaphors for dominance versus submission, dominant individuals attended upward in visual space, and submissive individuals attended downward. We have yet to show that such biases upward or downward in visual space predict more specific social behaviors, but this direction of future research can be advocated. For example, those biased upward in vertical attention may also engage in more coercive and domineering relationship behaviors and exhibit greater confrontation and less appeasement in response to provocations in daily life (Moskowitz, 2010). It is also seems consistent with Fiske's (1993) theory of power to suggest that placing individuals in more dominant (versus submissive) social roles may alter their vertical attention in an upward-favoring direction.

Although our depression- (Meier & Robinson, 2006) and dominance-related (Robinson et al., 2008) findings might be linked, we are inclined to suggest that they are not. The fact is that the up–down dimension appears to be recruited for multiple metaphoric purposes, including in morality, spirituality, happiness, and dominance domains (Meier, Hauser, Robinson, Friesen, & Schjeldahl, 2007). Individual differences in spirituality, for example, might also predict vertical selective attention, although results of this type would not likely be due to covarying levels of depression or dominance. It would seem useful to conduct a study in which multiple individual differences of a verticality type are assessed at the same time, thereby permitting multiple regression tests of which dimension or set of dimensions is the most consequential one for vertical selective attention.

Prosocial Personality and Sweet Taste Preferences

We refer to nice gestures as *sweet,* nice people as *sweet,* and terms of endearment among relationship partners often borrow from this root conceptual metaphor (e.g., *cupcake, honey, sugar, sweetheart*). Sweet tastes, of course, are gustatory in nature, whereas people are not entities to be eaten. Nonetheless, the ubiquity of such linguistic expressions suggested to us that the psychological domain of interpersonal niceness would draw from the metaphoric domain of sweet taste experiences. In Study 1 of Meier, Moeller, Riemer-Peltz, and Robinson (2012), pictured individuals stated liking a particular food item and one whose primary taste was sweet (e.g., ice cream), sour (e.g., lemons), bitter (e.g., grapefruit), salty (e.g., beef jerky), or spicy (e.g., curry). Persons expressing liking for a sweet food (but not other foods) were judged to be more agreeable (i.e., nice, friendly) but not more extraverted or neurotic.

The remaining studies focused on individual difference predictions, broadly construed. In Study 2 (Meier et al., 2012), we assessed the personality trait of agreeableness (e.g., *am interested in people, have a soft heart*). Higher levels of the personality trait of agreeableness predicted higher levels of liking for sweet foods, but not sour, bitter, salty, or spicy foods. We believe such results occurred not because agreeable individuals actually eat sweet foods more often, although they might, but rather because their typical thoughts are of a prosocial type (Graziano & Eisenberg, 1997). Such prosocial thoughts, in turn, are likely to recruit metaphoric interests consistent with them. It is for this reason, we suggest, that the food preferences of agreeable individuals gravitate toward sweet foods via a cognitive consistency mechanism (Gawronski & Strack, 2012).

The goals of Study 3 of Meier et al. (2012) were more ambitious. In this study, we dispensed with measuring agreeableness by self-report. Instead, the sole personality variable was the extent to which people liked sweet foods (e.g., candy, honey, maple syrup, sugar). The laboratory session was one in which people could volunteer to help others in concrete ways. The first dependent measure asked individuals whether they would commit to flood cleanup efforts in the Fargo–Moorhead community, which had a historic flood during the time of the study. At the end of the study, we told participants that their extra credit was assured but that an English professor needed volunteers to complete a media survey and deposit it three floors above the psychology department. We surreptitiously monitored which participants completed and deposited this optional survey. We found that greater liking for sweet foods predicted both of these prosocial behaviors. Those who like sweet foods to a greater extent thus appear inclined and compelled to help others in the absence of significant incentives for doing so, an important criterion of prosocial functioning (Dovidio, Piliavin, Schroeder, & Penner, 2006).

Studies 4 and 5 of Meier et al. (2012) were manipulation studies, and we highlight the results of Study 4 here. The personality literature has increasingly suggested that there are personality states as well as personality traits. For example, McNiel and Fleeson (2006) showed that extraverted behaviors have the same correlates—and particularly positive affect—whether manipulated (by instructions to "act extraverted") or measured in trait-related terms. Accordingly, we thought it possible that a sweet taste experience would render individuals psychologically more agreeable. Participants were randomly assigned to taste a sweet (Hershey's Kisses) or less sweet (Altoid's Tangerine Sours) candy before reporting on their personality levels of agreeableness. As hypothesized, participants randomly assigned to the sweet taste condition reported higher levels of agreeableness subsequently. This study, like the previous studies, provides support for the metaphoric mapping of agreeableness to sweetness, but does so in causal terms.

As others do (e.g., Bolger, Davis, & Rafaeli, 2003), we regard tendencies manifest in everyday life as the ultimate phenomenon to be explained by personality assessments. Although not yet published, we can report that sweet taste preferences predict prosocial reactions in everyday life. In a relevant study, we asked individuals to report on their liking of sweet, sour, bitter, salty, and spicy foods. Subsequently, the same individuals completed a 14-day experience-sampling study over the Internet. Among other findings, it was found that sweet-preferring individuals experienced greater positive emotions on days when they engaged in prosocial behaviors (e.g., helped others) but that this same within-subject profile was markedly diminished among those not liking sweet foods. This illustrative finding is displayed in Figure 7.1. The important point here is that the individual difference assessments of Meier et al. (2012) should have wide utility in understanding individual differences in daily social functioning.

Rationality Versus Emotionality and the Head-Heart Metaphor

Human beings are relatively unique animals in that they have capacities to apprehend the world and behave in both rational and emotional manners. Rational thinking is rule-driven, nonemotional, and intellectual (Kahneman, 2003). Emotional thinking is intuitive, impressionistic, and reactive (Epstein, 1994). Neither one is necessarily better. Rational thinking helps one solve important intellectual problems, but not all problems can be solved intellectually (Gigerenzer & Goldstein, 1996). Emotional thinking is reactive and

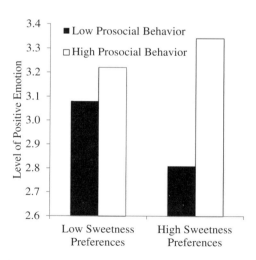

Figure 7.1. Liking of sweet foods as a predictor of relations between daily prosocial behavior and daily levels of positive emotion.

error prone (Epstein, 1994), but there is wisdom to emotional thinking, perhaps most prominently highlighted in the work of Damasio (1994) and in the emotional intelligence literature (Zeidner, Matthews, & Roberts, 2009). Rational and emotional thinking would seem fundamental in understanding differences between people, yet this distinction is not well captured by trait approaches to personality (Epstein, 1994).

Traditional attempts to understand this rational versus emotional distinction rely on brain process considerations. Rational, logical thinking styles are purportedly left hemispheric and emotional, reactive thinking styles are purportedly right hemispheric. It is true that the right hemisphere decodes emotion better (Heller, Schmidtke, Nitschke, Koven, & Miller, 2002), but attempts to link these two processing styles to left versus right hemispheric activity have not resulted in a strong set of findings (Corballis, 1999). Alternatively, rational thinking is said to be cortical, and emotional thinking is said to be subcortical (Miller & Cohen, 2001). Among human beings, however, these are highly interactive systems, and it would be an oversimplification at best to suggest that the rational–emotional distinction can be mapped onto activation in cortical versus subcortical structures (Pessoa, 2009). For example, the frontal cortex plays a much more dominant role in generating emotional responding than can be appreciated on the basis of such brain-based frameworks (e.g., Canli et al., 2001).

As an alternative explanatory framework, we suggest that the classic metaphoric distinction between the head and the heart (mentioned by Plato, Shakespeare, and many others; see Swan, 2009, for a review) may have considerable value. Linguistically, we refer to rational individuals as *having their head on straight* and we encourage smarter decisions with the suggestion to *use your head*. By contrast, we refer to emotional individuals as *having a great heart* and encourage smarter decisions of this emotional type with the suggestion *follow your heart*. Fetterman and Robinson (in press) created a one-item metaphor questionnaire by asking the following question: "Irrespective of what you know about biology, which body part do you more closely associate with yourself?" Participants had to choose the *brain* or the *heart*. The *brain* rather than the *head* was used because the brain, like the heart, is a particular bodily organ.

Across the six studies in which this measure was administered, two striking initial patterns were evident. The first was that a relatively equal number of people indicated that the self was located in the brain versus the heart. For example, in Study 1 of this work, 58 (48%) participants picked the brain organ as the location of the self, whereas 62 (52%) picked the heart organ as the location of the self. Second, and consistent with gender stereotypes depicting women as the more "emotional" sex (Robinson & Clore, 2002), all six studies found that there were significant gender differences. For example, in Study 1, it was found that male participants thought the self was located in the brain to a greater extent (58%), whereas female participants thought that the self was located in the heart to a greater extent (63%).

Of more importance were the outcomes predicted. In Study 1, heart-located individuals reported higher levels of affect intensity, femininity, and liking of intimacy. In Study 2, heart-located individuals reported higher levels of attention to emotion (Salovey, Mayer, Goldman, Turvey, & Palfai, 1995) and greater experiential (Epstein, Pacini, Denes-Raj, & Heier, 1996) thinking styles. In Study 3, heart-located individuals reported greater levels of agreeableness, emotionality, and warmth, along with lower levels of logical thinking. These studies, then, converge on the idea that a novel, metaphor-informed individual difference measure has great potential in understanding the relative emotionality of different individuals, at least in self-reported terms. Two further points can be made. The first is that heart-located individuals reported greater levels of emotionality but also greater levels of agreeableness and warmth. Overall, then, we might wish to have heart-located individuals as interaction partners, despite their apparent tendencies toward greater emotionality. The second important point is that the vast majority of such relations remained significant when controlling for participant sex.

Study 4 examined outcomes that should be higher among "head" people. Those who located the self in the head had higher GPAs and did better on trivia problems. Thus, there is evidence in favor of their greater intellectual functioning. Study 5 sought to pit rational versus emotional thinking tendencies against each other in a common set of social judgment problems. In this study, we administered moral dilemmas such as the classic trolley problem asking people whether they would actively kill one person to save several other individuals. Being an active agent in the death of the one person is a rational solution to the problem, but emotional considerations discourage such an act of calculated killing (Greene & Haidt, 2002). As hypothesized, head-located individuals were more likely to solve these problems in a rational manner, whereas heart-located individuals were more likely to solve these problems in an emotional manner. Thus, a simple one-item metaphor-informed individual difference variable was of substantial value in understanding social decision making.

Studies 1 through 3 had suggested that heart-located individuals are more emotional, but there was an important limitation to these results in that they all relied on trait-reported emotional tendencies. Such trait-reported tendencies often fail to predict how individuals react to emotion-relevant events in daily life (Barrett, Robin, Pietromonaco, & Eyssell, 1998). In Study 6, therefore, we administered a daily diary protocol. We highlight one particular result here. For 14 days in a row, participants reported on the

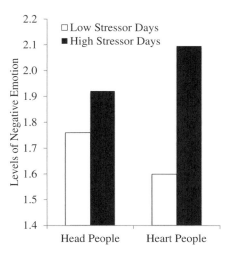

Figure 7.2. Head versus heart self-locations as a predictor of relations between daily stressors and daily levels of negative emotion.

extent to which particular days were low or high in the occurrence of stressful events (e.g., "had a lot of responsibilities"). They also reported on their daily levels of negative emotion because stressors are a common elicitor of such negative emotional reactions (Chamberlain & Zika, 1990). Consistent with the purported emotionality of heart-located individuals, they, relative to head-located individuals, exhibited stronger relations between daily stressors and daily negative emotion levels (see Figure 7.2). We emphasize the importance of these results in understanding the differential functioning of heart-versus head-located individuals in their daily lives.

Individuals are not differentially located in their hearts or heads, but they believe that they are, and such beliefs are predictive of multiple outcomes in a metaphor-consistent direction. Additionally, the results of Studies 1 through 6 suggest that a manipulation of differential attention to the heart versus the head might alter decision making in an emotional versus rational manner. In Study 7 (Fetterman & Robinson, in press), we introduced a cover story stating that our interest was in understanding responding using one's nondominant hand. In a between-subjects manipulation, some individuals were asked to place their dominant index fingers on their temples and others over their hearts, in both cases to eliminate the temptation to use their dominant hands in responding. Thereafter, they completed trivia problems and moral dilemmas. As hypothesized, head-pointing individuals did better on the trivia problems, and heart-pointing individuals were more likely to solve moral dilemmas in an emotion-favoring manner. Altogether, the findings of

Fetterman and Robinson (in press), like those of Meier et al. (2012), establish the relevance of metaphoric considerations in understanding personality processes in a manner that greatly extends the earlier results of Meier and Robinson (2006) and Robinson et al. (2008).

We can also emphasize the broader significance of these findings. We did not ask individuals whether they were rational or emotional but rather assessed such tendencies in an implicit, metaphor-informed manner. Doing so, we suggest, bypasses perennial concerns such as the social desirability of trait responding (Edwards, 1957). Of perhaps more importance, this single-item measure was consequential in its predictive value across many individual differences, such as sex differences, thinking style preferences, emotionality, femininity, emotional intelligence, intellectual performance, that have hitherto been treated as largely separate literatures. From this perspective, the findings of Fetterman and Robinson (in press) possess an integrative predictive value that is largely unprecedented in the personality literature. Finally, of course, these findings point to the value of a metaphor-informed personality psychology, perhaps even more so than any previous investigations.

INVESTIGATING METAPHORIC PROCESSES IN PERSONALITY

Landau et al. (2010) were able to review many studies in favor of a metaphor-enriched view of social psychology. In fact, social psychologists have conducted the vast majority of work in this area, as highlighted in the present volume. Personality psychology has lagged behind, and it is probably safe to say that there are few investigators of metaphor whose primary interest is individual differences. This is true of the present authors as well, despite the fact that we are self-described personality psychologists first and social psychologists second. There are challenges in translating the metaphor representation perspective to personality psychology, unanswered questions, and wisdom that we have only recently acquired. In this section, we consider such issues.

In a sense, every experiment is also a potential individual difference study (Kosslyn et al., 2002) and this is true in the metaphoric realm as well. One only has to examine variations across participants to realize that some individuals exhibit the predicted social cognitive pattern and others do not. In metaphor-related studies of a cognitive type, we have examined the potential moderating role of individual differences in visual imagery (Marks, 1973) on the basis of the idea that imagistic thinkers might be more metaphoric in their thinking (Paivio, 2007). We have yet to find moderating effects of this type. Many of our investigations have focused on affective processes (Meier

& Robinson, 2005). For this reason, we have examined the potential moderating role of attention to emotion (Salovey et al., 1995) in several studies. We have yet to find moderating effects of the latter type either.

Instead, our thinking is that individual differences in metaphoric cognition need to be examined more directly than in past studies—for example, on the basis of appreciation for conceptual metaphors. We are just beginning this line of research and have crafted a relevant questionnaire, which is preliminary at the present time. It will ask individuals to decide whether an initial statement (e.g., related to sad feelings) is better characterized in literal or metaphoric terms. By including a number of such items, we hope to develop a reliable and valid scale of individual differences in metaphoric thinking. We hypothesize that a greater frequency of metaphor-related endorsements may moderate many of the metaphoric effects documented in the social psychology literature (Landau et al., 2010), although this has yet to be determined.

By contrast, the assessment of individual differences of a metaphor-specific type might be served by assessing the extent to which the individual displays preferences consistent with prominent metaphors. For example, Meier et al. (2012) asked individuals to self-report their liking for sweet foods. Those who liked sweet foods to a greater extent were more prosocial in their personalities and behaviors. It therefore appears to be fruitful to extend this line of research in assessing other metaphor-specific individual differences. For example, the color black has been shown to facilitate negative evaluations (Meier, Robinson, & Clore, 2004), speed categorizations involving immoral words (Sherman & Clore, 2009), and result in more aggressive behavior (Frank & Gilovich, 1988). Accordingly, asking individuals whether they prefer the color black or the color white may have untapped value in diverse outcome domains. We are currently developing a number of individual difference measures of this type and expect them to have predictive value in future personality-related studies.

Additionally, it is notable that metaphors for the same concept often seem to possess very different implications. It would therefore be of value to pit different metaphors against each other in the study of individual differences. Fetterman and Robinson (in press) essentially did so by asking individuals whether they thought of the self as a heart- or head-located entity. Individuals differed quite a bit in how the self was conceptualized, and such differences had systematic implications for their personality traits, emotionality, thinking styles, and intellectual performance. This assessment approach can be extended. For example, we would expect individuals viewing love as a *game* to be more promiscuous and less committed to their romantic partners than those viewing love as a *flower* (Lakoff & Johnson, 1999). Similarly, we might expect individuals viewing anger as a *beast* to be less prone to aggression than those viewing anger as *fire* because beast-related metaphors are arguably more pejorative (Gibbs, 1994). In short, there appears to be value in contrasting different metaphors for the same concept by asking individuals to choose which conceptual metaphor seems more apt. There is little doubt, to us at least, that investigations of this type would yield additional insights into the manner in which individual differences function.

Although the focus of the present chapter was on our own investigations, necessarily so because they have been unique in focusing on vertical attention, taste preferences, and head–heart metaphors, individual differences have proven their worth in other investigations in the embodiment literature. Perhaps most straightforwardly, Stefanucci and Proffitt (2009) found that people fearing heights to a greater extent were more prone to overestimating distances downward from a high vertical position. Schnall, Haidt, Clore, and Jordan (2008) found that disgust manipulations (e.g., completing the study in a filthy room) led to harsher moral judgments, particularly among individuals higher in sensitivity to their own bodily sensations. More recently, Bargh and Shalev (2012) found that especially lonely individuals seek (Study 1) and benefit (e.g., Study 3) from physical warmth sensations. Whether all such individual difference findings converge is arguable because they seem to be focusing on different mechanisms and processes. Regardless, findings from our investigations converge with these other investigations in highlighting the importance of individual differences in understanding how and why metaphor-consistent manipulations work.

Conceptual metaphors are likely to have a bodily basis (Tolaas, 1991). This bodily basis may yield other directions for individual differences research. For example, what is important is big according to prominent metaphors (Lakoff & Johnson, 1999). For this reason, tall, big people may come to have a greater sense of social potency and others may treat them with greater respect than short, small people. White is good and black is bad according to prominent metaphors (Meier & Robinson, 2005). Such considerations may help explain why darker skinned individuals are the frequent target of prejudice and discrimination. There are multiple other ways in which bodies differ, such as their strength, perceptual acuity, and age, that also may prove explanatory in the individual difference realm. Concretely so, Bhalla and Proffitt (1999) found that stronger, more fit individuals were less likely to overestimate the slant of a hill (Study 3) and that older individuals (Study 4) were more likely to overestimate the slant of especially steep hills. Although their explanation was based on bodily resources and capacities, their findings encourage a broader focus on how differences between bodies, perhaps through the locus of the metaphor representation perspective, may influence judgment and decision making in ways that have yet to be determined.

CONCLUSION

We believe that the metaphor representation perspective (Lakoff & Johnson, 1980, 1999) can provide many insights into personality functioning that a trait self-report perspective cannot. In this sense, we echo earlier calls for a multimethod assessment of personality (Allport, 1937; Bruner, 1951; McClelland, 1951), but we do so in a novel and metaphor-informed manner. In the present chapter, we focused primarily on the results of four investigations, but also considered the interface of personality and social psychology, the optimal manner in which personality processes of a metaphoric type can be assessed, and the limitations of standard assessment approaches in personality psychology. In the latter case, for example, there are significant concerns that trait-outcome relations may often reflect tautologies, such as when (trait) self-reported negative affect predicts (state) self-reported negative affect (Cervone, 1999). A metaphoric view of personality processes can avoid such tautological relations. In addition, it can provide potential insights into how a history of bodily experiences (e.g., those linking low energy levels to lower vertical positions, as in fatigued states or sleep) are drawn on in conceptualizing one's personality tendencies.

Moreover, individual difference investigations can point to novel social cognitive manipulations. Studies 2 and 3 of Meier et al. (2012) revealed that individuals who liked sweet foods to a greater extent were more prosocial in nature. Such results led to manipulation studies in which participants savored either a sweet or nonsweet food, and this manipulation caused individuals to be more prosocial. It is doubtful whether results of this type would have been found as quickly were it not for the individual difference findings. Similarly, the multiple individual difference findings of Fetterman and Robinson (in press) led to a manipulation study in which individuals pointed to their heads or hearts before completing trivia problems and moral dilemmas. Were it not for the earlier individual difference findings, Study 7 of this work would not have been conducted. In sum, a personality-process perspective of conceptual metaphor can result in novel manipulations and findings that might not be discovered otherwise.

Of final importance, we emphasize the value of individual difference studies for two additional reasons. First, there are always concerns as to whether social cognitive manipulation effects (perhaps excepting reaction time effects) are due to demand characteristics. An individual difference perspective can circumvent such concerns because relevant relations are established in the absence of potentially more transparent priming manipulations (Robinson & Neighbors, 2006). Second, although individual difference results are ambiguous with respect to cause and effect (McNiel & Fleeson,

2006), such studies are beneficial in establishing that a relevant relationship is actually consequential to the manner in which individuals live their lives (Robinson & Compton, 2008). For such reasons, we advocate future studies of the metaphor representation perspective in which individual differences are accorded a central role.

REFERENCES

Allport, G. W. (1937). *Personality: A psychological interpretation*. Oxford, England: Holt.

Bargh, J. A., & Shalev, I. (2012). The substitutability of physical and social warmth in daily life. *Emotion, 12*, 154–162. doi:10.1037/a0023527

Barrett, L. F., Robin, L., Pietromonaco, P. R., & Eyssell, K. M. (1998). Are women the "more emotional" sex? Evidence from emotional experiences in social context. *Cognition and Emotion, 12*, 555–578. doi:10.1080/026999398379565

Bhalla, M., & Proffitt, D. R. (1999). Visual-motor recalibration in geographical slant perception. *Journal of Experimental Psychology: Human Perception and Performance, 25*, 1076–1096. doi:10.1037/0096-1523.25.4.1076

Bolger, N., Davis, A., & Rafaeli, E. (2003). Diary methods: Capturing life as it is lived. *Annual Review of Psychology, 54*, 579–616. doi:10.1146/annurev.psych.54.101601.145030

Bruner, J. S. (1951). Personality dynamics and the process of perceiving. In R. R. Blake & G. V. Ramsey (Eds.), *Perception: An approach to personality* (pp. 121–147). New York, NY: Ronald Press. doi:10.1037/11505-005

Canli, T., Zhao, Z., Desmond, J. E., Kang, E., Gross, J., & Gabrieli, J. D. E. (2001). An fMRI study of personality influences on brain reactivity to emotional stimuli. *Behavioral Neuroscience, 115*, 33–42. doi:10.1037/0735-7044.115.1.33

Cervone, D. (1999). Bottom-up explanation in personality psychology: The case of cross-situational coherence. In D. Cervone & Y. Shoda (Eds.), *The coherence of personality: Social-cognitive bases of consistency, variability, and organization* (pp. 303–341). New York, NY: Guilford Press.

Chamberlain, K., & Zika, S. (1990). The minor events approach to stress: Support for the use of daily hassles. *British Journal of Psychology, 81*, 469–481. doi:10.1111/j.2044-8295.1990.tb02373.x

Corballis, M. C. (1999). Are we in our right minds? In S. D. Sala (Ed.), *Mind myths: Exploring popular assumptions about the mind and the brain* (pp. 25–41). New York, NY: Wiley.

Damasio, A. R. (1994). *Descartes' error: Emotion, reason and the human brain*. New York, NY: Grosset/Putnam.

Dovidio, J. F., Piliavin, J. A., Schroeder, D. A., & Penner, L. A. (2006). *The social psychology of prosocial behavior*. Mahwah, NJ: Erlbaum.

Edwards, A. L. (1957). *The social desirability variable in personality assessment and research.* Ft. Worth, TX: Dryden Press.

Epstein, S. (1994). Integration of the cognitive and the psychodynamic unconscious. *American Psychologist, 49,* 709–724. doi:10.1037/0003-066X.49.8.709

Epstein, S., Pacini, R., Denes-Raj, V., & Heier, H. (1996). Individual differences in intuitive-experiential and analytical-rational thinking styles. *Journal of Personality and Social Psychology, 71,* 390–405. doi:10.1037/0022-3514.71.2.390

Fetterman, A. K. & Robinson, M. D. (in press). Do you use your head or follow your heart? Self-location predicts personality, emotion, decision making, and performance. *Journal of Personality and Social Psychology.*

Fiske, S. T. (1993). Controlling other people: The impact of power on stereotyping. *American Psychologist, 48,* 621–628. doi:10.1037/0003-066X.48.6.621

Frank, M. G., & Gilovich, T. (1988). The dark side of self- and social perception: Black uniforms and aggression in professional sports. *Journal of Personality and Social Psychology, 54,* 74–85. doi:10.1037/0022-3514.54.1.74

Gawronski, B., & Strack, F. (2012). *Cognitive consistency: A fundamental principle in social cognition.* New York, NY: Guilford Press.

Gibbs, R. W., Jr. (1994). *The poetics of mind: Figurative thought, language, and understanding.* New York, NY: Cambridge University Press.

Gigerenzer, G., & Goldstein, D. G. (1996). Reasoning the fast and frugal way: Models of bounded rationality. *Psychological Review, 103,* 650–669. doi:10.1037/0033-295X.103.4.650

Graziano, W. G., & Eisenberg, N. (1997). Agreeableness: A dimension of personality. In R. Hogan, J. A. Johnson, & S. R. Briggs (Eds.), *Handbook of personality psychology* (pp. 795–824). San Diego, CA: Academic Press. doi:10.1016/B978-012134645-4/50031-7

Greene, J., & Haidt, J. (2002). How (and where) does moral judgment work? *Trends in Cognitive Sciences, 6,* 517–523. doi:10.1016/S1364-6613(02)02011-9

Heller, W., Schmidtke, J. I., Nitschke, J. B., Koven, N. S., & Miller, G. A. (2002). States, traits, and symptoms: Investigating the neural correlates of emotion, personality, and psychopathology. In D. Cervone & W. Mischel (Eds.), *Advances in personality science* (pp. 106–126). New York, NY: Guilford Press.

IJzerman, H., & Semin, G. R. (2009). The thermometer of social relations: Mapping social proximity on temperature. *Psychological Science, 20,* 1214–1220. doi:10.1111/j.1467-9280.2009.02434.x

Kahneman, D. (2003). A perspective on judgment and choice: Mapping bounded rationality. *American Psychologist, 58,* 697–720. doi:10.1037/0003-066X.58.9.697

Kenrick, D. T., & Funder, D. C. (1988). Profiting from controversy: Lessons from the person-situation debate. *American Psychologist, 43,* 23–34. doi:10.1037/0003-066X.43.1.23

Kosslyn, S. M., Cacioppo, J. T., Davidson, R. J., Hugdahl, K., Lovallo, W. R., Spiegel, D., & Rose, R. (2002). Bridging psychology and biology: The analysis of individuals in groups. *American Psychologist, 57,* 341–351. doi:10.1037/0003-066X.57.5.341

Lakoff, G., & Johnson, M. (1980). *Metaphors we live by.* Chicago, IL: University of Chicago Press.

Lakoff, G., & Johnson, M. (1999). *Philosophy in the flesh.* Chicago, IL: University of Chicago Press.

Landau, M. J., Meier, B. P., & Keefer, L. A. (2010). A metaphor-enriched social cognition. *Psychological Bulletin, 136,* 1045–1067. doi:10.1037/a0020970

MacLeod, C., Koster, E. H. W., & Fox, E. (2009). Whither cognitive bias modification research? Commentary on the special section articles. *Journal of Abnormal Psychology, 118,* 89–99. doi:10.1037/a0014878

Marks, D. F. (1973). Visual imagery differences in the recall of pictures. *British Journal of Psychology, 64,* 17–24. doi:10.1111/j.2044-8295.1973.tb01322.x

McClelland, D. C. (1951). *Personality.* New York, NY: William Sloane Association. doi:10.1037/10790-000

McNiel, J. M., & Fleeson, W. (2006). The causal effects of extraversion on positive affect and neuroticism on negative affect: Manipulating state extraversion and state neuroticism in an experimental approach. *Journal of Research in Personality, 40,* 529–550. doi:10.1016/j.jrp.2005.05.003

Meier, B. P., Hauser, D. J., Robinson, M. D., Friesen, C. K., & Schjeldahl, K. (2007). What's "up" with God? Vertical space as a representation of the divine. *Journal of Personality and Social Psychology, 93,* 699–710. doi:10.1037/0022-3514.93.5.699

Meier, B. P., Moeller, S. K., Riemer-Peltz, M., & Robinson, M. D. (2012). Sweet taste preferences and experiences predict prosocial inferences, personalities, and behaviors. *Journal of Personality and Social Psychology, 102,* 163–174. doi:10.1037/a0025253

Meier, B. P., & Robinson, M. D. (2004). Why the sunny side is up: Associations between affect and vertical position. *Psychological Science, 15,* 243–247. doi:10.1111/j.0956-7976.2004.00659.x

Meier, B. P., & Robinson, M. D. (2005). The metaphorical representation of affect. *Metaphor and Symbol, 20,* 239–257. doi:10.1207/s15327868ms2004_1

Meier, B. P., & Robinson, M. D. (2006). Does "feeling down" mean seeing down? Depressive symptoms and vertical selective attention. *Journal of Research in Personality, 40,* 451–461. doi:10.1016/j.jrp.2005.03.001

Meier, B. P., Robinson, M. D., & Clore, G. L. (2004). Why good guys wear white: Automatic inferences about stimulus valence based on brightness. *Psychological Science, 15,* 82–87. doi:10.1111/j.0963-7214.2004.01502002.x

Miller, E. K., & Cohen, J. D. (2001). An integrative theory of prefrontal cortex function. *Annual Review of Neuroscience, 24,* 167–202. doi:10.1146/annurev.neuro.24.1.167

Mischel, W. (1968). *Personality and assessment.* Hoboken, NJ: Wiley.

Mischel, W. (2009). From *Personality and Assessment* (1968) to personality science, 2009. *Journal of Research in Personality, 43,* 282–290. doi:10.1016/j.jrp.2008.12.037

Moskowitz, D. S. (2010). Quarrelsomeness in daily life. *Journal of Personality, 78,* 39–66. doi:10.1111/j.1467-6494.2009.00608.x

Ozer, D. J., & Benet-Martinez, V. (2006). Personality and the prediction of consequential outcomes. *Annual Review of Psychology, 57,* 401–421. doi:10.1146/annurev.psych.57.102904.190127

Paivio, A. (2007). *Mind and its evolution: A dual coding theoretical approach.* Mahwah, NJ: Erlbaum.

Pessoa, L. (2009). How do emotion and motivation direct executive control? *Trends in Cognitive Sciences, 13,* 160–166. doi:10.1016/j.tics.2009.01.006

Robinson, M. D., & Clore, G. L. (2002). Belief and feeling: Evidence for an accessibility model of emotional self-report. *Psychological Bulletin, 128,* 934–960. doi:10.1037/0033-2909.128.6.934

Robinson, M. D., & Compton, R. J. (2008). The happy mind in action: The cognitive basis of subjective well-being. In M. Eid & R. J. Larsen (Eds.), *The science of subjective well-being* (pp. 220–238). New York, NY: Guilford Press.

Robinson, M. D., & Gordon, K. H. (2011). Personality dynamics: Insights from the personality and social cognitive literature. *Journal of Personality Assessment, 93,* 161–176. doi:10.1080/00223891.2010.542534

Robinson, M. D., & Neighbors, C. (2006). Catching the mind in action: Implicit methods in personality research and assessment. In M. Eid & E. Diener (Eds.), *Handbook of multimethod measurement in psychology* (pp. 115–125). Washington, DC: American Psychological Association. doi:10.1037/11383-009

Robinson, M. D., Zabelina, D. L., Ode, S., & Moeller, S. K. (2008). The vertical nature of dominance-submission: Individual differences in vertical attention. *Journal of Research in Personality, 42,* 933–948. doi:10.1016/j.jrp.2007.12.002

Ross, L., & Nisbett, R. E. (1991). *The person and the situation: Perspectives of social psychology.* New York, NY: McGraw-Hill.

Salovey, P., Mayer, J. D., Goldman, S. L., Turvey, C., & Palfai, T. P. (1995). Emotional attention, clarity, and repair: Exploring emotional intelligence using the Trait Meta-Mood Scale. In J. W. Pennebaker (Ed.), *Emotion, disclosure, and health* (pp. 125–154). Washington, DC: American Psychological Association. doi:10.1037/10182-006

Schnall, S., Haidt, J., Clore, G. L., & Jordan, A. H. (2008). Disgust as embodied moral judgment. *Personality and Social Psychology Bulletin, 34,* 1096–1109. doi:10.1177/0146167208317771

Schubert, T. W. (2005). Your highness: Vertical positions as perceptual symbols of power. *Journal of Personality and Social Psychology, 89,* 1–21. doi:10.1037/0022-3514.89.1.1

Schwartz, B. (1981). *Vertical classification: A study in structuralism and the sociology of knowledge*. Chicago, IL: The University of Chicago Press.

Searle, J. (1998). *Mind, language and society: Philosophy in the real world*. New York, NY: Basic Books.

Segal, Z. V., & Swallow, S. R. (1994). Cognitive assessment of unipolar depression: Measuring products, processes and structures. *Behaviour Research and Therapy, 32*, 147–158. doi:10.1016/0005-7967(94)90097-3

Sherman, G. D., & Clore, G. L. (2009). The color of sin: White and black are perceptual symbols of moral purity and pollution. *Psychological Science, 20*, 1019–1025. doi:10.1111/j.1467-9280.2009.02403.x

Stefanucci, J. K., & Proffitt, D. R. (2009). The roles of altitude and fear in the perception of height. *Journal of Experimental Psychology: Human Perception and Performance, 35*, 424–438. doi:10.1037/a0013894

Swan, T. (2009). Metaphors of body and mind in the history of English. *English Studies, 90*, 460–475. doi:10.1080/00138380902796292

Tolaas, J. (1991). Notes on the origin of some spatialization metaphors. *Metaphor & Symbolic Activity, 6*, 203–218. doi:10.1207/s15327868ms0603_4

Wiggins, J. S., Trapnell, P., & Phillips, N. (1988). Psychometric and geometric characteristics of the Revised Interpersonal Adjective Scale (IAS-R). *Multivariate Behavioral Research, 23*, 517–530. doi:10.1207/s15327906mbr2304_8

Wilkowski, B. M., Meier, B. P., Robinson, M. D., Carter, M. S., & Feltman, R. (2009). "Hot-headed" is more than an expression: The embodied representation of anger in terms of heat. *Emotion, 9*, 464–477. doi:10.1037/a0015764

Williams, L. E., Huang, J. Y., & Bargh, J. A. (2009). The scaffolded mind: Higher mental processes are grounded in early experience of the physical world. *European Journal of Social Psychology, 39*, 1257–1267. doi:10.1002/ejsp.665

Zeidner, M., Matthews, G., & Roberts, R. D. (2009). *What we know about emotional intelligence: How it affects learning, work, relationships, and our mental health*. Cambridge, MA: MIT Press.

8

THE ROLE OF METAPHORS IN INTERGROUP RELATIONS

ANNE MAASS, CATERINA SUITNER, AND LUCIANO ARCURI

Do metaphors play a role in intergroup relations? Are they used to maintain a positive image of the ingroup and to denigrate the outgroup? Do they shape our stereotypes and inform our decisions and behaviors? We believe they do, starting from the very definition of *stereotype*. When Lippmann (1922) proposed his seminal concept of a social category, he decided to synthesize this complex concept by way of a metaphoric image, that of a stereotype, that is, a mold or a stamp. The image effectively integrates two important features of social categories—namely, that they are represented in the mind of people as a rigid container and that they denote many exemplars with the same characteristics. The term *stereotype* derives from the combination of two Greek words, *stereos*, which means "solid," and *typos*, which means "a model." Stereotype therefore refers to a solid model, like the metal plate used to print pages in the old printing houses. According to Miller (1982),

http://dx.doi.org/10.1037/14278-008
The Power of Metaphor: Examining Its Influence on Social Life, M. J. Landau, M. D. Robinson, and
B. P. Meier (Editors)

this term underlines two characteristics: rigidity and replication of sameness. When applied to groups of people, stereotypes act as rigid boundaries, within which the same characteristics are applied to all members of the group. The metaphoric use of the term *stereotype* illustrates the importance of this figure of speech in social cognition. In line with the historical origin of the word, stereotypes are indeed often expressed by means of metaphors.

In the context of social cognition, metaphors represent a meaningful interface between the categorical knowledge that is linguistically expressed by a stereotype and the vividness of the emotive and sensory aspects of perceptual experience. Among the fuzzy and flexible linguistic tools used to describe the world, the metaphor is the one that best allows people to express multiple characteristics in a concise and effective way, suggesting the subset of features associated with the stereotype.

In this chapter, we discuss what functions metaphors fulfill and what aspects of intergroup relations are likely to be affected. We first illustrate the prevalence and origins of intergroup metaphors and reflect about the reasons why they are so widely used. In the subsequent parts of this chapter, we argue that metaphors are potentially relevant at different levels—the individual, the interpersonal, and the broader societal level. Starting from the individual level, we first show that metaphors affect all stages of social cognition as they guide categorization, enhance the perception of groups as homogenous entities, and facilitate inferences of stereotype-congruent information. At the interpersonal level, metaphors are often used strategically to justify the status quo, such as when outgroup members are dehumanized and when unpleasant aspects of reality (e.g., suffering caused by war) are downplayed. At the broadest, societal level, metaphors have tangible effects on how social problems are framed and resolved. In the final section of this chapter, we discuss open questions and propose new avenues for the small but growing research area on metaphors in intergroup relations.

Throughout this chapter, we provide empirical evidence concerning either *embodied metaphors* that are closely linked to bodily experiences (such as vertical position or height, e.g., *upper class*) or classical *resemblance metaphors* (e.g., *lawyers are sharks*). Although these two types of metaphors may well be processed differently, for the aims of this chapter, we treat the two as largely interchangeable. Also, we focus mainly on conventionalized metaphors with meaning that is socially shared; we largely ignore novel metaphors that are sophisticated but comparably rare communication devices, estimated to constitute only about 5% of all metaphors (Steen, 2011). According to Bowdle and Gentner's (2005) *career of metaphor hypothesis*, compared with novel metaphors, socially shared conventional metaphors are processed more easily (no comparison is needed) and faster and are automatically more available to thought, such that they are as familiar and accessible as category names. These characteristics make conventional metaphors a particularly relevant tool in intergroup discourse.

METAPHORS IN INTERGROUP RELATIONS

Metaphors are here defined as figures of speech in which relatively concrete, tangible concepts (referred to as *source concepts*) are used to represent more abstract concepts (referred to as *target concepts*). Such metaphors generally associate a concrete object, image, or event to a social category that typically (but not exclusively) occurs in the role of target domain. Importantly, target and source concepts generally refer to different categories of stimuli that have nothing literally to do with each other.

Types of Intergroup Metaphors

There is an almost unlimited variety of metaphoric labels applied to social groups, ranging from basic spatial metaphors (*down* for clinically depressed and *out of their mind* for mentally ill), references to the animal world (*beast* for criminal offenders, *ape* for African American, or *loan shark* for Jew) and contamination (*pestilence* for immigration; see O'Brien, 2003), and references to the presumed social function of the category, as in *anchor baby*, a metaphor applied to children of noncitizens born in the United States, presumably facilitating immigration.

However, not all figurative descriptions of outgroups are metaphors in a strict sense—that is, comparisons to literally unrelated concepts. At times, outgroups are referred to by features that are directly linked to the group, such as historical events or food preferences. Such expressions may best be subsumed under the label *metonym*—a figure of speech in which a specific exemplar or attribute of an object comes to represent the entire object (e.g., *Hollywood* becomes a metonym for the American film industry[1]). For instance, outgroups are frequently labeled by reference to historical events involving that group, as illustrated by the English term *Christ killer* used to refer to Jews (see Durante, Volpato, & Fiske, 2010, for an analysis of the depictions of Jews during fascism) or by the Italian expression *l'ultimo giapponese* (the last Japanese) used to describe a person or group fighting a losing battle.[2]

---

[1]There is considerable debate about the appropriateness of distinguishing metaphor and metonymy (see Barnden, 2010, for a recent review of the controversy). Although debatable and fuzzy, the distinction may be conceptually useful in the context of intergroup relations because metonyms are generally defined by greater contiguity between source and target domain.
[2]The metaphor derives from the historical fact that small groups of Japanese soldiers held out in remote areas because they were entirely unaware that the Second World War had ended.

Interestingly, some historically based intergroup metonyms become entirely conventionalized and survive for centuries even when the event that originally gave rise to their use is no longer part of the collective memory. For instance, the common Italian metaphor *fare il portoghese* (in English: *to play the Portuguese*), which stands for a dishonest person trying to receive a service without paying, derives from an event that took place in Rome during the 18th century, when the Portuguese ambassador organized a theatre play that was offered for free to all Portuguese citizens of Rome. That night many natives of Rome entered the theatre claiming to be Portuguese. Ironically, it was the Romans, rather than the Portuguese, who cheated.[3] Another example of conventionalized metaphors is the terms *right wing* versus *left wing*, which originated from a practical matter of spatial organization during the French Revolution. It was in 1789 when the king of France called the Estates General, and the liberal deputies of the Third Estate sat to the left of the president, whereas the nobility sat to the right side. Since then, *right wing* has become a synonym for conservative political attitudes and *left wing* for liberalism. The step from the distribution of bodies in space to a metaphoric representation of political ideology was short, and *la gauche et la droite* are now much more than mere spatial coordinates. Although anchored in specific historical events, these metaphors (*fare il portoghese* and *right wing–left wing*) are used frequently without speakers and listeners being aware of their derivation, which illustrates that they are conventionalized to the point of losing their metaphoric origins.

Metonyms are particularly common in disparaging references to social groups, where the entire category is identified with some physical feature (e.g., *skinhead* for members of the hard mod movement in the United Kingdom or *redneck* for the rural population of the United States), food habit (*kraut* for German or *macaroni* for Italians), typical name (*Guido* for Italians), characteristic behavior (*holy roller* for ritualistic protestants in the United States), or phonetic feature of native language (*ching chong* for Americans of Chinese descent).

An important question is whether there are source concepts that are intrinsically suited to become metaphors or metonyms, in which case one would expect a considerable overlap across cultures and languages. It is our impression that metonymic stereotypes tend to be more culturally specific, whereas metaphoric stereotypes are more likely to be shared across cultures, presumably because they are grounded in universal features of bodily experience and worldly knowledge. In line with this idea, cross-cultural and

---

[3]This example illustrates that social groups (in this case, nationality) may also occur in the role of source concept. In the current example, the Portuguese metaphorically represent the concept of dishonesty or cheating. Occasionally social categories may represent both source and target concepts, for example, "this surgeon is a butcher."

cross-linguistic studies generally show a certain degree of overlap, especially for those metaphors that are strongly anchored in spatial or bodily experiences (Emanatian, 1995; Yu, 1995) or that are linked to shared experiences with nature. An English–Persian comparison study conducted by Talebinejad and Dastjerdi (2005) found a total or partial overlap in meaning for about three fourths of the 44 animal metaphors included in the study but different meanings in the remaining fourth. For instance, *chicken* stands for fear in English but for stupidity in Italian, *turkey* refers to a stupid person in English but to a hypocrite in Persian, and *owl* represents wisdom in most European languages[4] but is associated with death in some African cultures and considered a bad omen in the Middle East. Also, the core message of fairy tales is often quite similar across cultures, yet they may involve different (local) animals to represent the same human characteristics (e.g., fear, cleverness, pride; see Satta, 2011). As these examples illustrate, there is some variation in the specific source–target pairing, yet the very principle that human groups or human traits are represented by metaphors such as animals seems universal. We argue here that, even where the specific content varies across language communities, the very mechanism and the cognitive consequences of metaphors are shared across cultures. Given the greater cultural–historical ubiquity of metaphors (compared with metonyms), in this chapter we mainly focus on metaphoric stereotypes.

Functions of Metaphors in Social Discourse

The main question arising is, what are social metaphors for? *Conceptual metaphor theory* (Lakoff & Johnson, 1980) states that metaphors are a tool of thought rather than of language and that they play a crucial role in concept understanding and knowledge building. Indeed, they are often referred to as *conceptual metaphors* to distinguish them from the linguistic expressions that are their representing instances (see Chapters 1 and 2, this volume). To exemplify this concept, the linguistic expression "the project gets on the road" or "has a head start" refers to a conceptual metaphor that explains the *project* (the target) in terms of a *journey* (the source). Importantly, this cognitive account of metaphors implies that, like schemas (Allbritton, 1995), metaphors are used automatically and without effort (Lakoff, 1993). In the social realm, they therefore fulfill similar functions and respond to similar cognitive needs as stereotypes.

---

[4]The origin of this metaphor is generally attributed to the fact that the owl was the symbol of Athena, the goddess of wisdom, in ancient Greece, although the association between owl and wisdom may date back to earlier times.

But why would metaphors be so common in intergroup discourse? We argue that metaphors are particularly powerful social tools because they allow generalizations across all members of a given category while communicating concrete and vivid images. This unique combination of abstraction and concreteness derives from the paradox of metaphor raised by Gibbs (2008), who underlined the twofold nature of metaphors. On one hand, metaphors create a new and creative vision of a given target and "allows us to transcend the mundane" (p. 5). On the other hand, metaphors are deeply rooted in bodily experience and worldly knowledge and hence offer a more concrete vehicle to represent the target. Therefore, metaphor is concrete and abstract at the same time, and this paradox is particularly relevant for social metaphors. Take, for example, the metaphor that is widely endorsed in Italy according to which Chinese people are *ants*. The metaphor is abstract because it captures the generalizability of the stereotype that Chinese are many, crowded, and hardworking. At the same time, it is concrete because the content of the stereotype is easily represented with a concrete image (e.g., the anthill). This twofold nature of the metaphor is particularly important from a social point of view because it promotes a social categorization that is abstract and general, able to include a wide number of instances, but at the same time it also is graspable and catchy. We therefore propose here that metaphors are a powerful social tool for facilitating categorization, creating and maintaining stereotypes, and justifying the existing social system.

To explain the capacity of metaphors to facilitate social categorization and stereotypic inferences, we can refer to a useful conceptual scheme suggested by Ortony (1975) that underlines three crucial qualities of metaphors: compactness, inexpressibility, and vividness. *Compactness* refers to the capacity to communicate multiple characteristics in a single expression that would otherwise require a long list of properties. For instance, the metaphor *shark* implies, in a single word, a whole chunk of features such as *aggressive*, *vicious*, *cruel*, *unscrupulous*, *merciless*, and *tenacious*. Thus, metaphors are quick, concise, and effective communication devices. The second attribute acknowledged by Ortony is the metaphor's capacity to express the *inexpressible*. Metaphors step in where literal language fails. Whereas some metaphors can be translated into literal equivalents (e.g., *rearranging the deckchairs on the Titanic* may be translated into *performing futile actions in times of crisis*), others offer a unique possibility to give shape to the unnameable. For instance, it is difficult to talk about time without reference to space and, within the confines of a given language, some metaphors (e.g., *the last Japanese)* can only be translated into yet another metaphor (*fighting a lost battle*).

Finally, according to Ortony (1975), the metaphor lies much closer to perceived experience than a nonmetaphoric equivalent. Thanks to its *vividness*, the metaphor enables the communication of ideas with the richness of details, much less likely to come about in the normal course of events. In sum, metaphors represent stronger labels able to broaden the boundaries of the category, narrow its characteristics, and communicate these characteristics in an efficient and vivid manner.

In the subsequent parts of the chapter, we analyze at which points metaphors come into play and what effects they may exert on the intraindividual level, how they are used in interpersonal discourse, and how they may affect policy decisions at a broader societal level.

SOCIAL COGNITIVE CONSEQUENCES OF METAPHORIC LANGUAGE

Looking first at the intraindividual level, metaphors have been shown to affect different stages of social cognition, namely, initial categorization, perceived homogeneity, and stereotyping.

Social Categorization

Many natural and social phenomena are continuous, such as time, color, and race, yet they are mentally and linguistically represented as discrete categories, such as *spring* and *summer, blue* and *green,* and *Black* and *White.* Language is a discrete symbol system through which we convey what is usually some kind of continuum (see Labov, 1973). However, this system is incapable of literally capturing every conceivable aspect of an object, event, or experience that one might wish to describe. Ortony (1975) suggested that metaphors make up for this deficiency.

According to Gentner and Wolff (1997), the processing of metaphors occurs mainly by structural alignment. According to this model, the elaboration and understanding of a metaphor implies the matching of the similar features of the source and the target (i.e., alignment). The features that have been filtered in the initial phase according to context and *systematicity* (i.e., maximizing the commonalities between source and target) are then structurally matched in source and target, completing the inference process and the mapping procedure. Once a metaphor has completed its career and is widely socially shared, familiar, and conventionalized, it can be processed by an abstraction-driven elaboration, in which the source domain works as an abstract representation whose features are projected into the target.

This model accounts for several properties of metaphors. Particularly important for social cognition is the role that metaphors play in categorization. If metaphors are "categorical, class-inclusion assertions" as suggested by Glucksberg (2008, p. 69), then they should facilitate the inclusion of stimuli in a given category. In line with this idea, Jones and Estes (2005) showed that participants primed with a metaphor are more likely to include a target word in the class promoted by the metaphor. For example, being primed by *that desk is a junkyard* increases the likelihood that *desks* are included in the class *junkyards* compared with a literal (e.g., *that desk is from a junkyard*) or no prime. Similarly, after being primed by the metaphor *the argument is war*, participants included the target *argument* in the class of *war* more easily than after being primed by the literal *that argument started a war*. If we apply this finding to social targets, the expected effect is that metaphors facilitate the categorization of a target person with respect to a social group and, as a consequence, also the attribution to stereotypical characteristics (an issue we come back to in the next section).

The role of metaphors in the categorization of groups has been investigated by several scholars who have mainly focused on spatial metaphors and, in particular, on the horizontal and the vertical position in space. Many social concepts (e.g., good vs. bad, happy vs. sad, god vs. devil) map onto the vertical space, but the one that is most relevant to intergroup relations is clearly the concept of power. This metaphor is evident in common references to social status such as the *upper class, moving up the social latter,* or *your highness.* Schubert (2005) found that the vertical metaphor of power influences the elaboration of social information and facilitates social categorization. In particular (Schubert, 2005, Experiment 2), social categorization of targets as more powerful (or as less powerful) was facilitated when the target word occurred in the metaphor-coherent position, with the powerful group occupying a spatially higher and the powerless a lower position in the visual field. This confirms that the *power = up* metaphor is active even when not expressed linguistically and that it affects categorization even if not directly relevant to the task at hand. Importantly, these facilitation effects occur more strongly when a comparative framework (e.g., powerful vs. powerless) is activated (Lakens, Semin, & Foroni, 2011), suggesting that spatial metaphors are, at least in part, based on contrasts rather than on absolute positions.

In these studies, the mapping of power onto the vertical space was grounded in the perceivers' physical experience with space (e.g., children experience that adults who tower over them tend to be more powerful). Quite different is the case of horizontal mapping of political orientation that has recently been investigated by Farias, Garrido, and Semin (2013). As explained at the beginning of this chapter, the terms *right wing* and *left wing* derive from a particular historical incident, but they have become a conventional metaphor for political orientation in many languages. In one of Farias et al.'s (2013) studies (Experiment 3), participants were asked to categorize photos of well-known politicians as either socialist or conservative (without any mention of the spatial terms *left wing* or *right wing*). In line with conceptual metaphor theory, they were faster in classifying group members when the photo appeared in the metaphor-consistent position (socialists to the left and conservatives to the right). Similarly, van Elk, van Schie, and Bekkering (2010) found faster reactions to party acronyms when either the response key (Experiments 1–3) or the spatial position on the screen (Experiment 4) matched the political orientation of the party. Thus, Farias et al.'s and van Elk et al.'s studies concur that spatial metaphors associated with political parties guide the processing of information regarding these parties and their members, facilitating recognition in spatially congruent positions and interfering with recognition in incongruent positions.

Together, the studies on vertical and horizontal asymmetries reported here suggest that metaphors do indeed facilitate (or hamper) processing by creating metaphoric categories that make the shared characteristics of source and target more salient (Gentner & Wolff, 1997). Depending on whether exemplars occur in a metaphor-congruent or incongruent position, their categorization is facilitated or not. Interestingly, such metaphor-driven facilitation in categorization was found both for metaphors that are grounded in bodily experiences (power = up) and for those that are purely language-driven (left wing vs. right wing).

Perception of Group Homogeneity

If metaphors are structural mappings that promote the comparisons and selection of the elements that a source and a target have in common, they should also emphasize the similarity of intraclass targets and the differences of interclass targets by virtue of the filtering process of relevant features in the structural representation. This effect has been observed for literal category labels, with evidence showing that they are able to shape the perception of the described objects. For example, Roberson, Davidoff, Davies, and Shapiro (2005) showed that the name of a color can influence its evaluation, with visual stimuli that belong to the same linguistic category being judged as more similar compared with stimuli that belong to different categories (irrespective of their actual similarity).

In the case of social membership, categorization is known to produce similar effects, with members of the same group being perceived as more similar than members of different groups, even when the targets are randomly assigned to the groups in a minimal group paradigm (Billig & Tajfel, 1973). Interestingly, the degree to which exemplars are seen as similar depends on the strength of the category label under which they are subsumed, as recently demonstrated by Foroni and Rothbart (2011). Participants viewed silhouettes of women differing in weight (from very slim to greatly overweight) and asked to judge the similarity of pairs of target women. Not only were similarity judgments greater when the two targets were subsumed under the same label, but similarity judgments increased as a function of the strength of the verbal label. For instance, the same two body shapes were perceived as more similar when subsumed under the label *anorexic* rather than *below average*.

Applying this same principle, one may hypothesize that metaphors ("this lawyer is a *shark*"), compared with semantically similar literal descriptions ("this lawyer is *merciless*"), will increase the perceived homogeneity of category members with respect to the relevant trait. This argument is based on the assumption that metaphors, compared with nonmetaphoric equivalents, represent stronger labels able to both broaden the boundaries of the category and narrow its characteristics. By broadening the boundaries of a category, we mean that a metaphor should enhance the likelihood that a member is included in the category. For example, under the metaphor *dolly*, we can include any pretty, cute, and lovely woman, from a wide age range. A literal correspondent (e.g., cute girls, sexy women) would limit the inclusion of some members. At the same time, the characteristics that are defined and selected by the metaphor are extremely precise and vivid, making the group homogeneous.

To test this hypothesis, the authors of this chapter recently conducted a study in which participants read a four-sentence description of a lawyer and of a politician including either a metaphoric or a semantically similar, nonmetaphoric statement that was stereotypical of the category.[5] The lawyer was either described as a *shark* or as *unscrupulous*, the politician either as *fox* or as *shrewd*. Subsequently, participants (none of whom were lawyers or politicians) were asked to estimate what percentage of the entire category of lawyers or of politicians were similar to the target person. As can be seen in Figure 8.1, in both cases, participants exposed to the metaphor perceived the social category as more homogeneous compared to those who had been exposed to a semantically similar trait adjective. Although more systematic research is needed, these first observations suggest that metaphors may indeed enhance the perceived homogeneity of outgroups.

Metaphor-Driven Stereotyping

Besides driving categorization and influencing perceived homogeneity, metaphors fulfill a third function in intergroup settings: They guide stereotypic inferences. Looking first at embodied metaphors that are grounded in physical experiences, there is evidence that people inadvertently rely on spatial metaphors when making inferences about social targets. To cite just

---

[5]We thank Angela Alessandrini for kindly collecting the data.

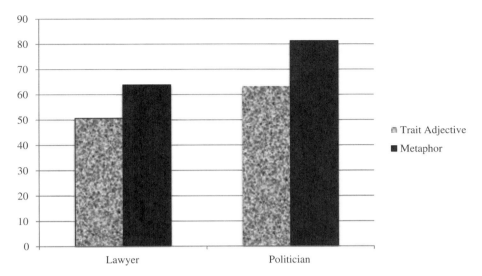

Figure 8.1. Percentage of lawyers or politicians who share the characteristics of the target person as a function of type of description (trait adjective or metaphor).

one example, leaders are generally perceived as powerful, but the degree to which people infer power depends critically on how the leader's position is represented in space. Giessner and Schubert (2007) varied systematically the vertical distance between leaders and lower level personnel in a fictitious organizational chart. The greater the distance, the more participants believed that the leader was powerful,[6] supporting the idea that metaphor-consistent spatial information enhances stereotypical inferences.

Even more interesting is the case of classical resemblance metaphors (e.g., those that associate the category *surgeon* to *butchers*). As stated earlier, such metaphors generally imply great generality across category members, combined with the potential to provide a clear image of relevant traits. In fact, the metaphor represents a meaningful interface between the categorical knowledge that is linguistically expressed by a stereotype and the vividness of the emotive and sensory aspects appearing in the perceptual experience of people. In the flow of the fuzzy and flexible linguistic tools used to describe the world, the metaphor enables people to combine characteristics in a concise and effective way, suggesting the subset of features associated to the stereotype.

This dual effect can be illustrated analyzing the social metaphor *lawyers are well-paid sharks* (Glucksberg, 2008). The source *shark* represents a literally

[6]Somewhat inconsistent with metaphor theories (Sperber & Wilson, 2008), this research also found that unrelated priming of longer (vs. shorter) vertical distance had similar effects on power judgments.

unrelated category—namely, predators—whose selected features (e.g., cruel, ferocious) are filtered and projected to the target category, *lawyers*. Through the use of this metaphor, the traits of law professionals that are also typical of predators (e.g., being merciless and aggressive) come to the forefront, whereas other traits typical of lawyers but unrelated to the metaphor are pushed into the background (e.g., being eloquent). At the same time, this metaphor-relevant image is applied to the entire category of lawyers, without exceptions and without differences in degree.

However, one may wonder whether a similar result could also be obtained by affirming that lawyers are unscrupulous, aggressive, and merciless. The difference between a metaphor and a list of traits is threefold. First, a single incisive word (metaphor) conveys a broad and flexible range of information that otherwise requires that each piece of information is specified separately (see Ortony, 1975). In other words, metaphors are economic vehicles to communicate stereotypes because they provide an efficient synthesis of the most relevant characteristics. Second, metaphors often take the form of nouns, which have been shown to facilitate stereotypical inferences and to inhibit counter-stereotypical inferences much more than comparable traits do (Carnaghi et al., 2008). Third, related to the above argument, trait adjectives allow for different degrees (a specific lawyer may be more or less *merciless*), whereas metaphoric nouns are either–or statements (a specific lawyer either is a *shark* or he is not). As a consequence, metaphors may induce stronger stereotypical inferences than semantically similar trait descriptions.

We addressed the question of whether intergroup metaphors affect listeners above and beyond the effects of nonmetaphoric trait descriptions in the new study just mentioned. Applying widely shared stereotypes according to which lawyers are unscrupulous and politicians are shrewd, we varied the last statement contained in the descriptions using either a metaphor (lawyer: "his colleagues describe him as a *shark*"; politician: "his colleagues describe him as a *fox*") or an equivalent nonmetaphoric adjective (lawyer: "his colleagues describe him as *unscrupulous*"; politician: "his colleagues describe him as *shrewd*"). In the control condition, the final statement was omitted. Participants then rated each of the two target persons on a number of scales, including scrupulousness (immoral, merciless, daring), and shrewdness (astute, cunning, sly). Unsurprisingly, the target persons were perceived more in line with the stereotype when the additional, stereotype-relevant information was provided. More important, as can be seen in Figure 8.2, this effect was stronger when the information was communicated through a metaphor compared with a semantically similar adjective. If confirmed across larger and more representative sets of stimuli, this would suggest that metaphors may be particularly powerful tools of communicating stereotypes as listeners

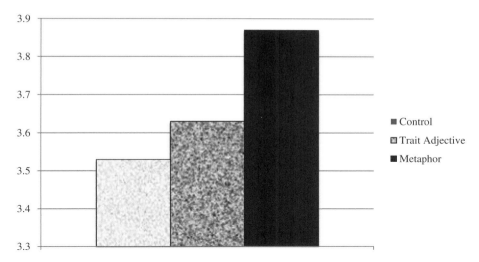

Figure 8.2. Attribution of stereotypical traits (either shrewdness or unscrupulousness) as a function of condition.

draw stronger stereotype-consistent inferences from such metaphors than from equivalent trait terms.

Extending the foregoing argument, one may even hypothesize that metaphors affect self-stereotyping. Thus, specific metaphors may increase the likelihood that people attribute to themselves those traits that align with the activated metaphor. Indirect evidence for this idea comes from a study by Oppenheimer and Trail (2010) in which spatially rightward- (or leftward-) oriented participants reported more conservative (or liberal) political attitudes. Apparently, the left–right metaphor affected people's political attitudes through direct bodily experiences—namely, body inclination. In this case, self-perception changed as a function of the metaphor, but the opposite may also be envisaged, suggesting that the relation between metaphors and self-perception is bidirectional. In line with this idea, Duguid and Goncalo (2012) showed that people who were made to feel powerful overestimated their own height. Although, to our knowledge, there is currently no research evidence for the relation between metaphor and self-stereotyping, these two studies provide at least indirect evidence for a (bidirectional) link between metaphors and self-perception.

Together, the small but growing body of research reported in this section shows that the exposure to metaphoric language affects the way listeners elaborate social information. In the following section, we look at how metaphors are used to describe ingroup and outgroup and which functions they are likely to fulfill in intergroup contexts, thus focusing on the speaker rather than the listener.

THE USE OF METAPHORS IN INTERPERSONAL DISCOURSE

Metaphors are often used in interpersonal discourse as well as in mass communication with the explicit or implicit intent to delegitimize the outgroup or conceal illegitimate behaviors of the ingroup.

Delegitimization and Dehumanization

Frequently metaphors are used in intergroup relations with the intention of dehumanizing the outgroup. In his seminal work on delegitimization strategies, Bar-Tal (1989) argued that dehumanization frequently involves the use of labels that either describe the outgroup as subhuman (e.g., as animals) or as superhuman creatures (e.g., as monsters or demons). In line with Haslam (2006), we may add a third form of dehumanization that links social groups to objects or automata (e.g., robots or machines). What these three types of metaphors (subhuman, superhuman, and automata) have in common is that they place the outgroup outside the boundaries of the category *human being,* thus paving the way for treating its members as not human. An extreme historical example of denial of humanity is Hitler's reference to Jews as *parasites* or *rats,* a rhetorical tool aimed at encouraging moral disengagement and ultimately justifying genocide. Contrary to the wishful thinking of the democratically minded reader, the use of dehumanizing animal metaphors is by no means a phenomenon of the past. To cite just one example, the Italian chapter of the Stormfront Internet forum (http://www.stormfront.org/forum/f148/),[7] considered the most popular White supremacy hate site worldwide, recently invited its readership to watch the TV program of a successful Jewish journalist in the following way: "We may observe, just as one observes rats in the laboratory, how the Jew lies and distorts reality. . . . Unfortunately these Jewish pigs are very capable of making people believe whatever they want" (December 20, 2011).

Bar-Tal and Hammack (2012) argued that delegitimization strategies such as these "free human beings from the normative and moral restraints and justify participation in violence, including the most evil actions" (p. 29). According to these authors, dehumanizing narratives, such as those containing animal metaphors, fulfill multiple functions including the facilitation of moral disengagement, the justification of discriminatory acts and of social exclusion of the outgroup, and the maintenance of the ingroup's feeling of superiority.

---

[7]Stormfront was founded and is run by the American White nationalist Don Black.

Although we are not aware of research that has systematically investigated the entire range of functions hypothesized by Bar-Tal (1989), there is strong evidence that outgroups are not only perceived as less human but also as more animal-like than ingroups. On one side, the steadily growing field of infrahumanization has provided consistent evidence that people deny outgroups uniquely human, secondary emotions (such as pride), whereas primary emotions, shared with the animal world (such as fear), are approximately equally assigned to ingroup and outgroups (for recent reviews, see Leyens, Demoulin, Vaes, Gaunt, & Paladino, 2007; Vaes, Leyens, Paladino, & Miranda, in press). On the other side, there is evidence that outgroups are not only perceived as less human but also associated with animal images. For instance, Viki et al. (2006) found that people associated the outgroup more with animal-related words (and less with human-related words) than the ingroup. Using an Implicit Association Test procedure (Study 1) Viki et al. found that people provided faster responses when outgroup and animal words (vs. ingroup and human words) shared the same response key than vice versa. Importantly, the association of outgroups with the animal world held not only for negative (e.g., *creature, carnivore, primal*) but also for positive concepts (e.g., *instinct, earthy, nature*; Viki et al., 2006, Experiment 4). Similarly, Pérez, Moscovici, and Chulvi (2007) found that Gypsies were associated with wild animals, and Boccato, Capozza, Falvo, and Durante (2008), using a priming procedure, observed that outgroup members were more associated with animality than with humanity, whereas ingroup members were primarily associated with humanity (see Capozza, Boccato, Andrighetto, & Falvo, 2009, for a related study using ambiguous human–ape faces). Particularly striking is the fact that, even today, Blacks are implicitly associated with apes even in people denying such associations at an explicit level. Goff, Eberhart, Williams, and Jackson (2008) ran a series of studies showing that White Americans, regardless of their racial attitudes, associate "Black" with "ape" and that this association is distinct in the sense that it was not observed for other social groups, nor were Blacks associated with animals other than apes (e.g., feline). Similarly, Saminaden, Loughan, and Haslam (2010), using a go/no-go procedure, found that traditional or indigenous (vs. industrialized) cultures are associated both with animals (vs. persons) and with children (vs. adults). According to Saminaden et al., this illustrates that even today traditional cultures are metaphorically dehumanized by placing them in either a phylogenetically (animals) or an ontogenetically (children) inferior position. This was true regardless of whether traditional versus industrialized cultures were presented in the form of verbal labels (*tribal, traditional* vs. *industrial, civilized*, etc.) or images.

This latter finding is important because it shows that dehumanizing metaphoric rhetoric may rely on not only verbal concepts but also images. In line with this idea, Volpato, Durante, Gabbiadini, Andrighetto, and Mari (2010) reported an impressive archive analysis of visual images published in *La difesa della razza*, a pseudo-scientific journal supportive of racist policies in Italy (1938–1943), finding that Jews were frequently portrayed as vultures, spiders, parasites, microbes, or devils (approximately 4% of all images describing Jews), whereas Blacks were primarily associated with apes or were objectified by showing only body parts such as hands or feet (approximately 2% of all images describing Blacks). Volpato et al. observed that, at least for Jews, metaphoric associations with animals were actually more frequent in visual materials than in the text. Thus, intergroup metaphors need no language; they may be expressed as efficiently or even more potently through images.

Although dehumanization often relies on animal metaphors, not all animal metaphors are offensive. Some animal metaphors signal positive affect (e.g., a woman calling her partner *panda* or a father referring to his daughter as *Spatz*, the German world for *sparrow*), others describe acceptable social behaviors. For instance, the verb *scimmiottare* (in Italian), "to ape" (English) or *nachäffen* (in German) may be used with a negative connotation, but it may also describe the playful synchronization behavior typically shown by children when they mimic one another.[8] So what makes an animal metaphor offensive? Haslam, Loughnan, and Sun (2011) investigated this question, finding that animal metaphors were considered particularly offensive when (a) they involve disliked or disgusting animals (e.g., rats, vultures, cockroaches, or worms rather than kittens, puppies, or rabbits) and (b) when they imply a high degree of dehumanization, suggesting that the target-person is indeed animal-like. Interestingly, animal metaphors do not become more offensive the greater the phylogenetic distance to human beings. As the authors observe, among the most offensive metaphors are animals that are distant (e.g., worms, parasites) but also some (e.g., pigs, rats, apes) that are close relatives of human beings. Together, these findings suggest that the offensiveness of animal metaphors may derive from two distinct sources: disgust (often involving phylogenetically distant animals) and falling short of full humanity (often involving phylogenetically close animals, e.g., apes or dogs).

Also, looking at the great variety of animal metaphors used in intergroup contexts, one may roughly distinguish two large groups, those that are broadly offensive without referring to any specific trait (e.g., *rat, dog*) and those that are narrower in meaning and are synonyms for specific human traits. Examples for this latter category, taken from the Italian language, are *bradipo* (bradypus) for slow, *asino* (donkey) for stupid, *volpe* (fox) for shrewd, and *squalo* (shark) for unscrupulous. Although we cannot cite any empirical evidence in favor of this hypothesis, we suspect that the former type of

---

[8]Haslam et al. (2011) found that, among the 40 animal metaphors considered in this research, approximately 20% were nonoffensive, whereas the large majority (80%) served hostile intentions.

metaphor has a primary function in dehumanization, whereas the latter is more closely related to stereotyping.

Another largely unexplored issue regards the cognitive and behavioral consequences of dehumanizing metaphors. There is evidence that metaphors do affect people's thinking, as illustrated by Goff et al.'s (2008, Experiment 5) finding that participants primed with ape words were more likely to condone violence against Blacks. Yet to our knowledge, many other consequences of the exposure to dehumanizing metaphors, such as moral disengagement and discriminatory behavior, remain to be explored.

Hiding and Deemphasizing Reality Through Metaphors

The systematic and coherent way in which we are able to comprehend one aspect of a concept in terms of another will necessarily hide other aspects of the concept. Consider the following sentence produced by a person involved in an intense discussion with a challenger: "He (she) *attacked* every weak point in my argument." Through this metaphor, the activity of "carrying on a discussion" is partially structured by the source concept *war*. In allowing us to focus on one aspect of a target concept (e.g., battling aspects of arguing), a metaphoric source can prevent us from focusing on the other aspects of the target that are not coherent with the metaphor. In this example, we may lose sight of the more cooperative aspects involved in an argument, such as comparing opinions or identifying logical flaws.

Allbritton (1995) argued that one of the central functions of metaphors is to filter information, promoting the selection and interpretation of information in a way that is coherent with the metaphor. Just as stereotypes tend to channel the interpretation of events (Bodenhausen & Wyer, 1985), metaphors tend to direct attention to certain aspects while detracting attention from others.

Looking at the use of metaphors in everyday talk, Cameron (2008) maintained that people use metaphors to think, to explain themselves to others, and to organize their discourse. Their choice of metaphor often reveals not only their conceptualization but also, and perhaps more important for human communication, their attitudes and values. Listening to and visualizing metaphors coined by others may help us to broaden our vision. Metaphors describe the world in a vivid yet familiar way, enabling us to see events from a specific perspective.

Metaphors carry not only ideational content but also information about the speaker's attitudes and values with respect of that content. The affective potential connected to a particular metaphor is crucial in understanding the reason a speaker decides to use it to influence the listener's attitudes about groups or social categories. According to Graumann (1990), three dimensions of affect help to analyze how speakers' choices contribute to the affective functioning of a metaphor: alignment–distancing, positive–negative evaluation, and emphasis–deemphasis. In particular, when the topic of discourse is uncomfortable for speakers in some way, metaphor helps to distance speaker and listener from the event and to deemphasize its unpleasant aspects.

Consider as an example the problem of social conflicts between national groups. At times, the course of the events culminates in real war. In this case, it becomes extremely important to distinguish what is metaphoric from what is not. Pain, death, hunger, and injury of loved ones are not metaphoric; they are real, and, in a war, they trouble hundreds of thousands of real human beings (Lakoff & Johnson, 1980). However, to hide the atrocious aspects of this social scenario from the public opinion, political leaders and military strategists at times translate the war into a sort of competitive game like chess or into a sport like football or boxing. An expression like *the arms race* refers to a metaphoric representation of a competitive game in which the opponents are fighting for the possession of a trophy without the actual use of deadly weapons.

It is a metaphor in which there is a clear winner and loser, and a clear end to the game. The metaphor highlights strategic thinking, team-work, preparedness, the spectators in the world arena, the glory of winning and the shame of defeat. This metaphor takes away the images of death and mourning and emphasizes a more acceptable view of the conflict. The public is primed to accept this clean scenario, providing a moral justification of the war.

Another metaphor hiding the real state of affairs is the term *side effects* to indicate that a war is producing blameless victims. In medicine, a side effect is an effect, typically adverse, that is secondary to the one intended; the term is predominantly used to describe adverse consequences of the use of a drug. In the case of a war, the air raids that cause death and destruction in the civil population are justified by means of the expression *side effects*. It associates the concept of war to an important and functional therapeutic procedure that unfortunately produces unwanted but expected injuries: the death of innocents.

During the conflict in the former Yugoslavia, the proposed strategy of the Serbian army against the Muslim minority was based on the systematic assassination of people (men, women, old people, children) living in rural communities. To hide the criminal nature of this conduct, the expression used by Serbian politician to portray this strategy was *ethnic cleansing*. This metaphoric image directs the attention of the unaware listener toward a worldview based on the following idea: In a confusing social and political reality that is not easy to understand, the best way to impose order and transparency on the ethnic environment is through a sort of physical cleaning up. Following the same logic, the German Nazi regime during the Second World War alluded to the design of the systematic elimination of the Jewish people using the expression *final solution*. In terms of Graumann's (1990) work, all these examples represent an attempt to affectively deemphasize a representation of social reality by means of a metaphor, ultimately justifying existing social, economic, or political arrangements (for a more detailed discussion of metaphoric framing effects in the political realm, see Chapter 9, this volume).

METAPHORIC FRAMING OF INTERGROUP RELATIONS AND POLICY DECISIONS

As the foregoing examples show, metaphors do not always refer to any specific social group but rather to intergroup relations in a wider sense. When talking about immigration, acculturation, racism, diversity, equity, power, hostile intergroup relations, international negotiation, or impermeable national boundaries, we tend to make use of metaphors such as *melting pot, colorblindness, Cold War, iron curtain, ping-pong or chess*, or simply to spatial relative positions that represent these abstract concepts. For instance, Henze (2005) found that school leaders in the United States tend to mentally represent the concept of "diversity" with reference to horizontal space. Also, *nation* is often envisaged as a *home* or as a physical *body* (Levine, 1995; O'Brien, 2003), and international negotiations are often framed as chess games, with politicians making wrong moves, worsening their position with every move, ending up in a stalemate, or being grandmasters who handle the endgame well or offer a draw at the right time (Mišić Ilic, 2008).

A number of authors (e.g., O'Brien, 2003) have argued that metaphors are intentionally used in public debate concerning immigration to create a fearful climate and to justify restrictive policies. Particularly common in this context are disease-related metaphors (e.g., immigration as *pestilence, plague,* or as a *cancer)* as well as natural-catastrophe metaphors (e.g., immigration as a *flood,* a *tide* against which *dams* must be erected).

Are metaphors such as these able to shift public opinion and to influence social policy? An interesting recent set of studies by Thibodeau and Borodistky (2011) suggests that metaphors may indeed shape the framing of and the solution to social problems. In this research, participants received a fictitious news article describing the increasing crime rate in a North American city, using either an animal (a *wild beast*) or a disease metaphor (a *virus* infecting the city) to refer to criminality. Participants were then asked to propose intervention strategies to counter the increase in crimes. The solutions that participants proposed were in line with the metaphor: Compared with the wild animal metaphor, the disease metaphor elicited more prevention-focused and fewer punishment-focused interventions. Thus, metaphoric framing does seem to have tangible consequences for public opinion attitudes.

CONCLUSIONS AND FUTURE RESEARCH

This brief review of the literature suggests that metaphors play a relevant role in intergroup relations by affecting various cognitive (categorization, homogeneity perception, stereotyping) as well as more motivational aspects. Social categorization comes easier when the immediate context is metaphor-congruent (e.g., when categorizing targets in powerful vs. powerless groups, located, respectively, in the upper or lower position). Not only do metaphors facilitate the classification of exemplars, they also make exemplars appear more similar to each other, thus enhancing group homogeneity. Metaphors also shift interpretation and inferences such that metaphor-consistent aspects of a social group come to the foreground, whereas other features are ignored. Importantly, this shift in interpretation appears more potent when elicited by a metaphor than by a semantically similar trait adjective. As we have seen, this hiding or filtering function becomes an important tool when trying to distort reality and to justify hostile intergroup behaviors, including war. Finally, metaphors provide a critical tool in dehumanizing propaganda, where outgroups are associated with subhuman beings (animals), superhuman creatures (devils), or automata (robots) and hence mentally excluded from the human race and often treated accordingly.

Although the small but growing literature on intergroup metaphors suggests that metaphors should have a definite place in theorizing and research on language and social cognition, many aspects remain to be explored. First of all, research should focus on the basic question of whether metaphors affect listeners above and beyond nonmetaphoric discourse and whether they operate by similar or distinct mechanisms. Also, the relation between metaphoric and nonmetaphoric representations remains to be explored (e.g., see Loughnan, Haslam, & Kashima, 2009, for the mutual influence between metaphor-based and attribute-based dehumanization).

Second, it remains to be seen whether speakers use metaphors differentially when talking about ingroups versus outgroups. Similar to the linguistic intergroup bias (Maass, 1999), according to which positive ingroup and negative outgroup behaviors are described more abstractly than negative ingroup and positive outgroup behaviors, one may suspect that metaphors are used in a strategic way to differentiate the ingroup favorably from the outgroup. Thus, metaphors may be handy tools of communication when describing positive characteristics of the ingroup or negative characteristics of the outgroup.

Third, assuming that metaphors function much like schemata, as suggested by Allbritton (1995), there seems to be a striking parallelism between the cognitive functions of metaphors and those of stereotypes. In our opinion, the interplay between the two remains to be explored. We suspect that a metaphoric framing of stereotypes will greatly increase their impact.

Fourth, it has been argued that metaphors reduce uncertainty. The first empirical evidence for the relation between metaphors and uncertainty came from research by Keefer, Landau, Sullivan, and Rothschild (2011), who showed that the accessibility of a metaphor (such as *life is a path*) affected subsequent cognition only when people were in a state of subjective uncertainty. Specifically, the metaphor *life is a path* enhanced participants' perception of autobiographical continuity only when personal uncertainty was salient. Although Keefer and colleagues have shown that uncertainty moderates the effect of metaphoric thinking, to our knowledge, there is as yet no direct evidence that metaphors actually reduce uncertainty. If metaphors were to reduce uncertainty, then any target that creates uncertainty should be particularly likely to be described by a metaphor. This possibility seems interesting in relation to uncertainty identity theory, according to which uncertainty reduction represents the motivational component of social identification and drives subsequent intergroup behaviors (Hogg, 2007).

Fifth, relatively little is known about the communicative functions of metaphors in intergroup discourse. Allbritton (1995) and others have suggested that metaphors promote intimacy and closeness because they highlight the shared knowledge among the speakers. Similarly, Castelli, Arcuri, and Zogmaister (2003) showed that stereotypes are a social tool that enhances the perception of closeness and similarity among group members. Thus, it remains to be seen whether metaphors fulfill this social function above and beyond that of stereotype sharing.

At the most general level, many studies reported here aimed primarily at investigating intergroup phenomena—for instance, by testing whether outgroups are denied the same degree of humanity that is generally granted to ingroups. As a consequence, a considerable portion of the research discussed here was framed within social-psychological theory (e.g., infrahumanization or dehumanization models), rather than within metaphor theory. We believe that research in this area would benefit from a more explicit reference to theoretical concepts and experimental designs used in the metaphor literature.

REFERENCES

Allbritton, D. W. (1995). When metaphors function as schemas: Some cognitive effects of conceptual metaphors. *Metaphor & Symbolic Activity, 10,* 33–46. doi:10.1207/s15327868ms1001_4

Barnden, J. A. (2010). Metaphor and metonymy: Making their connections more slippery. *Cognitive Linguistics, 21,* 1–34.

Bar-Tal, D. (1989). Delegitimization: The extreme case of stereotyping and prejudice. In D. Bar-Tal, C. Graumann, A. W. Kruglanski, & W. Stroebe (Eds.),

Stereotyping and prejudice: Changing conceptions (pp. 169–188). New York, NY: Springer Verlag.

Bar-Tal, D., & Hammack, P. L. (2012). Conflict, delegitimization, and violence. In L. R. Tropp (Ed.), *Oxford handbook of intergroup conflict* (pp. 29–52). New York, NY: Oxford University Press.

Billig, M., & Tajfel, H. (1973). Social categorization and similarity in intergroup behaviour. *European Journal of Social Psychology, 3,* 27–52. doi:10.1002/ejsp.2420030103

Boccato, G., Capozza, D., Falvo, R., & Durante, F. (2008). The missing link: Ingroup, outgroup and the Human species. *Social Cognition, 26,* 224–234. doi:10.1521/soco.2008.26.2.224

Bodenhausen, G. V., & Wyer, R. S. (1985). Effects of stereotypes in decision making and information-processing strategies. *Journal of Personality and Social Psychology, 48,* 267–282. doi:10.1037/0022-3514.48.2.267

Bowdle, B. F., & Gentner, D. (2005). The career of metaphor. *Psychological Review, 112,* 193–216. doi:10.1037/0033-295X.112.1.193

Cameron, L. (2008). Metaphor and talk. In R. W. Gibbs (Ed.), *The Cambridge handbook of metaphor and thought* (pp. 197–211). New York, NY: Cambridge University Press. doi:10.1017/CBO9780511816802.013

Capozza, D., Boccato, G., Andrighetto, L., & Falvo, R. (2009). Categorization of ambiguous human/ape faces: Protection of ingroup but not outgroup humanity. *Group Processes & Intergroup Relations, 12,* 777–787. doi:10.1177/1368430209344868

Carnaghi, A., Maass, A., Gresta, S., Bianchi, M., Cadinu, M., & Arcuri, L. (2008). Nomina sunt omina: On the inductive potential of nouns and adjectives in person perception. *Journal of Personality and Social Psychology, 94,* 839–859. doi:10.1037/0022-3514.94.5.839

Castelli, L., Arcuri, L., & Zogmaister, C. (2003). Perceiving ingroup members who use stereotypes: Implicit conformity and similarity. *European Journal of Social Psychology, 33,* 163–175. doi:10.1002/ejsp.138

Duguid, M. M., & Goncalo, J. A. (2012). Living large: The powerful overestimate their own height. *Psychological Science, 23,* 36–40. doi:10.1177/0956797611422915

Durante, F., Volpato, C., & Fiske, S. T. (2010). Using the stereotype content model to examine group depictions in Fascism: An archival approach. *European Journal of Social Psychology, 40,* 465–483.

Emanatian, M. (1995). Metaphor and the expression of emotion: The value of cross-cultural perspectives. *Metaphor & Symbolic Activity, 10,* 163–182. doi:10.1207/s15327868ms1003_2

Foroni, F., & Rothbart, M. (2011). Category boundaries and category labels: When does a category name influence the perceived similarity of category members? *Social Cognition, 29,* 547–576. doi:10.1521/soco.2011.29.5.547

Farias, A. R., Garrido, M. V., & Semin, G. R. (2013). Converging modalities ground abstract categories: The case of politics. *PLoS ONE, 8*(4), e60971. doi:10.1371/journal.pone.0060971

Gentner, D., & Wolff, P. (1997). Alignment in the processing of metaphor. *Journal of Memory and Language, 37*, 331–355. doi:10.1006/jmla.1997.2527

Gibbs, R. W. (2008). (Ed.). *The Cambridge handbook of metaphor and thought*. New York, NY: Cambridge University Press.

Giessner, S. R., & Schubert, T. (2007). High in hierarchy: How vertical location and judgments of leaders' power are interrelated. *Organizational Behavior and Human Decision Processes, 104*, 30–44. doi:10.1016/j.obhdp.2006.10.001

Glucksberg, S. (2008). How metaphors create categories—quickly. In R. W. Gibbs (Ed.), *The Cambridge handbook of metaphor and thought* (pp. 67–83). New York, NY: Cambridge University Press. doi:10.1017/CBO9780511816802.006

Goff, P. A., Eberhart, J. L., Williams, M. J., & Jackson, M. C. (2008). Not yet human: Implicit knowledge, historical dehumanization, and contemporary consequences. *Journal of Personality and Social Psychology, 94*, 292–306. doi:10.1037/0022-3514.94.2.292

Graumann, C. (1990). Perspective structure and dynamics in dialogues. In I. Markova & K. Foppa (Eds.), *The dynamics of dialogue* (pp. 105–126). London, England: Harvester Wheatsheaf.

Haslam, N. (2006). Dehumanization: An integrative review. *Personality and Social Psychology Review, 10*, 252–264. doi:10.1207/s15327957pspr1003_4

Haslam, N., Loughnan, S., & Sun, P. (2011). Beastly: What makes animal metaphors offensive? *Journal of Language and Social Psychology, 30*, 311–325. doi:10.1177/0261927X11407168

Henze, R. (2005). Metaphors of diversity, intergroup relations, and equity in the discourse of educational leaders. *Journal of Language, Identity, and Education, 4*, 243–267. doi:10.1207/s15327701jlie0404_1

Hogg, M. A. (2007). In M. P. Zanna (Ed.), *Advances in experimental social psychology: Vol. 39. Uncertainty-identity theory* (pp. 69–126). San Diego, CA: Academic Press.

Jones, L. L., & Estes, Z. (2005). Metaphor comprehension as attributive categorization. *Journal of Memory and Language, 53*, 110–124. doi:10.1016/j.jml.2005.01.016

Keefer, L. A., Landau, M. J., Sullivan, D., & Rothschild, Z. K. (2011). Exploring metaphor's epistemic function: Uncertainty moderates metaphor-consistent priming effects on social perceptions. *Journal of Experimental Social Psychology, 47*, 657–660. doi:10.1016/j.jesp.2011.02.002

Labov, W. (1973). The boundaries of words and their meanings. In C. Bailey & R. Shuy (Eds.), *New ways of analyzing variations in English* (pp. 340–373). Washington, DC: Georgetown University Press.

Lakens, D., Semin, G. R., & Foroni, F. (2011). Why your highness needs the people: Comparing the absolute and relative representation of power in vertical space. *Social Psychology, 42*, 205–213. doi:10.1027/1864-9335/a000064

Lakoff, G. (1993). The contemporary theory of metaphor. *Metaphor and Thought, 2*, 202–251.

Lakoff, G., & Johnson, M. (1980). *Metaphors we live by*. Chicago, IL: University of Chicago Press.

Levine, D. N. (1995). The organism metaphor in sociology. *Social Research, 62,* 239–265.

Leyens, J. P., Demoulin, S., Vaes, J., Gaunt, R., & Paladino, M. P. (2007). Infrahumanization: The wall of group differences. *Journal of Social Issues and Policy Review, 1,* 139–172. doi:10.1111/j.1751-2409.2007.00006.x

Lippmann, W. (1922). *Public opinion*. New York, NY: Harcourt Brace.

Loughnan, S., Haslam, N., & Kashima, Y. (2009). Understanding the relationship between attribute-based and metaphor-based dehumanization. *Group Processes & Intergroup Relations, 12,* 747–762. doi:10.1177/1368430209347726

Maass, A. (1999). In M. Zanna (Ed.), *Advances in experimental social psychology: Vol. 31. Linguistic intergroup bias: Stereotype-perpetuation through language* (pp. 79–121). San Diego, CA: Academic Press.

Miller, A. G. (1982). Historical and contemporary perspectives on stereotyping. In A. G. Miller (Ed.), *In the eye of the beholder: Contemporary issues in stereotyping* (pp. 1–40). New York, NY: Praeger.

Mišić Ilic, B. (2008). Chess-related metaphors—gens una sumus. *Facta Universitatis: Linguistics and Literature, 6,* 15–26.

O'Brien, G. V. (2003). Indigestible food, conquering hordes, and waste materials: Metaphors of immigrants and the early immigration restriction debate in the United States. *Metaphor and Symbol, 18,* 33–47. doi:10.1207/S15327868MS1801_3

Oppenheimer, D. M., & Trail, T. E. (2010). Why leaning to the left makes you lean to the left: Effect of spatial orientation on political attitudes. *Social Cognition, 28,* 651–661. doi:10.1521/soco.2010.28.5.651

Ortony, A. (1975). Why metaphors are necessary and not just nice. *Educational Theory, 25,* 45–53. doi:10.1111/j.1741-5446.1975.tb00666.x

Pérez, J. A., Moscovici, S., & Chulvi, B. (2007). The taboo against group contact: Hypothesis of Gypsy ontologization. *British Journal of Social Psychology, 46,* 249–272. doi:10.1348/014466606X111301

Roberson, D., Davidoff, J. B., Davies, I. R. L., & Shapiro, L. R. (2005). Color categories: Evidence for the cultural relativity hypothesis. *Cognitive Psychology, 50,* 378–411. doi:10.1016/j.cogpsych.2004.10.001

Saminaden, A., Loughan, S., & Haslam, N. (2010). Afterimages of savages: Implicit associations between "primitives," animals and children. *British Journal of Social Psychology, 49,* 91–105. doi:10.1348/014466609X415293

Satta, A., (2011). *Ci sarà una volta: Favole e mamme in ambulatorio*. Castel Gandolfo, Italy: Libri Infinito.

Schubert, T. W. (2005). Your highness: Vertical positions as perceptual symbols of power. *Journal of Personality and Social Psychology, 89,* 1–21. doi:10.1037/0022-3514.89.1.1

Sperber, D., & Wilson, D. (2008). A deflationary account of metaphors. In Gibbs Jr., R. W. (Ed.), *The Cambridge handbook of metaphor and thought* (pp. 84–105). New York, NY: Cambridge University Press.

Steen, G. (2011). Metaphor, language and discourse processes. *Discourse Processes, 48,* 585–591. doi:10.1080/0163853X.2011.606424

Talebinejad, M. R., & Dastjerdi, H. V. (2005). A cross-cultural study of animal metaphors: When owls are not wise! *Metaphor and Symbol, 20,* 133–150. doi:10.1207/s15327868ms2002_3

Thibodeau, P. H., & Borodistky, L. (2011). Metaphors we think with: The role of metaphor in reasoning. *PLoS ONE, 6,* e16782. doi:10.1371/journal.pone.0016782

Vaes, J., Leyens, J., Paladino, M. P., & Miranda, M. P. (in press). We are human, they are not: Driving forces behind outgroup dehumanization and the humanization of the ingroup. *European Review of Social Psychology.*

van Elk, M., van Schie, H. T., & Bekkering, H. (2010). From left to right: Processing acronyms referring to names of political parties activates spatial associations. *The Quarterly Journal of Experimental Psychology: Human Experimental Psychology, 63,* 2202–2219. doi:10.1080/17470218.2010.495160

Viki, G. T., Winchester, L., Titshall, L., Chasing, T., Pina, A., & Russell, R. (2006). Beyond secondary emotions: The infrahumanization of outgroups using human-related and animal-related words. *Social Cognition, 24,* 753–775. doi:10.1521/soco.2006.24.6.753

Volpato, C., Durante, F., Gabbiadini, A., Andrighetto, L., & Mari, S. (2010). Picturing the other: Targets of delegitimization across time. *International Journal of Conflict and Violence, 4,* 269–287.

Yu, N. (1995). Metaphorical expressions of anger and happiness in English and Chinese. *Metaphor and Symbolic Activity, 10,* 59–92. doi:10.1207/s15327868ms1002_1

9

THE METAPHORIC FRAMING MODEL: POLITICAL COMMUNICATION AND PUBLIC OPINION

VICTOR OTTATI, RANDALL RENSTROM, AND ERIKA PRICE

This chapter develops a comprehensive model of metaphor effects within the domain of political communication and political cognition. We begin by considering the nature and prevalence of metaphor commonly appearing in political rhetoric. We then provide an overarching theoretical perspective that conceptualizes metaphoric political rhetoric as a form of political framing. This *metaphoric framing model* posits that a communication or situational cue initially activates a *root metaphor* in the mind of the message recipient. This root metaphor contains an image, central theme, or storyline that is associated with the political entity, event, or issue being described. This metaphoric image influences the message recipient's attitudes and opinions regarding the event or issue. The psychological nature of this influence is presumed to be multifaceted, encompassing a variety of mediating psychological

This chapter was funded by a National Science Foundation grant awarded to the first author (Grant 0518007).

http://dx.doi.org/10.1037/14278-009
The Power of Metaphor: Examining Its Influence on Social Life, M. J. Landau, M. D. Robinson, and B. P. Meier (Editors)

process mechanisms. These include metaphoric framing effects that are mediated by information seeking, selective information processing, interpretation of ambiguous information, as well as metaphor-guided attribution, inference, and elaboration. The metaphoric framing model also posits that metaphoric language can influence the message recipient's cognitive processing style en route to deriving a political opinion or attitude.

NATURE AND PREVALENCE OF METAPHOR IN POLITICAL COMMUNICATION

A metaphor contains two fundamental components. The *target* (*topic*) of the metaphor is simply the object, event, or issue being described (Lakoff, 1993; Richards, 1936). The *source* (*vehicle*) is some other object or event that conveys a certain meaning about the target (topic). For example, *pollution is a disease* contains *pollution* as the target (topic) and *disease* as the source (vehicle). Many researchers have suggested that metaphor comprehension entails mapping semantic and evaluative connotations of the source (e.g., *disease*) on to the metaphor target (e.g., *pollution*). Thus, *pollution is a disease* might convey that pollution is a source of sickness, weakness, decay, and death.

Metaphor is prevalent in many forms of communication, including both spoken and written discourse (Gibbs, 1994; Graesser, Long, Mio, 1989; Lakoff, 1987; Landau, Meier, & Keefer, 2010; Mio & Katz, 1996). Although often viewed as a literary device reserved for extraordinary or poetic utterances, metaphor also pervades ordinary and conventional forms of communication (Lakoff, 1993). Research confirms that metaphor is commonly used in literature (Kreuz & Roberts, 1993; Kreuz, Roberts, Johnson, & Bertus, 1996), advertising and marketing (Arndt, 1985; Hunt & Menon, 1995), interpersonal communication (Fussell & Moss, 1998), and psychotherapy (McMullen, 1989). In many instances, metaphors describe an abstract entity or issue in terms of more concrete aspects of human experience (Landau, Sullivan, & Greenberg, 2009). Thus, it is not surprising that metaphors are highly prevalent in the political realm (Howe, 1988; Lakoff, 2004; Mio, 1996, 1997).

Politicians use metaphors to characterize themselves (e.g., Sarah Palin as a *mama grizzly*), their opponents (e.g., Tony Blair as Bush's *lap dog*), and their political agendas (e.g., *New Deal, Bridge to the Twenty-First Century*). Charismatic presidents are more likely to use metaphoric language in their inaugural addresses, suggesting that metaphors can inspire the electorate (Mio, Riggio, Levin, & Reese, 2005). Indeed, metaphoric language is used to great effect during public policy debates, often to persuade the public toward a certain viewpoint (e.g., social services are abused by *welfare queens*) or to explain a particular policy stance (e.g., *domino theory* to justify U.S. involvement in Vietnam). Metaphors are also used by the media when reporting on elections and political candidates (e.g., *horse race, dark horse candidate, riding the president's coattails, mudslinging, landslide victory*).

Several types of metaphor are used in political communication, including those involving war, sports, family, and nature (S. Gilbert, 1979; Howe, 1988). Metaphors involving war, conflict, and violence are particularly prevalent (Eubanks, 2000; Howe, 1988) For example, the *trade is war* metaphor is often used by politicians to suggest there are *winners* and *losers* when it comes to international trade and as such may influence the public's attitudes toward protectionism, tariffs, and free-trade bills in Congress. The *war on drugs* metaphor provides another prominent example. Many have argued that this metaphor increased incarceration rates for illegal drug users, culminating in the overcrowding of U.S. prisons. War metaphors are also used during political campaigns. For example, Sarah Palin encouraged her conservative supporters not to retreat but to *reload* in the run-up to the 2010 elections (for related examples, see Martin, 2011). Sports metaphors are as prevalent as war metaphors, if not more so (Howe, 1988). Politicians play *hardball*. When they advance a particular policy, they bring out their *heavy hitters*. During debates, candidates *come out swinging*, don't *pull any punches*, and land a *knockout punch*. Such metaphors may provide an apt description for many political events, but because men often have a greater interest in sports than women do, sports metaphors may turn women off to political communications or arguments (Howe, 1988; but see Ottati, Rhoads, & Graesser, 1999).

In contrast to war and sports metaphors, family metaphors are often used to bring people together. Reagan often used sports metaphors during the 1984 campaign, referring to the *Washington tax increase team* and the *grassroots opportunity team* (Howe, 1988). There were also allusions to Reagan being a *quarterback* and America *scoring touchdowns again*. In contrast, during the primaries, Mario Cuomo spoke of Americans being a *family* and *bound to one another*, and Jesse Jackson described his multiethnic campaign as a *rainbow coalition* (Howe, 1988). Many other metaphors are also prevalent in politics. For example, machine metaphors describe Congress and the lawmaking process (the *sausage-making factory*), and political bosses are said to run political *machines* in large cities that produce votes for candidates the *boss* supports. Cancer metaphors have long been used to describe political problems (e.g., *Watergate is a cancer on the presidency*). Likewise, metaphors that reference the body—*three arms of government, heads of state, brain trust*—are prevalent. We even refer to our organized political system itself as the *body politic*.

AGENDA-SETTING, PRIMING, AND
METAPHORIC POLITICAL PRIMING

How do political metaphors influence public opinion? To address this question, it is important to consider metaphor effects in the context of a larger body of work regarding the effects of political communication. Early analysis of political communication, although often based on anecdotal evidence, characterized the mass media as exercising a powerful influence on public opinion. However, empirically oriented researchers eventually rejected this claim. Indeed, academic orthodoxy came to emphasize that the media produces "minimal effects" on public opinion (Klapper, 1960). During this *minimal effects* era, it was suggested that political opinions are, in large part, determined by long-standing political predispositions. The political campaign and media were viewed as short-term forces that failed to modify deeply entrenched, long-standing political predispositions. This research era ended, however, when researchers documented the presence of *agenda-setting* and *priming effects*.

Agenda-setting research demonstrated that the media are effective in telling the public what to think *about* (Behr & Iyengar, 1985; Rössler & Schenk, 2000; Soroka, 2003; Sutherland & Galloway, 1981). That is, by giving extensive coverage to certain political issues and less coverage to other issues, the media influence the relative salience and importance of political issues in the mind of the public (Bizer & Krosnick, 2001; Iyengar, Kinder, Peters, & Krosnick, 1984). This agenda-setting effect, in turn, gives rise to a media priming effect. That is, media coverage of an issue increases the likelihood that voters will rely on that issue when they derive their overall evaluation of a politician's performance (Behr & Iyengar, 1985; Iyengar et al., 1984; Soroka, 2003). Thus, for example, prominent and frequent coverage of domestic economic issues increases the weight ascribed to the president's economic performance when voters derive their global evaluation of the president (Iyengar et al., 1984).

The *minimal effects* assumption was also challenged by research documenting media *framing* effects. Whereas agenda-setting determines *what* the public thinks about, media framing influences *how* individuals think about an issue. More specifically, news frames emphasize, prime, or highlight certain aspects of a political event while deemphasizing or ignoring others (Dimitrova & Stromback, 2005; Entman, 1993, 2004). In doing so, frames increase the accessibility or importance of certain aspects of a news event and decrease the accessibility or importance of other aspects of a news event (Druckman, 2001; Iyengar, 1991; Nelson, Oxley, & Clawson, 1997). A news frame consists of words and phrases that highlight and select what is most relevant, notable, or important about a news event (Druckman, 2001; Entman,

1993). It often provides a central theme or storyline that organizes and adds coherence to specific information pertaining to a news event (Berinsky & Kinder, 2006; Druckman, 2001). This central theme or storyline promotes a particular construal of the news event (e.g., referring to the Iraq War as an *occupation* versus a *liberation;* Pfau et al., 2005; Semetko & Valkenburg, 2000). Comprehension, interpretation, and opinion formation regarding a news event are thereby shaped by the manner in which the media frames the news event (Nelson et al., 1997). For example, public opinion regarding a Ku Klux Klan rally depends on whether the news event is framed in terms of freedom of speech, racism, or public safety (Druckman, 2001).

This chapter conceptualizes metaphor in political communication as *metaphoric political framing.* From this perspective, metaphoric political utterances function as communication frames that elicit many of the effects produced by political frames more generally. Notably, however, metaphoric political frames are often more subtle and are therefore difficult for citizens to detect or control (Bougher, 2012; Thibodeau & Boroditsky, 2011).

THE METAPHORIC FRAMING MODEL

The metaphoric framing model can be applied to a variety of domains. These include therapist–client interaction, parent–child interaction, interpersonal communication in close relationships, persuasion, advertising, political communication, and other forms of mass communication. This chapter applies the model to examine the effects of metaphoric statements contained in news stories, political speeches, news interviews, and other forms of mass political communication. The metaphoric framing model is inspired by theory and research in psychology, political science, and communication. Its psychological foundations can be found in conceptual metaphor theory (Lakoff, 1993; Lakoff & Johnson, 1980), research regarding the cognitive representation of events (Pennington & Hastie, 1986), as well as in social psychological models of persuasion (Chaiken, 1980; Petty & Cacioppo, 1986), impression formation (Wyer & Srull, 1989), and stereotyping (e.g., Bodenhausen & Macrae, 1998; D. Gilbert & Hixon, 1991). Political communication research regarding framing effects also provides a foundation for the model (e.g., Entman, 2004; Iyengar, 1991).

The metaphoric framing model attempts to integrate the implications of these various theoretical approaches to provide a more comprehensive and overarching conceptualization of metaphor effects. In doing so, it also provides an explicit account of many psychological processes that are yet to be fully illuminated in the metaphor literature. These include a fivefold typology of metaphor activation, an explicit distinction between metaphor activation

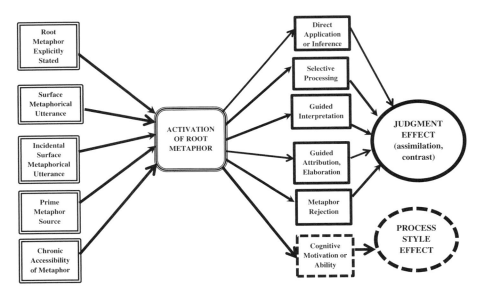

Figure 9.1. The metaphoric framing model.

and application, an explicit distinction between metaphor-induced judgment effects and metaphor-induced process style effects, as well as a more fully articulated model of the psychological process mechanisms that mediate the effect of metaphor on judgment and process style.

The metaphoric framing model contains two basic stages of cognitive processing: metaphor activation and application (see Figure 9.1). The first stage involves *activation* of a root metaphor. This occurs when, either explicitly or implicitly, a root metaphor is activated that links the communication target to a metaphor vehicle or source (e.g., *Operation Desert Storm is a football game*). As will soon become apparent, there are at least five psychological routes to activating a root metaphor. The root metaphor typically contains a concrete entity, event, or storyline (e.g., *football game*) that is associated with the target of the communication (e.g., *Operation Desert Storm*). Often, this central theme or storyline can be conceptualized as a prototypic event schema or script (e.g., an event in which fans are loyal to their preferred team, the coach is in charge of the game plan, offensive maneuvers are based on both a ground and passing game strategy, nonessential personnel sit on the sidelines). The second stage involves *application* of the metaphor. At this stage, the central theme or storyline influences the individual's impression of the target event or topic being described in the communication (e.g., *Israel remained on the sidelines* produces the belief that Israel did not directly participate in the military operation). This can occur in a relatively direct or indirect manner. In what follows, we describe each stage of the metaphoric framing model in more detail.

Activation of the Root Metaphor

In accordance with the implications of conceptual metaphor theory (Lakoff, 1993; Lakoff & Johnson, 1980), the metaphoric framing model presumes that verbal statements (e.g., "the allied force included special teams") *activate* an underlying metaphor in the mind of the message recipient (e.g., *war is a football game*). The underlying conceptual metaphor can be activated by a diverse set of surface metaphoric utterances and functions as the root origin of a diverse set of cognitive entailments (e.g., *civilians are merely spectators, remain loyal to your team!*). For these reasons, the metaphoric framing model uses the term *root metaphor* to identify the underlying conceptual metaphor that is activated. As previously noted, the root metaphor contains a target, source, and a linkage that implies the target is the source. For example, the root metaphor *Operation Desert Storm is a football game* contains *Operation Desert Storm* as the target (topic), *football game* as the source (vehicle), and *is a* as the linkage between the target and source.

According to the metaphoric framing model, the root metaphor can be activated in at least five ways. First, it is possible that the root metaphor is directly and explicitly stated in a communication. For example, a political commentator might argue that *the presidential campaign is a beauty contest* and provide specific examples of campaign events that support this cynical construal of a presidential contest. Explicit metaphoric expressions of this nature significantly influence the message recipient's reasoning regarding social and political issues. For example, Thibodeau and Boroditsky (2011) provided information with statistical information regarding crime rates that was preceded by *crime is a virus* or, alternatively, *crime is a beast*. Individuals exposed to the former metaphor recommended crime solutions analogous to viral epidemic solutions (e.g., "investigate source," "institute programs that will decrease the spread of crime"). Individuals exposed to the later metaphor recommended crime solutions that are analogous to those often prescribed for dangerous animals (e.g., "hunt down, capture, and cage the criminals").

Often, however, a root metaphor is activated in the listener's mind even when the communication fails to contain any direct or explicit mention of the root metaphor. This more implicit avenue of activation emerges when a communication contains *surface utterances* that imply (but do not directly state) the root metaphor. For example, a description of Operation Desert Storm might indicate that the allied attack featured a *ground game* as well as the use of *special teams* to execute a successful *end sweep* strategy (Beer & de Landtsheer, 2004). Although not explicitly stated, the root metaphor

Operation Desert Storm is a football game is clearly implied by this description. As such, this description will presumably activate this root metaphor in the mind of the listener. Research confirms that this avenue of activation can serve as an effective means of political persuasion. As one example, Bowers and Osborn (1966) activated a *death* metaphor to persuade participants to cut government aid to needy students. Although they never explicitly stated *government aid is death*, such a metaphor was implied by the language in the persuasive communication (e.g., *allow our government to slowly strangle individuality, permit the basis of our national strength to rot, the death rattle of liberty*). Compared with a literal communication, those who were exposed to the communication containing the death metaphor showed greater attitude change.

A third avenue of activation is even more subtle (or implicit) than the one just described. In this case, a root metaphor is activated by *incidental*, surface metaphoric utterances that are not even part of a communication regarding the specific target of evaluation. Evidence for this process is provided by Landau et al. (2009). Specifically, American participants were initially exposed to information that increased or decreased motivation to avoid bodily contamination. Next, some participants read an essay description of the United States containing surface metaphoric expressions that compared the United States to a physical body. Importantly, none of this information specifically pertained to immigration (the target of evaluation). Nevertheless, this information influenced attitudes toward immigration. Namely, increased motivation to avoid bodily contamination predicted more negative attitudes toward immigration and immigrants. For these participants, the root metaphor *my country is a body* was incidentally activated by the essay. As a consequence, among these participants, motivation to avoid viral invasion of the body was associated with more negative attitudes toward immigration. In the control condition, participants initially read a parallel essay that described the Unites States in literal terms. Among these participants, motivation to avoid bodily contamination had no impact on attitudes toward immigration.

A fourth avenue of activation is potentially the most subtle of all. In this case, the context incidentally primes the metaphor vehicle (source), without implying or mentioning a link between the source and target. When subsequently considering the target, however, the individual *spontaneously* links the target to the recently activated source, thereby producing activation of the metaphor. Effects of this nature can emerge when the metaphor source is activated by a physical cue. For example, when holding a warm (as opposed to cold) cup of coffee, participants are more likely to rate a target person as *warm* (Williams & Bargh, 2008). In this case, the physical cue does not state or imply the root metaphor (i.e., *interpersonal warmth is physical warmth*). Nevertheless, this root metaphor is spontaneously activated when participants rate the target person. An analogous effect might emerge in the political domain. For example, participants might spontaneously activate the *war is a football game* metaphor when viewing news coverage of a war immediately following a televised football game (even if the news program fails to mention or imply a link between *football* and *war*). Effects of this nature may be limited, however. Thibodeau and Boroditsky (2011), for example, found that *crime is a virus* elicited metaphor-consistent reasoning regarding crime policy. In contrast, a condition that simply primed *virus* failed to produce this effect.

The previously described avenues of metaphor activation involve situational cues (e.g., physical cues, surface metaphoric utterances) that prime a metaphor when an individual thinks about the target. A fifth avenue of metaphor activation involves individual differences in chronic accessibility. From this perspective, the accessibility of a metaphor is significantly influenced by chronic predispositions (Bougher, 2012; Lakoff & Johnson, 1980). For example, some individuals might chronically construe public policy regarding drug abuse in terms of a *war on drugs*. Other individuals might chronically construe this public policy in terms of a *medical epidemic*. Individual differences of this nature are presumably associated with a variety of political predispositions (e.g., ideology, partisanship), worldviews (e.g., social dominance orientation), personality characteristics (e.g., authoritarianism), values (e.g., egalitarianism, freedom), and cultural orientations (e.g., individualism, collectivism, modernity). If a metaphor regarding a topic is chronically accessible, it might be automatically activated by the mere mention of the topic. For example, among conservatives, the simple mention of *taxation* might automatically activate metaphors involving physical burden, socialism, or robbery.

The Nature of the Activated Representation

Activation of the root metaphor does not simply produce a comparison between one entity (e.g., *virus*) and another (e.g., *crime*). On the contrary, the root metaphor maps an entire conceptual *domain* on to another conceptual *domain* (Bowdle & Gentner, 2005; Lakoff, 1993). Thus, the metaphor *crime is a virus* maps a series of cognitive entailments associated with *virus* onto *crime* (e.g., *education inoculates youth against a criminal lifestyle, urban youth programs prevent the spread of crime*). Moreover, in addition to activating a comparison between entities or objects, metaphors can activate an entire storyline or narrative (Stone, 1988). This narrative storyline can be conceptualized as an event representation or script that guides comprehension, understanding, and inferences that are derived on the basis of a communication (for related conceptualizations, see Berinsky & Kinder, 2006; Pennington & Hastie, 1986).

Consider, for example, the following description of U.S. military action during Operation Desert Storm: "The Highway of Death was a death camp. It was Auschwitz on a road." This description activates the root metaphor

Operation Desert Storm was genocide. This metaphor contains a *genocide* script or event representation possessing some rather notable elements. Genocide is a morally repugnant, barbaric, inhumane, and egregious practice. Perpetrators of genocide commonly elicit intense feelings of disgust, repulsion, and anger. Victims of genocide are, in most cases, completely helpless and unable to defend themselves. In light of this genocide script, Operation Desert Storm might be viewed as a merciless, gruesome, and inhumane attack on a helpless and powerless group of Iraqis. This view of Operation Desert Storm should engender negative attitudes toward the military operation.

In comparison, consider a description of Desert Storm that indicates "Desert Storm was Bush's Emancipation Proclamation. The imprisonment of Kuwait was diverted." This description activates the root metaphor *Operation Desert Storm was a liberation of captives.* This metaphor contains the *captive liberation* script, a prototypic event representation possessing a drastically different set of implications. In this storyline, the Kuwaiti "captives" are innocent and powerless victims who have been unfairly treated by hostile and unfriendly Iraqi "captors." The U.S. "liberators" are heroes who rescue and release the captives. In this captive liberation script, the U.S. invasion is perceived to be a heroic action that freed innocent Kuwaiti citizens. Clearly, the genocide and captive liberation scripts activate divergent stories of the U.S. war in Iraq. Once activated, these images or storylines serve as cognitive frames that can influence public opinion regarding U.S. military action in Operation Desert Storm.

Effect of Metaphor on Political Judgment

The effect of metaphoric political framing on the public's attitudes and opinions is potentially mediated by a variety of psychological process mechanisms (Ottati & Renstrom, 2010; for a related discussion, see Ottati, 2001). Some of these psychological process mechanisms involve relatively direct effects of the activated cognitive frame on citizens' political judgments. In other cases, however, the metaphoric political framing effect is postulated to be more indirect (Ottati & Renstrom, 2010). In these instances, metaphoric statements activate a cognitive frame, storyline, or expectancy that influences cognitive processing of other information pertaining to the target. These effects on cognitive processing, in turn, elicit effects on political judgment.

Direct Application Hypothesis

Metaphor comprehension entails mapping informational implications of the source onto the target (Gentner, 1983; Gibbs, 1994; Ortony, Reynolds,

& Arter, 1978; but see Gineste, Indurkhva, & Scart, 2000). In accordance with this perspective, the *direct application hypothesis* presumes that the message recipient takes information contained in the source and directly applies it to form an impression of the target. Thus, if a description of Desert Storm activates the genocide script, the message recipient might directly infer that U.S. soldiers ruthlessly killed Iraqis who were helpless and unable to defend themselves. This *direct inference* can serve to "fill in missing data" if the message recipient receives no other information that more directly and explicitly describes U.S. soldiers' behavior during the military operation. Individuals who adopt this belief are, of course, likely to derive a negative evaluation of Operation Desert Storm. In this fashion, the direct application process should ultimately produce an effect on the public's attitudes and opinions regarding Operation Desert Storm. In accordance with this formulation, research confirms that metaphors can produce an assimilation effect on political judgment. That is, metaphors containing positive vehicles elicit positive evaluations of political entities and policies, whereas metaphors containing negative vehicles produce the opposite effect (Johnson & Taylor, 1981).

It is important to note that the metaphor source is not simply an abstract schematic category that includes the target as an exemplar (Landau et al., 2010). On the contrary, the source and target constitute distinct categories or concepts that contain both shared and unshared attributes. Only the shared attributes are potentially mapped onto the target (Hitchon, 1997; Kintsch, 2001). Thus, the metaphor *Operation Desert Storm is a football game* does not lead the receiver to infer that U.S. soldiers wore football uniforms, drank Gatorade during timeouts, or spiked a ball when they penetrated enemy lines. Individuals fail to generate these inferences because they involve features of a football game that are clearly not shared by a military action. However, such a communication may well lead the American public to avoid criticism of the war and to remain loyal to the U.S. military. It may also promote a sanitized view of the war that neglects the physical pain, suffering, and death caused by the military action. After all, good football fans should remain loyal to their preferred team, and although football is an aggressive sport, football players rarely kill each other.

Importantly, direct application does not necessarily produce an effect on attitudes toward the communication target that is congruent with the overall valence of the metaphor source (vehicle). In some cases, the evaluative implication of features shared by the target and source is not equivalent to evaluation of the source taken as a whole. Consider, for example, President Reagan's claim that the government is a *baby*. Although most people evaluate babies positively overall, the positive features of a baby (e.g., cute, lovable, cuddly, fresh) are not easily attributed to government. That is, the positive features of a baby are not the *shared* features. However, negative features of a baby are readily attributed to the government. For example, the government can be construed as irresponsible, lacking restraint, failing to clean up after itself, and so on. A baby and the government potentially share all of these negative features. Thus, when Reagan described the government as a baby, direct application of the shared features would have negatively influenced the public's attitude toward government.

Direct application should be most likely to occur when the message recipient has little prior knowledge of the news event. Under such conditions, the implications of the activated metaphor can be directly applied without any "interference" from the message recipient's prior knowledge of the news event. Thus, metaphoric activation of the genocide script might engender negative opinions regarding Operation Desert Storm mostly among individuals who have incomplete knowledge of the U.S. soldiers' actual behavior during the operation. This effect might be weaker among message recipients who can rely on detailed prior knowledge of the military operation to derive an opinion, assuming of course, that such knowledge contradicts the implications of the genocide script. Individuals who have detailed prior knowledge might also rely on a previously established issue frame that is chronically accessible and consistent with their prior political predispositions (Hansen, 2007). Consistent with this conceptualization, research suggests political experts are resistant to influence elicited by issue frames that contradict their prior predispositions (Hansen, 2007; but see Johnson & Taylor, 1981).

Selective Processing Hypothesis

To persuade the public, metaphors can be used in political communications to selectively highlight certain information while overlooking information that contradicts a politician's primary argument (Lakoff & Johnson, 1980). As Edelman (1971) famously noted:

> Metaphor . . . defines the pattern of perception to which people respond. To speak of deterrence and strike capacity is to perceive war as a game; to speak of legalized murder is to perceive war as a slaughter of human beings. . . . Each metaphor intensifies selected perceptions and ignores others, thereby helping one to concentrate upon desired consequences of favored public policies and helping one to ignore their unwanted, unthinkable, or irrelevant premises and aftermaths. Each metaphor can be a subtle way of highlighting what one wants to believe and avoiding what one does not wish to face. (p. 67)

In this fashion, politicians use metaphor to set the frame of the debate, emphasizing information and arguments they promote while obscuring information and arguments they prefer to ignore.

The *trade is war* metaphor described earlier effectively highlights certain aspects of free trade (i.e., free trade causes countries to compete for cheap or skilled workers, with some countries winning and others losing) while ignoring or disregarding others aspects of free trade (i.e., most countries prosper from free trade either through increased jobs or decreased prices for imports). A candidate advocating an antitrade position can use the *trade is war* metaphor and highlight the negative competitive aspects of free trade. In contrast, a candidate who wishes to convince his or her constituents that free trade is beneficial would seek to avoid such a metaphor, instead selecting a metaphor that emphasizes the shared prosperity of free trade and downplays or ignores any aspects involving competition between nations for jobs (e.g., *free trade is a rising tide that lifts all boats*). In this fashion, metaphors can distill an intricate and multifaceted policy into a simpler (and often one-sided) issue description. When metaphor selectively highlights only one side of an issue, it may lead the public to derive their policy opinion on the basis of an incomplete, limited, or biased set of considerations. Political candidates can use this to their advantage to promote themselves or their policies.

It is likely that metaphoric framing produces selectivity effects at many stages of information processing. A metaphoric news frame, by highlighting certain aspects of a news story and ignoring others, essentially constitutes a form of selective news presentation. Thus, the metaphoric political framing effect is, by definition, mediated by the message recipient's selective exposure to information pertaining to the news event. Because the news consumer does not directly control how a news source chooses to frame a news story, this is essentially an *involuntary* form of selective exposure (see Ottati, 2001). Research suggests that metaphoric framing can also elicit a *voluntary* selective exposure effect when individuals actively seek out or selectively attend to information pertaining to the target. Specifically, Thibodeau and Boroditsky (2011) presented experimental participants with information that activated the *crime is a virus* or *crime is a beast* metaphor. When given an opportunity to seek out additional information pertaining to crime, participants sought out information that confirmed the validity of the metaphor. This finding identifies a process in which metaphoric communication might amass long-term effects on social policy reasoning that increase over time.

Metaphoric political framing effects might also be mediated by selective encoding. Once activated, a metaphoric image might facilitate the encoding of subsequent literal information that is consistent with the image. For example, reference to *welfare queens* might increase the likelihood that citizens encode subsequently encountered examples of welfare abuse or decrease the likelihood that citizens encode subsequently encountered examples of welfare success stories (e.g., an individual who rises from poverty to economic success). Effects of this nature, which involve selective encoding of information into long-term memory, might emerge even when controlling for the previously described effects of selective exposure and attention.

Metaphoric political framing effects might also be mediated by selective retrieval of previously acquired information pertaining to a political issue. Thus, references to welfare queens might increase the likelihood that previously encountered examples of welfare abuse are recalled or decrease the likelihood that previously encountered examples of welfare success are recalled. That is, metaphoric framing might highlight previously acquired issue information that is metaphor-consistent and reduce the accessibility of previously acquired information that is metaphor-inconsistent. Here, the highlighting function of metaphor is retrospective.

Guided Interpretation Hypothesis

Previous theory and research suggests that metaphoric statements provide a schematic framework that guides cognitive processing of other, literal statements contained in a communication (Billow, 1977; Mio, 1993, 1996; Read, Cesa, Jones, & Collins, 1990; see also Srull & Wyer, 1979). When a metaphor precedes literal statements about a political issue, it can serve as a cognitive expectancy that influences the interpretation of subsequent information. This metaphor-guided interpretation effect might, in turn, produce an effect on the message recipient's attitudes and opinions regarding the issue. This effect should be especially likely to emerge when the subsequently encountered news information is ambiguous and, therefore, open to alternative interpretations. In accordance with this assumption, Renstrom, Krumdick, and Ottati (2008) found that individuals rated ambiguously hostile behaviors enacted by a target person, Donald, much more negatively if the description of those behaviors was accompanied by a hostile metaphor ("Donald is a Nazi") versus a neutral control metaphor. However, this effect emerged only when the hostile metaphor preceded (as opposed to followed) the ambiguous behavioral description, suggesting that the metaphor acted as a frame that guided the interpretation of the rest of the descriptive communication.

A similar effect might emerge in the political domain. Suppose "Congressman Jones is a rock star" precedes the literal statement "He accumulated more than a million dollars in contributions last quarter." In this case, the literal statement is interpreted to suggest Congressman Jones attracted financial support due to his charisma and popular support. In contrast, if "Congressman Jones is a puppet" precedes the literal statement, a different interpretation is likely to emerge. Namely, the literal statement will be interpreted in a negative fashion (i.e., the congressman is bought and controlled by rich contributors or lobbyists).

Guided Attribution and Elaboration

Although yet to be tested, it seems likely that metaphor guides attribution. For example, the *welfare queen* metaphor might elicit dispositional attributions for unemployment whereas the *ailing economy* metaphor might elicit situational attributions for unemployment. These attributions, in turn, should increase the likelihood that individuals endorse metaphor-consistent policy solutions for the unemployment problem. Consistent with this claim, Thibodeau and Boroditsky (2011) demonstrated that metaphors influence proposed solutions to the crime problem. Namely, as noted previously, *crime is a beast* elicited crime proposals that focus on enforcement, punishment, and incarceration. In contrast, *crime is a virus* elicited proposals for social reform that focus on addressing the social causes of crime (e.g., poverty) and preventing the spread of crime.

In a related fashion, it can be anticipated that metaphor will elicit a metaphor-consistent pattern of cognitive elaboration. For example, individuals who view unemployment as a *symptom of an ailing economy* should generate pro-arguments in responses to a proposal to introduce a federally funded job creation program. In contrast, individuals who view the unemployed as *parasites* should generate counterarguments in response to such a proposal.

Metaphor Rejection

The previously described hypotheses presume that individuals, either consciously or unconsciously, accept the validity of the activated metaphoric proposition. In some cases, however, individuals may actively reject a metaphoric proposition. When this occurs, it can be anticipated that the metaphoric framing effect will be reduced, eliminated, or even reversed (see Schwarz & Bless, 2007, for a related conceptualization). Consider, for example, a communication containing the statement "CNN is Nazi propaganda promulgated by big business." Although some individuals will regard this as an apt metaphor, many will consider it to be an extreme, unfair, and inappropriate characterization of CNN news (or big business). How does this latter group of individuals respond to this communication?

Inspired by theory and research regarding the effects of context on judgment (e.g., Schwarz & Bless, 2007), the metaphoric framing model presumes that one of three psychological processes will ensue. First, these individuals may simply discount the implications of the metaphor when deriving a judgment. If this occurs, the aforementioned metaphor should elicit ratings of CNN bias that are no different from ratings obtained in a control condition that excludes the metaphor. Second, these individuals might derive an initial judgment that is biased in the direction of the metaphor. After doing so, however, these individuals might attempt to correct for the biasing influence of the metaphor. If they undercorrect, the metaphor framing effect should be reduced (but not eliminated). If they correct in an appropriate fashion, the metaphor framing effect should be eliminated. If they overcorrect, the effect should be reversed. In this latter case, presentation of "CNN news is Nazi propaganda promulgated by big business" should reduce ratings of CNN news bias relative to a control condition.

A third process might ensue when the source of the metaphor is perceived to be overly extreme. In this case, the source may function as a standard of comparison when individuals rate the target. Thus, a respondent might reason that, compared with Nazi propaganda, CNN is a decidedly fair and unbiased purveyor of news. As a consequence, the metaphor "CNN news is Nazi propaganda" might elicit judgments that are opposite to the implications of the metaphor.

Effects of Metaphor on Process Style

Basic research confirms that metaphor can significantly influence cognitive style when individuals process other literal information contained in a communication. Inspired by dual-process models of persuasion (Chaiken, 1980; Petty & Cacioppo, 1986), Ottati et al. (1999) demonstrated that metaphors influence the degree to which message recipients systematically process other, literal statements in a communication. Systematic processing occurs when the message recipient carefully attends to, scrutinizes, and elaborates on the literal statements. It is marked by increased generation of message-relevant cognitive responses, a more complex and organized representation of the target, and increased sensitivity to argument strength when listeners derive their evaluation of the target (Chaiken, 1980; Gernsbacher, 1991; Graesser, Singer, & Trabasso, 1994; Petty & Cacioppo, 1986).

It is important to note that this effect of metaphor on *cognitive style* is not equivalent to the previously described effects of metaphor on political judgment (Ottati et al., 1999; Ottati & Renstrom, 2010). When metaphor influences cognitive style, the evaluative impact of the metaphor is determined by the strength of the literal statements, not the valence of the metaphor source. Careful scrutiny of strong literal arguments produces positive cognitive responses (pro-arguments), whereas careful scrutiny of weak literal arguments produces negative cognitive responses (counterarguing). A metaphor that promotes systematic processing should therefore produce positive attitudes toward the target if the literal message arguments are strong but produce negative attitudes toward the target if these arguments are weak. A metaphor that reduces central processing should produce an obverse pattern of effects (Ottati et al., 1999).

Motivation to Systematically Process

On the basis of these considerations, Ottati et al. (1999) developed the *motivational resonance model*. This model proposes that metaphor increases systematic processing when it contains content that is of personal interest to the message recipient but decreases systematic processing when it contains content that alienates or disinterests the message recipient. Accordingly, Ottati et al. reported that a sports metaphor increases systematic processing among sports enthusiasts, but decreases systematic processing among listeners who dislike sports (for related conceptualizations, see McGuire, 2000; McQuarrie & Mick, 1999). Although this model has yet to be tested using a political communication, it is potentially influential in this domain. As previously noted, sports metaphors are extremely prevalent, for example, when military missions are described by politicians, political analysts, and military leaders (Beer & de Landtsheer, 2004). According to the motivational resonance model, this reliance on sports metaphors might promote a more sophisticated, elaborate, and complex understanding of military operations among sports enthusiasts. However, it should produce the opposite effect, and alienate individuals who dislike sports.

Ability to Systematically Process

Metaphor might also influence the message recipient's *ability* to engage in systematic processing. Some theory and research suggests that a metaphor can increase the coherence of a communication, providing an overarching schematic framework that guides interpretation, facilitates organization, and facilitates central processing of literal statements (Billow, 1977; Krumdick, Renstrom, Aalai, & Ottati, 2007; Mio, 1993, 1996; Read et al., 1990). For example, Read et al. (1990) demonstrated that metaphor facilitates encoding and recall of subsequently presented literal political information, presumably because metaphor activates a cognitive structure that facilitates comprehension and organization of related literal political information. According to this view, metaphor should increase systematic processing of other, literal statements contained in a communication.

Alternatively, as previously noted, metaphor might promote selective processing that leads the message recipient to ignore important information. When this is the case, metaphor might produce a one-sided and oversimplified view of a political issue (Landau et al., 2009; Thompson, 1996). Moreover, if the metaphor *fails* to afford clear linkages with the literal statements contained in a communication, it might confuse or distract the listener and thereby reduce systematic processing of the literal communication arguments (Billow, 1977; Frey & Eagly, 1993; Mio, 1996; Mio & Lovrich, 1998). Although research has yet to determine *when* each of these effects will emerge, effects of this nature should be extremely relevant to understanding the role of metaphor in political communication.

MULTIPLE METAPHORS

In democracies characterized by electoral competition, the public is confronted with multiple (and often conflicting) metaphoric frames (Hansen, 2007). Often, individuals also possess chronically accessible metaphoric frames that are spontaneously activated by the mere mention of a political issue. Thus, multiple metaphors are often activated when an individual thinks about a political issue or derives a political judgment. Although research regarding multiply activated metaphors is limited, related theory and research regarding priming effects provides a basis for generating some plausible hypotheses. Specifically, it can be hypothesized that the relative influence of a given metaphor will be a joint function of the accessibility and perceived aptness of the metaphor (see Higgins, 1996, for a related priming model).

When multiple metaphoric utterances converge on the same root metaphor, each utterance can be viewed as a repetition of one and the same conceptual prime. Under such conditions, multiple utterances should increase the accessibility of the root metaphor and thereby increase the magnitude of the metaphoric framing effect. Thus, for example, a communication containing multiple utterances that activate the *war is a football game* metaphor should elicit a stronger metaphoric framing effect than a communication that contains only one such utterance (for related evidence in the priming literature, see Balota & Paul, 1996; Srull & Wyer, 1979).

What happens, however, when two or more distinct conceptual metaphors are activated at the time an individual derives a political judgment? This can occur when a communication activates multiple conceptual metaphors or when a communication activates a metaphor that is distinct from a metaphor that is chronically accessible in the message recipient. Under these conditions, an important question involves the relative weight ascribed to each metaphor in determining the message recipient's reasoning and judgment regarding the target issue. One possibility is that each metaphor will be weighted equally. This should yield reinforcing effects when the metaphors imply a similar judgmental conclusion and cancellation effects when the metaphors imply opposite judgmental conclusions (Hansen, 2007). It seems likely, however, that the metaphors will be unequally weighted. That is, as previously suggested, metaphors that are high in accessibility and perceived aptness (i.e., perceived semantic fit with the target issue) will be weighted more heavily than metaphors that are low in accessibility or perceived aptness. This unequally weighted approach can be derived from related research that examines the effect of dual-framed messages that imply opposite judgmental conclusions. This research suggests that dual-framed messages usually produce predisposition-consistent effects on political opinion (Hansen, 2007). Apparently, individuals give more weight to the predisposition-consistent frame than the predisposition-inconsistent frame when deriving political judgments. Presumably, this is because the predisposition-consistent frame is high in chronic accessibility and perceived to be "well fitting" by the message recipient. However, activation of the predisposition-inconsistent frame may be suppressed by the (competing) consistent frame (for related evidence, see Balota & Paul, 1996; Gernsbacher, 1991). Moreover, as previously suggested, the message recipient might actively reject a predisposition-inconsistent frame because it is perceived to be low in aptness (i.e., perceived to provide a poor fit). For these reasons, it stands to reason that predisposition-consistent frames will often be given more weight than predisposition-inconsistent frames when individuals derive political judgments.

CONCLUSION

The metaphoric framing model provides a basis for understanding the effects of metaphor in political communication. According to this model, political communications can implicitly or explicitly activate a root metaphor (e.g., *Operation Desert Storm is a football game*). This root metaphor links the message target (e.g., *Operation Desert Storm*) to the metaphor source (e.g., *a football game*). The source contains a series of cognitive entailments that are potentially mapped on to the target. This multifaceted image can directly determine the listener's impression of the news event. Or it can indirectly influence this impression by guiding processing of other literal information pertaining to the news event. Under appropriate circumstances, metaphoric language may also influence the message recipient's motivation or ability to systematically process a political communication.

REFERENCES

Arndt, J. (1985). On making marketing science more scientific: Role of orientations, paradigms, metaphors, and puzzle solving. *Journal of Marketing, 49,* 11–23. doi:10.2307/1251612

Balota, D. A., & Paul, S. T. (1996). Summation of activation: Evidence from multiple primes that converge and diverge within semantic memory. *Journal of Experimental Psychology: Learning, Memory, and Cognition, 22,* 827–845. doi:10.1037/0278-7393.22.4.827

Beer, F. B., & de Landtsheer, C. (2004). *Metaphorical world politics*. East Lansing: Michigan State Press.

Behr, R. L., & Iyengar, S. (1985). Television news, real-world cues, and changes in public agenda. *Public Opinion Quarterly, 49*, 38–57. doi:10.1086/268900

Berinsky, A. J., & Kinder, D. R. (2006). Making sense of issues through media frames: Understanding the Kosovo crisis. *The Journal of Politics, 68*, 640–656. doi:10.1111/j.1468-2508.2006.00451.x

Billow, R. M. (1977). Metaphor: A review of the psychological literature. *Psychological Bulletin, 84*, 81–92. doi:10.1037/0033-2909.84.1.81

Bizer, G. Y., & Krosnick, J. (2001). Exploring the structure of strength-related attitude features: The relation between attitude importance and attitude accessibility. *Journal of Personality and Social Psychology, 81*, 566–586. doi:10.1037/0022-3514.81.4.566

Bodenhausen, G. V., & Macrae, N. (1998). Stereotype activation and inhibition. In R. S. Wyer, Jr., (Ed.), *Advances in social cognition* (Vol. 11, pp. 1–52). Mahwah, NJ: Erlbaum.

Bougher, L. D. (2012). The case for metaphor in political reasoning and cognition. *Political Psychology, 33*, 145–163. doi:10.1111/j.1467-9221.2011.00865.x

Bowdle, B. F., & Gentner, D. (2005). The career of metaphor. *Psychological Review, 112*, 193–216. doi:10.1037/0033-295X.112.1.193

Bowers, J. W., & Osborn, M. M. (1966). Attitudinal effects of selected types of concluding metaphors in persuasive speeches. *Speech Monographs, 33*, 147–155. doi:10.1080/03637756609375490

Chaiken, S. (1980). Heuristic versus systematic information processing and the use of source versus message cues in persuasion. *Journal of Personality and Social Psychology, 39*, 752–766. doi:10.1037/0022-3514.39.5.752

Dimitrova, D. V., & Stromback, J. (2005). Mission accomplished? Framing of the Iraq War in the elite newspapers in Sweden and the United States. *International Communication Gazette, 67*, 399–417. doi:10.1177/0016549205056050

Druckman, J. N. (2001). The implications of framing effects for citizen competence. *Political Behavior, 23*, 225–256. doi:10.1023/A:1015006907312

Edelman, M. (1971). *Politics as symbolic action*. Chicago, IL: Marham.

Entman, R. M. (1993). Framing: Towards clarification of a fractured paradigm. *Journal of Communication, 43*, 51–58. doi:10.1111/j.1460-2466.1993.tb01304.x

Entman, R. M. (2004). *Projections of power: Framing news, public opinion, and U.S. foreign policy*. Chicago, IL: University of Chicago Press.

Eubanks, P. (2000). *A war of words in the discourse on trade: The rhetorical constitution of metaphor*. Carbondale: Southern Illinois University Press.

Frey, K. P., & Eagly, A. H. (1993). Vividness can undermine persuasiveness of messages. *Journal of Personality and Social Psychology, 65*, 32–44. doi:10.1037/0022-3514.65.1.32

Fussell, S. R., & Moss, M. M. (1998). Figurative language in emotional communication. In S. R. Fussell & R. J. Kreuz (Eds.), *Social and cognitive approaches to interpersonal communication* (pp. 113–141). Mahwah, NJ: Erlbaum.

Gentner, D. (1983). Structure-mapping: A theoretical framework for analogy. *Cognitive Science, 7,* 155–170. doi:10.1207/s15516709cog0702_3

Gernsbacher, M. A. (1991). Cognitive processes and mechanisms in language comprehension: The structure building framework. *Psychology of Learning and Motivation, 27,* 217–263. doi:10.1016/S0079-7421(08)60125-5

Gibbs, R. W. (1994). *The poetics of mind: Figurative thought, language, and understanding.* New York, NY: Cambridge University Press.

Gilbert, D. J., & Hixon, J. G. (1991). The trouble of thinking: Activation and application of stereotypic beliefs. *Journal of Personality and Social Psychology, 60,* 509–517. doi:10.1037/0022-3514.60.4.509

Gilbert, S. F. (1979). The metaphorical structuring of social perceptions. *Soundings, 62,* 166–186.

Gineste, M., Indurkhya, B., & Scart, V. (2000). Emergence of features in metaphor comprehension. *Metaphor and Symbol, 15,* 117–135. doi:10.1207/S15327868 MS1503_1

Graesser, A. C., Long, D., & Mio, J. (1989). What are the cognitive and conceptual components of humorous texts? *Poetics, 18,* 143–164. doi:10.1016/0304-422X(89)90026-0

Graesser, A. C., Singer, M., & Trabasso, T. (1994). Constructing inferences during narrative text comprehension. *Psychological Review, 101,* 371–395. doi:10.1037/0033-295X.101.3.371

Hansen, K. M. (2007). The sophisticated public: The effect of competing frames on public opinion. *Scandinavian Political Studies, 30,* 377–396. doi:10.1111/j.1467-9477.2007.00185.x

Higgins, E. T. (1996). Knowledge activation: Accessibility, applicability, and salience. In E. T. Higgins & A. Kruglanski (Eds.), *Social psychology: Handbook of basic principles* (pp. 133–168). New York, NY: Guilford Press.

Hitchon, J. C. (1997). The locus of metaphorical persuasion: An empirical test. *Journalism & Mass Communication Quarterly, 74,* 55–68. doi:10.1177/107769909707400105

Howe, N. (1988). Metaphor in contemporary American political discourse. *Metaphor and Symbolic Activity, 3,* 87–104. doi:10.1207/s15327868ms0302_2

Hunt, S. D., & Menon, A. (1995). Metaphors and competitive advantage: Evaluating the use of metaphors in theories of competitive strategy. *Journal of Business Research, 33,* 81–90. doi:10.1016/0148-2963(94)00057-L

Iyengar, S. (1991). *Is anyone responsible? How television frames political issues.* Chicago, IL: University of Chicago Press. doi:10.7208/chicago/9780226388533.001.0001

Iyengar, S., Kinder, D. R., Peters, M. D., & Krosnick, J. A. (1984). The evening news and presidential evaluations. *Journal of Personality and Social Psychology, 46,* 778–787. doi:10.1037/0022-3514.46.4.778

Johnson, J. T., & Taylor, S. E. (1981). The effect of metaphor on political attitudes. *Basic and Applied Social Psychology, 2,* 305–316. doi:10.1207/s15324834 basp0204_6

Kintsch, W. (2001). Predication. *Cognitive Science, 25,* 173–202. doi:10.1207/s15516709cog2502_1

Klapper, J. T. (1960). *The effects of mass communication.* New York, NY: Free Press.

Kreuz, R. J., & Roberts, R. M. (1993). The empirical study of figurative language in literature. *Poetics, 22,* 151–169. doi:10.1016/0304-422X(93)90026-D

Kreuz, R. J., Roberts, R. M., Johnson, B. K., & Bertus, E. L. (1996). Figurative language occurrence and co-occurrence in contemporary literature. In R. J. Kreuz & M. S. MacNealy (Eds.), *Empirical approaches to literature and aesthetics* (pp. 83–97). New York, NY: Ablex.

Krumdick, N. D., Renstrom, R. A., Aalai, A., & Ottati, V. C. (2007, May). *Metaphor and persuasion: Effects of cognitive coherence.* Poster presented at the annual meeting of the Midwest Psychological Association, Chicago, IL.

Lakoff, G. (1987). *Women, fire and dangerous things: What categories reveal about the mind.* Chicago, IL: University of Chicago Press. doi:10.7208/chicago/9780226471013.001.0001

Lakoff, G. (1993). The contemporary theory of metaphor. In A. Ortony (Ed.), *Metaphor and thought* (pp. 202–251). Cambridge, England: Cambridge University Press. doi:10.1017/CBO9781139173865.013

Lakoff, G. (2004). *Don't think of an elephant: Know your values and frame the debate.* White River Junction, VT: Chelsea Green.

Lakoff, G., & Johnson, M. (1980). *Metaphors we live by.* Chicago, IL: University of Chicago Press.

Landau, M. J., Meier, B. P., & Keefer, L. A. (2010). A metaphor-enriched social cognition. *Psychological Bulletin, 136,* 1045–1067. doi:10.1037/a0020970

Landau, M. J., Sullivan, D., & Greenberg, J. (2009). Evidence that self-relevant motivations and metaphoric framing interact to influence political and social issues. *Psychological Science, 20,* 1421–1427. doi:10.1111/j.1467-9280.2009.02462.x

Martin, J. (2011, January 10). Tucson shooting marks turning point for Sarah Palin. *Politico.* Retrieved from http://www.politico.com/news/stories/0111/47351.html

McGuire, W. J. (2000). Standing on the shoulders of ancients: Consumer research, persuasion, and figurative language. *Journal of Consumer Research, 27,* 109–114. doi:10.1086/314312

McMullen, L. (1989). Use of figurative language in successful and unsuccessful cases of psychotherapy: Three comparisons. *Metaphor and Symbolic Activity, 4,* 203–225. doi:10.1207/s15327868ms0404_1

McQuarrie, E. F., & Mick, D. G. (1999). Verbal rhetoric in advertising: Test-interpretive, experimental, and reader-response analyses. *Journal of Consumer Research, 26*, 37–54. doi:10.1086/209549

Mio, J. S. (1993, August). *Responding to metaphors in the context of political debate.* Paper presented at the 101st Annual Convention of the American Psychological Association, Toronto, Canada.

Mio, J. S. (1996). Metaphor, politics, and persuasion. In J. S. Mio & A. N. Katz (Eds.), *Metaphor: Implications and applications* (pp. 127–145). Mahwah, NJ: Erlbaum.

Mio, J. S. (1997). Metaphor and politics. *Metaphor and Symbol, 12*, 113–133. doi:10.1207/s15327868ms1202_2

Mio, J. S., & Katz, A. N. (Eds.). (1996). *Metaphor: Implications and applications.* Mahwah, NJ: Erlbaum.

Mio, J. S., & Lovrich, N. P. (1998). Men of zeal: Memory for metaphors in the Iran-Contra hearings. *Metaphor and Symbol, 13*, 49–68. doi:10.1207/s15327868 ms1301_4

Mio, J. S., Riggio, R. E., Levin, S., & Reese, R. (2005). Presidential leadership and charisma: The effects of metaphor. *The Leadership Quarterly, 16*, 287–294. doi:10.1016/j.leaqua.2005.01.005

Nelson, T. E., Oxley, Z., & Clawson, R. A. (1997). Toward a psychology of framing effects. *Political Behavior, 19*, 221–246. doi:10.1023/A:1024834831093

Ortony, A., Reynolds, R. E., & Arter, J. A. (1978). Metaphor: Theoretical and empirical research. *Psychological Bulletin, 85*, 919–943. doi:10.1037/0033-2909.85.5.919

Ottati, V., Rhoads, S., & Graesser, A. (1999). The effect of metaphor on processing style in a persuasion task: A motivational resonance model. *Journal of Personality and Social Psychology, 77*, 688–697. doi:10.1037/0022-3514.77.4.688

Ottati, V. C. (2001). The psychological determinants of political judgment. In A. Tesser & N. Schwarz (Eds.), *Blackwell handbook of social psychology: Intra-individual processes* (pp. 615–632). Oxford, England: Blackwell.

Ottati, V. C., & Renstrom, R. A. (2010). Metaphor and persuasive communication: A multi-functional approach. *Social and Personality Psychology Compass, 4*, 783–794. doi:10.1111/j.1751-9004.2010.00292.x

Pennington, N., & Hastie, R. (1986). Evidence evaluation in complex decision making. *Journal of Personality and Social Psychology, 51*, 242–258. doi:10.1037/0022-3514.51.2.242

Petty, R. E., & Cacioppo, J. T. (1986). *Communication and persuasion: Central and peripheral routes to attitude change.* New York, NY: Springer-Verlag.

Pfau, M., Haigh, M., Logsdon, L., Perrine, C., Baldwin, J. P., Breitenfeldt, R. E., . . . Romero, R. (2005). Embedded reporting during invasion and occupation of Iraq: How the embedding of journalists affects television news reports. *Journal of Broadcasting & Electronic Media, 49*, 468–487. doi:10.1207/s15506878 jobem4904_7

Read, S. J., Cesa, I. L., Jones, D. K., & Collins, N. L. (1990). When is the federal budget like a baby? Metaphor in political rhetoric. *Metaphor and Symbolic Activity, 5,* 125–149. doi:10.1207/s15327868ms0503_1

Renstrom, R. A., Krumdick, N. D., & Ottati, V. C. (2008, May). *Metaphorical communication: The effects of figurative language on impression formation.* Paper presented at the 58th Annual Meeting of the International Communication Association, Montreal, Canada.

Richards, I. A. (1936). *The philosophy of rhetoric.* London, England: Oxford University Press.

Rössler, P., & Schenk, M. (2000). Cognitive bonding and the German reunification: Agenda-setting and persuasion effects of mass media. *International Journal of Public Opinion Research, 12,* 29–47. doi:10.1093/ijpor/12.1.29

Schwarz, N., & Bless, H. (2007). Mental construal processes: The inclusion/exclusion model. In D. A. Stapel & J. Suls (Eds.), *Assimilation and contrast in social psychology* (pp. 119–141). Philadelphia, PA: Psychology Press.

Semetko, H. A., & Valkenburg, P. M. (2000). Framing European politics: A content analysis of press and television news. *Journal of Communication, 50,* 93–109. doi:10.1111/j.1460-2466.2000.tb02843.x

Soroka, S. N. (2003). Media, public opinion, and foreign policy. *The International Journal of Press/Politics, 8,* 27–48. doi:10.1177/1081180X02238783

Srull, T. K., & Wyer, R. S. (1979). The role of category accessibility in the interpretation of information about persons: Some determinants and implications. *Journal of Personality and Social Psychology, 37,* 1660–1672. doi:10.1037/0022-3514.37.10.1660

Stone, D. A. (1988). *Policy paradox and political reason.* Glenview, IL: Scott Foresman.

Sutherland, M., & Galloway, J. (1981). Role of advertising: Persuasion or agenda setting? *Journal of Advertising Research, 21,* 25–29.

Thibodeau, P. H., & Boroditsky, L. (2011). Metaphors we think with: The role of metaphor in reasoning. *PLoS ONE, 6*(2), e16782. doi:10.1371/journal.pone.0016782

Thompson, S. (1996). Politics without metaphors is like a fish without water. In J. S. Mio & A. N. Katz (Eds.), *Metaphor: Implications and applications* (pp. 185–201). Mahwah, NJ: Erlbaum.

Williams, L. E., & Bargh, J. A. (2008). Experiencing physical warmth promotes interpersonal warmth. *Science, 322,* 606–607. doi:10.1126/science.1162548

Wyer, R. S., & Srull, T. K. (1989). *Memory and cognition in its social context.* Hillsdale, NJ: Erlbaum.

III

CURRENT ISSUES AND DIRECTION FOR FUTURE RESEARCH

10

DO EVALUATIVE METAPHORS SHAPE EMOTIONAL THOUGHT? A CALL FOR NEW EVIDENCE

GARY D. SHERMAN AND GERALD L. CLORE

In the realm of emotion, metaphors abound. This is true of how people talk about emotion (Kövecses, 2000) and perhaps of how people think about, and experience, emotion. Indeed, this is the central claim of conceptual metaphor theory (CMT; Lakoff & Johnson, 1980, 1999)—that metaphor is more than a linguistic phenomenon. In the current chapter, we examine this claim with respect to a particular often-studied type of emotion metaphor—*dimensional evaluative metaphors*. Dimensional evaluative metaphors involve the mapping between the valence dimension of emotion—good–bad—and a concrete physical dimension such as *up–down, bright–dark,* or *big–small* (Crawford, 2009). Evaluative–experiential mappings of this form have been the focus of most psychological research on the topic of emotion and metaphor. In this chapter, we review what is known about these mappings, focusing on what it would mean for them to function as metaphors in the sense articulated by CMT.

http://dx.doi.org/10.1037/14278-013
The Power of Metaphor: Examining Its Influence on Social Life, M. J. Landau, M. D. Robinson, and B. P. Meier (Editors)

EVALUATIVE–EXPERIENTIAL MAPPINGS AS METAPHORS: STRUCTURING ABSTRACT THOUGHT

Metaphors clarify the meaning of an abstract, unfamiliar concept through comparison with a more concrete, familiar concept (Boroditsky, 2000; Gentner, 1983; Lakoff & Johnson, 1980, 1999). More specifically, metaphor involves a structural or relational mapping that allows for the importing of knowledge or meaning from a well-understood domain into a less well-understood domain. For example, by thinking about arguments through the lens of war ("she attacked my opinion"), one comes to understand that arguments have similar attributes to war (e.g., they are zero-sum games; Lakoff & Johnson, 1980). For evaluative–experiential mappings to be metaphoric in this sense, it would mean that people think of, and experience, goodness and badness as akin to the experiential dimensions to which they are linked. For example, to call the goodness–brightness mapping a metaphor implies that people conceive of goodness as being akin to brightness—that is, as having similar attributes. One interpretation is that how someone evaluates the world—the way he or she thinks about and experiences goodness or badness—will be shaped by the particular mappings that are operating in any given context. A critical question we address in this chapter is whether the available evidence supports this interpretation, and if not, what sort of evidence would be needed to bolster such a view.

CORRELATIONS BETWEEN VALUE AND PHYSICAL ATTRIBUTES

An alternative explanation for people's tendency to find evaluative meaning in dimensions of experience is that value and certain physical attributes covary. Evaluative reactions are concerned with identifying which entities are desired and which are undesired—that is, which to be approached or avoided (Chen & Bargh, 1999). To aid in this process, people may infer value on the basis of physical cues, such as an object's appearance or location. Indeed, goodness has concrete, physical correlates, or at least people tend to assume that it does. For example, it is common for people to believe that good things tend to be elevated or brightly colored; conversely, people often assume that objects low in space or dark are inherently less valuable or even overtly harmful. For example, in many societies, such as among the Hua of New Guinea, food taboos specifically discourage eating foods that grow on the ground (e.g., some species of taro) or have dark interiors resembling dirt (Meigs, 1984). This association between the goodness and badness of foods and their spatial origins and brightness may derive from the fact that the ground is a source of physical contamination. Given these patterns of covariation, the mental mapping of evaluation to experience (e.g., good–bad to light–dark) can then act as a useful judgment heuristic. According to this explanation, there is no importing of knowledge from one domain to another. One need not see goodness as somehow akin to "highness" or "brightness." Rather, highness and brightness are simply attributes that covary with goodness in experience and are therefore used heuristically to infer the presence of valued or desired attributes.

EVALUATIVE METAPHORS AND TYPES OF GOODNESS

In contrast, if evaluative–experiential mappings are metaphoric, and not merely associations reflecting the physical correlates of goodness, what particular function might they serve? As many theorists have argued, affect is ultimately about value—the goodness and badness of events, actions, and objects (Clore & Tamir, 2002; Ortony, Clore, & Collins, 1988). Critically, there are many ways in which something or someone may be good or bad. For example, a person may violate a moral standard (e.g., by cheating) or a performance standard (e.g., by failing a test). An observer would evaluate both of these actions, and the individual, negatively. How the observer treats the individual, however, and the particular character inferences made, will depend on the particular type of badness under consideration. Dimensional evaluative metaphors, by specifying a detailed set of entailments and associated attributes, could play a particularly important role in this process. For example, if the good thing—such as one's elevated moral standing—is a state that is particularly fleeting and hard to maintain, then a certain metaphoric framework may encourage treating it as fragile and transient. Testable hypotheses like this one, which outline a specific pattern of metaphor-consistent changes in emotional thought, do not follow parsimoniously from a purely associative account. For this reason, we think it is most useful to try to unpack the various dimensional evaluative metaphors with regard to specific attributes and specific valenced concepts, such as moral standing, social status, or intelligence. Importantly, although the dimensions tend to line up in an affectively consistent way— with higher moral standing, greater social status, and greater intelligence all being typically considered good—this is not necessary. For example, one may think that power is bad and yet still represent power metaphorically in terms of greater size or elevated physical position. Mapping the social concept onto the concrete experiential dimension clarifies the concept itself and not necessarily its value. In other words, as we argue here, people associate greater social status with greater physical size not because powerful people are good but because powerful people are influential.

To explore the potential metaphoric function of the various evaluative– experiential mappings, we consider three well-studied mappings (verticality, brightness, and size), focusing on whether evidence supports the claim that such mappings function as metaphors. First, we review evidence that the mapping exists. We then ask what entailments of the experiential dimension are psychologically salient (i.e., features that people grasp intuitively) and therefore plausible as candidates for structuring concepts of goodness. These entailments may be specific attributes or causal schemas associated with the dimension (Morris, Sheldon, Ames, & Young, 2007). Finally, we propose ways of testing these entailments and the extent to which metaphoric importing occurs. In each case, the proposed studies would test whether (a) strengthening, or simply making salient, the low-level evaluative–experiential associations or (b) giving participants direct physical experience with the experiential dimension (e.g., brightness, verticality) increases the likelihood that one thinks about goodness in a metaphor-consistent manner.

In their review of the role of metaphor in social cognition, Landau, Meier, and Keefer (2010) articulated this empirical strategy, which they called the *metaphoric transfer strategy*. We agree that this strategy is critical for providing support for CMT. We do not believe, however, that most of the empirical studies conducted on evaluative–experiential mappings qualify as tests of whether metaphoric transfer has occurred. Instead, these studies primarily demonstrate the existence and relative automaticity of the evaluative–experiential mappings. The question of whether metaphoric transfer occurs in these cases is largely untested. Devising direct, compelling tests of metaphoric transfer will be critical for evaluating whether these associations operate as metaphors. When testing for metaphor transfer, the choice of dependent variable is critical. The outcome cannot simply be a measure of whether the target domain is active or accessible (e.g., elevated vertical position facilitating judgments of positivity)—a purely associative, nonmetaphoric link could account for the same effect. Instead, the outcome must assess a particular feature or aspect of the target domain that directly follows from one or more of the entailments of the experiential dimension. In other words, the test should not be whether, for example, experiencing or priming the idea of elevated physical position makes people think of positivity but rather whether doing so makes people think of positivity *in a certain way* (i.e., as having similar attributes to elevated entities).

Verticality

In everyday language, it is common to refer to affectively valenced concepts using language that references vertical space. The ubiquity of these valence–verticality associations has been demonstrated numerous times. Wapner, Werner, and Krus (1957) found that after experiencing success (vs. failure), participants tended to adjust their gaze upward. Meier and Robinson

(2004) provided additional evidence that people automatically associate high vertical position and positivity. They found that participants were faster to recognize good words as good when those words appeared at the top of the computer screen and faster to recognize bad words as bad when those words appeared at the bottom of the computer screen. Later research demonstrated that these associations can influence memory (Crawford, Margolies, Drake, & Murphy, 2006): Participants viewed positive and negative images in various locations. When asked to recall the location of each image, their memory for positive images was biased upward, and their memory for negative images was biased downward.

The influence of these associations can extend to other sensory modalities. In one series of studies, participants categorized positive and negative words (Weger, Meier, Robinson, & Inhoff, 2007). After each word, they heard and judged a tone. Positive words biased judgments toward higher pitch. Testing the opposite direction of influence, Horstmann and colleagues (Horstmann, 2010; Horstmann & Ansorge, 2011) found that the ability to mimic a smile was enhanced by a high-pitch tone, whereas the ability to mimic a frown was enhanced by a low-pitch tone. Supporting evidence also comes from research taking an individual differences approach. For example, individuals prone to depression are particularly likely to attend to lower regions of vertical space (Meier & Robinson, 2006). Similar associations with vertical space have been found for specific social concepts such as divinity (Meier, Hauser, Robinson, Friesen, & Schjeldahl, 2007) and power (Giessner & Schubert, 2007; Schubert, 2005). That power shows the same pattern of associations is instructive because high power is not universally considered good. Power's consistent link to highness regardless of its perceived valence suggests that the power–verticality link emerges not because highness is a symbol or correlate of goodness but because highness implies certain attributes, which are orthogonal to valence.

Because verticality involves spatial relations along a single spatial dimension, the most psychologically salient entailments of verticality are centered on changes in physical position, such as the nature and origin of the forces necessary to initiate a change in position and the ease of movement in different directions. As a result, the good–up mapping may be representative of a broader metaphor in which one's level of an abstract, continuous, affectively valenced attribute, such as moral goodness or social influence, is treated as if it were akin to a "position" along a vertically oriented physical dimension (Brandt & Reyna, 2011; Haidt, 2003; Schubert, 2005). In this metaphor, the entailments of verticality provide structure for thinking about changes in one's position, which are treated as if they are movements along a vertical dimension in space. One's position may change; one may move up or down on the dimension. Elevated position on this dimension is a status that may be attained or lost, as people "rise" and "fall" along the dimension. This metaphor gives life to phrases such as *climbing the corporate ladder* and *a fall from grace*. It is clear that people talk about various forms of status in terms of vertical position, but if this metaphor is a way of thinking about status and not just a way of talking about it, then people's basic conception of moral standing, power, and similar concepts should be shaped by the various entailments of verticality.

We identify several psychologically salient features of verticality, many of which derive from the fact the vertical dimension is aligned with gravitational force. For example, on account of gravity, there is an asymmetry in the ease of movement along the vertical dimension, such that moving up (*rising*) is harder than moving down (*falling*). People appear to intuitively grasp this asymmetry, given the frequency of metaphoric sayings that use the term *uphill* to convey difficulty or resistance (e.g., "she's fighting an uphill battle"). This fact may influence how people conceive of certain forms of social status such as power and moral standing. Descents—movements from up to down—should be thought of as easier, more natural, and more likely than ascents, which must work against the force of gravity. For example, a loss of moral standing due to a moral transgression is commonly referred to as a *fall from grace*. If a loss of standing is a fall, it should be thought of as rapid and hard to reverse once initiated. This metaphoric mapping could lead to the perception of power and moral standing as precarious states that are hard to achieve and easy to lose (Rozin & Royzman, 2001).

In a similar vein, because gravity impedes ascents but facilitates descents, movement up and down a vertical dimension may naturally engender different causal schemas (Morris et al., 2007). That is, descents (e.g., *falls*) are largely passive events and can happen without the aid of willful, intentional intervention. Conversely, ascents may evoke an agentic causal model in which movement up the dimension (e.g., a *climb*) is considered to be caused by the internal motivation and attributes of the individual. Within this general metaphoric framework, there may be some flexibility. For example, one may conceive of an ascent as a *rise* rather than a *climb*, thereby implying a more passive path to status in which the causal force may be attributed more to external, than internal, forces.

Finally, physical highness may imply certain physical attributes that are seen as consistent with that position, such as weight (highness implies lightness, lowness implies heaviness; Yu, 1995). Likewise, because *down* is typically anchored on the ground and *up* is anchored on the sky, lowness may be associated with physical dirtiness (e.g., the phrase *down and dirty*) and darkness.

Analyses of the various entailments of verticality, such as the one discussed here, provides a starting point for testing whether the tendency to associate goodness with highness (Crawford et al., 2006; Meier & Robinson, 2004; Weger et al., 2007) reflects a metaphor. If these associations reflect the conceptual structure of such valenced attributes as moral goodness, then they should shape how one thinks about those attributes. A number of testable hypotheses follow from this. For example, if individuals differ in the tendency to associate morality with up and down, then individuals with accessible or strong associations should regard moral goodness as a precarious state that is hard to achieve and easy to lose. Moreover, priming the associations experimentally may strengthen this particular conceptualization. Whereas most previous research has focused on whether priming *up* activates *virtue* (and vice versa), the critical question for the metaphor interpretation is whether priming verticality changes how one thinks about virtue. For example, if verticality is primed, will people be especially likely to perceive a loss of moral standing as *like a fall* (i.e., rapid, hard to reverse, etc.)? More generally, this approach would seek to answer the question "When the experiential dimension is primed, is one more likely to make metaphor-consistent inferences about the particular type of goodness (or badness) under consideration?"

This paradigm could be used to pit the two accounts against each other. Specifically, one could include general outcome measures that assess whether judgments of goodness are facilitated and specific questions that assess whether specific metaphor-consistent ways of thinking about goodness are facilitated. If the up = good mapping reflects not a metaphor but the use of concrete physical attributes to infer goodness or badness, then priming elevated physical position will facilitate judgments of goodness but will not encourage one particular conceptualization of goodness over another.

In sum, it is clear that the associations exist and that they run deep; it is not entirely clear that they reflect conceptual metaphor. Is the way people think about goodness different because of these associations, as CMT asserts? Answering this question requires an examination of the various entailments of verticality that appear to be central to people's experience of highness and lowness. See Table 10.1 with reference to this point.

Brightness

Many studies have shown that people tend to associate positive concepts with brightness and the color white and negative concepts with darkness and the color black. Meier, Robinson, and Clore (2004) found that participants were faster to categorize good words as good when those words appeared in white and faster to categorize bad words as bad when those words appeared in black. This effect extends to affectively valenced concepts such as morality (Sherman & Clore, 2009) and can influence perceptual judgments as well. For example, studies have found that participants judge (a) smiling faces as brighter than frowning faces (Song, Vonasch, Meier, & Bargh, 2012), (b) a shade of gray as darker after having categorized a negative

TABLE 10.1

Entailments and Implicated Properties of the Experiential Dimensions of Verticality, Brightness, and Size

Properties	Verticality	Brightness		Size
		Luminance	Reflectance	
Physical	Asymmetry of movement (it is easier to fall than to rise) Visual salience (high = salient)	Effect on visibility (brightness illuminates) Differences in energy (light as energy source) Visual salience (bright = salient)	Asymmetry and directionality of influence (dark substances have disproportionate, irreversible effect)	Asymmetry in influence (large things assumed to be heavier and stronger than small things) Visual salience (large = salient)
Psychological	Precariousness, prominence	Ability to guide or reveal, energy, prominence	Purity, fragility	Influence, permanence, prominence

Experiential dimension

word (Meier, Robinson, Crawford, & Ahlvers, 2007), and (c) a room as darker after recalling an unethical transgression (Banerjee, Chatterjee, & Sinha, 2012).

The ability of the darkness to prime "immorality" extends to moral behavior and decision making. In the domain of sports, several studies have found that athletes wearing darker uniforms are more likely to engage in aggressive or competitive behavior (Frank & Gilovich, 1988; Webster, Urland, & Correll, 2012). Likewise, another study found that participants were more likely to engage in unethical behavior if they were in a dimly lit room or wearing sunglasses (Zhong, Bohns, & Gino, 2010).

What are the psychologically salient features of the light–dark dimension that might be applied metaphorically to understand the good–bad dimension? Answering this question requires first recognizing that darkness may refer to the (a) *luminance*, the amount of ambient light in a given space (e.g., a dimly vs. brightly lit room), or (b) *reflectance*, the amount of incident light a surface reflects (e.g., a black vs. white shirt).

In the former sense, darkness impairs visibility and, as a result, serves a concealing function that may produce a sense of ignorance (e.g., "she was kept in the dark") or anonymity (Zhong et al., 2010). In this sense, light reveals truth or insight (e.g., "my experience was illuminating"), providing a basis for concepts such as *enlightenment* (Lakoff & Johnson, 1999). Additionally, light is a form of energy and so brightness may suggest a high energy state. Finally, bright things are highly visible, salient, and, therefore likely to grab one's attention. For example, to call someone a *bright spot* is to say that this person stands out in his or her goodness.

In the second sense of darkness (i.e., the relative lightness or darkness of physical material), the colors black and white play a central role, with white implying physical purity and cleanliness as well as innocence, youth, and fragility (Grieve, 1991; Sherman & Clore, 2009; Sherman, Haidt, & Clore, 2012; Williams, Morland, & Underwood, 1970). Conversely, blackness may imply physical contamination, decay, or filth (Duncan, 1994). On account of their associations with cleanliness and filth, the entailments of white and black are essentially the entailments of the psychology of purity and contagion. A central feature of contagion is the marked asymmetry between positive and negative forces, with negative forces being far more potent (Rozin & Royzman, 2001). For example, as the principle of negativity dominance articulates, an otherwise appetizing substance can be thoroughly spoiled by the introduction of a negligible amount of an offending substance (Rozin & Royzman, 2001). Indeed, people are largely insensitive to degree of contamination: One drop of the offending substance is nearly as bad as 100 drops, a phenomenon termed *dose insensitivity* (Rozin & Nemeroff, 2002). The upshot of negativity dominance and dose insensitivity is that pure entities, often represented with the color white, are regarded as fragile and easily ruined. Altogether, the white–black dimension seems to readily imply various purity-related attributes.

On account of the purity-related entailments of the black–white dimension, any valenced concepts linked to that dimension should recruit the psychology of purity such that these concepts are conceptualized and experienced through the lens of purity. For example, a moral value that is extremely highly valued may become linked to the color white, a metaphoric mapping that would encourage thinking of that value as "sacred" or off limits from being traded off with other kinds of value (Baron & Spranca, 1997; Tetlock, Kristel, Elson, Green, & Lerner, 2000).

The critical question becomes to what extent are these features of lightness, in either sense, applied to clarify various manifestations of positivity? What types of goodness evoke the metaphor most commonly? There are two types of goodness that seem most likely to be structured in terms of the light–dark dimension: moral standing ("he has a black heart") and intelligence ("she is very bright").

Morality

People typically conceive of knowledge in terms of brightness (Lakoff & Johnson, 1980). As a result, any domain that draws on the concepts of knowledge and ignorance will typically make use of the luminance dimension. With this in mind, the metaphor of moral goodness as bright may reflect a metaphor in which good and evil are competing "forces." In this battle, evil is a form of ignorance that only the illuminating power of good can counteract.

Besides the metaphor of moral goodness as an illuminating force, there is at least one other metaphor linking morality to darkness. Drawing on the second meaning of darkness (i.e., reflectance, or the relative darkness of material), the association of moral goodness with the color white (e.g., Sherman & Clore, 2009) may reflect a broader purity metaphor, in which moral virtue is regarded as a "pure" state akin to physical cleanliness. There is ample evidence that people indeed think of morality in this way (Schnall, Benton, & Harvey, 2008; Zhong & Liljenquist, 2006; Zhong, Strejcek, & Sivanathan, 2010). The critical question, however, is whether the concrete physical experience of white and black and the automatic associations revealed in the aforementioned empirical research play a direct causal role in encouraging this conceptualization of morality. For example, does giving people experience with the colors black and white increase the tendency to think of moral transgressions as imparting an irreversible stain on one's moral reputation? Likewise, would manipulations that strengthen the low-level mental associations (virtue = white, sin = black), such as in an associative learning paradigm (Paivio, 1969), similarly encourage one to think and reason about morality in purity-centered ways?

The fact that there appear to be at least two moral metaphors linking morality to the light–dark dimension provides an opportunity to use the *alternate source strategy* (Landau et al., 2010), which pits two metaphors against each other. In this case, one could randomly assign people to receive one of two possible experiences: (a) an experience with luminance (e.g., have participants attend to fluctuations in the amount of ambient light in a room) or (b) an experience with reflectance (e.g., having participants attend to, or interact with, white and black substances). Afterward, participants would be asked to make a variety of judgments about a given moral transgression. The particular physical experience that participants have should influence the specific moral inferences and judgments that they make. For example, because a loss of brightness (as luminance) is experienced as reversible (e.g., one simply needs to locate a light source to make a dark room bright), exposure to this experiential dimension should encourage the view of a moral transgressor's reputation as reversible. A loss of whiteness (as reflectance), on the other hand, is commonly seen as impossible to regain once lost (e.g., once even a drop of black paint is added to a cup of white paint, there is nothing that can be done to return it to a "pure" white state), so that exposure to reflectance should lead participants to see such reputational damage as irreversible.

Intelligence

The association between good–bad and light–dark is not limited to morality. Because brightness provides a metaphoric grounding for thinking about knowledge, the trait of intelligence is frequently cast in terms of brightness. To be smart is to be "bright." It has been found, for example, that exposure to an illuminated light bulb can increase the ability to solve problems that require insight (Slepian, Weisbuch, Rutchick, Newman, & Ambady, 2010). This mapping between knowledge and brightness may encourage thinking of intelligence as a quality that illuminates. In this view, intelligence and knowledge serve a guiding function that enables one to venture into otherwise unexplored places. To test this possibility experimentally, one could give people physical experiences with lightness and darkness, effectively priming the experiential dimension, and then test whether these experiences increase the likelihood that one will perceive intelligent individuals as capable of serving as guides (i.e., leaders). Because luminance provides physical guidance, priming luminance should increase the perception of intelligence as congruent with leadership (a form of social guidance).

Additionally, light is a form of energy, and people experience the dimming of brightness (e.g., a dying flame) as a loss of energy. Consequently, if one conceives of intelligence as spanning a dimension from *dim* to *bright*, one may infer that intelligent people are prone to high energy states. Thus, when the metaphor is active, there may be a tendency to assume that *bright* individuals are energetic and that *dim* individuals are slow, lethargic, or otherwise marked by low energy.

Experimentally, one could test whether priming brightness increases the perception of intelligence as congruent with high energy. However, if priming brightness only facilitates judgments of intelligence but does not systematically alter *how* one thinks about intelligence, it would lend support to the possibility that the mappings are merely associative, perhaps arising from an inherent confounding of goodness and brightness in experience, and not metaphoric.

Size

In a common idiom, bigger is said to be better. Consistent with this saying, people display a relatively basic size preference. Preference for larger objects has been found even for abstract geometric shapes and even in children as young as 3 years old (Silvera, Josephs, & Giesler, 2002). Other research presented positive and negative words in different font sizes and found that positive words could be identified as positive more quickly and accurately when presented in a larger font (Meier, Robinson, & Caven, 2008). In addition, this study found that the intensity of evaluation was also affected by size, with positive words presented in larger fonts being seen as more positive.

Although people associate positivity and largeness, it is not clear that this means that they think of goodness as similar to largeness. If this association is indeed indicative of a metaphor, what are the psychologically salient attributes of largeness that might be used to clarify goodness? Compared with small things, large things take up a lot of space and, as a result, are visually salient. Given that people infer that large entities are heavy (Charpentier, 1891; Kloos & Amazeen, 2002), large things are also typically thought of as capable of exerting substantial force on other objects. That is, all things being equal, largeness may imply strong causal force. As a consequence, physical size is used to convey information about importance and influence. To say that someone is big in a social sense (e.g., "he's a big shot") implies that he or she exerts great influence just as physically large objects do. Similarly, because large entities are typically hard to move, physical largeness may imply some degree of permanence.

Power

Given these entailments, it is not surprising that power seems to be the social dimension most commonly linked to physical size in figurative language. Invoking the physical size metaphor may encourage thinking of an individual as both influential and firmly entrenched in his or her position. Empirically, an open question is whether priming individuals with physical largeness, or strengthening the good = large association, facilitates thinking about social status or power in this way. For example, one such study could have participants handle objects of various size, making the small–large dimension salient, and then have people estimate how difficult it would be to remove a given high status individual from their particular position. The prediction would be that priming people with physical size will encourage them to think about social status in terms of physical size, and that this in turn will lead them to regard high status individuals as particularly hard to displace.

Morality

Beyond its role in how people talk and perhaps think about power, references to physical size are a common feature of how people talk about certain forms of moral goodness. For example, terms such as *largesse* and *magnanimous,* which are derived from Latin terms for large (e.g., *magna*), are often used to describe acts of generosity. These instances suggest that the metaphor operates in morality as it does for power: as a way of implying impact or influence. If so, then priming people with size before reading about an act of charity could alter how they think about that act's potential impact and effectiveness. Moreover, if it is generosity in particular that is conceptualized in terms of size, then priming size may not affect how people think about other moral concepts such as honesty or compassion.

METAPHORIC TRANSFER AND ATTRIBUTION

One way to distinguish the associative and metaphoric accounts we have discussed might involve their relative susceptibility to attributional alteration. It seems possible that a metaphoric mapping of concrete experience onto value might not be easily changed by an attributional manipulation. Consider an example in which experiences of lightness and darkness affect judgments of value. If a word (e.g., *honesty*) printed in a white font were evaluated as more moral than otherwise, one might explain the effect by assuming that the moral meaning implied by whiteness had been misattributed to (and added to) the moral meaning already inherent in the word.

The process would be similar to the case in which positive affect elicited by warm and sunny spring weather was found to influence judgments of life satisfaction (Schwarz & Clore, 1983). That experiment included an attributional manipulation in which the sunny weather was made salient for one group just before participants rated their life satisfaction. Making salient the true cause of their positive feelings in this way then eliminated any effect of mood on judgments of life satisfaction. The authors concluded that the mood effects had depended on misattributions so that affect from an irrelevant source (the weather) had been experienced as part of their assessment of their life satisfaction. Returning to the font color example, would a similar pattern be found if the whiteness (or the moral connotation) of the font were made salient before participants made judgments of the moral meanings of the words? Would participants be able to separate their experience of the two sources of moral meaning? If a common pattern in such attributional studies prevailed, it is possible that the word *honesty*, for example, would be rated as less moral because the now-salient whiteness of the font would be experienced as the source of the moral connotation.

Evidence is lacking concerning whether attribution plays a role in perceptions of goodness as up, bright, or big. However, research has recently been done on the effect of experiencing something as physically heavy or weighty and inferring that it is therefore important (Chandler, Reinhard, & Schwarz, 2012). The experimenters found that handling a copy of a novel (*Catcher in the Rye*) with a weight inside led people to see it as especially important in American literature. Of special interest is the fact that the experimenters did a subsequent study (Reinhard, Chandler, & Schwarz, 2012) in which they cautioned participants that the book was a display copy with a weight in it to allow it to stand unsupported in a display. When this alternative cause for the experience of weightiness was made salient, it was not mapped onto the idea of literary importance. It might be useful to determine the role of such misattributions in other examples of the effects of perceptual grounding on judgment, including those of the effects of experiencing things as up, bright, and big on evaluation.

Of course, it is quite possible that such attributional manipulations would have no effect in the examples we are considering. What if being up, bright, and big were not merely associated with goodness but were linked metaphorically? If an attribute suggests goodness metaphorically (white suggesting purity, bigness suggesting influence, and elevated location suggesting precariousness), then the source of one's sense of purity, power, or precariousness might not be apparent. Unlike mood that can be experienced as distinct and rated explicitly, the purity implied by light color is perhaps only implicitly inferred and not really experienced, so that it is not easily discounted through an attributional manipulation.

If the relationship is metaphoric, an attribution manipulation might be successful only when applied upstream, with regard to whether the whiteness is allowed to be experienced as purity rather than simply as a color in the first place (and bigness as powerful, rather than just as sizable, and elevation as dominance rather than simply a location). If so, perhaps part of the power of metaphor lies in the fact that it is difficult for the buyer to be wary of what he or she is buying because the entailments of metaphors are inherent in the metaphoric meaning and cannot be easily appreciated once the metaphor has transformed the object in the gestalt-like fashion that it has. Having seen the object in the new light provided, one cannot easily go back or make after-the-fact alterations.

The point of an attribution manipulation in such situations would not be to get participants to undo the associations learned over a lifetime. Attributional discounting might occur if one became aware that one's perception of goodness might not have come from relevant qualities of the judgment object but merely from the object being up, bright, or big. For an attributional manipulation to have such a debiasing effect, however, the perceiver would have to see, at some level, how such an extraneous factor might bias experience or judgment.

In a related way, misattribution manipulations tend to be ineffective when the biasing stimulus is presented unconsciously (Winkielman, Zajonc, & Schwarz, 1997) because without access to the biasing stimulus, there is no way for it to be disaggregated from more relevant factors. It might be similarly difficult for judges to perceive an experience as potentially biasing if the connection that would create bias is a metaphor rather than a more transparent association. For an attribution manipulation to be successful, it must provide a basis for parsing potentially biasing experiences from judgment-relevant experiences. All such parsing activity (whether before or after a judgment is formed) should depend on the transparency of the connection that gives the extraneous stimulus the potential for bias. We suggest the possibility, therefore, that mere associations may be more transparent and hence provide a more successful basis for attributional inoculation. In the Schwarz and Clore (1983) weather study, the potentially biasing effect of foul weather on judgments of life satisfaction was avoided when participants were asked to evaluate the weather before evaluating their life satisfaction. To our knowledge, no investigator has asked whether preliminary judgments of the goodness of being up, bright, or big would serve to cleanse the affective palettes of judges in a similar way.

CONCLUSION

In this chapter, we have reviewed three common mappings between concrete experience and evaluative processing (good = up, good = bright, and good = big). We have attempted to address the important question of whether these mappings reflect (a) metaphors that help clarify the nature of the particular form of goodness under consideration or (b) associations between value and physical attributes that aid in inferring the presence of desired entities. The basic experimental paradigms that we have outlined could provide a starting point for future research that evaluates which account—the metaphoric account or the associative account—can best explain the observed mappings. The rationale behind each proposed experiment is the same. If a given mapping is merely associative, priming one aspect of the concrete dimension (e.g., elevated position) should activate the corresponding aspect of the abstract dimension (e.g., goodness), thereby facilitating relevant evaluative processing or judgment (e.g., categorizing positive words as positive). It should not, however, affect the particular way in which one conceptualizes the abstract dimension. In other words, it should affect *whether* one thinks of that aspect or dimension but not *how* one thinks about it. Alternatively, if the mappings are metaphoric, in the sense articulated by CMT (Lakoff & Johnson, 1980; 1999), we believe it will be because the experiential dimensions imply specific attributes, such as precariousness, purity, and influence, that are transferred to the target domain, shaping how one thinks and reasons about abstract concepts such as intelligence, morality, and power.

REFERENCES

Banerjee, P., Chatterjee, P., & Sinha, J. (2012). Is it light or dark? Recalling moral behavior changes perception of brightness. *Psychological Science, 23*, 407–409. doi:10.1177/0956797611432497

Baron, J., & Spranca, M. (1997). Protected values. *Organizational Behavior and Human Decision Processes, 70*, 1–16. doi:10.1006/obhd.1997.2690

Boroditsky, L. (2000). Metaphoric structuring: Understanding time through spatial metaphors. *Cognition, 75*, 1–28. doi:10.1016/S0010-0277(99)00073-6

Brandt, M. J., & Reyna, C. (2011). The chain of being: A hierarchy of morality. *Perspectives on Psychological Science, 6*, 428–446. doi:10.1177/1745691611414587

Chandler, J., Reinhard, D., & Schwarz, N. (2012). To judge a book by its weight you need to know its content: Knowledge moderates the use of embodied cues. *Journal of Experimental Social Psychology, 48*, 948–952. doi:10.1016/j.jesp.2012.03.003

Charpentier, A. (1891). Analyse experimentale de quelques elements de la sensation de poids [Experimental study of some aspects of weight perception]. *Archives de Physiologie Normales et Pathologiques, 3*, 122–135.

Chen, M., & Bargh, J. A. (1999). Consequences of automatic evaluation: Immediate behavioral predispositions to approach or avoid the stimulus. *Personality and Social Psychology Bulletin, 25*, 215–224. doi:10.1177/0146167299025002007

Clore, G. L., & Tamir, M. (2002). Affect as embodied information. *Psychological Inquiry, 13*, 37–45.

Crawford, L. E. (2009). Conceptual metaphors of affect. *Emotion Review, 1*, 129–139. doi:10.1177/1754073908100438

Crawford, L. E., Margolies, S. M., Drake, J. T., & Murphy, M. E. (2006). Affect biases memory of location: Evidence for the spatial representation of affect. *Cognition and Emotion, 20*, 1153–1169. doi:10.1080/02699930500347794

Duncan, M. G. (1994). In slime and darkness: The metaphor of filth in criminal justice. *Tulane Law Review, 68*, 725–802.

Frank, M. G., & Gilovich, T. (1988). The dark side of self and social perception: Black uniforms and aggression in professional sports. *Journal of Personality and Social Psychology, 54*, 74–85. doi:10.1037/0022-3514.54.1.74

Gentner, D. (1983). Structure-mapping: A theoretical framework for analogy. *Cognitive Science, 7*, 155–170. doi:10.1207/s15516709cog0702_3

Giessner, S. R., & Schubert, T. W. (2007). High in the hierarchy: How vertical location and judgments of leaders' power are interrelated. *Organizational Behavior and Human Decision Processes, 104*, 30–44. doi:10.1016/j.obhdp.2006.10.001

Grieve, K. W. (1991). Traditional beliefs and colour perception. *Perceptual and Motor Skills, 72*, 1319–1323. doi:10.2466/pms.1991.72.3c.1319

Haidt, J. (2003). Elevation and the positive psychology of morality. In C. L. M. Keyes & J. Haidt (Eds.), *Flourishing: Positive psychology and the life well-lived* (pp. 275–289). Washington, DC: American Psychological Association. doi:10.1037/10594-012

Horstmann, G. (2010). Tone-affect compatibility with affective stimuli and affective responses. *The Quarterly Journal of Experimental Psychology: Human Experimental Psychology, 63*, 2239–2250. doi:10.1080/17470211003687538

Horstmann, G., & Ansorge, U. (2011). Compatibility between tones, head movements, and facial expressions. *Emotion, 11*, 975–980. doi:10.1037/a0023468

Kloos, H., & Amazeen, E. L. (2002). Perceiving heaviness by dynamic touch: An investigation of the size–weight illusion in preschoolers. *British Journal of Developmental Psychology, 20*, 171–183. doi:10.1348/026151002166398

Kövecses, Z. (2000). *Metaphor and emotion: Language, culture and body in human feeling*. New York, NY: Cambridge University Press.

Lakoff, G., & Johnson, M. (1980). *Metaphors we live by*. Chicago, IL: University of Chicago Press.

Lakoff, G., & Johnson, M. (1999). *Philosophy in the flesh: The embodied mind and its challenge to western thought*. New York, NY: Basic Books.

Landau, M. J., Meier, B., & Keefer, L. (2010). A metaphor-enriched social cognition. *Psychological Bulletin, 136*, 1045–1067. doi:10.1037/a0020970

Meier, B. P., Hauser, D. J., Robinson, M. D., Friesen, C. K., & Schjeldahl, K. (2007). What's "up" with God? Vertical space as a representation of the divine. *Journal of Personality and Social Psychology, 93*, 699–710. doi:10.1037/0022-3514.93.5.699

Meier, B. P., & Robinson, M. D. (2004). Why the sunny side is up. *Psychological Science, 15*, 243–247. doi:10.1111/j.0956-7976.2004.00659.x

Meier, B. P., & Robinson, M. D. (2006). Does "feeling down" mean seeing down? Depressive symptoms and vertical selective attention. *Journal of Research in Personality, 40*, 451–461. doi:10.1016/j.jrp.2005.03.001

Meier, B. P., Robinson, M. D., & Caven, A. J. (2008). Why a Big Mac is a good mac: Associations between affect and size. *Basic and Applied Social Psychology, 30*, 46–55. doi:10.1080/01973530701866516

Meier, B. P., Robinson, M. D., & Clore, G. L. (2004). Why good guys wear white: Automatic inferences about stimulus valence based on brightness. *Psychological Science, 15,* 82–87. doi:10.1111/j.0963-7214.2004.01502002.x

Meier, B. P., Robinson, M. D., Crawford, L. E., & Ahlvers, W. J. (2007). When "light" and "dark" thoughts become light and dark responses: Affect biases brightness judgments. *Emotion, 7,* 366–376. doi:10.1037/1528-3542.7.2.366

Meigs, A. S. (1984). *Food, sex, and pollution: A New Guinea religion.* New Brunswick, NJ: Rutgers University Press.

Morris, M. W., Sheldon, O. J., Ames, D. R., & Young, M. J. (2007). Metaphors and the market: Consequences and preconditions of agent and object metaphors in stock market commentary. *Organizational Behavior and Human Decision Processes, 102,* 174–192. doi:10.1016/j.obhdp.2006.03.001

Ortony, A., Clore, G. L., & Collins, A. (1988). *The cognitive structure of emotions.* New York, NY: Cambridge University Press. doi:10.1017/CBO9780511571299

Paivio, A. (1969). Mental imagery in associative learning and memory. *Psychological Review, 76,* 241–263. doi:10.1037/h0027272

Reinhard, D., Chandler, J., & Schwarz, N. (2012, January). *Knowing what's inside counts: Prime awareness diminishes effects of embodied metaphors.* Hot topic talk at the embodiment preconference of the Society for Personality and Social Psychology, San Diego, CA.

Rozin, P., & Nemeroff, C. (2002). Sympathetic magical thinking: The contagion and similarity "heuristics." In T. Gilovich, D. Griffin, & D. Kahneman (Eds.), *Heuristics and biases. The psychology of intuitive judgment* (pp. 201–216). Cambridge, England: Cambridge University Press. doi:10.1017/CBO9780511808098.013

Rozin, P., & Royzman, E. B. (2001). Negativity bias, negativity dominance, and contagion. *Personality and Social Psychology Review, 5,* 296–320. doi:10.1207/S15327957PSPR0504_2

Schnall, S., Benton, J., & Harvey, S. (2008). With a clean conscience: Cleanliness reduces the severity of moral judgments. *Psychological Science, 19,* 1219–1222. doi:10.1111/j.1467-9280.2008.02227.x

Schubert, T. W. (2005). Your highness: Vertical positions as perceptual symbols of power. *Journal of Personality and Social Psychology, 89,* 1–21. doi:10.1037/0022-3514.89.1.1

Schwarz, N., & Clore, G. L. (1983). Mood, misattribution, and judgments of well-being: Informative and directive functions of affective states. *Journal of Personality and Social Psychology, 45,* 513–523. doi:10.1037/0022-3514.45.3.513

Sherman, G. D., & Clore, G. L. (2009). The color of sin: White and black are perceptual symbols of moral purity and pollution. *Psychological Science, 20,* 1019–1025. doi:10.1111/j.1467-9280.2009.02403.x

Sherman, G. D., Haidt, J., & Clore, G. L. (2012). The faintest speck of dirt: Disgust enhances the detection of impurity. *Psychological Science, 23,* 1506–1514. doi:10.1177/0956797612445318

Silvera, D. H., Josephs, R. A., & Giesler, R. B. (2002). Bigger is better: The influence of physical size on aesthetic preference judgments. *Journal of Behavioral Decision Making, 15*, 189–202. doi:10.1002/bdm.410

Slepian, M. L., Weisbuch, M., Rutchick, A. M., Newman, L. S., & Ambady, N. (2010). Shedding light on insight: Priming bright ideas. *Journal of Experimental Social Psychology, 46*, 696–700. doi:10.1016/j.jesp.2010.03.009

Song, H., Vonasch, A. J., Meier, B. P., & Bargh, J. A. (2012). Brighten up: Smiles facilitate perceptual judgment of facial lightness. *Journal of Experimental Social Psychology, 48*, 450–452. doi:10.1016/j.jesp.2011.10.003

Tetlock, P. E., Kristel, O. V., Elson, S. B., Green, M. C., & Lerner, J. S. (2000). The psychology of the unthinkable: Taboo trade-offs, forbidden base rates, and heretical counterfactuals. *Journal of Personality and Social Psychology, 78*, 853–870. doi:10.1037/0022-3514.78.5.853

Wapner, S., Werner, H., & Krus, D. M. (1957). The effect of success and failure on space localization. *Journal of Personality, 25*, 752–756. doi:10.1111/j.1467-6494.1957.tb01563.x

Webster, G., Urland, G. R., & Correll, J. (2012). Can uniform color color aggression? Quasi-experimental evidence from professional ice hockey. *Social Psychological and Personality Science, 3*, 274–281. doi:10.1177/1948550611418535

Weger, U. W., Meier, B. P., Robinson, M. D., & Inhoff, A. W. (2007). Things are sounding up: Affective influences on auditory tone perception. *Psychonomic Bulletin & Review, 14*, 517–521. doi:10.3758/BF03194100

Williams, J. E., Morland, J. K., & Underwood, W. L. (1970). Connotations of color names in the United States, Europe, and Asia. *The Journal of Social Psychology, 82*, 3–14. doi:10.1080/00224545.1970.9919925

Winkielman, P., Zajonc, R. B., & Schwarz, N. (1997). Subliminal affective priming resists attributional interventions. *Cognition and Emotion, 11*, 433–465. doi:10.1080/026999397379872

Yu, N. (1995). Metaphorical expressions of anger and happiness in English and Chinese. *Metaphor and Symbolic Activity, 10*, 59–92. doi:10.1207/s15327868ms1002_1

Zhong, C. B., Bohns, V. K., & Gino, F. (2010). Good lamps are the best police: Darkness increases dishonesty and self-interested behavior. *Psychological Science, 21*, 311–314. doi:10.1177/0956797609360754

Zhong, C. B., & Liljenquist, K. A. (2006). Washing away your sins: Threatened morality and physical cleansing. *Science, 313*, 1451–1452. doi:10.1126/science.1130726

Zhong, C. B., Strejcek, B., & Sivanathan, N. (2010). A clean self can render harsh moral judgment. *Journal of Experimental Social Psychology, 46*, 859–862. doi:10.1016/j.jesp.2010.04.003

11

ARE THERE BASIC METAPHORS?

SIMONE SCHNALL

More than 20 years ago, Paul Ekman provocatively asked whether there were basic emotions (Ekman, 1992a, 1992b). He argued that specific facial expressions and underlying physiological reactions involved in emotional experiences suggest that the answer to this question is yes. Ekman, and many others who noted the universality of emotion, attributed to physical experience a fundamental role in emotion. Although some of the questions posed at the time are still heavily discussed and disputed (Barrett, 2006; Panksepp, 2007), contemporary social psychologists have taken Ekman's lead and considered the role of physical experiences not only in emotion but more generally in shaping the cognitive processing of social phenomena. Following researchers in other areas of cognitive science (e.g., Barsalou, 1999, 2008; Glenberg, 1997; Lakoff & Johnson, 1980), social psychologists have started

The preparation of this chapter was supported by Economic and Social Research Council grant RES-000-22-4453.

http://dx.doi.org/10.1037/14278-010
The Power of Metaphor: Examining Its Influence on Social Life, M. J. Landau, M. D. Robinson, and B. P. Meier (Editors)

to emphasize the benefits of an embodied view of cognition, based on the notion that functioning in the world with specific bodily capabilities fundamentally constrains cognitive processes (e.g., Meier, Schnall, Schwarz, & Bargh, 2012; Niedenthal, Barsalou, Winkielman, Krauth-Gruber, & Ric, 2005; Smith & Semin, 2004; Spellman & Schnall, 2009).

In contrast to traditional theories of cognition, embodied approaches posit that cognitive processes do not have the goal of arriving at a mirror image of the world but rather serve to facilitate people's action in their physical and social environments. This view has some early precursors (see, e.g., Gibson, 1979; Merleau-Ponty, 1962); however, cognitive scientists have largely studied *high-level* cognitive processes as divorced from any *low-level* perceptual or motor input processes (for a history of *disembodied* cognitive science, see Johnson, 1987; Spellman & Schnall, 2009). In contrast, with conceptual structures that are defined by *interactional* (Lakoff & Johnson, 1980) or *experiential* (Varela, Thompson, & Rosch, 1991) properties of the world, the boundaries between perception, cognition, and action become increasingly fluid (Barsalou, 1999; Clark, 1997). Because mental representations that are due to interactions with the environment retain the modality of perceptual experience, the resulting concepts are considered to involve reenactments, or simulations of such perceptual processes (Barsalou, 1999; Glenberg, 1997).

One of the earliest embodied approaches originated within cognitive linguistics in the form of conceptual metaphor theory (Lakoff & Johnson, 1980, 1999), which proposed that bodily processes shape and constrain cognitive information processing. *Metaphor*, defined as "*understanding and experiencing one kind of thing in terms of another*" (Lakoff & Johnson, 1980, p. 5, emphasis in original) does not only concern the use of language but is also informative about underlying cognitive structure, because abstract concepts that are described metaphorically often reflect basic physical experiences (for more background on the theory, see Chapter 2, this volume).

Whereas early work on conceptual metaphor theory was primarily confined to linguistics and involved cataloguing lists of metaphoric expressions and their potential links to basic physical experience, recent empirical research in social psychology has increasingly confirmed the metaphoric basis of many cognitive processes (for a review, see Landau, Meier, & Keefer, 2010). Testing the potential existence of embodied metaphors has become a highly productive enterprise, with research papers on new metaphoric connections between physical experiences and social phenomena accumulating at a rapid pace. However, although this growing literature supports the notion that embodied metaphors play a critical role in social thought and behavior, a wide range of metaphors has been examined without much consideration regarding which specific ones might constitute basic, or *core* metaphors. Indeed, critical discussions have pointed to the short-lived strategy of moving from metaphor to metaphor without taking into account what underlying processes and mechanisms might be at play (Landau et al., 2010; Meier et al., 2012). In particular, if metaphors are indeed the building blocks of cognitive representation, how many and which such metaphors are required to arrive at a comprehensive conceptual structure? Given the vast number of bodily experiences to draw on for mappings of physical concepts onto abstract target concepts, are there any bodily experiences that are more fundamental than others? In other words, given the evidence, is there any reason to believe that there are basic embodied metaphors?

The goal of this chapter is to extract a number of basic metaphors to guide future empirical investigations. What is first needed, however, is a working definition of what might make certain embodied concepts especially central, or basic. Ultimately, cross-cultural investigations and longitudinal studies following children's early development will need to establish the extent to which some physical experiences, and their applications to abstract concepts, are universal. To date, however, such investigations have been scarce (but see Chapter 12, this volume). In the meantime, one possibility to determine which metaphors can be considered basic is to examine the extent to which a given *source concept*, that is, a representation of a concrete physical experience, can be used to understand a wide range of *target concepts*, namely, superficially dissimilar, relatively abstract concepts that otherwise are difficult to understand. Thus, for a given bodily concept to be a good candidate for a basic metaphor, it should have applicability to a wide range of target concepts and therefore be instrumental in understanding and influencing a variety of cognitive, behavioral, and social phenomena related to those abstract concepts.

This chapter reviews the evidence for the existence of a number of putatively basic bodily metaphors, based on the following two fundamental observations: First, the body is a container with a clear boundary that keeps it separate from other people and objects; second, the body is situated in space and moves in it while maintaining varying distances to objects and people. From these basic properties of the body, the following metaphors are derived that may be considered as relatively basic: First, verticality provides a source domain to distinguish between good and bad entities in multiple contexts; second, the fact that the body is a container is implicit in the conceptualization of many social and emotional processes; and third, spatial distance contrasts things and people that are close from those that are distant and remote. Physical closeness in social relationships is also associated with physical warmth and therefore indicates a positive social contact. Considerable evidence has accumulated to support the existence of these metaphors. Before I review this work, however, I discuss the theoretical framework that provided much of the basis for such investigations.

METAPHORIC GROUNDINGS:
CONCEPTUAL METAPHOR THEORY

According to the conceptual metaphor theory (Lakoff & Johnson, 1980), the body is a source of knowledge, and by means of conceptual metaphors, basic *embodied* concepts are mapped onto more abstract concepts. For instance, the spatial metaphor of verticality is used to contrast good and bad things, such as emotional feelings. For example, I might say that "I'm on top of the world" or "feeling up" or, in contrast, note that "I'm down in the dumps" or "fell into a depression." Those mappings of physical body states are not arbitrary but are correlated with what happens with the human body when one feels a certain emotion: an upright, relaxed posture when feeling happy versus a slumped, drooping posture when feeling depressed.

Embodied metaphors are ubiquitous in everyday talk, even if the bodily origin is often not easily evident. Those origins can be inferred, however, by observing that metaphoric linguistic expressions are usually not isolated instances but instead are organized into highly coherent and elaborate systems (Lakoff & Johnson, 1980). For example, some expressions emphasize that time is a limited resource (e.g., *using up time*, *wasting time*), whereas other expressions emphasize that time is a valuable resource (e.g., *Thank you for your time*). Both implications reflect aspects of the overall metaphor *time is money*, which implies that people think of "using up" time in the same way as "using up" other resources, such as money. Importantly, the metaphoric expressions that treat abstract entities, such as time, as tangible things are not arbitrarily constructed but are grounded in basic experiences of how the body interacts with the physical world. For example, a body uses resources, such as by eating and breathing, and thus, using up resources is a basic embodied concept. Although some metaphors might at first glance not have much of a bodily grounding, a closer examination can reveal that even seemingly abstract expressions relate back to specific physical experiences: By likening them to resources, abstract things, such as time, are talked about in the same way as the concrete things that the body consumes, such as food or air.

However, the similarities used for mapping structural relations from one concept to another are not objectively inherent in concepts or categories but are the result of interactions with the world. This is a central point. Lakoff and Johnson (1980) challenged the view that category membership is determined by objective, inherent properties of objects and instead proposed that properties emerge from interactions with the physical and social environment. Those *interactional properties* of objects can include perceptual properties (e.g., what an apple looks like), functional properties (the apple satisfies an appetite), motor-activity properties (what it feels like to hold an apple in your hand while taking a bite of it), and purposive properties (eating fruit to stay healthy). Categories based on interactional properties do not have sharp boundaries but are relatively open-ended. For example, tossing an apple from hand to hand can fall into the category "ball," even though an apple typically does not normally fall into that category. Thus, in their *experientialist* approach, Lakoff and Johnson (1980, 1999) claimed that objects can only be understood in relation to a particular perceptual and conceptual apparatus of the human body.

Central to Lakoff and Johnson's theory is the concept of *image schema* (Johnson, 1987), which describes a pattern of perceptual experience that emerges from basic bodily activities and is nonpropositional and analogue in nature. Image schemas result in mental representations with a level of abstractness less concrete than a mental picture, or a "rich" image, but still less abstract than propositional knowledge. The sensorimotor experience of using resources is one example of such an image schema; additional examples are the concepts of *containment*, which is derived from the basic understanding of the human body as a container (some things are inside of the body, others are outside of it) and *verticality* (people are usually situated in an upright position within space, with a clear up–down orientation).

Of course, the proposal that sensorimotor experiences and actions shape cognitive structure is not a new invention of cognitive science but has been a prominent theme in developmental psychology for quite some time (e.g., Werner & Kaplan, 1963). Based on a constructivist framework, Piaget (1980) was one of the pioneers to argue that information does not exist independently from the perceptual and interpretive cognitive system but that the construction of meaning necessitates an active individual. Through direct, physical action with an object, very young children are able to abstract cognitive schemes that serve as *templates* against which new objects are standardized or *assimilated*. New information derived from other objects allows for the scheme to be modified or *adapted*, a process that becomes possible only through the active, constructive role of the individual. Similarly, Mandler (1992) outlined a theory of *perceptual analysis* through which children actively restructure, or redescribe, conceptual information abstracted from perceptual information. The outcome of this process, which takes place as early as in 3 to 4 month olds, is compacted preverbal information units and what Lakoff and Johnson (1980) termed *image schemas*, which involve mappings from sensorimotor activities. Recent work in social psychology has built on such early investigations, and, for example, has applied the developmental notion of *scaffolding* (Bruner, 1978; Vygotsky, 1978) to the learning processes that map physical experiences early in life to social phenomena (Williams, Huang, & Bargh, 2009). However, as noted earlier, it would be helpful to know which embodied metaphors matter most in the sense of influencing cognitive processes with relation to many different abstract target concepts.

TABLE 11.1
Basic Embodied Source Domains and Corresponding Abstract Target Domains

Source domain	Aspect of source domain	Target domain	Sample articles
Verticality			
		Valence	Meier & Robinson (2004)
		Power	Schubert (2005)
		Morality	Meier, Sellbom, & Wygant (2007)
		Divinity	Meier, Hauser, et al. (2007)
Container			
	Depth of Container	Emotion	Kövecses (2000)
	Heat of Fluid in Container	Anger	Wilkowski et al. (2009)
	Maintaining Boundaries	Disgust	Schnall, Haidt, et al. (2008)
		Cleanliness	Zhong & Liljenquist (2006)
Distance			
	Closeness	Intimacy	Argyle & Dean (1965)
	Warmth	Intimacy	Williams & Bargh (2008)
	Distance	Abstraction	Trope & Liberman (2010)

When examining the possibility of basic metaphors, it is useful to consider which image schemas might enjoy a special status, based on which certain relatively universal metaphors might have evolved. On the most basic level, the human body is a particular object—namely, a container with a discrete surface that delineates it from other objects and other people. Two fundamental properties of this container relate to how it is situated in space and how it moves in space. Thus, the following three image schemas might be especially central: First, the body functions in an upright, vertical position; second, it is a container that is separate from other entities; and third, the body maintains a given distance from other people and objects while moving in space. The meaning and ramifications of these image schemas (listed in Table 11.1) are now discussed in turn.

VERTICALITY: BEING UPRIGHT IN SPACE

Lakoff and Johnson (1980) articulated a theory on the basis of which they developed a rich repertoire of metaphors. These include, for example, describing an argument as war, love as a journey, or time as money. Lakoff and Johnson (1980) proposed that a certain set of metaphors uses space as organizing principle in what they refer to as *orientational metaphors*. One central orientational metaphor is verticality. Experience in space, and spatial metaphors, are likely to serve a central function within metaphoric structure. Some of the spatial metaphors proposed by Lakoff and Johnson (1980) were indeed the earliest conceptual metaphors to be put to the test by social psychologists. For example, Meier and Robinson (2004) demonstrated that people represent good things as spatially up and bad things as spatially down. In their work, participants were faster to categorize positive words such as *love* or *candy* as "good" when they were presented in the top section of a computer screen, and negative words such as *danger* or *spider* as "bad" when they were presented in the bottom section. Similarly, being powerful is associated with being high up in space, whereas being powerless is comparatively low (Schubert, 2005).

Consistent with Lakoff and Johnson's (1980) early proposal, the vertical dimension that pulls the mind up to higher values originates from the basic physical experience of verticality: People use the vertical dimension to contrast moral virtue and vice when talking about *high-minded* and *upstanding* citizens, versus the *lowlife* of society. However, moral considerations and verticality are not as strongly associated for people who are not concerned with social norms—namely, those scoring high on measures of psychopathy (Meier, Sellbom, & Wygant, 2007). Furthermore, when people feel metaphorically *uplifted* and *elevated* because of having witnessed another person's morally exemplary behavior, they are more likely to engage in prosocial behavior themselves (Schnall & Roper, 2012; Schnall, Roper, & Fessler, 2010). Moreover, participants considering acts of moral excellence not only express more *high-level* concepts such as abstract values, they also gaze up more in space while doing so than participants considering acts of nonmoral excellence (Pavarini, Schnall, & Immordino-Yang, 2012). Beyond valence, power, and morality, an additional target concept that maps onto verticality is divinity: Participants associate God with being high up in the sky, and the Devil as being down low in the underworld (Meier, Hauser, Robinson, Friesen, & Schjeldahl, 2007).

All this evidence suggests that one single source concept, verticality, is sufficient to make sense of a broad variety of target concepts. Thus, verticality may be considered a central, core embodied concept, on the basis of which many abstract concepts can be understood. Indeed, given the limited number of direct physical experiences relative to the almost unlimited number of abstract concepts, it is remarkable how efficiently the same source concept can be applied to vastly different abstract concepts. Another such example of an embodied source concept with wide applicability is the notion of the body as a specific kind of object.

THE BODY AS A CONTAINER

Drawing the Line Between *In* and *Out*

The fact that the body can be considered a container with an inside and an outside has several implications. First, the language reflecting control and responsibility often describes the lack thereof as a force coming over, or getting into, a person ("What has gotten into him?!"). In particular, emotions that are considered to involve the lack of rational thinking are talked about as some force acting within the bodily confines of a person. Within cognitive linguistics, the most comprehensive account of such embodied emotion metaphors was developed by Zoltan Kövecses (1990, 2000). While investigating the general metaphors used in talking about emotions, he noted the centrality of the container metaphor in providing the basis for conceptualizing all kinds of objects as containers, with having an *inside* and *outside*. In the context of emotions, two spatial metaphors make use of the image schema of containment—namely, that emotions are fluids in a container and that emotions relate to the heat of the fluid in a container. The latter is especially important because it yields a number of metaphoric consequences, by describing emotions that involve a lack of control and that are often regarded as "typical" emotions, because they interrupt and disturb everyday functioning, such as anger or hatred.

The metaphors referring to anger tend to reflect its physiological effects, such as feeling hot and flushed. Heat of a fluid in a container is the source concept for the target concept of anger, and various *entailments* (Lakoff & Johnson, 1980) follow from that mapping. For example, when a person explodes, the *inside* of the person comes to the surface, suggesting that an authentic aspect of the person emerges that was previously *deep down* and hidden. Similar to anger, metaphors about fear correspond to physiological and behavioral aspects of fear. The notion of fluid in a container is used as well, but in contrast to anger, the fluid is not hot. Again, this is no coincidence but correlates with the bodily experience of those emotions: Anger is experienced as hot and is characterized by an increase in skin temperature, whereas the opposite is the case for fear (e.g., Ekman, Levenson, & Friesen, 1983). In the case of anger, the emotion develops inside the container, whereas in the case of fear, the emotion appears to be independent of the person and then moves into the body as a result of some force (Kövecses, 1990).

If embodied metaphors indeed reflect the physiological experiences when feeling an emotion, then the same source domain (e.g., heat, when describing anger) should be used across cultures. Indeed, cross-language comparisons show that the concept of heat is central in linguistic expressions of anger not only in English but also in Chinese (Yu, 1995), Japanese, Hungarian, Wolof, Zulu, and Polish (Kövecses, 2000). Similarly, if heat and anger are conceptually related, then activating one should simultaneously activate the other, and this has in fact been shown. Participants are better at categorizing anger-related word when presented with a background involving heat, compared with a cold or neutral background image.

Furthermore, participants primed with anger provided higher estimates of average annual temperature for unfamiliar cities than participants primed with fear, or neutral words (Wilkowski, Meier, Robinson, Carter, & Feltman, 2009). The reverse relationship also holds: Priming participants with heat activates thoughts related to anger and aggression (DeWall & Bushman, 2009). Because one metaphoric entailment of anger and heat is the association with the color red, priming participants with the concept of anger, or inducing the emotional state of anger, facilitates the perception of redness (Fetterman, Robinson, Gordon, & Elliot, 2011).

The container metaphor, especially when the fluid in the container is conceptualized as hot, mirrors the control aspect of emotion: The level of a fluid in a container rises as the intensity of the emotion rises, and as it gets too intense, the container explodes, reflecting that the person has to give up control over the emotion. Notably, it is perhaps less common to talk about the body as a container for emotions that do not involve high levels of physiological arousal, such as pride or respect (Kövecses, 1990), nor do they usually exert a disturbing influence on everyday actions, and thus they are considered less prototypical or less "good" examples of emotion.

Not only specific emotions are talked about with reference to the metaphor of the body as a container, but language used to talk about emotions more generally consists of spatial language, such as *deep* feelings. The usage of this particular type of language can be traced back to properties of a container, because the deeper the container, the more substance in the form of fluid it can hold (Kövecses, 1990). In addition to more intense, *deep* can also mean "more sincere" and is reflected in the fact that points farther away from the container surface are deep inside the container. Using the container metaphor thus exemplifies the more general principle of *more is up:* More fluid in the container stands for higher intensity of the emotion, or conversely, a lack of fluid ("I feel empty") indicates a lack of emotion.

Keeping One's Boundaries

The emotion that is most clearly concerned with maintaining the boundaries of the bodily container is disgust. On its most basic level, disgust has a functional role in the context of food consumption, that is, when it comes to which substances to physically incorporate by ingesting (Rozin, Haidt, & McCauley, 2008). The rejection of potentially edible items that look, taste, or smell bad is adaptive because it reduces the likelihood of consuming food that may be harmful to one's health. Similarly, the potential of coming into contact with contaminated objects and surfaces is reduced in the face of reluctant physical contact due to feelings of disgust and repulsion. Behavioral responses of literally expelling bad-tasting food by spitting it out or pulling up the nose in disgust to reduce the amount of airflow stemming from the contaminant (Susskind et al., 2008) further ensure that potentially harmful substances do not enter the bodily container. The role of disgust in protecting the body of harm and contamination therefore has a clear bodily basis.

Built on this, however, is a sense of disgust that goes beyond the realm of the bodily container because it extends to metaphoric contamination: It is not only bad food that makes us feel repulsed and sick to the stomach, the same is the case for bad people and their bad, repulsive behaviors. In other words, in addition to physical disgust another sense of disgust involves moral disgust (Rozin et al., 2008), and it is likely that the two have a close metaphoric link. Indeed, functional neuroimaging studies suggest that the same brain structures may be implicated in the experience of physical and moral disgust (Moll et al., 2005; Schaich Borg, Lieberman, & Kiehl, 2008). Furthermore, inductions of physical disgust change judgments and decisions involving moral disgust (Schnall, Haidt, Clore, & Jordan, 2008; Wheatley & Haidt, 2005). For example, in one study, my colleagues and I exposed some participants to a bad smell in the form of "fart spray." Participants who sensed this disgusting smell judged various moral transgressions, such as falsifying a resume or not returning a lost wallet, to be more wrong than participants who were not exposed to the smell. Similarly, in a different study, participants who happened to sit at a disgusting table and were surrounded by dirty pizza boxes and used tissues made more severe moral judgments than participants sitting at the same table when it was clean and untainted (Schnall, Haidt, et al., 2008). Furthermore, people's spontaneous facial expressions are similar toward physically and morally disgusting stimuli (Cannon, Schnall, & White, 2011; Chapman, Kim, Susskind, & Anderson, 2009). These findings suggest that people often equate physical disgust and moral disgust, such as when experimentally induced feelings of repulsion are taken as evidence of moral condemnation. The conflation of physical and social disgust seems to take place especially when the metaphor of the body as a container is made salient. Landau, Sullivan, and Greenberg (2009) showed that after describing the United States in ways that highlighted its properties as a bodily entity, participants exposed to contamination fears were especially likely to express concerns about foreign immigration. Thus, physical and metaphoric notions of containment are closely linked (see Chapter 6, this volume).

Related to the function of disgust as guardian of the body's actual and metaphoric boundaries against physical and moral contamination, studies have investigated the link between physical and moral purity. Experiments have documented the *Macbeth effect*, named after Lady Macbeth, who attempted to rinse off the imaginary stains of murder. After having considered their past immoral actions, participants found cleansing products to be more attractive and expressed a greater desire to wash themselves (Zhong &

Liljenquist, 2006). Furthermore, different types of transgression lead to different kinds of cleansing desires: After speaking immoral things, people want to use mouthwash, but after typing something immoral using a computer keyboard, people want to use a hand sanitizer (Lee & Schwarz, 2010a). Similarly, being primed with words related to cleanliness or engaging in handwashing can influence moral judgments and make them less harsh when participants interpret feelings of cleanliness to be relevant to specific transgressions (Schnall, Benton, & Harvey, 2008) but more harsh when the cleanliness is seen as indicative of one's own superior moral standing (Zhong, Strejcek, & Sivanathan, 2010). Furthermore, cleanliness in other people may indicate the fact that they possess close social contacts and that therefore they may be good cooperative partners (Schnall, 2011).

Moving beyond the immediate need to protect one's bodily boundaries, recent findings suggest that the effects of cleansing can go beyond the moral domain. For example, a form of cognitive dissonance—namely, nagging doubts about whether one made the right decision, can be reduced by handwashing (Lee & Schwarz, 2010b; see also Chapter 5, this volume). However, not only negative states can be removed; physical cleansing can also get rid of positive states, such as one's sense of having a *lucky streak* (Xu, Zwick, & Schwarz, 2012). In this sense, physically cleansing the body can serve as a "reset" button for the mind.

ACTUAL AND METAPHORIC DISTANCE IN SPACE AND TIME

As reviewed in the previous section, on a basic level, the human body is a container with a clearly delineated inside and outside. A related, also basic embodied concept is self–other overlap: Once another person is "close," the distinction between self and body, and that of the other, breaks down (Aron, Aron, Tudor, & Nelson, 1991; Smith, 2008). Terms such as *ingroup* and *outgroup* further denote the distinction between those who we keep so close that they almost seem part of the self, compared with those who are not. Because each person is separated from the surrounding world by a skin, we see objects as possessing boundaries even if they are not clearly defined: A peak in a mountain range might appear as a distinct entity and be labelled as such, even if its boundary from the rest of the geological structure is fuzzy at best. Overall, the tendency to impose real and metaphoric boundaries implies that some things are close, whereas others are not.

On the most basic level, physical distance reflects the extent to which objects and people are brought close and within reach or are kept at *arm's length*. Indeed, approach and avoidance are considered some of the most basic behavioral tendencies (e.g., Elliot, 2008). Distance is further used metaphorically to denote social relationships, for example, by speaking of a *close* contact or a *distant* acquaintance. These metaphors reflect how people move and act in space as a reflection of specific social relationships. Indeed, people get close to intimate others to whom they feel close (Patterson, 1977; Willis, 1966), but they literally distance themselves from others who are seen as less attractive, such as people marked by a physical stigma (Kleck, 1968), as if one is afraid that too close of a contact might literally pose the danger of the stigma "rubbing off."

In general, people feel highly protective of the area of space immediately around them that has been termed *personal space* (Hall, 1968). Discomfort results when this space is invaded, and people engage in compensatory behaviors by reducing other indicators of intimacy, such as eye gaze (Argyle & Dean, 1965). Thus, social factors constrain how people act and move in physical space, and this has consequences for how this space is perceived. Distances are perceived differently depending on whether they imply entities that are considered part of one's ingroup or, instead, an outgroup (Burris & Branscombe, 2005; Kerkman, Stea, Norris, & Rice, 2004). For instance, distances that involve crossing the borders between one's home country (e.g., the United States) into a foreign country (e.g., Mexico) are estimated as greater than distances within the home country (Burris & Branscombe, 2005). Similarly, study participants estimate distances between city pairs that used to be separated by the Iron Curtain, with one city located within East Germany and the other city located within West Germany, to be greater than distances of cities located within the same areas of Germany (Carbon & Leder, 2005). This overestimation was greatest for participants who had a negative attitude toward the reunification of Germany, presumably reflecting a strong personal sense of the country's social and political boundaries.

Findings such as these suggest that rather than being objectively determined by a low-level modular process that takes place in a *computationally encapsulated* (Fodor, 1983) manner, visual processes such as estimating small-scale distances on maps are constrained by various contextual factors, which can include social and cognitive variables. On a broader level, visual perceptions of various kinds, including those of the physical environment, relate back to how people and their bodies use space and how they act in space. Such considerations can shape how close or far objects appear because the visual perception of distance takes into account how easy or difficult it would be to reach a target object, given one's bodily capabilities (Proffitt, 2006). For example, while participants wore a heavy backpack, objects placed within a few meters of them appeared farther away than when no such backpack was worn (Proffitt, Stefanucci, Banton, & Epstein, 2003). Presumably, the physical state of being weighted down is indicative of how easy or difficult it would be to cover a distance, and it therefore shapes how close or far a given target appears. Similarly, because the effort involved in throwing a heavy ball is greater than the effort involved in throwing a light ball, after throwing the heavy ball, distances appear to be farther (Witt, Proffitt, & Epstein, 2004). In addition to relative difficulty or effort of engaging with an object, motivational states relating to the desirability to objects also change perceptual affordances. Balcetis and Dunning (2010) showed that desirable objects, such as a glass of water when one is thirsty, appear closer than undesirable objects; such a perceptual bias would presumably facilitate the goal-relevant action of approaching the object, such as grabbing the glass of water to quench one's thirst.

Psychological Distance

As this chapter has reviewed in detail, the theory of conceptual metaphor (Lakoff & Johnson, 1980, 1999) proposes that physical experiences are linked with abstract concepts through embodied metaphors. Thus, there is a basic distinction between a concrete experience, for example, the actual distance to an object in space, and an abstract concept, for example, the subjective valence assigned to this object. In a somewhat similar way, construal level theory (Liberman & Trope, 2008; Trope & Liberman, 2010) proposes a fundamental distinction regarding what is termed *psychological distance*: Experiences can be concrete, immediate and happening at the present moment, or in contrast, be abstract, distant and remote. As a consequence, psychological distance involves different mental representations of events, such that thinking about the here and now involves concrete, low-level construals tied to direct perceptual experience, whereas thinking about distant places, other people, or one's future self involves abstract, high-level construals that are detached from current experience.

Accumulating evidence suggests that people process the same kind of information differently depending on metaphoric distance and resulting construal level. Relative to events and situations that are psychologically *close*, taking a more *removed* psychological perspective facilitates abstract and global processing (e.g., Henderson, Fujita, Trope, & Liberman, 2006; Liberman & Förster, 2009). For example, abstract moral principles are more likely to be emphasized over situational constraints when participants use a high-level rather than a low-level construal (Eyal, Liberman, & Trope, 2008), and moral transgressions are condemned more in the distant future than in the near future, presumably because high-level construals make abstract moral values especially salient (Agerström & Björklund, 2009). Furthermore, increased psychological distance can lead to better economic decisions, such as a greater focus on long-term over short-term benefits (Kim, Schnall, & White, 2013) or the enhanced goal of maximizing financial gains in an economic game (Kim, Schnall, Yi, & White, 2012). These findings suggest that a distant psychological perspective and its associated high-level construal may literally help people "step back" from the immediate concerns and instead, focus on more abstract, *higher level* goals.

Construal level theory notes that the central construct of psychological distance manifests itself in various domains, including space (close vs. far), time (now vs. later), social distance (self vs. other), and hypothetical distance (likely vs. unlikely; Liberman, Trope, & Stephan, 2007). Indeed, all four dimensions of psychological distance are highly correlated (Fiedler, Jung, Wänke, & Alexopoulos, 2012). Liberman and Förster (2011), however, raised the issue of whether spatial distance might be more primary and therefore more basic than other types of psychological distance. As reviewed above, this is likely to be the case, given that physical space provides the perceptual source domain for many other target domains. Thus, spatial distance serves as the source domain for other, more metaphoric types of psychological distance, such as temporal distance or social distance. Indeed, the way in which space facilitates thinking about time is well documented (Boroditsky, 2000; Boroditsky & Ramscar, 2002). Overall, findings derived from the construal level framework suggest that psychological distance is a fundamental dimension that is used to organize experiences and concepts, thus lending support to the notion that distance, whether concrete or abstract, constitutes a fundamental embodied metaphor.

Being Close = Being Warm

As noted previously, physical and metaphoric closeness is indicative of immediate experiences and concerns. Because it means potentially putting oneself in danger, we only let those people get close toward whom we are favorably disposed. Being close therefore often coincides with close bodily contact, or touching. In his seminal work, Bowlby (1969) noted that the close relationship between infant and caregiver provides a critical relationship template for future romantic relationships, and such close primary relationships are characterized by close physical contact and warmth. Thus, from very early on in childhood, feeling warm becomes synonymous with being cared for and loved by others. Indeed, Fiske, Cuddy, and Glick (2007) proposed that when making evaluations about other people, one of the two most basic dimensions, along with judgments of competence, is the judgment of how warm and friendly that person is. Thus, warmth is a basic perceptual concept that grows out of the understanding that, relative to one's own bodily boundaries, we keep those whom we like so close that we can sense the warmth radiating from them.

Just like physical and moral purity can become conflated, as noted earlier (Schnall, Benton, & Harvey, 2008; Zhong & Liljenquist, 2006), physical and interpersonal warmth can become conflated. For example, after holding a cup containing a hot drink, research participants rated a neutral stranger as more warm and friendly than they did after holding a cold drink (Williams & Bargh, 2008). Similarly, research participants express more relational thinking in a warm relative to a cold room (IJzerman & Semin, 2009). Looking at the reverse relationship, participants who were made to feel lonely and excluded rated the ambient room temperature to be colder than those who felt accepted, and presumably "warm" (Zhong, & Leonardelli, 2008). As a means of emotional self-regulation, experienced loneliness can be ameliorated by seeking out warm comfort in the form of a hot bath or shower (Bargh & Shalev, 2012).

Thus, interpersonal closeness seems to be closely associated with warmth. Fay and Maner (2012) found direct evidence for precisely this link. They had participants hold a warm or cold cup of coffee and then estimate the distance to the cup. Participants low in avoidant attachment saw the warm cup as closer than the cold cup, whereas participants high in avoidant attachment showed the opposite effect. A second study showed that when feelings of warmth were induced, participants were more likely to report a desire to be close to others, but again this effect was moderated by attachment style, with only participants low in avoidant attachment demonstrating this connection. The association between warmth and proximity and the moderating effect of attachment styles indicates that such a connection is not innate or invariate but is at least to some extent shaped by specific experience. Thus, warmth originating from a caregiver early in life is the result of being "close" to this person.

OTHER BASIC METAPHORS

I have argued for a given set of bodily image schemas and resulting metaphoric concepts to be central. However, what is the reason to believe that other embodied concepts are less central? Much of what was discussed concerned potential basic metaphors derived from how the human body is situated and functions within space. In addition, information from different sensory modalities may provide fundamental source domains for potential use with abstract target domains. Although human beings take in information about the surrounding world through five distinct senses—vision, hearing, taste, smell, and touch—it is well established that vision is much more important for human beings than is hearing or smell. As a consequence, it is likely that specific visual experiences, such as the light of dawn and sunshine, are experienced positively across practically all cultures, whereas the darkness and potential danger of night are universally experienced negatively.

A reflection of this importance of telling light from dark, such as day from night, is that all language communities studied to date have distinct terms for *black* and *white*, even if they lack words for other colors (Berlin & Kay, 1969). Thus, it is likely that findings with Western samples suggesting a positive valence of brightness relative to darkness (Meier, Robinson, & Clore, 2004; Sherman & Clore, 2009) also hold for non-Western samples. However, the recent observation that a black and white visual contrast leads to more polarized, extreme judgments (Zarkadi & Schnall, 2013) may be limited to cultures that have specific linguistic expressions about *black and white thinking*.

Visual cues of light and dark are more likely to cross-culturally represent similar metaphoric ideas than, for example, specific smells that are associated with moral connotations. Indeed, Lee and Schwarz (2012; see also Chapter 5, this volume) recently showed that although the specific smell of "fishy" is linked with something being suspicious, this expression is not necessarily universal across cultures. Thus, it may be that unpleasant smells of various kinds are linguistically reflected as spelling trouble, but because the sense of smell is less central than the sense of vision, there is cultural variability in what particular type of smell has a suspicious meaning attached to it.

Most important in this context will be cross-cultural investigations using the metaphoric transfer strategy described by Landau and colleagues (2010) that has been so productively used with Western samples. As reviewed elsewhere (Leung, Qiu, Ong, & Tam, 2011; see Chapter 12, this volume), some findings already suggest that some embodied metaphors hold across various cultural communities.

CONCLUSION

Embodied approaches to language and cognition propose that all thought processes need to be conceptualized as taking place in the service of embodied action that is contextually constrained. Such a view suggests that cognition depends heavily on perceptual and interactional processes of the human body in the physical world. The most fundamental such bodily experiences are based on the fact that the body is a container that moves in space. It is a bounded entity that has a surface. Objects and people are positioned at varying distances to the body, and the distance to them is manipulated depending on action goals. This chapter has proposed a list of potentially basic metaphors that result from these sets of fundamental image schemas that are grounded in physical experience. In contrast to Ekman's (1992b) forceful conclusion that there definitely are basic emotions, for now, the conclusion regarding the existence of basic metaphors needs to remain somewhat more tentative and speculative. On the basis of existing evidence, a number of metaphors seem to be basic in the sense defined here, but additional evidence for such proposed universality is needed.

REFERENCES

Agerström, J., & Björklund, F. (2009). Temporal distance and moral concerns: Future morally questionable behavior is perceived as more wrong and evokes stronger prosocial intentions. *Basic and Applied Social Psychology, 31,* 49–59. doi:10.1080/01973530802659885

Argyle, M., & Dean, J. (1965). Eye-contact, distance and affiliation. *Sociometry, 28,* 289–304. doi:10.2307/2786027

Aron, A., Aron, E. N., Tudor, M., & Nelson, G. (1991). Close relationships as including other in the self. *Journal of Personality and Social Psychology, 60,* 241–253. doi:10.1037/0022-3514.60.2.241

Balcetis, E., & Dunning, D. (2010). More desirable objects are seen as closer. *Psychological Science, 21,* 147–152. doi:10.1177/0956797609356283

Bargh, J. A., & Shalev, I. (2012). The substitutability of physical and social warmth in everyday life. *Emotion, 12,* 154–162. doi:10.1037/a0023527

Barrett, L. F. (2006). Are emotions natural kinds? *Perspectives on Psychological Science, 1,* 28–58. doi:10.1111/j.1745-6916.2006.00003.x

Barsalou, L. W. (1999). Perceptual symbol systems. *Behavioral and Brain Sciences, 22,* 577–660.

Barsalou, L. W. (2008). Grounded cognition. *Annual Review of Psychology, 59,* 617–645. doi:10.1146/annurev.psych.59.103006.093639

Berlin, B., & Kay, P. (1969). *Basic color terms: Their universality and evolution.* Berkeley and Los Angeles: University of California Press.

Boroditsky, L. (2000). Metaphoric structuring: Understanding time through spatial metaphors. *Cognition, 75,* 1–28. doi:10.1016/S0010-0277(99)00073-6

Boroditsky, L., & Ramscar, M. (2002). The roles of body and mind in abstract thought. *Psychological Science, 13,* 185–189. doi:10.1111/1467-9280.00434

Bowlby, J. (1969). *Attachment and loss.* London, England: Hogarth Press.

Bruner, J. (1978). The role of dialogue in language acquisition. In A. Sinclair, R. Jarvella, & W. J. M. Levelt (Eds.), *The child's conception of language* (pp. 241–256). Berlin, Germany: Springer.

Burris, C. T., & Branscombe, N. R. (2005). Distorted distance estimation induced by a self-relevant national boundary. *Journal of Experimental Social Psychology, 41,* 305–312. doi:10.1016/j.jesp.2004.06.012

Cannon, P. R., Schnall, S., & White, M. (2011). Transgressions and expressions: Affective facial muscle activity predicts moral judgments. *Social Psychological and Personality Science, 2,* 325–331. doi:10.1177/1948550610390525

Carbon, C. C., & Leder, H. (2005). The wall inside the brain: Overestimation of distances crossing the former Iron Curtain. *Psychonomic Bulletin & Review, 12,* 746–750. doi:10.3758/BF03196767

Chapman, H. A., Kim, D. A., Susskind, J. M., & Anderson, A. K. (2009). In bad taste: Evidence for the oral origins for moral disgust. *Science, 323,* 1222–1226. doi:10.1126/science.1165565

Clark, A. (1997). *Being there: Putting brain, body and world together again.* Cambridge, MA: MIT Press.

DeWall, C. N., & Bushman, B. J. (2009). Hot under the collar in a lukewarm environment: Words associated with hot temperature increase aggressive thoughts and hostile perceptions. *Journal of Experimental Social Psychology, 45,* 1045–1047. doi:10.1016/j.jesp.2009.05.003

Ekman, P. (1992a). Are there basic emotions? *Psychological Review, 99,* 550–553. doi:10.1037/0033-295X.99.3.550

Ekman, P. (1992b). An argument for basic emotions. *Cognition and Emotion, 6,* 169–200. doi:10.1080/02699939208411068

Ekman, P., Levenson, R. W., & Friesen, W. V. (1983). Autonomic nervous system activity distinguishes among emotions. *Science, 221,* 1208–1210. doi:10.1126/science.6612338

Elliot, A. J. (2008). Approach and avoidance motivation. In A. J. Elliot (Ed.), *Handbook of approach and avoidance motivation* (pp. 3–14). New York, NY: Psychology Press.

Eyal, T., Liberman, N., & Trope, Y. (2008). Judging near and distant virtue and vice. *Journal of Experimental Social Psychology, 44,* 1204–1209. doi:10.1016/j.jesp.2008.03.012

Fay, A. J., & Maner, J. K. (2012). Warmth, spatial proximity, and social attachment: The embodied perception of a social metaphor. *Journal of Experimental Social Psychology, 48,* 1369–1372. doi:10.1016/j.jesp.2012.05.017

Fetterman, A. K., Robinson, M. D., Gordon, R. D., & Elliot, A. J. (2011). Anger as seeing red: Perceptual sources of evidence. *Social Psychological and Personality Science, 2,* 311–316. doi:10.1177/1948550610390051

Fiedler, K., Jung, J., Wänke, M., & Alexopoulos, T. (2012). On the relations between distinct aspects of psychological distance: An ecological basis of construal-level theory. *Journal of Experimental Social Psychology, 48,* 1014–1021. doi:10.1016/j.jesp.2012.03.013

Fiske, S. T., Cuddy, A. J. C., & Glick, P. (2007). Universal dimensions of social cognition: Warmth and competence. *Trends in Cognitive Sciences, 11,* 77–83. doi:10.1016/j.tics.2006.11.005

Fodor, J. A. (1983). *Modularity of mind.* Cambridge, MA: MIT Press.

Gibson, J. J. (1979). *The ecological approach to visual perception.* Boston, MA: Houghton Mifflin.

Glenberg, A. M. (1997). What memory is for. *Behavioral and Brain Sciences, 20,* 1–55.

Hall, E. T. (1968). Proxemics. *Current Anthropology, 9*, 83–95. doi:10.1086/200975

Henderson, M. D., Fujita, K., Trope, Y., & Liberman, N. (2006). Transcending the "Here": The effect of spatial distance on social judgment. *Journal of Personality and Social Psychology, 91*, 845–856. doi:10.1037/0022-3514.91.5.845

IJzerman, H., & Semin, G. R. (2009). The thermometer of social relations: Mapping social proximity on temperature. *Psychological Science, 20*, 1214–1220. doi:10.1111/j.1467-9280.2009.02434.x

Johnson, M. (1987). *The body in the mind: The bodily basis of meaning, imagination, and reason.* Chicago, IL: University of Chicago Press.

Kerkman, D. D., Stea, D., Norris, K., & Rice, J. L. (2004). Social attitudes predict biases in geographic knowledge. *The Professional Geographer, 56*, 258–269.

Kim, H., Schnall, S., & White, M. P. (2013, May 7). Similar psychological distance reduces temporal discounting. *Personality and Social Psychology Bulletin.* Advance online publication. doi: 10.1177/0146167213488214

Kim, H., Schnall, S., Yi, D., & White, M. P. (2012). *Psychological distance increases responders' acceptance in the Ultimatum Game.* Manuscript submitted for publication.

Kleck, R. E. (1968). Effects of stigmatizing conditions on the use of personal space. *Psychological Reports, 23*, 111–118. doi:10.2466/pr0.1968.23.1.111

Kövecses, Z. (1990). *Emotion concepts.* New York, NY: Springer. doi:10.1007/978-1-4612-3312-1

Kövecses, Z. (2000). *Metaphor and emotion: Language, culture, and body in human feeling.* New York, NY: Cambridge University Press.

Lakoff, G., & Johnson, M. (1980). *Metaphors we live by.* Chicago, IL: University of Chicago Press.

Lakoff, G., & Johnson, M. (1999). *Philosophy in the flesh: The embodied mind and its challenge to Western thought.* New York, NY: Basic Books.

Landau, M. J., Meier, B. P., & Keefer, L. A. (2010). A metaphor-enriched social cognition. *Psychological Bulletin, 136*, 1045–1067. doi:10.1037/a0020970

Landau, M. J., Sullivan, D., & Greenberg, J. (2009). Evidence that self-relevant motivations and metaphoric framing interact to influence political and social issues. *Psychological Science, 20*, 1421–1427. doi:10.1111/j.1467-9280.2009.02462.x

Lee, S. W. S., & Schwarz, N. (2010a). Of dirty hands and dirty mouths: Embodiment of the moral purity metaphor is specific to the motor modality involved in moral transgression. *Psychological Science, 21*, 1423–1425. doi:10.1177/0956797610382788

Lee, S. W. S., & Schwarz, N. (2010b). Washing away postdecisional dissonance. *Science, 328*, 709. doi:10.1126/science.1186799

Lee, S. W. S., & Schwarz, N. (2012). Bidirectionality, mediation, and moderation of metaphorical effects: The embodiment of social suspicion and fishy smells. *Journal of Personality and Social Psychology, 103*, 737–749.

Leung, A. K.-y., Qiu, L., Ong, L., & Tam, K.-P. (2011). Embodied cultural cognition: Situating the study of embodied cognition in socio-cultural contexts. *Social and Personality Psychology Compass, 5,* 591–608. doi:10.1111/j.1751-9004.2011.00373.x

Liberman, N., & Förster, J. (2009). Distancing from experienced self: How global-versus-local perception affects estimation of psychological distance. *Journal of Personality and Social Psychology, 97,* 203–216. doi:10.1037/a0015671

Liberman, N., & Förster, J. (2011). Estimates of spatial distance: A construal level perspective. In A. Maas & T. W. Schubert (Eds.), *Spatial dimensions of social thought* (pp. 109–128). Berlin, Germany: Mouton de Gruyter.

Liberman, N., & Trope, Y. (2008). The psychology of transcending the here and now. *Science, 322,* 1201–1205. doi:10.1126/science.1161958

Liberman, N., Trope, Y., & Stephan, E. (2007). Psychological distance. In A. W. Kruglanski & E. T. Higgins (Eds.), *Social psychology: Handbook of basic principles* (2nd ed., pp. 353–383). New York, NY: Guilford Press

Mandler, J. M. (1992). How to build a baby: II. Conceptual primitives. *Psychological Review, 99,* 587–604. doi:10.1037/0033-295X.99.4.587

Meier, B. P., Hauser, D. J., Robinson, M. D., Friesen, C. K., & Schjeldahl, K. (2007). What's "up" with God? Vertical space as a representation of the divine. *Journal of Personality and Social Psychology, 93,* 699–710. doi:10.1037/0022-3514.93.5.699

Meier, B. P., & Robinson, M. D. (2004). Why the sunny side is up: Associations between affect and vertical position. *Psychological Science, 15,* 243–247. doi:10.1111/j.0956-7976.2004.00659.x

Meier, B. P., Robinson, M. D., & Clore, G. L. (2004). Why good guys wear white: Automatic inferences about stimulus valence based on brightness. *Psychological Science, 15,* 82–87. doi:10.1111/j.0963-7214.2004.01502002.x

Meier, B. P., Schnall, S., Schwarz, N., & Bargh, J. A. (2012). Embodiment in social psychology. *Topics in Cognitive Science, 4,* 705–716. doi:10.1111/j.1756-8765.2012.01212.x

Meier, B. P., Sellbom, M., & Wygant, D. B. (2007). Failing to take the moral high ground: Psychopathy and the vertical representation of morality. *Personality and Individual Differences, 43,* 757–767. doi:10.1016/j.paid.2007.02.001

Merleau-Ponty, M. (1962). *Phenomenology of perception.* London, England: Routledge.

Moll, J., de Oliveira-Souza, R., Moll, F., Ignacio, F., Bramati, I., Caparelli-Daquer, E., & Eslinger, P. J. (2005). The moral affiliations of disgust: A functional MRI study. *Cognitive and Behavioral Neurology, 18,* 68–78. doi:10.1097/01.wnn.0000152236.46475.a7

Niedenthal, P. M., Barsalou, L. W., Winkielman, P., Krauth-Gruber, S., & Ric, F. (2005). Embodiment in attitudes, social perception, and emotion. *Personality and Social Psychology Review, 9,* 184–211. doi:10.1207/s15327957pspr0903_1

Panksepp, J. (2007). Neurologizing the psychology of affects: How appraisal-based constructivism and basic emotion theory can coexist. *Perspectives on Psychological Science, 2,* 281–296. doi:10.1111/j.1745-6916.2007.00045.x

Patterson, M. L. (1977). Interpersonal distance, affect, and equilibrium theory. *The Journal of Social Psychology, 101*, 205–214. doi:10.1080/00224545.1977.9924008

Pavarini, G., Schnall, S., & Immordino-Yang, M. H. (2012). *Looking up to virtuous others: Gaze aversion and cognitive abstraction distinguish moral elevation from admiration for skill*. Unpublished manuscript.

Piaget, J. (1980). The psychogenesis of knowledge and its epistemological significance. In M. Piatelli-Palmarini (Ed.), *Language and learning: The debate between Jean Piaget and Noam Chomsky* (pp. 23–34). Cambridge, MA: Harvard University Press.

Proffitt, D. R. (2006). Embodied perception and the economy of action. *Perspectives on Psychological Science, 1*, 110–122. doi:10.1111/j.1745-6916.2006.00008.x

Proffitt, D. R., Stefanucci, J., Banton, T., & Epstein, W. (2003). The role of effort in perceived distance. *Psychological Science, 14*, 106–112. doi:10.1111/1467-9280.t01-1-01427

Rozin, P., Haidt, J., & McCauley, C. R. (2008). Disgust. In M. Lewis & J. M. Haviland (Eds.), *Handbook of emotions* (3rd ed., pp. 757–776). New York, NY: Guilford Press.

Schaich Borg, J., Lieberman, D., & Kiehl, K. (2008). Infection, incest, and iniquity: Investigating the neural correlates of disgust and morality. *Journal of Cognitive Neuroscience, 20*, 1529–1546. doi:10.1162/jocn.2008.20109

Schnall, S. (2011). Clean, proper and tidy are more than the absence of dirty, disgusting and wrong. *Emotion Review, 3*, 264–266. doi:10.1177/1754073911402397

Schnall, S., Benton, J., & Harvey, S. (2008). With a clean conscience: Cleanliness reduces the severity of moral judgments. *Psychological Science, 19*, 1219–1222. doi:10.1111/j.1467-9280.2008.02227.x

Schnall, S., Haidt, J., Clore, G. L., & Jordan, A. H. (2008). Disgust as embodied moral judgment. *Personality and Social Psychology Bulletin, 34*, 1096–1109. doi:10.1177/0146167208317771

Schnall, S., & Roper, J. (2012). Elevation puts moral values into action. *Social Psychological and Personality Science, 3*, 373–378. doi:10.1177/1948550611423595

Schnall, S., Roper, J., & Fessler, D. M. T. (2010). Elevation leads to altruistic behavior. *Psychological Science, 21*, 315–320. doi:10.1177/0956797609359882

Schubert, T. W. (2005). Your highness: Vertical positions as perceptual symbols of power. *Journal of Personality and Social Psychology, 89*, 1–21. doi:10.1037/0022-3514.89.1.1

Sherman, G. D., & Clore, G. L. (2009). The color of sin: White and black are perceptual symbols of moral purity and pollution. *Psychological Science, 20*, 1019–1025. doi:10.1111/j.1467-9280.2009.02403.x

Smith, E. R. (2008). An embodied account of self-other "overlap" and its effects. In G. R. Semin & E. R. Smith (Eds.), *Embodied grounding: Social, cognitive, affective, and neuroscientific approaches* (pp. 148–159). New York, NY: Cambridge University Press. doi:10.1017/CBO9780511805837.007

Smith, E. R., & Semin, G. R. (2004). Socially situated cognition: Cognition in its social context. In M. P. Zanna (Ed.), *Advances in Experimental Social Psychology*. San Diego, CA: Academic Press. doi:10.1016/S0065-2601(04)36002-8

Spellman, B. A., & Schnall, S. (2009). Embodied rationality. *Queen's Law Journal, 35,* 117–164.

Susskind, J. M., Lee, D. H., Cusi, A., Feiman, R., Grabski, W., & Anderson, A. K. (2008). Expressing fear enhances sensory acquisition. *Nature Neuroscience, 11,* 843–850. doi:10.1038/nn.2138

Trope, Y., & Liberman, N. (2010). Construal-level theory of psychological distance. *Psychological Review, 117,* 440–463. doi:10.1037/a0018963

Varela, F. J., Thompson, E., & Rosch, E. (1991). *The embodied mind: Cognitive science and human experience*. Cambridge, MA: MIT Press.

Vygotsky, L. S. (1978). *Mind in society: The development of higher psychological processes*. Cambridge, MA: Harvard University Press.

Werner, H., & Kaplan, B. (1963). *Symbol formation*. New York, NY: Wiley.

Wheatley, T., & Haidt, J. (2005). Hypnotic disgust makes moral judgments more severe. *Psychological Science, 16,* 780–784. doi:10.1111/j.1467-9280.2005.01614.x

Wilkowski, B. M., Meier, B. P., Robinson, M. D., Carter, M. S., & Feltman, R. (2009). "Hot-headed" is more than an expression: The embodied representation of anger in terms of heat. *Emotion, 9,* 464–477. doi:10.1037/a0015764

Williams, L. E., & Bargh, J. A. (2008). Experiencing physical warmth promotes interpersonal warmth. *Science, 322,* 606–607. doi:10.1126/science.1162548

Williams, L. E., Huang, J. Y., & Bargh, J. A. (2009). The scaffolded mind: Higher mental processes are grounded in early experience in the physical world. *European Journal of Social Psychology, 39,* 1257–1267. doi:10.1002/ejsp.665

Willis, R. N. (1966). Initial speaking distance as a function of the speaker's relationship. *Psychonomic Science, 5,* 221–222.

Witt, J. K., Proffitt, D. R., & Epstein, W. (2004). Perceiving distance: A role of effort and intent. *Perception, 33,* 577–590. doi:10.1068/p5090

Xu, A. J., Zwick, R., & Schwarz, N. (2012). Washing away your (good or bad) luck: Physical cleansing affects risk-taking behavior. *Journal of Experimental Psychology: General, 141,* 26–30. doi:10.1037/a0023997

Yu, N. (1995). Metaphorical expressions of anger and happiness in English and Chinese. *Metaphor and Symbolic Activity, 10,* 59–92. doi:10.1207/s15327868ms1002_1

Zarkadi, T., & Schnall, S. (2013). "Black and white" thinking: Visual contrast polarizes moral judgment. *Journal of Experimental Social Psychology, 49,* 355–359. doi:10.1016/j.jesp.2012.11.012

Zhong, C. B., & Leonardelli, G. J. (2008). Cold and lonely: Does social exclusion literally feel cold? *Psychological Science, 19*, 838–842. doi:10.1111/j.1467-9280.2008.02165.x

Zhong, C. B., & Liljenquist, K. A. (2006). Washing away your sins: Threatened morality and physical cleansing. *Science, 313*, 1451–1452. doi:10.1126/science.1130726

Zhong, C. B., Strejcek, B., & Sivanathan, N. (2010). A clean self can render harsh moral judgment. *Journal of Experimental Social Psychology, 46*, 859–862. doi:10.1016/j.jesp.2010.04.003

12

EXPERIENTIAL ORIGINS OF MENTAL METAPHORS: LANGUAGE, CULTURE, AND THE BODY

DANIEL CASASANTO

People not only talk metaphorically, they also think metaphorically. Where do our mental metaphors come from? Metaphor theorists posit that hundreds of metaphors in language and thought have their basis in bodily interactions with the physical world. Yet the origins of most mental metaphors are difficult to discern because the patterns of linguistic, cultural, and bodily experience that could give rise to them appear mutually inextricable. This chapter highlights three mental metaphors for which the contributions of language, culture, and the body can be distinguished unambiguously. By analyzing the distinct ways in which *politics*, *time*, and *emotional valence* come to be metaphorized in terms of left–right space, it is possible to illustrate the

Thanks to Laura Staum Casasanto and Roberto Bottini for comments and discussion. This research was supported in part by a grant from the Consejería de Innovación, Ciencia y Empresa, Junta de Andalucía and the European Regional Development Fund (P09-SEJ-4772) and by a James S. McDonnell Foundation Scholar Award.

http://dx.doi.org/10.1037/14278-011
The Power of Metaphor: Examining Its Influence on Social Life, M. J. Landau, M. D. Robinson, and B. P. Meier (Editors)

distinct linguistic, cultural, and bodily origins of the mental metaphors that scaffold our thoughts, feelings, and choices.

METAPHORS BEYOND LANGUAGE

At one time, the claim that people think metaphorically was supported only by patterns in language (Clark, 1973; Jackendoff, 1983; Lakoff & Johnson, 1980, 1999), but there is now behavioral evidence that source domain representations are activated with a high degree of automaticity when people think about abstract domains including time (Boroditsky, 2000), number (Dehaene, Bossini, & Giraux, 1993), similarity (Casasanto, 2008), emotional attachment (Williams & Bargh, 2008), and power (Schubert, 2005; for a review of more than 40 studies validating metaphor theory, see Landau, Meier, & Keefer, 2010). People think in mental metaphors even when they are not using language (Casasanto & Boroditsky, 2008; Dolscheid, Shayan, Majid, & Casasanto, 2013). That is, when people conceptualize domains such as time, number, or emotion, their conceptualizations may be partly constituted by mental metaphors: implicit, analog mappings between nonlinguistic mental representations in a concrete "source domain" (e.g., space, force, motion) and a relatively abstract or unfamiliar "target domain."[1] Mental metaphors import the relational structure of source domains such as space into target domains, allowing us to envision, measure, and compare the "height" of people's excitement, the "depth" of their sadness, or the "breadth" of their compassion (Boroditsky, 2000; Casasanto, 2009; Lakoff & Johnson, 1999).

In their groundbreaking book, *Metaphors We Live By*, Lakoff and Johnson (1980) wrote: "We do not know very much about the experiential bases of metaphors," noting that "our physical and cultural experience provides many possible bases" (p. 19). Two decades later, however, Lakoff and Johnson (1999) were no longer circumspect about the origins of mental

---

[1]The term *conceptual metaphor* is often used ambiguously, even by metaphor theorists: Sometimes the term refers to expressions in language, other times to hypothetical nonlinguistic mental representations, and still other times to both linguistic and nonlinguistic mappings. These ambiguities complicate discussions of the relationship between metaphoric language and metaphoric thinking. I distinguish the linguistic and nonlinguistic components of conceptual metaphors by using the term *linguistic metaphor* to refer to words and expressions in language and the term *mental metaphor* to refer to the associations between nonlinguistic source and target domains, which are hypothesized to underlie linguistic metaphors (Casasanto, 2008, 2009). This terminological distinction becomes particularly important when discussing mental metaphors such as the left–right spatial mappings of *time* and of *valence* in left-handers, for which no corresponding linguistic metaphors exist, and discussing linguistic expressions such as *my right hand man* and *the right answer*, which people appear to use without activating any corresponding mental metaphor.

metaphors. They advanced a forcefully argued theory of how hundreds of primary metaphors, the basic building blocks of all mental metaphors, are inevitably acquired on the basis of bodily interactions with the physical environment.

On this proposal, mental metaphors arise due to the unavoidable conflation of two types of bodily experiences: subjective experiences in target domains and perceptuomotor experiences in source domains. For example, the metaphor *affection is warmth* arises in children's minds as a consequence of feeling the physical warmth of their caretakers' bodies as they are held and comforted. The metaphor *time is motion* arises as children subjectively experience the passage of time while watching moving objects travel through space. According to Lakoff and Johnson (1999),

> We do not have a choice as to whether to acquire and use primary metaphor. Just by functioning normally in the world, we automatically and unconsciously acquire and use a vast number of such metaphors. Those metaphors are realized in our brains *physically* and are mostly beyond our control. They are a consequence of the nature of our brains, our bodies, and the world we inhabit. (p. 59, italics in original)

Lakoff and Johnson's (1980) earlier suggestion that at least some basic metaphors could be grounded in cultural experiences was replaced by a monolithic argument for an "embodied" basis for mental metaphors, echoed subsequently by numerous books and papers in the literatures on embodied cognition in linguistics, philosophy, psychology, and cognitive neuroscience (for an overview, see Gibbs, 2006).

REASONS TO QUESTION THE EMBODIED BASIS OF MENTAL METAPHORS

Although Lakoff and Johnson's (1999) proposal has been widely accepted, there are at least four reasons to doubt that conflations between subjective and perceptuomotor experiences, which occur inevitably and universally during the course of early cognitive development, give rise to all (or *any*) of our basic mental metaphors. The first reason for skepticism is a simple lack of evidence. The evidence offered by Lakoff and Johnson (1999) is their interpretation of Christopher Johnson's (1999) survey of a single metaphor in a single child's speech input and output. They suggested that purely metaphoric uses of *to see* meaning *to know* (e.g., "I see what you're saying") were preceded by uses of *see* in which its literal (visual) and metaphoric (epistemic) meanings were conflated (e.g., "let's see [and thereby come to know] what's in the box"). Lakoff and Johnson (1999) suggested that *seeing* and *knowing* were initially fused in the child's mind due to their conflation in his experiences with vision and knowledge: Seeing things (perceptuomotor source domain) was correlated with knowing about them (subjective target domain), and thus seeing and knowing were "not experienced as separate" (p. 49). Eventually, after this period of conflation and fusion, *seeing* and *knowing* can be differentiated, but a source–target association remains.

Lakoff and Johnson's (1999) interpretation of Christopher Johnson's study appears to be at odds with Johnson's own interpretation: Johnson denied that *seeing* and *knowing* are ever conceptually fused in the child's mind (instead, he simply noted that they are conflated in adults' language).[2] Moreover, the logic by which the linguistic data support Lakoff and Johnson's ontogenetic claim about mental metaphors is elusive. The child used *see* most frequently in its visual senses (Johnson, 1999, Table 1). Yet if the ideas of *seeing* and *knowing* were initially fused, shouldn't *see* have been used indiscriminately, either to refer to acts of seeing or to acts of knowing? There may be a simple explanation for the observed longitudinal pattern in the use of *see:* Children may be able to talk, and think, about concrete acts of perception earlier than they can talk and think about abstract mental states (e.g., Aksu-Koç, Ögel-Balaban, & Alp, 2009). More broadly, there is an inescapable circularity to arguments about mental metaphors that are based on linguistic observations alone.

A second reason exists for skepticism about the proposed origin of mental metaphors: Even if children go through a developmental stage at which source and target domains are conflated in their minds, a proposal that is compatible with Piaget's (1927/1969) theorizing about cross-domain relationships, the existence of such a stage cannot be interpreted as evidence that children *learn* these conflations on the basis of bodily experience. In principle, source–target mappings that are important for reasoning about the physical and social world could have become part of our mind's "standard equipment" over the time course of human evolution, not of cognitive development: That is, they could be innate (Casasanto, 2010; Casasanto,

---

[2]George Lakoff and Mark Johnson (1999) appear to have interpreted Christopher Johnson's survey differently from how Johnson (1999) himself did. According to Lakoff and Johnson (1999), conflation is at the levels of direct experience and of conceptualization: "For young children, subjective (nonsensorimotor) experiences and judgments . . . and sensorimotor experiences . . . are so regularly conflated—undifferentiated in experience—that for a time children do not distinguish between the two when they occur together" (p. 46). For C. Johnson, however, the conflation is only at the level of language. Contra Lakoff and Johnson, he wrote that his conflation hypothesis "does *not* rely on the idea that [correlated experiences] are undifferentiated by children—more specifically *there is no claim* that children are incapable of distinguishing visual and mental experiences . . . rather that visual situations provide a good opportunity for adults to talk to children about mental experiences and as a result, children associate 'see' with situations that are both visual and mental" (1999, p. 168, italics added). Thus, it would appear that for C. Johnson, the "conflation hypothesis" refers to a process through which adults' use of metaphoric language influences the relationship between source and target domains in children's minds—not direct physical experience.

Fotakopoulou, & Boroditsky, 2010; Lourenco & Longo, 2011; Srinivasan & Carey, 2010). Increasingly, developmental experiments reveal cross-domain mappings that appear to function like metaphoric source–target relationships in the minds of infants. Ten-month-olds make inferences about social interactions that are consistent with the metaphor *physical size is social dominance* (Thomsen, Frankenhuis, Ingold-Smith, & Carey, 2011). Four-month-olds presented with visual and auditory stimuli appear to intuit the metaphor *spatial height is height in musical pitch* (Walker et al., 2010). The fact that these mappings are detectable in infants does not necessarily mean that they are innate; innateness claims are exceptionally hard to support experimentally. However, there is no evidence that many of the mappings Lakoff and Johnson (and others) attribute to bodily experience are *not* innate.

A third reason for skepticism: There is a plausible, well-developed alternative to the proposed *embodied* origin of mental metaphors. Rather than originating in correlations in bodily experience, mental metaphors could originate in correlations in linguistic experience. Consider the mental metaphor *good is up, bad is down*. According to Lakoff and Johnson (1999), this mapping is established as people implicitly learn associations between bodily actions and the emotional states that typically co-occur with them (e.g., standing tall when we feel proud, slouching when we feel dejected). As an alternative proposal, however, mental metaphors could be established through experience using linguistic metaphors. Using spatial words in both literal and metaphoric contexts (e.g., *on top* of the building; *on top* of the world) could cause structural elements of the source domain to be imported into target domain representations in the mind of the language learner, via analogical processes that are not necessarily "embodied" (see Boroditsky, 2000; Casasanto, 2009; French, 2002; Gentner, 1983). Linguistic conventions associating valence with vertical space are reinforced by other nonlinguistic cultural conventions, such as the *thumbs up* and *thumbs down* gestures that indicate approval and disapproval. Once these symbolic conventions exist in language and culture, they can serve as the basis for metaphoric mappings in the minds of individual learners, obviating any role for direct bodily experience in constructing mental metaphors. As humans, we learn a great deal from direct physical interactions with the environment, but we also learn from symbols—and particularly from language. Exposure to metaphors in language should be considered among the possible experiential origins of mental metaphors in individual learners' minds.[3]

---

[3]The proposal that correlations in linguistic experience give rise to mental metaphors such as *good is up* in the individual learner raises the question of how such linguistic metaphors arose in the first place and why they are so common across languages. It may be that correlations in direct bodily experience resulted in the construction of these linguistic conventions over the time course of biological or linguistic-cultural evolution. Yet even if direct bodily experience is necessary on one of these timescales, it may not be necessary on the timescale of conceptual development in the individual learner (Carey, 2009; Dehaene, 1999).

A fourth reason for skepticism: Some of the embodied experiential bases of metaphors proposed by Lakoff and Johnson (1999) are plausible (indeed, there is a correlation between upright posture and positive mood, which could give rise to the source–target relationship between vertical space and emotional valence in principle), but for other source–target relationships that are deeply entrenched in language and thought, this sort of embodied correlational origin is implausible. For example, behavioral studies have explored *weight* as a metaphoric source domain for *importance*. There is no doubt that people use linguistic metaphors linking weight and importance in English and other languages: a *weighty* opinion is an important opinion. Accordingly, in one experiment, participants rated the importance of messages that they read on either a heavy or a light clipboard. Fair decision-making procedures were judged to be more important when people read about them on a heavy clipboard than on a light one (Jostmann, Lakens, & Schubert, 2009). Jostmann et al. (2009) offered the following as the embodied, correlational basis of the mental metaphor *important is heavy*:

> Gravity is a ubiquitous force in nature that shapes people's bodies and behaviors in fundamental ways. . . . Depending on density and size, some objects are heavier than others, and interacting with heavy objects provides different affordances . . . than interacting with light objects. Being hit by a heavy object generally has more profound consequences than being hit by a light object, and the energetic costs of moving a heavy object are higher than those of moving a light object. Thus, on average, heavy objects have a greater impact on people's bodies than light objects do. Through repeated experiences with heavy objects since early childhood, people learn that dealing with heavy objects generally requires more effort, in terms of physical strength or cognitive planning, than dealing with light objects. People may thus associate the experience of weight with the increased expenditure of bodily or mental effort. (p. 1169)

All of this may be true, but none of this constitutes a plausible experiential basis for the relationship between weight and importance. These experiences could, in principle, form the embodied, correlational basis of a mapping such as *injurious is heavy* or *difficult is heavy*, but not *important is heavy*.

A moment's reflection suggests that if there is any experiential correlation between weight and importance, it is a negative correlation. What do people consider to be most important? Love, friendship, respect, meaningful work, a sense of humor—all weightless. Among physical entities, what do people consider most important: a wedding band, the photo of a soldier's sweetheart on his helmet, money (a $100 bill weighs four hundredths of an ounce—the same as a $1 bill)? Someone's car may be important, and it is heavy, but it is probably not important *because* it is heavy, and a heavier car would not necessarily be more important. How about the relationship between weight and importance for children during a putative *conflation* stage: Is Dad more important than Mom because he weighs more? Is the dictionary more important than a Dr. Seuss book?

It does not appear to be the case that more weight correlates with more importance in our ordinary physical experiences. It is possible that in previous eras, an experiential correlation between weight and importance was more evident, at least in some symbolic domains such as salary (when it was literally paid in salt) or coins (when they were made of precious metals of particular masses) or when the value of commodities was determined by their weights on balance scales. Expressions in modern languages that link weight with importance could be vestiges of these bygone physical experiences, and using these linguistic expressions could invite language learners to construct a mental metaphor, in which case, the experiential basis of our *importance is weight* mapping would be linguistic experience, not direct physical experience.

In summary, Lakoff and Johnson (1999) advanced the theory that basic mental metaphors are learned obligatorily during the course of cognitive development, on the basis of universally observable correlations between subjective experiences and perceptuomotor experiences. This proposal has been embraced by many scholars and is widely considered to be a fundamental tenet of metaphor theory and of embodied cognition. Yet this proposal has virtually no empirical support, it is implausible in some cases (i.e., where no correlation between source and target domains exists in our everyday experience), and there are at least two credible alternatives to this proposal (i.e., at least some mental metaphors are innate; at least some mental metaphors are learned via linguistic or cultural experience).

Contrary to appearances, we are, as a field, in very much the same situation Lakoff and Johnson described in 1980: We do not know much about the experiential bases of metaphors. And we are unlikely to make progress on the question "Where do our mental metaphors come from?" unless we acknowledge that (a) not all metaphors have an embodied basis and (b) this question has only just begun to be addressed. In what follows, I describe three metaphors that use the same source domain, the lateral (left–right) spatial continuum, which provide unusual theoretical leverage on questions about the experiential origins of metaphors in language and thought.

HOW LANGUAGE CREATES MENTAL METAPHORS: THE LEFT–RIGHT SPATIALIZATION OF POLITICS

In the late 18th century, the French Legislative Assembly was arranged such that the conservative members sat on the right side of the room and the liberal members on the left (Oppenheimer & Trail, 2010). This arrangement has had enduring consequences. More than 2 centuries later, liberal and conservative values are metaphorized on a left–right continuum, across many languages and cultures, as evidenced by English expressions such as "the liberal left," "centrist politics," and "right-wing conservatives."

These linguistic metaphors appear to correspond to active mental metaphors. In one experiment, U.S. students were asked to sit in a "broken" office chair while completing a political attitudes survey. Unbeknownst to participants, a wheel had been removed strategically from one side or the other, causing the chair to tilt leftward or rightward. Responses showed that, on average, participants who had been assigned to sit in the left-leaning chair expressed more agreement with Democrats (traditionally the more liberal party), whereas participants assigned to sit in the right-leaning chair tended to agree more strongly with Republicans (Oppenheimer & Trail, 2010).

The automaticity with which people activate an implicit left–right mapping of politics was confirmed in a series of reaction time studies in Dutch participants. Although The Netherlands has many political parties, which differ along multiple dimensions, the parties' liberality or conservativism is often described using left–right metaphors (Bienfait & van Beek, 2001). Accordingly, when presented with parties' acronyms, Dutch participants were faster to make judgments about more liberal parties with their left hand (or when the acronym appeared on the left of the screen), and faster to make judgments about more conservative parties with their right hand (or when the acronym appeared on the right of the screen; van Elk, van Schie, & Bekkering, 2010).

Where does this mental metaphor come from? Pointing to its historical roots does not answer this question: That is, the arrangement of 18th century French politicians does not explain how individuals come to intuit a mapping between politics and space today. The left–right mapping of politics is of theoretical interest because it appears to function much like other *orientational metaphors* (Lakoff & Johnson, 1980)—and yet this mapping in language and in thought cannot be acquired through incidental learning of correlations between politics and space in the natural world. It is extremely unlikely, for example, as we encounter others in our environment (e.g., at the dinner table, in the classroom, at the cinema, on the bus) that we see people with liberal views on our left and people with conservative views on our right with such regularity that politics becomes "inevitably" mapped onto left–right space.

Rather than correlations in bodily experience, the obvious origin of this mental metaphor is correlations in linguistic experience. Using the words *right* and *left* in both literal contexts (e.g., the can is *on the left* of the shelf) and metaphoric contexts (e.g., the candidate is *on the left* of the political spectrum) could cause structural elements of the source domain to be transferred to target domain representations in individual language users' minds, potentially via analogical processes such as those proposed by Gentner (1983).

Before accepting the conclusion that linguistic experience instills this metaphor in individuals' minds, it is important to consider other possibilities. First, in principle, the mapping could be innate (and this implicit mental metaphor biased the arrangement of the French Legislative Assembly). This proposal is dubious: It is unlikely that liberal and conservative political ideologies, or even the concepts of left and right (which are absent from some modern languages and cultures), arose early enough in human history to have been encoded in our genes and neurally hardwired. Second, and more plausibly, the mapping could arise via another source of experience: the spatialization of politics in nonlinguistic cultural conventions. Could it be the case that people acquire this mapping through exposure to graphic representations in the media?

This suggestion presupposes that liberal and conservative political parties or ideologies are, in fact, commonly represented on the left and right respectively, in graphic representations on TV or in newspapers and magazines. Is this true? For example, in the United States, donkeys and elephants symbolize the Democratic and Republican parties, respectively. Often the animals are depicted side by side, presumably to indicate opposition or competition between the parties or to represent the voters' two main alternatives. Is the donkey usually depicted on the left and the elephant on the right?

To address this question, I conducted a brief survey. I ran two queries of Google Images (http://www.google.com; August 24, 2012), using the Advanced Image Search function to restrict the search to U.S. websites. The search terms were *donkey elephant* for the first query and *elephant donkey* for the second. Each search yielded more than 3 million images. Visual inspection of the first 10 pages displayed for each query confirmed that the majority of the images conformed to the following criteria: (a) They showed exactly one donkey and one elephant, (b) one animal was clearly located to the right (or left) of the other, and (c) the depictions appeared to be intended to symbolize the Democratic and Republican parties (i.e., they were not nature photos that happened to contain these animals). For most images, this intention was clear from the blue and red colors of the donkey and elephant, stars and stripes motifs, political slogans, pugilistic attitudes of the animals toward each other, or the personification of the animals (e.g., dressing them in suits and ties, placing them under the Capitol dome). The images appeared to come from political cartoons, TV news backdrops, or campaign materials (e.g., hats, T-shirts, bumper stickers, posters).

To sample the images in an unbiased manner, I selected the first 50 images from each query that met the three criteria and that were not redundant with any previously selected image. I then tabulated and compared the number of images in which the donkey was on the left of the image and the elephant on the right (metaphor-congruent images) and the number in which the positions were reversed.

The results were clear. Of the 100 images sampled, 51 (51%) were metaphor-congruent and 49 (49%) were metaphor-incongruent (sign test $p = .92$). The order of the search terms did not significantly affect the metaphor-congruity of the images ("donkey elephant": 27 [54%] metaphor-congruent, 23 [46%] metaphor-incongruent; "elephant donkey": 24 [48%] metaphor-congruent, 26 [52%] metaphor-incongruent; $\chi^2(1) = 0.36$, $p = .55$).

The donkey and the elephant, the most widely recognizable nonlinguistic symbols of political orientation in U.S. politics, are often depicted side by side. Yet according to this (preliminary) survey, these depictions do not reliably spatialize the animals according to the left–right political metaphor that is found in Americans' language and thought. It is not clear why they do not: In some cases, other design constraints might outweigh spatializing the animals according to the left–right metaphor. Alternatively, unlike some other spatial relationships (e.g., up–down), right–left depends on perspective. In many images, the donkey and elephant are facing out of the page, toward the viewer. In such cases, an artist who wished to make their spatial locations congruent with the *left is liberal* convention would have to decide whether to place the donkey on the viewer's left or on the elephant's left (i.e., the viewer's right). The apparent randomness of the positions of the animals in the images surveyed could reflect artists expressing the left–right mental metaphor graphically but making different choices about whose left–right perspective to adopt. The ambiguity introduced by a reversible spatial perspective could also explain why candidates are not always placed in metaphor-congruent locations on our TV screens: In the last debate of the 2008 U.S. presidential campaign the Democrat (Barack Obama) was on the left and the Republican (John McCain) on the right, but in the first debate of the 2012 campaign the Republican (Mitt Romney) was on the left and the Democrat (Obama) on the right of the screen.[4]

Whatever the reason for the apparent lack of any systematic use of left–right space in these political depictions, the implications for the present

---

[4]The U.S. Senate and House are arranged similarly to the 18th century French Legislative Assembly, but people who are not members of the Senate or House are unlikely to be exposed to this spatialization of the political "left" and "right" with sufficient frequency to give rise to an implicit mental metaphor. Furthermore, the viewpoint from which the Senate or Congress are depicted varies between photographs and videos, sometimes showing the Democrats and Republicans in metaphor-congruent and sometimes in metaphor-incongruent sides of viewer-centered space.

question are clear. If political parties or ideologies are not systematically spatialized in the media and in nonlinguistic graphic conventions, these conventions cannot be responsible for establishing the spatial mappings in people's minds. It appears that talking about liberal and conservative political attitudes in terms of space is what causes people to think about them that way—a conclusion that awaits further experimental validation.

HOW THE BODY CREATES MENTAL METAPHORS: THE LEFT–RIGHT SPATIALIZATION OF VALENCE

Across many cultures, the right side is associated with things that are good and lawful and the left side with things that are dirty, bad, or prohibited. The association of *good* with *right* and *bad* with *left* is evident in positive and negative expressions like *my right-hand man* and *two left feet,* and in the meanings of English words derived from the Latin for *right* (dexter) and *left* (sinister).

Do people *think* about good and bad things in terms of left–right space? For example, do people tend to feel more positively about things that appear on one side of space and more negatively about things that appear on the other side? Until recently, the answer appeared to be no. According to Tversky (2001),

> despite the fact that most people are right-handed and terms like dexterity derived from "right" in many languages have positive connotations and terms like sinister derived from "left" have negative connotations, the horizontal axis in graphic displays seems to be neutral. (p. 101)

Some links between right–left space and positive and negative evaluation were documented (e.g., the preference for stockings hung on the right of a clothes hanger; Wilson & Nisbett, 1978), but such effects were unpredicted and explained post hoc in terms of temporal order, not spatial position.

More recently, however, studies have revealed that people *do* implicitly associate "positive" and "negative" emotional valence with "right" and "left" but not always in the way that linguistic and cultural conventions suggest. Rather, associations between valence and left–right space depend on the way people use their hands to interact with their physical environment (for a review, see Casasanto, 2011). In one series of experiments, when asked to decide which of two products to buy, which of two job applicants to hire, or which of two alien creatures looks more honest, intelligent, or attractive, right- and left-handers tended to respond differently: Right-handers tended to prefer the product, person, or creature presented on their right side, but left-handers tended to prefer the one on their left (Casasanto, 2009). This pattern persisted even when people made judgments orally, without using their hands to respond. Other experiments show that children as young as 5 years old already make evaluations according to handedness and spatial location, judging animals shown on their dominant side to be nicer and smarter than animals on their nondominant side (Casasanto & Henetz, 2012).

The implicit association between valence and left–right space influences people's memory and their motor responses as well as their judgments. In one experiment, participants were shown the locations of fictitious positive and negative events on a map and asked to recall the locations later. Memory errors were predicted by the valence of the event and the handedness of the participant: Right-handers were biased to locate positive events too far to the right and negative events too far to the left on the map, whereas left-handers showed the opposite biases (Brunyé, Gardony, Mahoney, & Taylor, 2012). In reaction time tasks, right- and left-handers were faster to classify words as positive when responding by pressing a button with their dominant hand and faster to classify words as negative when responding with their nondominant hand (de la Vega, de Filippis, Lachmair, Dudschig, & Kaup, 2012).

Associations of handedness with valence and space have been observed beyond the laboratory, in the speech and gestures of right- and left-handed U.S. presidential candidates during televised debates in 2004 and 2008 (Casasanto & Jasmin, 2010). In right-handers (Bush, Kerry), right-hand gestures were more strongly associated with positive-valence speech than left-hand gestures, and left-hand gestures were more strongly associated with negative-valence speech than right-hand gestures; the opposite associations between hand and valence were found in left-handers (McCain, Obama), despite the centuries-old tradition of training public speakers to gesture with the right hand for good things and the left hand for bad things (or not to use the left hand at all; Quintilianus, 1920).

Together, these data from studies using questionnaires, reaction time tasks, map tasks, and spontaneous gestures suggest that the mental metaphor *good is dominant side–bad is nondominant side* is habitually activated, with a high degree of automaticity, when people evaluate the positivity of stimuli or recall information with a positive or negative valence. These findings provide one line of support for the body-specificity hypothesis (Casasanto, 2009), which posits that people with different kinds of bodies should tend to think differently in predictable ways, specifically due to the ways their bodies constrain their interactions with the physical environment.

Where does this mental metaphor come from? Casasanto (2009) proposed that people come to associate *positive* with their dominant side of space because they can usually interact with their physical environment more fluently on this side, using their dominant hand. This proposal follows from the finding that fluent perceptuomotor interactions with the environment generally lead to more positive feelings, whereas disfluent interactions lead to more negative feelings and evaluations (e.g., Ping, Dhillon, & Beilock, 2009).

To test whether manual motor fluency drives associations between valence and left–right space, Casasanto and Chrysikou (2011) studied how people think about *good* and *bad* after their dominant hand had been impaired, reversing the usual asymmetry in motor fluency between their right and left hands. This reversal of motor fluency resulted in a reversal of behavioral responses: Natural right-handers whose right hand was permanently impaired by a unilateral stroke or temporarily by wearing a cumbersome glove on the right hand in the laboratory tended to associate *good* with the left side of space, like natural left-handers.

These results demonstrate a causal role for motor experience in determining the relationship between valence and left–right space in people's minds. In the short term, even a few minutes of acting more fluently with the left hand than the right can cause natural right-handers to associate *good* with *left*. The effects of short-term motor asymmetries are presumably temporary, but the same associative learning mechanisms that change people's judgments in the laboratory may result in the long-term changes found in stroke patients and may establish natural right- and left-handers' mental metaphors for valence in the course of ordinary motor experience.

Do regularities in language or culture contribute to the implicit left–right mapping of valence in people's minds? So far, there is no evidence that they do. Writing direction, for example, does not appear to have any effect on the strength of this mapping, nor does the presence of stringent taboos against use of the left hand, as evidenced by the finding of similar experimental results in Moroccan Arabs as in American, Spanish, and Dutch participants (de la Fuente, Casasanto, Román, & Santiago, 2011). It would be reasonable to posit that within a culture, influences of motor fluency and linguistic conventions could combine to shape people's left–right metaphors for valence. In principle, people could have *two* mental metaphors linking valence with left–right space: one based on patterns in language and culture and the other on patterns of direct bodily experience. If so, the two mappings would be congruent for right-handers (for whom both associate *good* with *right*) but incongruent for left-handers (for whom language and culture associate *good* with *right* but bodily experience associates *good* with *left*). This conjecture makes a prediction: Assuming the influences of the two metaphors on an individual's behavior are roughly additive, the *good is right* bias in right-handers should be stronger than the *good is left* bias in left-handers. Yet this prediction is disconfirmed by the results of numerous experiments (e.g., Casasanto, 2009; Casasanto & Henetz, 2012; Casasanto & Jasmin, 2010). Across studies, the body-specific *good is left* mapping tends to be stronger in left-handers than the *good is right* mapping in right-handers. To date, there is no evidence that *good is right* idioms in language or culture influence implicit left–right mental metaphors for valence.

Overall, these results cannot be explained by experience with language and culture, which consistently associate *good* with *right*. Linguistic and cultural experience, therefore, cannot be the origin of the robust association between *good* and *left* found in left-handers. Furthermore, the association of *good* with one side or the other cannot be (entirely) innate, because it has been shown to depend on long- and short-term motor experience. The body-specific left–right mapping of valence provides one example—arguably the *only* example to date—of a mental metaphor that can be shown to depend on correlations between subjective experiences (i.e., of valence) and motor experiences, learned implicitly as individuals interact with their physical environment.

Does the discovery of a body-based mapping between space and valence validate Lakoff and Johnson's (1999) proposal that mental metaphors originate in correlations between perceptuomotor and subjective experiences? In the broadest sense it does, but in the details it does not. There is no evidence, for example, that right-handed children go through a developmental phase of source–target conflation, during which their conceptions of *bad* and *leftward in space* are fused and gradually become differentiated; it would be surprising if this were the case. It would be even more surprising if such a process of conceptual conflation and differentiation were responsible for the reversal of the left–right valence mapping observed in unilateral stroke patients and in ski-glove-trained college students (Casasanto & Chrysikou, 2011). Rather than illustrating the specific process conflation-and-differentiation proposed by Lakoff and Johnson (1999), the left–right mapping of valence illustrates a more general process by which perceptuomotor and subjective experiences may become associated and used inferentially as a mental metaphor.

HOW CULTURE SHAPES MENTAL METAPHORS: THE LEFT–RIGHT SPATIALIZATION OF TIME

The left–right mappings of politics and of valence are special cases: A purely linguistic origin can be established for politics (or at least a largely linguistic origin, allowing for the possibility of as-yet-undetected influences of other cultural experiences), and a purely bodily origin can be established for valence. There may be no comparable case in which nonlinguistic cultural conventions can be shown to be responsible for establishing a mental metaphor, de novo. However, the left–right mapping of time provides an illustration of how culture can shape what may be preexisting mental metaphors, determining crucial aspects of implicit associations between time and space.

Often, the way people talk about time using spatial metaphors corresponds to the way they spatialize time in their minds. In English, spatial metaphors for temporal sequences suggest that events in time flow along the sagittal (front–back) axis: Deadlines lie *ahead of us* or *behind us*; we can *look forward* to our golden years or *look back* on our greener days (Clark, 1973). These linguistic metaphors appear to correspond to an active mental metaphor. In one study, for example, English speakers were found to lean forward when thinking about the future and lean backward when thinking about the past (Miles, Nind, & Macrae, 2010).

Yet the way people use space to talk about time is not necessarily the way they use space to think about it. No known spoken language uses the lateral (left–right) axis to talk about time conventionally, and invented left–right metaphors for time may sound nonsensical: Monday comes *before* Tuesday, not *to the left of* Tuesday (Casasanto & Jasmin, 2012; Cienki, 1998). Despite the total absence of left–right metaphors in spoken language, however, there is strong evidence that people implicitly associate time with left–right space. Furthermore, the direction in which events flow along people's imaginary timelines varies systematically across cultures. Events flow rightward in cultures whose literate members use a left-to-right orthography and leftward in cultures that use a right-to-left orthography (e.g., Fuhrman & Boroditsky, 2010; Ouellet, Santiago, Israeli, & Gabay, 2010; Tversky, Kugelmass, & Winter, 1991).

Does this mean that the left–right mapping of time in people's minds has its origin in the cultural practice of reading and writing? It is not possible to make this causal inference on the basis of cross-cultural data, which are correlational. In principle, a writing system could emerge with one directionality or another as a *consequence* of culture-specific conceptions of time—not a cause. Furthermore, cultural practices tend to covary. There are other well-established nonlinguistic cultural conventions by which time is habitually spatialized from left to right. These include spontaneous gestures and graphic conventions in calendars, graphs, and timelines.

Casasanto and Bottini (2013) conducted a series of experiments to investigate whether experience reading a particular orthography can determine the direction and orientation of the mental timeline. Dutch speakers performed space–time congruity tasks with the instructions and stimuli written in either standard, mirror-reversed, or rotated orthography. Reading requires scanning the page in a particular direction. Normally, for readers who use the Roman alphabet, reading each line of a text requires moving one's eyes (and one's attention) gradually from the left to the right side of the page or the computer screen. As such, moving rightward in space is tightly coupled with "moving" later in time. If the habit of reading from left to right contributes to an implicit left-to-right mapping of time in readers' minds, then practice reading in the opposite direction should eventually reverse this mapping. By the same logic, reading top-to-bottom or bottom-to-top should cause the usual space-time mapping to be rotated 90 degrees clockwise or counterclockwise.

Consistent with these predictions, when participants judged temporal phrases written in standard orthography, their reaction times were consistent with a rightward-directed mental timeline. After exposure to mirror-reversed orthography, however, participants showed the opposite pattern of reaction times; their implicit mental timelines were reversed, like those observed in members of right-to-left reading cultures. When standard orthography was rotated 90 degrees clockwise (downward) or counterclockwise (upward), reaction times indicated that participants' mental timelines were rotated accordingly. These results show that reading can play a causal role in shaping people's implicit time representations, even when other cultural, linguistic, and environmental factors are held constant. Exposure to a new orthography can change the direction and orientation of the mental timeline within minutes—even when the new space-time mapping directly contradicts the reader's usual mapping—illustrating both the automaticity and the flexibility with which people activate spatial schemas for temporal order.

The data showing that reading experience is sufficient to determine the orientation direction of the mental timeline should not be interpreted as indicating that reading or writing experience is *necessary* for fixing its direction or that reading and writing are the only cultural practices that could contribute to the specifics of the mental timeline beyond the laboratory. For the present discussion, it is important to note that the direction of the mental timeline could not be due to correlations in linguistic experience because time is not mapped to left–right space in spoken language. It could not be due to correlations in bodily experience with the natural environment because natural space–time correlations are not direction-specific (i.e., it is not the case that earlier events tend to occur on our left and later events on our right, or vice versa). The orientation and direction of the mental timeline must depend on *some* aspect (or aspects) of nonlinguistic cultural experience.

CONCLUSION

It is widely accepted that mental metaphors have an embodied origin: According to Lakoff and Johnson (1999), they are inevitably learned during the course of cognitive development, on the basis of correlations between subjective experiences and perceptuomotor experiences as children interact with the physical environment, due to universal properties of the body, brain, and world. Yet despite widespread acceptance of this view, there is little evidence to support it, and there is some clear evidence against it.

It may be difficult to determine the experiential origins of most of the mental metaphors that have been studied. Many metaphors are like *good is up:* They could be innate, or they could have their basis in linguistic experience (e.g., using expressions such as *feeling up* or *down*), cultural experience (e.g., using gestures such as *thumbs up*), or bodily experience (e.g., standing upright when we feel proud). Behavioral experiments validating the *good is up* mapping are consistent with all of these possibilities and are therefore uninformative about the origins of this mental metaphor, or others like it.

Fortunately, for at least a few mental metaphors, the experiential origins can be determined unambiguously, thus illustrating a range of possible origins for other mental metaphors. The left–right mapping of politics could not be based on correlations between subjective and perceptuomotor experiences with the natural environment, it is not likely to be innate, and it does not appear to be grounded in nonlinguistic cultural conventions; rather, it appears likely to arise, largely or entirely, on the basis of correlations in linguistic experience. By contrast, the left–right mapping of emotional valence could only arise from correlations in bodily experience (although not necessarily on the "conflation" of space in valence in early childhood, as posited by Lakoff & Johnson). The left–right mapping of time, in contrast, illustrates the role of nonlinguistic cultural practices in shaping preexisting source–target mappings and demonstrates how mental metaphors can be culture-specific at one level of analysis but may be universal at another.

Determining the experiential origins of our mental metaphors requires looking beyond the body and considering how our experiences of interacting with both the physical environment and social environment shape our minds.

REFERENCES

Aksu-Koç, A., Ögel-Balaban, H., & Alp, I. E. (2009). Evidentials and source knowledge in Turkish. In S. A. Fitneva & T. Matsui (Eds.), *Evidentiality: A window into language and cognitive development. New directions for child and adolescent development* (pp. 13–28). San Francisco, CA: Jossey-Bass.

Bienfait, F., & van Beek, W. E. A. (2001). Right and left as political categories: An exercise in "not-so-primitive" classification. *Anthropos: International Review of Anthropology and Linguistics, 96,* 169–178.

Boroditsky, L. (2000). Metaphoric structuring: Understanding time through spatial metaphors. *Cognition, 75,* 1–28. doi:10.1016/S0010-0277(99)00073-6 doi:10.1016/j.cognition.2010.09.010

Brunyé, T. T., Gardony, A., Mahoney, C. R., & Taylor, H. A. (2012). Body-specific representations of spatial location. *Cognition, 123*, 229–239. doi:10.1016/j.cognition.2011.07.013

Carey, S. (2009). *The origin of concepts.* New York, NY: Oxford University Press. doi:10.1093/acprof:oso/9780195367638.001.0001

Casasanto, D. (2008). Similarity and proximity: When does close in space mean close in mind? *Memory & Cognition, 36*, 1047–1056. doi:10.3758/MC.36.6.1047

Casasanto, D. (2009). Embodiment of abstract concepts: Good and bad in right- and left-handers. *Journal of Experimental Psychology: General, 138*, 351–367. doi:10.1037/a0015854

Casasanto, D. (2010). Space for thinking. In V. Evans & P. Chilton (Eds.), *Language, cognition, and space: State of the art and new directions* (pp. 453–478). London, England: Equinox.

Casasanto, D. (2011). Different bodies, different minds: The body-specificity of language and thought. *Current Directions in Psychological Science, 20*, 378–383. doi:10.1177/0963721411422058

Casasanto, D., & Boroditsky, L. (2008). Time in the mind: Using space to think about time. *Cognition, 106*, 579–593. doi:10.1016/j.cognition.2007.03.004

Casasanto, D., & Bottini, R. (2013, June 17). Mirror reading can reverse the flow of time. *Journal of Experimental Psychology.* Advance online publication. doi:10.1037/a0033297

Casasanto, D., & Chrysikou, E. (2011). When left is "right": Motor fluency shapes abstract concepts. *Psychological Science, 22*, 419–422. doi:10.1177/0956797611401755

Casasanto, D., Fotakopoulou, O., & Boroditsky, L. (2010). Space and time in the child's mind: Evidence for a cross-dimensional asymmetry. *Cognitive Science, 34*, 387–405. doi:10.1111/j.1551-6709.2010.01094.x

Casasanto, D., & Henetz, T. (2012). Handedness shapes children's abstract concepts. *Cognitive Science, 36*, 359–372. doi:10.1111/j.1551-6709.2011.01199.x

Casasanto, D., & Jasmin, K. (2010). Good and bad in the hands of politicians: Spontaneous gestures during positive and negative speech. *PLoS ONE, 5*, e11805. doi:10.1371/journal.pone.0011805

Casasanto, D., & Jasmin, K. (2012). The hands of time: Temporal gestures in English speakers. *Cognitive Linguistics, 23*, 643–674. doi:10.1515/cog-2012-0020

Cienki, A. (1998). Metaphoric gestures and some of their relations to verbal metaphoric expressions. In J.-P. Koening (Ed.), *Discourse and cognition: Bridging the gap* (pp. 189–204). Stanford, CA: CSLI.

Clark, H. H. (1973). Space, time, semantics and the child. In T. E. Moore (Ed.), *Cognitive development and the acquisition of language* (pp. 27–63). New York, NY: Academic Press.

Dehaene, S. (1999). *The number sense.* New York, NY: Penguin.

Dehaene, S., Bossini, S., & Giraux, P. (1993). The mental representation of parity and number magnitude. *Journal of Experimental Psychology: General, 122*, 371–396. doi:10.1037/0096-3445.122.3.371

de la Fuente, J., Casasanto, D., Román, A., & Santiago, J. (2011). Searching for cultural influences on the body-specific association of preferred hand and emotional valence. In L. Carlson, C. Holscher, & T. Shipley (Eds.), *Proceedings of the 33rd Annual Conference of the Cognitive Science Society* (pp. 2616–2620). Austin, TX: Cognitive Science Society.

de la Vega, I., de Filippis, M., Lachmair, M., Dudschig, C., & Kaup, B. (2012). Emotional valence and physical space: Limits of interaction. *Journal of Experimental Psychology: Human Perception and Performance, 38,* 375–385. doi:10.1037/a0024979

Dolscheid, S., Shayan, S., Majid, A., & Casasanto, D. (2013). The thickness of musical pitch: Psychophysical evidence for linguistic relativity. *Psychological Science, 24,* 613–621. doi:10.1177/0956797612457374

French, R. M. (2002). The computational modeling of analogy-making. *Trends in Cognitive Sciences, 6,* 200–205. doi:10.1016/S1364-6613(02)01882-X

Fuhrman, O., & Boroditsky, L. (2010). Cross-cultural differences in mental representations of time: Evidence from an implicit non-linguistic task. *Cognitive Science, 34,* 1430–1451. doi:10.1111/j.1551-6709.2010.01105.x

Gentner, D. (1983). Structure-mapping: A theoretical framework for analogy. *Cognitive Science, 7,* 155–170. doi:10.1207/s15516709cog0702_3

Gibbs, R. (2006). *Embodiment and cognitive science.* New York, NY: Cambridge University Press.

Jackendoff, R. (1983). *Semantics and cognition.* Cambridge, MA: MIT Press.

Johnson, C. (1999). Metaphor vs. conflation in the acquisition of polysemy: The case of *see.* In H. Massako, C. Sinha, & S. Wilcox (Eds.), *Cultural, psychological, and typological issues in cognitive linguistics* (pp. 155–170). Amsterdam, The Netherlands: John Benjamins.

Jostmann, N. B., Lakens, D., & Schubert, T. W. (2009). Weight as an embodiment of importance. *Psychological Science, 20,* 1169–1174. doi:10.1111/j.1467-9280.2009.02426.x

Lakoff, G., & Johnson, M. (1980). *Metaphors we live by.* Chicago, IL: Chicago University Press.

Lakoff, G., & Johnson, M. (1999). *Philosophy in the flesh: The embodied mind and its challenge to western thought.* Chicago, IL: University of Chicago Press.

Landau, M. J., Meier, B. P., & Keefer, L. A. (2010). A metaphor-enriched social cognition. *Psychological Bulletin, 136,* 1045–1067. doi:10.1037/a0020970

Lourenco, S. F., & Longo, M. R. (2011). Origins and the development of generalized magnitude representation. In S. Dehaene & E. Brannon (Eds.), *Space, time, and number in the brain: Searching for the foundations of mathematical thought* (pp. 225–244). Amsterdam, the Netherlands: Elsevier. doi:10.1016/B978-0-12-385948-8.00015-3

Miles, L. K., Nind, L. K., & Macrae, C. N. (2010). Moving through time. *Psychological Science, 21,* 222–223. doi:10.1177/0956797609359333

Oppenheimer, D. M., & Trail, T. (2010). When leaning to the left makes you lean to the left. *Social Cognition, 28,* 651–661. doi:10.1521/soco.2010.28.5.651

Ouellet, M., Santiago, J., Israeli, Z., & Gabay, S. (2010). Is the future the right time? *Experimental Psychology, 57,* 308–314. doi:10.1027/1618-3169/a000036

Piaget, J. (1969). *The child's conception of time.* New York, NY: Ballantine Books. Original work published in 1927.

Ping, R., Dhillon, S., & Beilock, S. L. (2009). Reach for what you like: The body's role in shaping preferences. *Emotion Review, 1,* 140–150. doi:10.1177/1754073908100439

Quintilianus, M. F. (1920). *Institutio oratoria.* Cambridge, MA: Harvard University Press.

Schubert, T. W. (2005). Your highness: Vertical positions as perceptual symbols of power. *Journal of Personality and Social Psychology, 89,* 1–21. doi:10.1037/0022-3514.89.1.1

Srinivasan, M., & Carey, S. (2010). The long and the short of it: On the nature and origin of functional overlap between representations of space and time. *Cognition, 116,* 217–241. doi:10.1016/j.cognition.2010.05.005

Thomsen, L., Frankenhuis, W., Ingold-Smith, M., & Carey, S. (2011). The big and the mighty: Preverbal infants represent social dominance. *Science, 331,* 477–480. doi:10.1126/science.1199198

Tversky, B. (2001). Spatial schemas in depictions. In M. Gattis (Ed.), *Spatial schemas and abstract thought* (pp. 79–112). Cambridge, MA: MIT Press.

Tversky, B., Kugelmass, S., & Winter, A. (1991). Cross-cultural and developmental trends in graphic productions. *Cognitive Psychology, 23,* 515–557. doi:10.1016/0010-0285(91)90005-9

van Elk, M., van Schie, H. T., & Bekkering, H. (2010). From left to right: Processing acronyms referring to names of political parties activates spatial associations. *The Quarterly Journal of Experimental Psychology: Human Experimental Psychology, 63,* 2202–2219. doi:10.1080/17470218.2010.495160

Walker, P., Bremner, J. G., Mason, U., Spring, J., Mattock, K., Slater, A., & Johnson, P. (2010). Preverbal infants' sensitivity to synaesthetic cross-modality correspondences. *Psychological Science, 21,* 21–25. doi:10.1177/0956797609354734

Williams, L. E., & Bargh, J. A. (2008). Keeping one's distance: The influence of spatial distance cues on affect and evaluation. *Psychological Science, 19,* 302–308. doi:10.1111/j.1467-9280.2008.02084.x

Wilson, T. D., & Nisbett, R. E. (1978). The accuracy of verbal reports about the effects of stimuli on evaluations and behavior. *Social Psychology, 41,* 118–131. doi:10.2307/3033572

13

METAPHOR RESEARCH IN SOCIAL-PERSONALITY PSYCHOLOGY: THE ROAD AHEAD

MARK J. LANDAU, MICHAEL D. ROBINSON, AND BRIAN P. MEIER

Lakoff and Johnson (1980) suggested that people think, feel, and behave in metaphoric terms. This is a fascinating perspective on human nature but one that has only recently been put to the test empirically. Despite the fact that such investigations have been recent—arguably less than 10 years old— an impressive body of evidence has supported conceptual metaphor theory (CMT; Landau, Meier, & Keefer, 2010). Each chapter in this volume shows, in its own way, that this emerging research area enhances our understanding of diverse social phenomena and, more generally, the cognitive underpinnings of human meaning making. Yet with each discovery, new research questions and theoretical controversies come to light. In this final chapter, we offer some suggestions that researchers might find useful as they create, refine, and test theories of metaphor's significance in social life. Some of these suggestions are inspired by CMT; others are based more generally on a critical

http://dx.doi.org/10.1037/14278-012
The Power of Metaphor: Examining Its Influence on Social Life, M. J. Landau, M. D. Robinson, and B. P. Meier (Editors)

survey of the contemporary empirical landscape. When possible, we discuss how researchers have already applied these suggestions to launch new and fruitful lines of empirical inquiry.

WIDENING THE EMPIRICAL LENS ON METAPHOR

In 2004, Meier and Robinson showed that people's judgments of affectively charged words such as *evil* and *hero* were influenced by the words' vertical position on the computer monitor (*up is good, down is bad*; Meier & Robinson, 2004) and font color (*white is good, black is bad*; Meier, Robinson, & Clore, 2004). The following year, Schubert (2005) reported a series of studies showing that groups and individuals were viewed as more powerful when they occupied higher regions of vertical space (*powerful is up, powerless is down*). These were among the first published studies that applied experimental methods to test CMT's claim that representations of abstract social concepts (referred to as *targets*) are partly structured around knowledge of superficially dissimilar, relatively more concrete concepts (*sources*).

This early work helped set the stage for the formalization of a broad empirical strategy for testing CMT-derived hypotheses, labeled the *metaphoric transfer strategy* (Landau et al., 2010). As we discussed in Chapter 1 of this volume, using this strategy (along with a toolbox of established methods) has enabled researchers to hurdle the limitations of previous research that looked for signs of conceptual metaphor in language use. In a nutshell, evidence for conceptual metaphor derived from the study of word etymology, patterns in metaphoric linguistic expressions, and language comprehension is regularly critiqued on the grounds that it tells us more about metaphor's prevalence in communication than its active influence in cognition and representational processes (see Chapter 2). Metaphor research in social psychology has sidestepped this critique by showing that people's perceptions, attitudes, and memories bear the stamp of metaphor's influence even in contexts in which people are not communicating or otherwise primed with metaphoric language.

As evidence for conceptual metaphor has increased, the metaphor-related basis of previous findings has increased as well. For example, hot temperatures render individuals more aggressive (Anderson, 2001), and we now know that at least part of this influence could be mediated by metaphors linking anger to heat (Wilkowski, Meier, Robinson, Carter, & Feltman, 2009). Aron, Aron, and Smollan (1992) showed that a nonverbal measure of interpersonal closeness—indicating the degree of overlap between circles representing the self and a relationship partner—is a powerful predictor of relationship outcomes. This effect likely derives from metaphoric influences linking physical and relational closeness (Williams & Bargh, 2008b). An early demonstration that the adjectives *warm* and *cold* are powerful influences on the favorability of personality impressions (Asch, 1946), too, has been reinterpreted in terms of the influence of temperature metaphors in forming impressions of others (Williams & Bargh, 2008a). We recommend that researchers continue to reexamine recent and classic findings in the literature through the lens of CMT.

Because CMT addresses the processes by which people make sense of abstract concepts, it can be applied to enhance the study of virtually any social and personality psychological phenomenon that involves people thinking, feeling, and acting in relation to abstract concepts. One need only observe the diversity of outcomes discussed in the chapters of this volume—ranging from consumer product choices to moral judgments—to appreciate CMT's broad relevance. As such, a straightforward future direction for metaphor research is to continue using the metaphoric transfer strategy to examine metaphors that have not yet been examined experimentally (e.g., does a sour taste experience lead to dissatisfaction with an interaction?) or outcomes that have not yet been investigated (e.g., do cold temperatures lead us to infer that crimes were committed in a "cold-blooded," calculating, and manipulative manner?).

Toward this end, a useful tool for hypothesis generation is to observe the expression of metaphor in ordinary language, images, ceremonies, and other practices by which people construct and communicate systems of cultural meaning. Researchers can turn to penetrating analyses of ordinary conversation (e.g., Gibbs, 1994; Kövecses, 2010; Lakoff & Johnson, 1980; Lakoff & Turner, 1989), commercial messaging and visual media (Forceville & Urios-Aparisi, 2009), and gesture (McNeill, 2005), or they can just listen carefully the next time they or anyone else opens their mouth, to observe how individuals and groups use metaphors to communicate about *events*, *causation*, *emotion*, *social organization*, and many other abstract social concepts. From there, researchers can formulate hypotheses about how those metaphors influence cognitive processes (e.g., inference making, attitude formation, memory) and behavior, and can then test those hypotheses using the metaphoric transfer strategy.

Such a focus on individual metaphors is necessary but limited. Although CMT inspires us to look for metaphors in every corner of social life, it leaves researchers all too free to jump from metaphor to metaphor—and there are plenty of them. Kövecses's (2010) introduction to contemporary metaphor research lists 347 conventional metaphors in its index, the majority of which are relevant to social thought, feeling, and action. The online *master metaphor list* compiled by Lakoff, Espenson, and Schwartz (1991) lists dozens more. Do people think about *balanced* political policies in terms of physical balance?

Do they conceptualize ideas as bits of food that that can be chewed up, swallowed, and regurgitated? Is guilt really experienced as a weight on one's shoulders? These are certainly interesting questions, but the totality of research along such lines may merely create a scattered list of isolated observations.

In this context, we recommend that researchers complement the study of individual metaphors with a more phenomenon-focused approach (for a further discussion, see Landau et al., 2010). This entails starting with a phenomenon of social- or personality-psychological interest, identifying the multiple metaphors observed in discourse surrounding that phenomenon, and then examining their disparate influences. For example, romantic courting may be viewed as a *game*, a *dance*, or a *conquest* (Lakoff & Johnson, 1999). Individuals viewing courting as a game should have shallower romantic relationships (e.g., Hendrick & Hendrick, 2006), those viewing courting as a dance should be more sensitive to their potential relationship partners, and we might expect Machiavellian individuals, as well as those prone to sexual harassment (Lee, Gizzarone, & Ashton, 2003), to more greatly endorse the idea that courtship involves conquest.

Although these specific predictions have not yet been tested, there are some empirical precedents for the *alternate source strategy*, which involves testing whether priming different metaphors for the same target (or a metaphor vs. a nonmetaphoric interpretation) produces divergent effects on target processing (Landau et al., 2010). In one relevant investigation, Landau, Sullivan, and Greenberg (2009) studied how metaphor influences Americans' attitudes toward immigration into the United States. A nation is often conceptualized metaphorically as a physical body (Lakoff & Johnson, 1980), and because bodies are known to be vulnerable to contaminating foreign agents, it is possible that people's motivation to protect their own bodies from contamination leads them to be vigilant about immigrants entering their nation.

To test this possibility, Landau et al. (2009) manipulated contamination concern by priming participants to view airborne bacteria in their environment as either harmful to their physical health or innocuous. Participants, all of whom were U.S. citizens, then read an ostensibly unrelated essay describing the United States. For half of the participants, the essay contained statements metaphorically framing the United States as a body (e.g., "The United States experienced an unprecedented *growth spurt*"); for the other participants, those metaphoric expressions were replaced with literal paraphrases (e.g., "The United States experienced an unprecedented *period of innovation*"). As expected, heightening participants' concerns with bodily contamination led them to express more hostility toward immigrants if they were primed to think of their nation as a physical body; in contrast, contamination threat did not influence immigration attitudes when the nation was framed in nonmetaphoric terms.

A phenomenon-focused approach to studying metaphor recommends the alternate source strategy in future research. It also recommends examining the factors of the person's social environment and personality that determine whether metaphors (vs. nonmetaphoric representations) are used to process information related to that phenomenon and which metaphors are used.

CONCEPTUAL METAPHOR VERSUS OTHER POTENTIAL MECHANISMS

We do not believe that the range of findings reviewed in the present volume can be understood in terms that are not metaphor related. However, other potential mechanisms are at least somewhat plausible, at least in relation to some findings. For this reason, and to highlight metaphor's unique influence on social thought, feeling, and behavior, we compare and contrast this mechanism with two other mechanisms that might be invoked.

Metaphoric Influence and Spreading Activation Processes

When many psychologists first hear about metaphoric transfer effects, they ask, "Aren't these just demonstrations of spreading activation?" We suspect that the reader is familiar with associative network models of semantic priming and spreading activation, given their central place in contemporary social psychology (e.g., Fiske & Taylor, 2008). The gist is that the activation of one thought in memory spreads to activate other thoughts that came to be associated through repeated pairings over time (Collins & Loftus, 1975). For example, priming the thought *salt* will likely render the thought *pepper* more accessible, presumably because these thoughts share a well-learned association. Perhaps metaphoric transfer effects simply involve spreading activation. More pointedly, embodied source primes (e.g., the sensation of physical warmth) may simply activate a polysemous concept (e.g., *warm*), which in turn influences perceptions related to abstract concepts (e.g., *friendliness*), potentially independent of metaphoric influences as characterized by CMT.

Can metaphoric influences be understood in terms of spreading activation processes? We believe that the most accurate answer to this question is "yes and no." Understood broadly, metaphor involves patterns of associations between pieces of knowledge, and metaphoric transfer effects involve spreading activation across some of these associations. A closer look, however, reveals three unique features of metaphor. The first thing to notice is that the concepts that participate in metaphor are *dissimilar*, at least at the surface level. It is sufficient to point out that most people interact with, say, salt and pepper in similar ways—both are commonly used as granulated substances for seasoning food. By comparison, consider a typical metaphor: *theories are buildings*. Although theories and buildings share some abstract qualities in common (e.g., both are created by human beings), people generally relate to exemplars of these categories in different ways. Despite this, metaphor enables people to use their well-structured knowledge of buildings as a framework for thinking about analogous aspects of theories: Theories must have a *solid foundation* and be *well-supported* by the data or they will *crumble*, and you can *construct* them from the *ground up*, *buttress* them with new findings, and then have your opponents *tear them down brick by brick*.

A second, related feature of metaphor is that the mapping between the source and the target is *partial*, meaning that not all elements of the source are used to structure representations of the target (e.g., people do not conventionally think about whether a theory's restrooms are handicapped accessible). Third, metaphors typically map structure from a concrete source to a relatively more abstract target but not the other way around. We can get a better grasp on theories by conceptualizing them in terms of buildings, but we do not normally rely on our knowledge of theories to think and talk about buildings. Although some (but not all) models of spreading activating could be retrofitted to accommodate these features—in sum, a partial and unidirectional mapping between dissimilar concepts—CMT specifies them a priori. In short, metaphoric transfer effects are indeed due to spreading activation but of a particular kind hitherto unappreciated in schema-based models of social cognition.

Metaphoric Influences and Embodied Simulation

There is considerable interest in embodied simulation in social psychology, typically following the lead of embodied theories of cognition. The best-known one, advanced by Barsalou (1999, 2008), holds that concepts contain representations of bodily states that regularly occur during interactions with relevant stimuli. As a result, processing those concepts involves the *simulation*, or reactivation, of associated bodily states. Conceptual metaphor and embodied simulation are both mechanisms by which representations of bodily states are informative concerning how people understand and process abstract concepts. Yet they are distinct. Embodied simulation is an *intraconceptual* mechanism—bodily states and experiences are represented as part of the concept they refer to, and they got there through direct perceptual and motor experiences with the surrounding environment. For example, smiling may trigger happy thoughts, and grasping may trigger thoughts consistent with tool use.

Metaphor does not necessarily possess either of these features. Most important, metaphor is an *interconceptual* mechanism—two concepts operate independently, but one can be used as a coherently organized schema for thinking about analogous elements of the other. Second, one does not need direct embodied experiences with the concrete concepts to use them in metaphor. For example, people can use their knowledge about computer hardware as a framework for thinking about how the mind works, or they can understand marital discord in terms of courtroom proceedings, even if they have no direct embodied interactions with motherboards or jury boxes. In these examples, thinking about abstract concepts is partly structured by schematic knowledge of a source concept's features, properties, and the relations that hold among them, and not necessarily the sensory and motor representations associated with them.

There are certainly embodied influences that are not metaphor related. For example, Niedenthal, Winkielman, Mondillon, and Vermeulen (2009) showed that participants making judgments about words related to emotion concepts (e.g., *joy*) exhibited facial muscle activity associated with those emotions. This evidence suggests that facial muscles that are customarily activated in response to emotion-eliciting stimuli constitute a portion of the content of respective emotion concepts. This evidence does not show, however, that these patterns of facial muscular activity are separate concepts that are used to think and talk metaphorically about emotions. In addition, there are also metaphoric influences that are not embodied. For example, people conceptualize their anger in terms of explosions (Gibbs, 1994), and yet bodies do not typically explode (if they did, such individuals would be dead rather than angry).

Thus, embodiment and metaphor-related theories both share the idea that perceptual representations are often co-opted to understand abstract concepts (e.g., emotions). In this important sense, both theories counter the idea that social cognition can be understood in terms of abstract, symbolic information processing independent of having the particular types of bodies that we have. Yet the mechanisms involved are conceptually distinct in many important respects, and it will be important to acknowledge these distinctions as theory and research on embodied social cognition progress.

FUTURE RESEARCH DIRECTIONS

There are discrepancies in the literature that need to be resolved. For example, Schnall, Benton, and Harvey (2008) found that cleansing the self resulted in more lenient moral judgments, whereas Zhong, Strejcek, and

Sivanathan (2010) found that cleansing the self resulted in harsher moral judgments. Williams and Bargh (2008a) found that a warm temperature experience resulted in greater perceptions of interpersonal warmth, but Bargh and Shalev (2012) found that more lonely people (who presumably lack interpersonal warmth in their lives) preferred and took longer warm baths and showers. Unpublished work in the Robinson laboratory has shown that people who prefer "light" to "dark" believe in God to a greater extent, but a subsequent manipulation of perceptual darkness resulted in higher levels of belief in God. What is missing is a systematic comparison of such apparently divergent effects in single research designs. In the present section, however, we emphasize more fundamental future research directions.

Personality Processes

Experimental demonstrations of CMT are valuable, but the effects may be short-lived. Therefore, there is a real need to show that metaphoric cognition can be used to understand relatively longer-lasting variations in thinking, feeling, and behavior, the focus of personality psychology. In their chapter, Robinson and Fetterman (Chapter 7, this volume) presented one general strategy for research studies of this type. Briefly, individuals can be asked which of two bipolar opposites that prominent metaphors suggest should be consequential—such as heart versus head, sweet versus bitter, light versus dark, and warm versus cold—they prefer. Individuals will naturally differ in their preferences and such differences should possess explanatory value in understanding and predicting a wide range of personality variables and outcomes. Extant studies using this strategy have shown that people higher in the personality trait of agreeableness prefer and perceive higher temperatures, relatively more dominant individuals prefer up to down, depressed individuals prefer down to up, people who have a higher preference for sweet foods are more prosocial, and people who view themselves as head-related entities are smarter. The evidence is preliminary, however, and a great deal more work would be useful in establishing what we term a metaphor-enriched view of personality psychology.

Metaphors and Relationship Outcomes

Many metaphors possess implications for relationship functioning. For example, we would typically prefer to interact with *warm* relative to *cold* people, and more intimate couples are described as *close* rather than *distant*. Experimental research confirms that priming perceptual warmth or closeness results in personality impressions consistent with perceiving people as friendly and promotes relationship attachment, respectively (Williams &

Bargh, 2008a, 2008b). Yet there have been no forays of CMT into the personal relationship literature that we know of.

The same metaphoric preference strategy identified earlier (see Chapter 7, this volume) can be used in the relationship domain. Among other predictions, we would expect warm-preferring individuals to display greater intimacy in their social interactions and to have romantic relationships that are longer-lived. It is in fact striking how seemingly metaphoric prominent relationship measures are (Aron et al., 1992; Berscheid, Snyder, & Omoto, 2004; Fletcher, Simpson, & Thomas, 2000; Rempel, Holmes, & Zanna, 1985). Accordingly, there are good reasons for thinking that metaphoric preferences and perceptions may possess considerable value in understanding relationship functioning, but the relevant studies have not been conducted.

Cross-Cultural Comparisons

We think it is an established fact that all cultures thus far examined use metaphors frequently in their everyday discourse (Asch, 1958; Kövecses, 2005). Furthermore, they often do so in a way that suggests equivalence across cultures. For example, there are reasons to think that multiple cultures conceptualize power in terms of higher vertical positions (Schwartz, 1981) and conceptualize interpersonal warmth in terms of physical warmth (Williams, Huang, & Bargh, 2009). Yet there are important differences across cultures as well. Anger is apparently viewed as a gas rather than a fluid in Eastern cultures (Yu, 1995), Eastern cultures apparently view linear time in terms of vertical rather than horizontal dimension (Boroditsky, 2001), and there may be reasons for thinking that perceptual redness has different connotations across cultures (Elliot & Maier, 2007). We therefore call for CMT-motivated studies in which cross-cultural comparisons are of central interest (see Chapter 12, this volume). Studies of this type may be invaluable in understanding whether metaphoric influences are culturally universal or vary by culture in accordance with the linguistic expressions that also vary by culture.

Light–Dark Metaphors and Racial Prejudice

In many of the major religious texts across the world, light–dark metaphors figure prominently. Darkness is associated with evil and ignorance, whereas lightness is associated with goodness and wisdom (for a partial review, see Meier et al., 2004). Such associations presumably occur because we are diurnal creatures who function effectively in daylight but ineffectively at nighttime (Tolaas, 1991). Such light–dark metaphors have systematic implications for understanding racial prejudice, but these systematic implications have yet to be pursued. What is known is that implicit evaluations of dark-skinned individuals are often negative (Fazio & Olson, 2003), sometimes even among African Americans (Greenwald, McGhee, & Schwartz, 1998), and that dark-skinned (e.g., Black) individuals are most definitely discriminated against (Dovidio & Gaertner, 2004). We suggest that conceptual metaphors may be implicated in these findings. If so, for example, individuals who prefer light to dark to a greater extent should be more racially prejudiced. Additionally, individuals who display priming effects consistent with white = positive and black = negative reaction time effects (Meier et al., 2004) should exhibit behaviors consistent with greater racial prejudice against black-skinned individuals. Again, such studies have not been performed.

The Multifaceted Nature of Conceptual Metaphor

Mappings between source and target concepts are likely multifaceted in nature. The same source concept (e.g., heat) appears to be recruited in understanding multiple social inferences (e.g., intimacy & hostility), and target concepts are often understood in terms of multiple source concepts. In some cases, the source concepts might result in similar inferences. For example, whether positive valence is understood in terms of whiteness or higher vertical positions, positive affective inferences are facilitated (Meier & Robinson, 2004; Meier et al., 2004). As a caveat, the positivity of upness may be more status-oriented (Schubert, 2005), whereas the positivity of whiteness may be more morality-based (Sherman & Clore, 2009).

More detailed investigations of these dynamic mappings would likely provide a richer picture of metaphoric influences on social behavior. Researchers should also focus more attention on variability in knowledge about concrete source concepts. To clarify, following the lead of CMT, metaphor research in social psychology has generally proceeded from the assumption that although abstract target concepts are ambiguous and open to multiple interpretations, everyone has more or less the same knowledge of concrete source concepts. This assumption is plausible because many aspects of our bodies and sensorimotor functioning are shared universally (e.g., we all generally face the direction in which we move; we experience warmth through physical contact with others). Still, social psychologists have long known that even "concrete" bodily experiences are subject to social and cultural influence (e.g., Bruner & Goodman, 1947). Thus, there may be room in metaphor research for even more contextual variability than has been examined thus far.

For example, metaphor theorists propose that knowledge of journeys— goal-directed motion along a path—is used to metaphorically conceptualize the time course of goal pursuits such as romantic relationships and business ventures. Furthermore, although some aspects of movement along a path are experienced universally, there are certainly important cultural and individual differences in people's knowledge of journeys. For example, individuals raised in rural settings, in which residences are located far apart, may be more likely than their urban-raised counterparts to expect journeys to require sustained effort, whereas urban individuals may expect journeys to be relatively more dangerous or unpleasant. Aside from physical ecology, experience with transportation technology likely changes how journeys are understood. Individuals with ready access to cars, trains, and airplanes may view journeys as relatively common.

The upshot of this variability in representations of concrete concepts is that when people apply these concepts to make sense of abstract concepts and experiences, they may exhibit different patterns of belief, attitudes, and behavior, despite using the "same" metaphor.

Along these lines, Zhong and House (Chapter 6, this volume) discussed how situational and dispositional variation in people's views of physical dirt influence their moral reasoning and judgment in a metaphor-consistent fashion.

A Call for Further Research on Alternate Sources

The *alternate source strategy* is based on CMT's claim that multiple different source concepts can be recruited to understand the same sort of target concept (Landau et al., 2010). For example, love can be likened to an irresistible force ("she was *swept off* her feet") or an entity that needs to be nurtured ("she *fueled* his passion"). The latter view of love is far more agentic in nature, and we would therefore expect that dispositional endorsement of that metaphor would positively predict proactive efforts to maintain and improve one's romantic relationships. In addition, we would expect that situationally priming different source concepts for a target concept will result in divergent, metaphor-consistent effects on target processing. Such effects have been demonstrated in a few previous studies (e.g., Landau et al., 2009; Morris, Sheldon, Ames, & Young, 2007; Thibodeau & Boroditsky, 2011), but more lines of research are necessary.

In particular, although there is strong evidence for immediate change in thought and behavior due to priming alternative metaphors, there have been few attempts to examine possible long-term consequences of such primes. Clinical practitioners often encourage their clients to change the established repertoire of metaphors with which they understand themselves and conduct their lifestyle, and they report that this approach is effective at least over the course of therapy (e.g., Kopp, 1995; Loue, 2008; McMullen, 2008). Nevertheless, we lack conclusive evidence that adopting different metaphors causes long-term change in the person. More refined methods (experiments and longitudinal designs) must be brought to bear on this question to address not only the length of time that an activated metaphor affects the individual but also the situational factors that may prolong or diminish this duration.

On the one hand, there are good reasons to think that the effects of an activated metaphor may be somewhat ephemeral. New embodied experiences are commonplace, as is exposure to new, and even competing, framings of abstract social concepts. We might expect that the effect of any given metaphor cue to be quickly subdued under a torrent of new cues.

On the other hand, because metaphor can be used to actively structure knowledge, its effects may persist indirectly by influencing how people respond to certain situations. For example, if individuals use the metaphor that *love is a journey*, they may find it easier to work through a particular conflict with their significant other, thereby resulting in long-term positive consequences for both them and their partner that might not have been possible without the metaphor. Even if the effect of a given embodied cue or framing may not extend beyond a given situation, that momentary change could have meaningful long-term consequences.

Motivation to Use (and Reject) Metaphor

Conceptual metaphor is arguably relied on because it reduces uncertainty in thinking about a target construct (Lakoff & Johnson, 1999). If so, individuals motivated to reduce uncertainty and ambiguity (Kruglanski, 1989) should be more likely to rely on metaphors that serve such valuable epistemic needs. In a test of this hypothesis, Keefer, Landau, Rothschild, and Sullivan (2011) primed need for closure among one group by asking partcipants to write about uncertainties concerning their personal identity. Following this manipulation, and orthogonal to it, participants were assigned to a journey-metaphoric framing condition (in which they visualized episodes from their past as progressing along a path) or to a control (nonmetaphor) condition. As hypothesized, the two manipulations interacted such that the benefits of viewing one's life as a journey for perceived continuity and meaning were seized on to a greater extent among individuals motivated to reduce uncertainty about their identity. Future research should extend this analysis. For example, we might expect individual differences in need for closure to moderate metaphoric transfer effects. Crawford (Chapter 4, this volume) offered other suggestions for further studying metaphor's uncertainty-reduction function.

Future research could also look beyond the motive to reduce general uncertainty to examine the motive to maintain specific beliefs and attitudes. We know from social cognition research that schema use is heavily influenced by this motive: Schemas are most likely to be activated and applied to interpret the present situation when they accord with previously held beliefs and attitudes. We would expect people to be similarly motivated to adopt metaphors that are compatible with their worldview, while rejecting metaphors that conflict with their worldview. For example, an individual with strong anti-immigration attitudes may be particularly drawn to thinking about their nation as a body, thereby supporting an inference consistent with their attitudes. Conversely, someone with more pro-immigration attitudes may be quick to point out relevant *dis*-analogies between a nation and a body. For concrete suggestions for future research along these lines, see Ottati, Renstrom, and Price (Chapter 9, this volume) and Maass, Suitner, and Arcuri (Chapter 8, this volume).

Implications for Attitude Stability and Change

As Ottati, Renstrom, and Price (Chapter 9, this volume) pointed out, metaphorically framed messages are commonly used in public discourse to communicate about practically important topics. They can be found in campaign slogans, consumer advertisements, news reports, educational materials, and the courtroom. Research is beginning to show that these messages are more than figures of speech—they lead people to unconsciously recruit their knowledge of a concrete concept to interpret and evaluate a target topic, even though the two concepts are unrelated at a surface level. This suggests that these widespread communications have powerful but largely unrecognized consequences for how people make judgments and decisions about practically important matters.

Research also suggests that, through the unconscious use of metaphor, people rely on their current bodily experiences to form attitudes and make decisions about practically important matters. Given the relatively subtle procedures that researchers have used to prime embodied experiences (e.g., holding warm coffee, being in a dirty office), physical ecology may play an underappreciated role in creating situational variability in people's thoughts and beliefs as they move from one physical setting to another. We can imagine, for instance, a person at the polls voting for tougher immigration policy based partly on bodily contamination concerns elicited by the funny-smelling tuna sandwich he or she just ate.

In short, exposure to metaphorically framed messages and embodied experiences can bias people's attitudes toward abstract issues by leading them to base their attitudes on knowledge of familiar concrete concepts, without due consideration of the unique properties and features of the abstract issues. The practical implication is that interventions designed to reduce bias in attitudes should pay particular attention to the metaphors individuals and groups use to frame discourse as well as individuals' physical ecology.

In addition to creating unrecognized sources of change in attitudes, metaphor may also create *stability* in attitudes. That is because metaphor transfers not only bits of knowledge from a concrete concept to an abstract concept but also the sheer *self-evident nature* of one's knowledge about the concrete concept. When people use that concrete knowledge as a framework for making sense of an abstract issue, they may be equally confident that their beliefs and attitudes toward that issue are correct.

To illustrate, it is obviously true that a baby requires constant care to survive and thrive. So what happens when people encounter a message that metaphorically frames the handling of the national economy in terms of baby care? We've already discussed the possibility that they will transfer knowledge of infant care to make sense of the economy, perhaps forming the attitude that the economy needs federal regulation to operate. Here we are adding a more subtle point: that the beliefs and attitudes they form about the economy using that metaphor will feel just as obvious, just as self-evident, as their beliefs and attitudes about what infants need to survive. This presents a paradox to consider when applying metaphor research to understand attitudes and attitude change: Metaphor can play a role at both ends of the continuum of ideological malleability, promoting change but, once in place, infusing attitudes with a subjective confidence that makes that highly resistant to change.

CONCLUSION

The picture emerging from this book is clear: People think, feel, and behave in terms of conceptual metaphors to a much larger extent than appreciated previously in social and personality psychology, and the cognitive mechanisms involved appear to be unique. As Lakoff and Johnson (1980) surmised, metaphors are not merely about language use but also capture important ways in which the human social animal thinks. This concluding chapter highlights multiple ways in which CMT can be extended in domains such as personality, relationship functioning, and intergroup dynamics. Furthermore, we advocate research designs that can move the field forward in understanding when, why, who, and to what effect conceptual metaphors are used by people in making sense of their social lives. At the risk of speaking metaphorically about metaphor, we envision a bright future for metaphor research in social-personality psychology.

REFERENCES

Anderson, C. A. (2001). Heat and violence. *Current Directions in Psychological Science, 10*, 33–38. doi:10.1111/1467-8721.00109

Aron, A., Aron, E. N., & Smollan, D. (1992). Inclusion of other in the self scale and the structure of interpersonal closeness. *Journal of Personality and Social Psychology, 63*, 596–612. doi:10.1037/0022-3514.63.4.596

Asch, S. E. (1946). Forming impressions of personality. *The Journal of Abnormal and Social Psychology, 41*, 258–290. doi:10.1037/h0055756

Asch, S. E. (1958). The metaphor: A psychological inquiry. In R. Tagiuri & L. Petrullo (Eds.), *Person perception and interpersonal behavior* (pp. 86–94). Stanford, CA: Stanford University Press.

Bargh, J. A., & Shalev, I. (2012). The substitutability of physical and social warmth in daily life. *Emotion, 12*, 154–162. doi:10.1037/a0023527

Barsalou, L. W. (1999). Perceptual symbol systems. *Behavioral and Brain Sciences, 22*, 577–660.

Barsalou, L. W. (2008). Grounded cognition. *Annual Review of Psychology, 59*, 617–645. doi:10.1146/annurev.psych.59.103006.093639

Berscheid, E., Snyder, M., & Omoto, A. M. (2004). Measuring closeness: The Relationship Closeness Inventory (RCI) revisited. In D. J. Mashek & A. Aron (Eds.), *The handbook of closeness and intimacy* (pp. 81–101). Mahwah, NJ: Erlbaum.

Boroditsky, L. (2001). Does language shape thought? English and Mandarin speakers' conception of time. *Cognitive Psychology, 43*, 1–22. doi:10.1006/cogp.2001.0748

Bruner, J. S., & Goodman, C. C. (1947). Value and need as organizing factors in perception. *The Journal of Abnormal and Social Psychology, 42*, 33–44. doi:10.1037/h0058484

Collins, A. M., & Loftus, E. (1975). A spreading-activation theory of semantic processing. *Psychological Review, 82*, 407–428. doi:10.1037/0033-295X.82.6.407

Dovidio, J. F., & Gaertner, S. L. (2004). Aversive racism. In M. P. Zanna (Ed.), *Advances in experimental social psychology* (pp. 1–52). San Diego, CA: Elsevier Academic Press.

Elliot, A. J., & Maier, M. A. (2007). Color and psychological functioning. *Current Directions in Psychological Science, 16*, 250–254. doi:10.1111/j.1467-8721.2007.00514.x

Fazio, R. H., & Olson, M. A. (2003). Implicit measures in social cognition research: Their meaning and uses. *Journal of Personality and Social Psychology, 54*, 297–327.

Fiske, S. T., & Taylor, S. E. (2008). *Social cognition: From brains to culture*. New York, NY: McGraw-Hill.

Fletcher, G. J. O., Simpson, J. A., & Thomas, G. (2000). Ideals, perceptions, and evaluations in early relationship development. *Journal of Personality and Social Psychology, 79*, 933–940. doi:10.1037/0022-3514.79.6.933

Forceville, C. J., & Urios-Aparisi, E. (Eds.). (2009). *Multimodal metaphor*. New York, NY: Mouton de Gruyter. doi:10.1515/9783110215366

Gibbs, R. W. (1994). *The poetics of mind*. Cambridge, England: Cambridge University Press.

Greenwald, A. G., McGhee, D. E., & Schwartz, J. L. K. (1998). Measuring individual differences in implicit cognition: The implicit association test. *Journal of Personality and Social Psychology, 74*, 1464–1480. doi:10.1037/0022-3514.74.6.1464

Hendrick, C., & Hendrick, S. S. (2006). Styles of romantic love. In R. Sternberg & K. Weis (Eds.), *The new psychology of love* (pp. 149–170). New Haven, CT: Yale University Press.

Keefer, L., Landau, M. J., Rothschild, Z., & Sullivan, D. (2011). Exploring metaphor's epistemic function: Uncertainty moderates metaphor-consistent priming effects on social perceptions. *Journal of Experimental Social Psychology, 47*, 657–660. doi:10.1016/j.jesp.2011.02.002

Kopp, R. R. (1995). *Metaphor therapy: Using client-generated metaphors in psychotherapy*. New York, NY: Brunner-Routledge.

Kövecses, Z. (2005). *Metaphor in culture: Universality and variation*. Cambridge, MA: Cambridge University Press. doi:10.1017/CBO9780511614408

Kövecses, Z. (2010). *Metaphor: A practical introduction*. New York, NY: Oxford University Press.

Kruglanski, A. W. (1989). *Lay epistemics and human knowledge: Cognitive and motivational bases*. New York, NY: Plenum.

Lakoff, G., Espenson, J., & Schwartz, A. (1991). *Master metaphor list*. Cognitive Linguistics Group, University of California–Berkeley. Retrieved from http://araw.mede.uic.edu/~alansz/metaphor/METAPHORLIST.pdf

Lakoff, G., & Johnson, M. (1980). *Metaphors we live by*. Chicago, IL: University of Chicago Press.

Lakoff, G., & Johnson, M. (1999). *Philosophy in the flesh*. New York, NY: Basic Books.

Lakoff, G., & Turner, M. (1989). *More than cool reason: A field guide to poetic metaphor*. Chicago, IL: University of Chicago Press. doi:10.7208/chicago/9780226470986.001.0001

Landau, M. J., Meier, B. P., & Keefer, L. A. (2010). A metaphor-enriched social cognition. *Psychological Bulletin, 136*, 1045–1067. doi:10.1037/a0020970

Landau, M. J., Sullivan, D., & Greenberg, J. (2009). Evidence that self-relevant motives and metaphoric framing interact to influence political and social attitudes. *Psychological Science, 20*, 1421–1427. doi:10.1111/j.1467-9280.2009.02462.x

Lee, K., Gizzarone, M., & Ashton, M. C. (2003). Personality and the likelihood to sexually harass. *Sex Roles, 49*, 59–69. doi:10.1023/A:1023961603479

Loue, S. (2008). *The transformative power of metaphor in therapy*. New York, NY: Springer.

McMullen, L. M. (2008). Putting it in context: Metaphor and psychotherapy. In R. W. Gibbs (Ed.), *The Cambridge handbook of metaphor and thought* (pp. 397–411). New York, NY: Cambridge University Press. doi:10.1017/CBO9780511816802.024

McNeill, D. (2005). *Gesture and thought.* Chicago, IL: University of Chicago Press. doi:10.7208/chicago/9780226514642.001.0001

Meier, B. P., & Robinson, M. D. (2004). Why the sunny side is up. *Psychological Science, 15,* 243–247. doi:10.1111/j.0956-7976.2004.00659.x

Meier, B. P., Robinson, M. D., & Clore, G. L. (2004). Why good guys wear white: Automatic inferences about stimulus valence based on brightness. *Psychological Science, 15,* 82–87. doi:10.1111/j.0963-7214.2004.01502002.x

Morris, M. W., Sheldon, O. J., Ames, D. R., & Young, M. J. (2007). Metaphors and the market: Consequences and preconditions of agent and object metaphors in stock market commentary. *Organizational Behavior and Human Decision Processes, 102,* 174–192. doi:10.1016/j.obhdp.2006.03.001

Niedenthal, P. M., Winkielman, P., Mondillon, L., & Vermeulen, N. (2009). Embodiment of emotion concepts. *Journal of Personality and Social Psychology, 96,* 1120–1136. doi:10.1037/a0015574

Rempel, J. K., Holmes, J. G., & Zanna, M. P. (1985). Trust in close relationships. *Journal of Personality and Social Psychology, 49,* 95–112. doi:10.1037/0022-3514.49.1.95

Schnall, S., Benton, J., & Harvey, S. (2008). With a clean conscience: Cleanliness reduces the severity of moral judgments. *Psychological Science, 19,* 1219–1222. doi:10.1111/j.1467-9280.2008.02227.x

Schubert, T. W. (2005). Your highness: Vertical positions as perceptual symbols of power. *Journal of Personality and Social Psychology, 89,* 1–21. doi:10.1037/0022-3514.89.1.1

Schwartz, B. (1981). *Vertical classification: A study in structuralism and the sociology of knowledge.* Chicago, IL: University of Chicago Press.

Sherman, G. D., & Clore, G. L. (2009). The color of sin: White and black are perceptual symbols of moral purity and pollution. *Psychological Science, 20,* 1019–1025. doi:10.1111/j.1467-9280.2009.02403.x

Thibodeau, P. H., & Boroditsky, L. (2011). Metaphors we think with: The role of metaphor in reasoning. *PLoS ONE, 6,* e16782. doi:10.1371/journal.pone.0016782

Tolaas, J. (1991). Notes on the origin of some spatialization metaphors. *Metaphor and Symbolic Activity, 6,* 203–218. doi:10.1207/s15327868ms0603_4

Wilkowski, B. M., Meier, B. P., Robinson, M. D., Carter, M. S., & Feltman, R. (2009). "Hotheaded" is more than an expression: The embodied representation of anger in terms of heat. *Emotion, 9,* 464–477. doi:10.1037/a0015764

Williams, L. E., & Bargh, J. A. (2008a). Experiencing physical warmth influences interpersonal warmth. *Science, 322,* 606–607. doi:10.1126/science.1162548

Williams, L. E., & Bargh, J. A. (2008b). Keeping one's distance: The influence of spatial distance cues on affect and evaluation. *Psychological Science, 19,* 302–308. doi:10.1111/j.1467-9280.2008.02084.x

Williams, L. E., Huang, J. Y., & Bargh, J. A. (2009). The scaffolded mind: Higher mental processes are grounded in early experience of the physical world. *European Journal of Social Psychology, 39,* 1257–1267. doi:10.1002/ejsp.665

Yu, N. (1995). Metaphorical expressions of anger and happiness in English and Chinese. *Metaphor and Symbol, 10,* 59–92. doi:10.1207/s15327868ms1002_1

Zhong, C. B., Strejcek, B., & Sivanathan, N. (2010). A clean self can render harsh moral judgment. *Journal of Experimental Social Psychology, 46,* 859–862. doi:10.1016/j.jesp.2010.04.003

INDEX

Natural-catastrophe metaphors, 171
Neal, D. T., 114
Negativity dominance, 213–214
Nemeroff, C., 121
The Netherlands, 256
Neuroscience research, 57, 234
Niedenthal, P. M., 275
Nietzsche, Friedrich, 5
Nocera, C. C., 90
Nuer people (Africa), 117, 120
Nussbaum, M. C., 113
Nystrom, L. E., 111

Obama, Barack, 17–18, 28
Objectification, of humans, 166
Ode, S., 137–138
Operation Desert Storm, 185–190
Oppenheimer, D. M., 165
Orientational metaphors
    defined, 66, 230
    examples of, 67
    functioning of, 256
    verticality. *See* Vertical orientation
        metaphors
Ortony, A., 158, 159
Osborn, M. M., 186
Other. *See also* Person perception
    identification and labeling of
        emotions in, 115
    metaphoric descriptions of, 56
Ottati, V. C., 192, 195, 281
Outgroups, 155, 235

Paivio, A., 76
Palin, Sarah, 181
Palma, T. A., 72
Parietal lobe damage, 78
Park, L., 113
Pearson, A. R., 52
Perception
    and cognition, 115
    influence of values on, 135
    and memory, 75, 76
    spatial. *See* Spatial perception
    visual, 236, 239–240, 251–252
Perceptual analysis, 229
Perceptuomotor experiences, 251, 252,
        261, 262
Pérez, J. A., 167

Permanence, in morality, 119–121
Personality psychology, 133–148. *See
    also* Social-personality psychology
    research
    depression and vertical attention in,
        136–137
    dominance-submission and vertical
        attention in, 137–138
    future directions for research on, 276
    and metaphor representation per-
        spective, 134–135, 147
    and person perception research, 56–57
    prosocial personality and sweet taste
        preferences in, 138–140, 145,
        147
    rationality vs. emotionality and
        head-heart metaphor in,
        140–144, 147
    support for a metaphoric-enriched,
        135–136, 144–146
Personal space, protection of, 236
Person perception, 43–57
    and conceptual metaphor theory,
        46–53
    defined, 44
    future directions for research on,
        57–58
    and personality psychology, 56–57
    pitfalls of conceptual metaphor
        theory and, 54–56
    promises of conceptual metaphor
        theory and, 56–57
    and schemas, 44–46
Person-situation controversy, 135
Phillips, N., 138
Physical attributes, 206–207
Physical experiences
    involved in person perception
        metaphors, 46–47
    with memory encoding and retrieval,
        76
    and self-perception, 55
Physical purity. *See* Cleanliness
    metaphors
Piaget, J., 229
Pizarro, D. A., 117
Political communication, 179–197
    activated representations in,
        187–188

Political communication, *continued*
    activation of root metaphor in, 179,
        184–187
    agenda-setting in, 182
    and metaphoric framing model,
        183–196
    nature of metaphor in, 180–181
    and political judgment, 188–194
    prevalence of metaphor in, 180
    priming in, 182–183
    and process style, 194–196
    use of multiple metaphors in, 196–197
Political orientation, 156, 160–161,
    165, 255–259
Pollution metaphors
    and morality, 116–119, 122–125
    in political communication, 180
Postdecisional dissonance, 97–98
Posture, 71–72
Power
    associations between vertical orien-
        tation and, 160, 209, 230, 270
    individual differences in, 138
    representations of, 207
    size metaphors related to, 216–217
Prejudice, 277–278
Price, E., 281
Primary metaphors
    appeal of, 20
    mappings underlying, 26
Priming
    in dehumanization research, 167
    in metaphor transfer research, 10–11
    in personality research, 137
    and person perception, 45, 46
    in political communication,
        182–183
    possible long-term consequences of,
        279–280
    and processing of idioms, 27
    in research on relationship outcomes,
        276
    in social-personality psychology
        research, 273–274
Processing. *See* Metaphor processing
Process-oriented research, 55
Proffitt, D. R., 146
Projective measures, 135
Prosocial personality, 56, 138–140,
    145, 147

Psycholinguistic research
    on embodied metaphor, 27
    on social nature of metaphoric
        thought, 30
    on thinking and verbal metaphor
        use, 26
Psychological distance, 237–238
Public policy
    individual differences in perception
        of, 187
    on intergroup relations, 171
    metaphoric communication used in,
        180–181
Purity. *See* Cleanliness metaphors;
    Morality
Purity-sanctity (moral domain), 112

Race and ethnicity, 52, 124
Racial segregation, 121
Ramscar, M., 78
Rationality, emotionality vs., 140–144,
    147
Rational thinking, 98
Read, S. J., 195
Reading, as cultural practice, 263–264
Reagan, Ronald, 189–190
Reality, 169–171
Reinhard, D., 93
Relationships
    as games, 272
    outcomes of, 270–271, 276–277
Religious concepts
    about washing and purification, 120
    and brightness, 276
    cleanliness metaphors, 116–117
    vertical orientation metaphors in,
        50–51, 67, 70
Renstrom, R. A., 192, 281
Resemblance metaphors, 154
Rholes, W. S., 45
Riemer-Peltz, M., 53, 138
Right-handedness, 259–262
Right-wing political orientation, 156,
    160–161, 165
Riskind, J. H., 71
Risk-taking behavior, 95–96
Rizzolatti, G., 57
Roberson, D., 161
Robinson, M. D.
    and personality psychology, 134,
        137–138, 141, 144, 147

ABOUT THE EDITORS

Mark J. Landau, PhD, is an associate professor of psychology at the University of Kansas. He received his doctorate from the University of Arizona in 2007. Dr. Landau has published many articles and chapters focused on metaphor's influence on social cognition and behavior and the role of existential motives in diverse aspects of human behavior. He has received funding from the National Science Foundation and serves on the editorial board of the *Journal of Experimental Psychology: General*.

Michael D. Robinson, PhD, is a professor of psychology at North Dakota State University. He received his doctorate in social psychology from the University of California, Davis, in 1996. Subsequently, he was trained in emotion in a 3-year national National Institute of Mental Health (NIMH) postdoc (advisors Richard Davidson and Gerald Clore). He has received funding from both the National Science Foundation and NIMH and has extensive editorial experience. Specifically, he has been an associate editor of the *Journal of Personality* and *Cognition & Emotion* and is now an associate editor of *Emotion*, the motivation/emotion section of *Social and Personality Psychology Compass*, and the *Journal of Personality and Social Psychology*. He publishes frequently in the areas of personality, cognition, and emotion.

Brian P. Meier, PhD, is an associate professor of psychology at Gettysburg College, where he teaches courses on general psychology, social psychology, and statistics. He received his doctorate in social psychology from North Dakota State University in 2005. His research is focused on social and personality psychology topics including embodiment, emotion, aggression, prosocial behavior, self-regulation, and mindfulness. Dr. Meier is a consulting editor for multiple journals and his research has been funded by multiple agencies.